# Solutions Manual

# Investment Analysis and Portfolio Management

## SIXTH EDITION

Prepared by **Jeanette Medewitz Diamond**

Frank K. Reilly
*University of Notre Dame*

Keith C. Brown
*University of Texas at Austin*

**HARCOURT COLLEGE PUBLISHERS**

Fort Worth  Philadelphia  San Diego  New York  Orlando  Austin  San Antonio
Toronto  Montreal  London  Sydney  Tokyo

**Cover Image:** FPG International.

ISBN: 0-03-025812-x

Portions of this work were published in previous editions.

*Address for Domestic Orders*
Harcourt, Inc., 6277 Sea Harbor Drive, Orlando, FL  32887-6777
800-782-4479

*Address for International Orders*
International Customer Service
Harcourt, Inc., 6277 Sea Harbor Drive, Orlando, FL  32887-6777
407-345-3800
(fax) 407-345-4060
(e-mail) hbintl@harcourtbrace.com

*Address for Editorial Correspondence*
Harcourt College Publishers, 301 Commerce Street, Suite 3700, Fort Worth, TX  76102

*Web Site Address*
http://www.harcourtcollege.com

Printed in the United States of America

1  2  3  4  5  6  7  8   202   9  8  7  6  5  4

# CONTENTS

**Harcourt**
**College Publishers**

## *Where Learning Comes to Life*

**TECHNOLOGY**

Technology is changing the learning experience, by increasing the power of your textbook and other learning materials; by allowing you to access more information, more quickly; and by bringing a wider array of choices in your course and content information sources.

Harcourt College Publishers has developed the most comprehensive Web sites, e-books, and electronic learning materials on the market to help you use technology to achieve your goals.

**PARTNERS IN LEARNING**

Harcourt partners with other companies to make technology work for you and to supply the learning resources you want and need. More importantly, Harcourt and its partners provide avenues to help you reduce your research time of numerous information sources.

Harcourt College Publishers and its partners offer increased opportunities to enhance your learning resources and address your learning style. With quick access to chapter-specific Web sites and e-books . . . from interactive study materials to quizzing, testing, and career advice . . . Harcourt and its partners bring learning to life.

Harcourt's partnership with Digital:Convergence™ brings :CRQ™ technology and the :CueCat™ reader to you and allows Harcourt to provide you with a complete and dynamic list of resources designed to help you achieve your learning goals. Just swipe the cue to view a list of Harcourt's partners and Harcourt's print and electronic learning solutions.

C 62 00 00 00 00 00 25 20

http://www.harcourtcollege.com/partners/

# CHAPTER 1

# THE INVESTMENT SETTING

## Answers to Questions

1.   When an individual's current money income exceeds his current consumption desires, he saves the excess. Rather than keep these savings in his possession, the individual may consider it worthwhile to forego immediate possession of the money for a larger future amount of consumption. This trade-off of present consumption for a higher level of future consumption is the essence of investment.

An investment is the current commitment of funds for a period of time in order to derive a future flow of funds that will compensate the investor for the time value of money, the expected rate of inflation over the life of the investment, and provide a premium for the uncertainty associated with this future flow of funds.

2.   Students in general tend to be borrowers because they are typically not employed so have no income, but obviously consume and have expenses. The usual intent is to invest the money borrowed in order to increase their future income stream from employment--i.e., students expect to receive a better job and higher income due to their investment in education.

3.   In the 20-30 year segment an individual would tend to be a net borrower since he is in a relatively low income bracket and has several expenditures--automobile, durable goods, etc. In the 30-40 segment again the individual would likely dissave since his expenditures would increase with the advent of family life, and conceivably, the purchase of a house. In the 40-50 segment, the individual would probably be a saver since income would have increased substantially with no increase in expenditures. Between the age of 50 and 60 the individual would typically be a strong saver since income would continue to increase and by now the couple would be "empty-nesters." After this, depending upon when the individual retires, the individual would probably be a dissaver as income decreases (transition from regular income to income from a pension).

4.   The saving-borrowing pattern would vary by profession to the extent that compensation patterns vary by profession. For most white-collar professions (e.g., lawyers) income would tend to increase with age. Thus, lawyers would tend to be borrowers in the early segments (when income is low) and savers later in life. Alternatively, blue-collar professions (e.g., plumbers), where skill is often physical, compensation tends to remain constant or decline with age. Thus, plumbers would tend to be savers in the early segments and dissavers later (when their income declines).

5.   The difference is because of the definition and measurement of return. In the case of the *WSJ*, they are only referring to the current dividend yield on common stocks versus the promised yield on bonds. In the University of Chicago studies, they are talking about the total rate of return on common stocks, which is the dividend yield plus the capital gain or

Harcourt, Inc.

loss during the period. In the long run, the dividend yield has been 4-5 percent and the capital gain has averaged about the same. Therefore, it is important to compare alternative investments based upon total return.

6.    The variance of expected returns represents a measure of the dispersion of actual returns around the expected value. The larger the variance is, everything else remaining constant, the greater the dispersion of expectations and the greater the uncertainty, or risk, of the investment. The purpose of the variance is to help measure and analyze the risk associated with a particular investment.

7.    An investor's required rate of return is a function of the economy's risk free rate (RFR), an inflation premium that compensates the investor for loss of purchasing power, and a risk premium that compensates the investor for taking the risk. The RFR is the pure time value of money and is the compensation an individual demands for deferring consumption. More objectively, the RFR can be measured in terms of the long-run real growth rate in the economy since the investment opportunities available in the economy influence the RFR. The inflation premium, which can be conveniently measured in terms of the Consumer Price Index, is the additional protection an individual requires to compensate for the erosion in purchasing power resulting from increasing prices. Since the return on all investments is not certain as it is with T-bills, the investor requires a premium for taking on additional risk. The risk premium can be examined in terms of business risk, financial risk, liquidity risk, exchange rate risk and country risk.

8.    Two factors that influence the RFR are liquidity (i.e., supply and demand for capital in the economy) and the real growth rate of the economy. Obviously, the influence of liquidity on the RFR is an inverse relationship, while the real growth rate has a positive relationship with the RFR--i.e., the higher the real growth rate, the higher the RFR.

      It is unlikely that the economy's long-run real growth rate will change dramatically during a business cycle. However, liquidity depends upon the government's monetary policy and would change depending upon what the government considers to be the appropriate stimulus. Besides, the demand for business loans would be greatest during the early and middle part of the business cycle.

9.    The five factors that influence the risk premium on an investment are business risk, financial risk, liquidity risk, exchange rate risk, and country risk.

      Business risk is a function of sales volatility and operating leverage and the combined effect of the two variables can be quantified in terms of the coefficient of variation of operating earnings. Financial risk is a function of the uncertainty introduced by the financing mix. The inherent risk involved is the inability to meet future contractual payments (interest on bonds, etc.) or the threat of bankruptcy. Financial risk is measured in terms of a debt ratio (e.g., debt/equity ratio) and/or the interest coverage ratio. Liquidity risk is the uncertainty an individual faces when he decides to buy or sell an investment. The two uncertainties involved are: (1) how long it will take to buy or sell this asset, and (2) what price will be received. The liquidity risk on different investments

1 - 2

can vary substantially (e.g., real estate vs. T-bills). Exchange rate risk is the uncertainty of returns on securities acquired in a different currency. The risk applies to the global investor or multinational corporate manager who must anticipate returns on securities in light of uncertain future exchange rates. A good measure of this uncertainty would be the absolute volatility of the exchange rate or its beta with a composite exchange rate. Country risk is the uncertainty of returns caused by the possibility of a major change in the political or economic environment of a country. The analysis of country risk is much more subjective and must be based upon the history and current environment in the country.

10.     The increased use of debt increases the fixed interest payment. Since this fixed contractual payment will increase, the residual earnings (net income) will become more variable. The required rate of return on the stock will change since the financial risk (as measured by the debt/equity ratio) has increased.

11.     According to the Capital Asset Pricing Model, all securities are located on the Security Market Line with securities' risk on the horizontal axis and securities' expected return on its vertical axis. As to the locations of the five types of investments on the line, the U.S. government bonds should be located to the left of the other four, followed by United Kingdom government bonds, low-grade corporate bonds, common stock of large firms, and common stocks of Japanese firms. U.S. government bonds have the lowest risk and required rate of return simply because they virtually have no default risk at all.

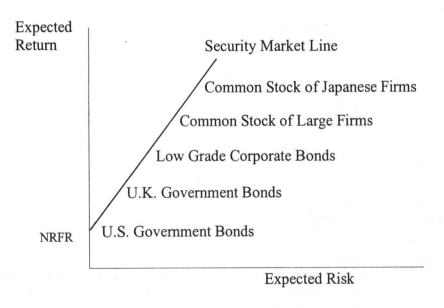

12.     If a market's real RFR is 4 percent, the investor will require a 4 percent return on an investment since this will compensate him for deferring consumption. However, if the inflation rate is 7 percent, the investor would be worse off in real terms if he invests at a rate of return of 4 percent--e.g., you would receive $104, but the cost of $100 worth of goods at the beginning of the year would be $107 at the end of the year, which means you could consume less real goods. Thus, for an investment to be desirable, it should have a return of 11.28 percent [(1.04 x 1.07) - 1]. Or an approximate return of 11 percent (4% + 7%).

1 - 3

13. Both changes cause an increase in the required return on all investments. Specifically, an increase in the real growth rate will cause an increase in the economy's RFR because of a higher level of investment opportunities. In addition, the increase in the rate of inflation will result in an increase in the nominal RFR. Because both changes affect the nominal RFR, they will cause an equal increase in the required return on all investments of 5 percent.

The graph should show a parallel shift upward in the capital market line of 5 percent.

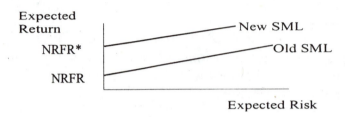

14. Such a change in the yield spread would imply a change in the market risk premium because, although the risk levels of bonds remain relatively constant, investors have changed the spreads they demand to accept this risk. In this case, because the yield spread (risk premium) declined, it implies a decline in the slope of the SML as shown in the following graph.

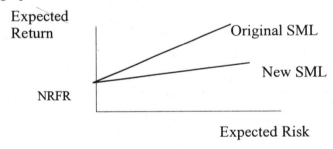

15. The ability to buy or sell an investment quickly without a substantial price concession is known as liquidity. An example of a liquid investment asset would be a United States Government Treasury Bill. A Treasury Bill can be bought or sold in minutes at a price almost identical to the quoted price. In contrast, an example of an illiquid asset would be a specialized machine or a parcel of real estate in a remote area. In both cases, it might take a considerable period of time to find a potential seller or buyer and the actual selling price could vary substantially from expectations.

# CHAPTER 1

## Answers to Problems

1.  $\text{HPR} = \dfrac{\text{Ending Value of Investment (including Cash Flows)}}{\text{Beginning Value of Investment}}$

$= \dfrac{39 + 1.50}{34} = \dfrac{40.50}{34} = 1.191$

$\text{HPY} = \text{HPR} - 1 = 1.191 - 1 = .191$

2.  $\text{HPR} = \dfrac{61 + 3}{65} = \dfrac{64}{65} = -.985$

$\text{HPY} = \text{HPR} - 1 = .985 - 1 = -.015$

3.  \$4,000 used to purchase 80 shares = \$50 per share

$\text{HPR} = \dfrac{(59 \times 80) + (5 \times 80)}{4,000} = \dfrac{4,720 + 400}{4,000} = \dfrac{5,120}{4,000} = 1.280$

$\text{HPY} = \text{HPR} - 1 = 1.280 - 1 = .280$

$\text{HPR (Price Increase Alone)} = \dfrac{59 \times 80}{4,000} = \dfrac{4,720}{4,000} = 1.180$

$\text{HPY (Price Increase Alone)} = 1.180 - 1 = .180$

therefore:  HPY (Total) = HPY (Price Increase) + HPY (Div)

.280 = .180 + HPY (Div)

.10 = HPY (Dividends)

4.  $\text{"Real" Rate of Return} = \dfrac{\text{Holding Period Return}}{1 + \text{Rate of Inflation}} - 1$

For Problem #1:  HPR = 1.191

at 4% inflation: $\dfrac{1.191}{1 + .04} - 1 = \dfrac{1.191}{1.04} - 1 = 1.145 - 1 = .145$

at 8% inflation: $\dfrac{1.191}{1 + .08} - 1 = \dfrac{1.191}{1.08} - 1 = 1.103 - 1 = .103$

For Problem #2: HPR = .985

at 4% inflation : $\dfrac{.985}{1.04} - 1 = .947 - 1 = -.053$

at 8% inflation : $\dfrac{.985}{1.08} - 1 = .912 - 1 = -.088$

For Problem #3: HPR = 1.280

at 4% inflation : $\dfrac{1.280}{1.04} - 1 = 1.231 - 1 = .231$

at 8% inflation : $\dfrac{1.280}{1.08} - 1 = 1.185 - 1 = .185$

5(a).  Arithemetic Mean (AM) $= \displaystyle\sum_{i=1}^{n} \dfrac{HPY_i}{n}$

$AM_T = \dfrac{(.19) + (.08) + (-.12) + (-.03) + (.15)}{5}$

$= \dfrac{.27}{5} = .054$

$AM_B = \dfrac{(.08) + (.03) + (-.09) + (.02) + (.04)}{5}$

$= \dfrac{.08}{5} = .016$

Stock T is more desirable because the arithmetic mean annual rate of return is higher.

5(b).  Standard Deviation $(\sigma) = \sqrt{\displaystyle\sum_{i=1}^{n} P_i [R_i - E(R_i)]^2}$

$\Sigma_T = (.19 - .054)^2 + (.08 - .054)^2 + (-.12 - .054)^2 + (-.03 - .054)^2 + (.15 - .054)^2$

$= .01850 + .0068 + .03028 + .00706 + .00922$

$= .06574$

$\sigma^2 = .06574 / 5 = .01315$

$\sigma_T = \sqrt{.01314} = .11467$

1 - 6

Harcourt, Inc.

$$\Sigma_B = (.08 - .016)^2 + (.03 - .016)^2 + (-.09 - .016)^2 + (.02 - .016)^2 + (.04 - .016)^2$$

$$= .00410 + .00020 + .01124 + .00002 + .00058$$

$$= .01614$$

$$\sigma^2 = .01614 / 5 = .00323$$

$$\sigma_T = \sqrt{.00323} = .05681$$

By this measure, B would be preferable

5(c).  Coefficient of Variation $= \dfrac{\text{Standard Deviation}}{\text{Expected Return}}$

$$CV_T = \frac{.11466}{.054} = 2.123$$

$$CV_B = \frac{.05682}{.016} = 3.5513$$

By this measure, T would be preferable.

5(d).  Geometric Mean (GM) $= \pi^{1/n} - 1$

where $\pi$ = Product of the HRs

$$GM_T = [(1.19)(1.08)(.88)(.97)(1.15)]^{1/5} - 1$$

$$= [1.26160]^{1/5} - 1 = 1.04757 - 1 = .04757$$

$$GM_B = [(1.08)(1.03)(.91)(1.02)(1.04)]^{1/5} - 1$$

$$= [1.07383]^{1/5} - 1 = 1.01435 - 1 = .01435$$

Stock T has more variability than Stock B. The greater the variability of returns, the greater the difference between the arithmetic and geometric mean returns.

6.  $E(R_{MBC})$ = $(.30)(-.10) + (.10)(0.00) + (.30)(.10) + (.30)(.25)$
    = $(-.03) + .000 + .03 + .075$ = $.075$

7.  $E(R_{FPC})$ = $(.05)(-.60) + (.20)(-.30) + (.10)(-.10) + (.30)(.20) + (.20)(.40) + (.15)(.80)$
    = $(-.03) + (-.06) + (-.01) + .06 + .08 + .12 = .16$

8.  The Fast and Powerful Computer Company presents greater risk as an investment because the range of possible returns is much wider.

1 - 7

9. $\text{Rate of Inflation} = \dfrac{CPI_{n+1} - CPI_n}{CPI_n}$

where CPI = the Consumer Price Index

$\text{Rate of Inflation} = \dfrac{172 - 160}{160} = \dfrac{12}{160} = .075$

$\text{Real Rate of Return} = \dfrac{HPR}{1 + \text{rate of inflation}} - 1$

$\text{U.S. Government T - Bills} = \dfrac{1.055}{1.075} - 1 = .9814 - 1 = -.0186$

$\text{U.S. Government LT bonds} = \dfrac{1.075}{1.075} - 1 = 0$

$\text{U.S. Common Stocks} = \dfrac{1.1160}{1.075} - 1 = 1.0381 - 1 = .0381$

10. $\text{NRFR} = (1 + .03)(1 + .04) - 1 = 1.0712 - 1 = .0712$
(An approximation would be growth rate plus inflation rate or $.03 + .04 = .07$.)

11. $\text{Return on common stock} = (1 + .0712)(1 + .05) - 1$
$= 1.1248 - 1 = .1248$ or $12.48\%$
(An approximation would be $.03 + .04 + .05 = .12$ or 12%.)

As an investor becomes more risk adverse, the investor will require a larger risk premium to own common stock. As risk premium increases, so too will required rate of return. In order to achieve the higher rate of return, stock prices should decline.

12. $\text{Nominal rate on T-bills (or risk-free rate)} = (1 + .03)(1 + .05) - 1$
$= 1.0815 - 1 = .0815$ or $8.15\%$
(An approximation would be $.03 + .05 = .08$.)

The required rate of return on common stock is equal to the risk-free rate plus a risk premium. Therefore the approximate risk premium for common stocks implied by these data is: $.14 - .0815 = .0585$ or 5.85%.

(An approximation would be $.14 - .08 = .06$.)

# APPENDIX 1

## Answers to Problems

1(a).    Expected Return = $\Sigma$(Probability of Return)(Possible Return)

$$E(R_{GDC}) = \sum_{i=1}^{n} P_i[R_i]$$

$$= (.25)(-.10) + (.15)(0.00) + (.35)(.10) + (.25)(.25)$$
$$= (-.025) + (.000) + (.035) + (.0625)$$
$$= (.0725)$$

$$\sigma^2 = \sum_{i=1}^{n} P_i[R_i - E(R_i)]^2$$

$$= (.25)(-.100 - .0725)^2 + (.15)(0.00 - .0725)^2 + (.35)(.10 - .0725)^2 + (.25)(.25 - .0725)^2$$
$$= (.25)(.02976) + (.15)(.0053) + (.35)(.0008) + (.25)(.0315)$$
$$= .0074 + .0008 + .0003 + .0079$$
$$= .0164$$

$$\sigma_{GDC} = \sqrt{.0164} = .128$$

1(b).    Standard deviation can be used as a good measure of relative risk between two investments that have the same expected rate of return.

1(c).    The coefficient of variation must be used to measure the relative variability of two investments if there are major differences in the expected rates of return.

2(a).    $E(R_{KCC})= (.15)(-.60) + (.10)(-.30) + (.05)(-.10) + (.40)(.20) + (.20)(.40) + (.10)(.80)$
$$= (-.09) + (-.03) + (-.005) + .08 + .08 + .08 = .115$$

$$\sigma^2 = (.15)(-.60 -.115)^2 + (.10)(-.30 -.115)^2$$
$$+ (.05)(-.10 -.115)^2 + (.40)(.20 -.115)^2$$
$$+ (.20)(.40 -.115)^2 + (.10)(.80 -.115)^2$$

$$= (.15)(-.715)^2 + (.10)(-.415)^2 + (.05)(-.215)^2$$
$$+ (.40)(.085)^2 + (.20)(.285)^2 + (.10)(.685)^2$$

$$= (.15)(.5112) + (.10)(.1722) + (.05)(.0462)$$
$$+ (.40)(.0072) + (.20)(.0812) + (.10)(.4692)$$

$$= .07668 + .01722 + .00231 + .00288 + .01624 + .04692$$
$$= .16225$$

$$\sigma_{KCC} = \sqrt{.16255} = .403$$

1 - 9

2(b). Based on [E(R$_j$)] alone, Kayleigh Computer Company's stock is preferable because of the higher return available.

2(c). Based on standard deviation alone, the Gray Disc Company's stock is preferable because of the likelihood of obtaining the expected return.

2(d). $\quad CV = \dfrac{Standard \quad Deviation}{Expected \quad Return}$

$$CV_{GDC} = \dfrac{.128}{.0725} = 1.77$$

$$CV_{KCC} = \dfrac{.403}{.115} = 3.50$$

Based on CV, Kayleigh Computer Company's stock return has approximately twice the relative dispersion of Gray Disc Company's stock return.

3(a). $\quad AM_{US} = \dfrac{.063 + .081 + .076 + .090 + .085}{5} = \dfrac{.395}{5} = .079$

$\quad AM_{UK} = \dfrac{.150 + (-.043) + .374 + .192 + (-.106)}{5} = \dfrac{.567}{5} = .113$

3(b). The average return of U.S. Government T-Bills is lower than the average return of United Kingdom Common Stocks because U.S. Government T-Bills are riskless, therefore their risk premium would equal 0. The U.K. Common Stocks are subject to the following types of risk: business risk, financial risk, liquidity risk, exchange rate risk, (and to a limited extent) country risk.

3(c). $\quad GM \quad = \pi^{1/n} - 1$

$\quad \pi_{US} \quad = (1.063)(1.081)(1.076)(1.090)(1.085) = 1.462$

$\quad GM_{US} = (1.462)^{1/5} - 1 = 1.079 - 1 = .079$

$\quad \pi_{UK} \quad = (1.150)(.957)(1.374)(1.192)(.894) = 1.611$

$\quad GM_{UK} = (1.1611)^{1/5} - 1 = 1.1 - 1 = .10$

In the case of the U.S. Government T-Bills, the arithmetic and geometric means are approximately equal (.079), therefore the standard deviations (using E(R$_j$) = .079) would be equal. The geometric mean (.10) of the U.K. Common Stocks is lower than the arithmetic mean (.113), and therefore the standard deviations will also differ.

1 - 10

# CHAPTER 2

# THE ASSET ALLOCATION DECISION

## Answers to Questions

1.  In answering this question, one assumes that the young person has a steady job, adequate insurance coverage, and sufficient cash reserves. The young individual is in the accumulation phase of the investment life cycle. During this phase, an individual should consider moderately high-risk investments, such as common stocks, because he/she has a long investment horizon and earnings ability.

2.  In answering this question, one assumes that the 63-year-old individual has adequate insurance coverage and a cash reserve. Depending on her income from social security, she may need some current income from her retirement portfolio to meet living expenses. At the same time, she will need to protect herself against inflation. Removing all her money from her company's retirement plan and investing it in money market funds would satisfy the investor's short-term current income needs. Investing in long-term investments, such as common stock mutual funds, would provide the investor with needed inflation protection.

3.  Typically investment strategies change during an individual's lifetime. In the accumulating phase, the individual is accumulating net worth to satisfy short-term needs (e.g., house and car purchases) and long-term goals (e.g., retirement and children's college needs). In this phase, the individual is willing to invest in moderately high-risk investments in order to achieve above-average rates of return.

    In the consolidating phase, an investor has paid off many outstanding debts and typically has earnings that exceed expenses. In this phase, the investor is becoming more concerned with long-term needs of retirement or estate planning. Although the investor is willing to accept moderate portfolio risk, he/she is not willing to jeopardize the "nest egg."

    In the spending phase, the typical investor is retired or semi-retired. This investor wishes to protect the nominal value of his/her savings, but at the same time must make some investments for inflation protection.

    The gifting phase is often concurrent with the spending phase. The individual believes that the portfolio will provide sufficient income to meet expenses, plus a reserve for uncertainties. If an investor believes there are excess amounts available in the portfolio, he/she may decide to make "gifts" to family or friends, institute charitable trusts, or establish trusts to minimize estate taxes.

4.  A policy statement is important for both the investor and the investment advisor. A policy statement assists the investor in establishing realistic investment goals, as well as, providing a benchmark by which a portfolio manager's performance may be measured.

Harcourt, Inc.

5. Student Exercise

6. The 45-year old uncle and 35-year old sister differ in terms of time horizon. However, each has some time before retirement (20 versus 30 years). Each should have a substantial proportion of his/her portfolio invested in equities, with the 35-year old sister possibly having more equity investments in small firms or international firms (i.e., can tolerate greater portfolio risk). These investors could also differ in current liquidity needs (such as children, education expenses, etc.), tax concerns, and/or other unique needs or preferences.

7. Before constructing an investment policy statement, the financial planner needs to clarify the client's investment objectives (e.g. capital preservation, capital appreciation, current income or total return) and constraints (e.g. liquidity needs, time horizon, tax factors, legal and regulatory constraints, and unique needs and preferences).

8. Student Exercise

9. CFA Examination III (1993)

9(a).. At this point we know (or can reasonably infer) that Mr. Franklin is:
- unmarried (a recent widower)
- childless
- 70 years of age
- in good health
- possessed of a large amount of (relatively) liquid wealth intending to leave his estate to a tax-exempt medical research foundation, to whom he is also giving a large current cash gift
- free of debt (not explicitly stated, but neither is the opposite)
- in the highest tax brackets (not explicitly stated, but apparent)
- not skilled in the management of a large investment portfolio, but also not a complete novice since he owned significant assets of his own prior to his wife's death
- not burdened by large or specific needs for current income
- not in need of large or specific amounts of current liquidity

Taking this knowledge into account, his Investment Policy Statement will reflect these specifics:

**Objectives**:

Return Requirements: The incidental throw-off of income from Mr. Franklin's large asset pool should provide a more than sufficient flow of net spendable income. If not, such a need can easily be met by minor portfolio adjustments. Thus, an inflation-adjusted enhancement of the capital base for the benefit of the foundation will be the primary return goal (i.e., real growth of capital). Tax minimization will be a continuing collateral goal.

2 - 2

Risk Tolerance: Account circumstances and the long-term return goal suggest that the portfolio can take somewhat above average risk. Mr. Franklin is acquainted with the nature of investment risk from his prior ownership of stocks and bonds, he has a still long actuarial life expectancy and is in good current health, and his heir—the foundation, thanks to his generosity-is already possessed of a large asset base.

**Constraints**:

Time Horizon: Even disregarding Mr. Franklin's still-long actuarial life expectancy, the horizon is long-term because the remainder of his estate, the foundation, has a virtually perpetual life span.

Liquidity Requirement: Given what we know and the expectation of an ongoing income stream of considerable size, no liquidity needs that would require specific funding appear to exist.

Taxes: Mr. Franklin is no doubt in the highest tax brackets, and investment actions should take that fact into account on a continuing basis. Appropriate tax-sheltered investment (standing on their own merits as investments) should be considered. Tax minimization will be a specific investment goal.

Legal and Regulatory: Investments, if under the supervision of an investment management firm (i.e., not managed by Mr. Franklin himself) will be governed by state law and the Prudent Person rule.

Unique Circumstances: The large asset total, the foundation as their ultimate recipient, and the great freedom of action enjoyed in this situation (i.e., freedom from confining considerations) are important in this situation, if not necessarily unique.

9(b).   Given that stocks have provided (and are expected to continue to provide) higher risk-adjusted returns than either bonds or cash, and considering that the return goal is for long-term, inflation-protected growth of the capital base, stocks will be allotted the majority position in the portfolio. This is also consistent with Mr. Franklin's absence of either specific current income needs (the ongoing cash flow should provide an adequate level for current spending) or specific liquidity needs. It is likely that income will accumulate to some extent and, if so, will automatically build a liquid emergency fund for Mr. Franklin as time passes.

Since the inherited warehouse and the personal residence are significant (15%) real estate assets already owned by Mr. Franklin, no further allocations to this asset class is made. It should be noted that the warehouse is a source of cash flow, a diversifying asset and, probably, a modest inflation hedge. For tax reasons, Mr. Franklin may wish to consider putting some debt on this asset, freeing additional cash for alternative investment use.

Harcourt, Inc.

Given the long-term orientation and the above-average risk tolerance in this situation, about 70% of total assets can be allocated to equities (including real estate) and about 30% to fixed income assets. International securities will be included in both areas, primarily for their diversification benefits. Municipal bonds will be included in the fixed income area to minimize income taxes. There is no need to press for yield in this situation, nor any need to deliberately downgrade the quality of the issues utilized. Venture capital investment can be considered, but any commitment to this (or other "alternative" assets) should be kept small.

The following is one example of an appropriate allocation that is consistent with the Investment Policy Statement and consistent with the historical and expected return and other characteristics of the various available asset classes:

|  | Range (%) | Current Target (%) |
|---|---|---|
| Cash/Money Market | 0 - 5 | 0 |
| U.S. Fixed Income | 10 – 20 | 15 |
| Non-U.S. Fixed Income | 5 – 15 | 10 |
| U.S. Stocks (Large Cap) | 30 – 45 | 30 |
| (Small Cap) | 15 – 25 | 15 |
| Non-U.S. Stocks | 15 – 25 | 15 |
| Real Estate | 10 – 15 | 15* |
| Other | 0 – 5 | 0 |
|  |  | 100 |

*Includes the Franklin residence and warehouse, which together comprise the proportion of total assets shown.

An alternate allocation could well be weighted more heavily to U.S. fixed income and less so to U.S. stocks, given the near equality of expected returns from those assets as indicated in Table 4.

Harcourt, Inc.

# CHAPTER 2

## Answers to Problems

1.  Most experts recommend that about 6 month's worth of living expenses be held in cash reserves. Although these funds are identified as "cash," it is recommended that they be invested in instruments that can easily be converted to cash with little chance of loss in value (e.g., money market mutual funds, etc.).

    Most experts recommend that an individual should carry life insurance equal to 7-10 times an individual's annual salary. An unmarried individual should have coverage equal to at least 7 times salary, whereas a married individual with two children should have more coverage (possibly 9-10 times salary).

2.  Married, filing jointly, $20,000 taxable income:
    Marginal tax rate = 15%
    Taxes due = $20,000 x .15 = $3,000
    Average tax rate = 3,000/20,000 = 15%

    Married, filing jointly, $40,000 taxable income:
    Marginal tax rate = 15%
    Taxes due = $40,000 x .15 = $6,000
    Average tax rate = 6,000/40,000 = 15%

    Married, filing jointly, $60,000 taxable income:
    Marginal tax rate = 28%
    Taxes due = $6,180 + .28($60,000 - $41,200)
               = $6,180 + $5,264 = $11,444
    Average tax rate = 11,444/60,000 = 19.07%

3.  Single with $20,000 taxable income:
    Marginal tax rate = 15%
    Taxes due = $20,000 x .15 = $3,000
    Average tax rate = 3,000/20,000 = 15%

    Single with $40,000 taxable income:
    Marginal tax rate = 28%
    Taxes due = $3,697.50 + .28($40,000 - $24,650)
               = $3,697.50 + $4,298 = $7,995.50
    Average tax rate = 7,995.50/40,000 = 19.99%

    Single with $60,000 taxable income:
    Marginal tax rate = 31%
    Taxes due = $13,525.50 + .31($60,000 - $59,750)
               = $13,525.50 + $77.50 = $13,603
    Average tax rate = 13,603/60,000 = 22.67%

4(a). $10,000 invested in 9 percent tax-exempt IRA (assuming annual compounding)

in 5 years:  $10,000(FVIF @ 9%) = $10,000(1.5386) = $15,386
in 10 years: $10,000(FVIF @ 9%) = $10,000(2.3674) = $23,674
in 20 years: $10,000(FVIF @ 9%) = $10,000(5.6044) = $56,044

4(b). After-tax yield = Before-tax yield (1 - Tax rate)
$$= 9\% \ (1 - .36)$$
$$= 5.76\%$$

$10,000 invested at 5.76 percent (assuming annual compounding)

in 5 years:  $10,000(FVIF @ 5.76%) = $13,231
in 10 years: $10,000(FVIF @ 5.76%) = $17,507
in 20 years: $10,000(FVIF @ 5.76%) = $30,650

5(a). $10,000 invested in 10 percent tax-exempt IRA (assuming annual compounding)

in 5 years:  $10,000(FVIF @ 10%) = $10,000(1.6105) = $16,105
in 10 years: $10,000(FVIF @ 10%) = $10,000(2.5937) = $25,937
in 20 years: $10,000(FVIF @ 10%) = $10,000(6.7275) = $67,275

5(b). After-tax yield = Before-tax yield (1 - Tax rate)
$$= 10\% \ (1 - .15)$$
$$= 8.50\%$$

$10,000 invested at 8.50 percent (assuming annual compounding)

in 5 years:  $10,000(FVIF @ 8.50%) = $15,037
in 10 years: $10,000(FVIF @ 8.50%) = $22,610
in 20 years: $10,000(FVIF @ 8.50%) = $51,120

Harcourt, Inc.

# CHAPTER 3

# SELECTING INVESTMENTS IN A GLOBAL MARKET

## Answers to Questions

1.  The major advantage of investing in common stocks is that generally an investor would earn a higher rate of return than on corporate bonds. Also, while the return on bonds is pre-specified and fixed, the return on common stocks can be substantially higher if the investor can pick a "winner" --i.e., if the company's performance turns out to be better than current market expectations. The main disadvantage of common stock ownership is the higher risk. While the income on bonds is certain (except in the extreme case of bankruptcy), the return on stocks will vary depending upon the future performance of the company and could well be negative.

2.  The three factors are:
    (1) Limiting oneself to the U.S. securities market would imply effectively ignoring approximately 50% of the world securities market. While the U.S. bond market is still the dominant sector, foreign bond markets have been growing in absolute and relative size since 1969.
    (2) The rates of return available on non-U.S. securities often have substantially exceeded those of U.S. securities.
    (3) Diversification with foreign securities reduces portfolio risk.

3.  International diversification reduces portfolio risk because of the low correlation of returns among the securities from different countries. This is due to differing international trade patterns, economic growth, fiscal policies, and monetary policies among countries.

4.  There are different correlations of returns between securities from the U.S. and alternate countries because there are substantial differences in the economies of the various countries (at a given time) in terms of inflation, international trade, monetary and fiscal policies and economic growth.

5.  The correlations between U.S. stocks and stocks for different countries should change over time because each country has a fairly independent set of economic policies. Factors influencing the correlations include international trade, economic growth, fiscal policy and monetary policy. A change in any of these variables will cause a change in how the economies are related. For example, the correlation between U.S. and Japanese stock will change as the balance of trade shifts between the two countries.

6.  The major risks that an investor must consider when investing in any bond issue are business risk, financial risk and liquidity risk. Additional risk associated with foreign bonds, such as Japanese or German bonds, are exchange rate risk and country risk. Country risk is not a major concern for Japanese or German securities. Exchange rate risk is the uncertainty which arises from floating exchange rates between the U.S. dollar and the Japanese yen or Deutsch mark.

Harcourt, Inc.

7. The additional risk that some investors believe international investing introduces include foreign exchange risk and country risk. For example, the domestic return on France bonds of 10.52% exceeded the U.S. return of 8.10%. The exchange rate effect of 2.00% increases the French franc return after conversion to U.S. dollars to 12.73%. (Table 3.1)

8. There are three alternatives to direct investment in foreign stocks available to investors:
   (1) purchase American Depository Receipts (ADRs)
   (2) purchase of American shares (issued by a transfer agent)
   (3) purchase of international mutual funds.

9. As opposed to corporate bonds, the interest earned on municipal bonds is exempt from taxation by the federal government and by the state that issued the bond, provided the investor is a resident of that state. Using the example presented in the text, a marginal tax rate of 30 percent means that a regular bond with an interest rate of 8 percent yields a net return after taxes of only 5.60 percent [.08 x (1 -.30)]. A tax-free bond with a 6 percent yield would be preferable.

10. The convertible bond of the growth company would have the lower yield. This is intuitive because there is a greater potential for the price of the growth company stock to increase, which would make the conversion feature of the bond extremely attractive. Thus, the investor would be willing to trade off the higher upside potential resulting from conversion for the lower yield.

11. Liquidity is the ability to buy or sell an asset quickly at a price similar to the prior price assuming no new information has entered the market. Common stocks have the advantage of liquidity since it is very easy to buy or sell a small position (there being a large number of potential buyers) at a price not substantially different from the current market price. Raw land is relatively illiquid since it is often difficult to find a buyer immediately and often the prospective buyer will offer a price that is substantially different from what the owner considers to be the true market value. A reason for this difference is that while common stock data are regularly reported in a large number of daily newspapers and several magazines and closely watched by a large number of individuals, raw land simply lacks this kind of interest. Further, the speculative nature of raw land investment calls for high risk and longer maturity before profits can be realized. Finally, the initial investment on a plot of raw land would be substantially greater than a round lot in most securities. As a result, the small investor is generally precluded from this kind of investment.

12. A stock warrant is an option issued by a corporation to buy a number of shares of the corporation's common stock at a specified price. Warrants typically have a life of several years and could even by perpetual.

    A call option is similar to a stock warrant with two essential differences. One is that the call option is not issued by the corporation but by an individual who "writes" it and stands behind it. The second difference is that a call option generally has a maturity of less than a year.

3 - 2

13. Art and antiques are considered illiquid investments because in most cases they are sold at auctions. The implication of being traded at auctions rather than on a developed exchange is that there is tremendous uncertainty regarding the price to be received and it takes a long time to contact a buyer who offers the "right" price. Besides, many buyers of art and antiques are accumulators rather than traders and this further reduces trading.

Coins and stamps are more liquid than art and antiques because an investor can determine the "correct" market price from several weekly or monthly publications. There is no such publication of current market prices of the numerous unique pieces of art and antiques and owners are forced to rely on dealer estimates. Further, while a coin or stamp can be readily disposed of to a dealer at a commission of about 10-15 percent, the commissions on paintings range from 30-50 percent.

To sale a portfolio of stocks that are listed on the New York Stock Exchange, an investor simply contacts his/her broker to sell the shares. Cost of trading stocks varies depending on whether the trade is handled by a full service broker or a discount broker.

14. The results of Table 3.8 would tend to support adding some gold to your portfolio. The table indicates a negative correlation with U.S. stocks (-0.088), which implies good diversification opportunities. It should also be noted that returns on gold are highly correlated with the rate of inflation, thus providing a hedge against the depreciating value of financial assets during inflationary times. Finally, the market for gold tends to be more liquid than other real assets.

15. Figure 3.6 indicates that an investment in American paintings during this period was a good investment. The geometric mean for American paintings (16.20%) was higher than that of U.S. common stocks, measured by the S&P 500 index (14.92%). In addition, risk as measured by standard deviation, was lower for American paintings (16.07%) than for the S&P 500 Index (17.57%).

16. CFA Examination I (1993)

16(a). International stocks versus U.S. stocks – Problems:

1. Information about foreign firms is often difficult to obtain on a timely basis and once obtained, can be difficult to interpret and analyze due to language and presentation differences.

2. Financial statements are comparable from country to country. Different countries use different accounting principles. Even when similar accounting methods are used, cultural, institutional, political and tax differences can make cross-country comparisons hazardous and misleading.

3. Stock valuation techniques useful in the United States may be less useful in other countries. Stock markets in different countries value different attributes.

4. Smith must consider currency risk in selecting non-U.S. stocks for his portfolio.

5. Increased costs: custody, management fees, and transactions expenses are usually higher outside the United States.

17.    CFA Examination III (1993)

17(a).  Arguments in favor of adding international securities include:
1.  Benefits gained from broader diversification, including economic, political and/or geographic sources.
2.  Expected higher returns at the same or lower (if properly diversified) level of portfolio risk.
3.  Advantages accruing from improved correlation and covariance relationships across the portfolio's exposures.
4.  Improved asset allocation flexibility, including the ability to match or hedge non-U.S. liabilities.
5.  Wider range of industry and company choices for portfolio construction purposes.
6.  Wider range of managers through whom to implement investment decisions.
7.  Diversification benefits are realizable despite the absence of non-U.S. pension liabilities.

At the same time, there are a number of potential problems associated with moving away from a domestic-securities-only orientation:

1.  Possible higher costs, including those for custody, transactions, and management fees.
2.  Possibly reduced liquidity, especially when transacting in size.
3.  Possible unsatisfactory levels of information availability, reliability, scope, timeliness and understand-ability.
4.  Risks associated with currency management, convertibility and regulations/controls.
5.  Risks associated with possible instability/volatility in both markets and governments.
6.  Possible tax consequences or complications.
7.  Recognition that EAFE has underperformed since 1989.

17(b).  A policy decision to include international securities in an investment portfolio is a necessary first step to actualization. However, certain other policy level decisions must be made prior to implementation. That set of decisions would include:

1.  What portion of the portfolio shall be invested internationally, and in what equity and fixed-income proportions?
2.  Shall all or a portion of the currency risk be hedged or not?
3.  Shall management of the portfolio be active or passive?
4.  Shall the market exposures be country/market-wide (top-down) or company/industry specific (bottom-up)?
5.  What benchmarks shall results be judged by?
6.  How will manager style be incorporated into the process?
7.  How will the process reflect/resolve the important differences in orientation between the international (non U.S.) major markets and the U.S. emerging markets perspectives?

Until decisions on these additional policy-level issues have been made, implementation of the basic decision to invest internationally cannot begin.

# CHAPTER 3

## Answers to Problems

1.  Student Exercise

2.  Student Exercise

3.  Student Exercise

4.  Student Exercise

5.  CFA Examination (Adapted)

5(a).  The arithmetic average assumes the presence of simple interest, while the geometric average assumes compounding or interest-on-interest. The geometric mean internal rate of return is a critical concept in security and portfolio selection as well as performance measurement in a multi-period framework.

5(b).  Ranking is best accomplished by using the coefficient of variation (standard deviation/ arithmetic mean, multiplied by 100):

> 1 - Real Estate        36.88
> 2 - Treasury Bills        48.93
> 3 - Long Gov't Bonds  104.92
> 4 - Common Stocks    164.37
> 5 - Long Corp. Bond   166.96

The coefficient of variation ranking methodology alternatively may be computed using the geometric mean (standard deviation – geometric mean multiplied by 100). This method provides a ranking almost identical to the prior method (with the 4th and 5th rankings reversed:

> 1 - Real Estate        37.08
> 2 - Treasury Bills        49.31
> 3 - Long Gov't Bonds  108.29
> 4 - Long Corp. Bonds  179.44
> 5 - Common Stocks    191.83

In both cases, a lower ratio indicates a higher return for risk.

Or, a somewhat different ranking methodology utilizes Sharpe's reward for risk-taking measure using the arithmetic mean return minus the risk free rate divided by the standard deviation multiplied by 100. The ranking using this measure would be as follows:

> 1 - Real Estate        84.29
> 2 - Common Stocks    22.13
> 3 - Treasury Bills        0.00
> 4 - Long Gov't Bonds   -6.88
> 5 - Long Corp. Bonds   -8.23

Harcourt, Inc.

Under this reward-for-risk ranking methodology, the higher the ratio, the higher the return per unit of risk. The arithmetic mean was used in this computation; however, the geometric mean also could be used to calculate this ranking.

5(c)(1). Expected mean plus or minus two standard deviations:
Arithmetic: 10.28% +/-16.9%(2) = -23.52% to +44.08%
Geometric: 8.81% +/-16.9%(2) = -24.99% to +42.61%

5(c)(2). Ninety-five percent of the area under the normal curve lies between +/- two standard deviations of the mean. Since the mean minus two standard deviations (9.44 - 7.0 = 2.44) is positive, one may conclude that the probability of breaking even is greater than 95%.

5(d). It seems at first that government bonds offer less return and more risk than real estate. However, real estate and government bonds might provide a good combination if the two do not fluctuate in a similar fashion, so that the variability of the portfolio is less than the variability of the individual investments. If the correlation coefficient applicable to this pair of investments is known and is not highly positive, the combination would be advantageous.

6(a). (1) Common Stock Risk Premium
= Return Common Stock - Return of U.S. Gov't T-bills
= 12.50 - 4.50
= 8.00%

(2) Small Firms Stock Risk Premium
= Return of Small Capitalization Common Stock
 - Return of Total Stocks (S&P 500)
= 14.60 - 12.50
= 2.10%

(3) Horizon (Maturity) Premium
= Return on Long-term Gov't Bonds
 - Return on U.S. Gov't T-bills
= 5.10 - 4.50
= 0.60%

(4) Default Premium
= Return on Long-term Corporate Bonds
 - Return on Long-term Gov't Bonds
= 5.80 - 5.10
= 0.70%

Harcourt, Inc.

6(b).　If Inflation = 4%

$$\text{"Real" rate of return} = \frac{\text{Holding Period Return}}{1 + \text{rate of inflation}} - 1$$

US T-bills
Real Rate of Return $= \dfrac{1 + .045}{1 + .04} - 1 = .0048$ or 0.48%

Common Stock
Real Rate of Return $= \dfrac{1 + .125}{1 + .04} - 1 = .0817$ or 8.17%

L-T Corporate Bonds
Real Rate of Return $= \dfrac{1 + .058}{1 + .04} - 1 = .0173$ or 1.73%

L-T Government Bonds
Real Rate of Return $= \dfrac{1 + .051}{1 + .04} - 1 = .0106$ or 1.06%

Small Cap Common Stock
Real Rate of Return $= \dfrac{1 + .1460}{1 + .04} - 1 = .1019$ or 10.09%

# APPENDIX 3

## Answers to Problems

1.  Lauren's average return

    $$\bar{L} = \frac{(5 + 12 - 11 + 10 + 12)}{5}$$

    $$= 28/5 = 5.6$$

    Kayleigh's average return

    $$\bar{K} = \frac{(5 + 15 + 5 + 7 - 10)}{5}$$

    $$= 22/5 = 4.4$$

| $L - \bar{L}$ | | $K - \bar{K}$ | |
|---|---|---|---|
| 5 - 5.6 = | -0.6 | 5 - 4.4 = | 0.6 |
| 12 - 5.6 = | 6.4 | 15 - 4.4 = | 10.6 |
| -11 - 5.6 = | -16.6 | 5 - 4.4 = | 0.6 |
| 10 - 5.6 = | 4.4 | 7 - 4.4 = | 2.6 |
| 12 - 5.6 = | 6.4 | -10 - 4.4 = | -14.4 |

$$COV_{LK} = \frac{\Sigma(L - \bar{L})(K - \bar{K})}{N}$$

$$= \frac{(-.6)(.6) + (6.4)(10.6) + (-16.6)(.6) + (4.4)(2.6) + (6.4)(-14.4)}{5}$$

$$= \frac{-23.2}{5} = -4.64$$

2.  Calculation of Correlation Coefficient

| Observation | $L - \bar{L}$ | $(L - \bar{L})^2$ | $(K - \bar{K})$ | $(K - \bar{K})^2$ |
|---|---|---|---|---|
| 1 | -.06 | .36 | 0.6 | .36 |
| 2 | 6.4 | 40.96 | 10.6 | 112.36 |
| 3 | -16.6 | 275.56 | 2.6 | 6.76 |
| 4 | 4.4 | 19.36 | 0.6 | 0.36 |
| 5 | 6.4 | 40.96 | -14.4 | 207.36 |
| | | 377.20 | | 327.20 |

3 - 8

$$\sigma_L^2 = \frac{377.2}{5} = 75.44 \qquad\qquad \sigma_K^2 = \frac{327.2}{5} = 65.44$$

$$\sigma_L = \sqrt{75.44} = 8.69 \qquad\qquad \sigma_K = \sqrt{65.44} = 8.09$$

$$r_{LK} = \frac{COV_{LK}}{\sigma_{:L}\sigma_K} = \frac{-4.64}{(8.69)(8.09)} = -.066$$

While there is a slight negative correlation, the two securities are essentially uncorrelated. Thus, even though the two companies produce similar products, their historical returns suggest that holding both of these securities would help reduce risk through diversification.

# CHAPTER 4

# ORGANIZATION AND FUNCTIONING OF SECURITIES MARKETS

## Answers to Questions

1. A market is a means whereby buyers and sellers are brought together to aid in the transfer of goods and/or services. While it generally has a physical location it need not necessarily have one. Secondly, there is no requirement of ownership by those who establish and administer the market—they need only provide a cheap, smooth transfer of goods and/or services for a diverse clientele.

   A good market should provide accurate information on the price and volume of past transactions, and current supply and demand. Clearly, there should be rapid dissemination of this information. Adequate liquidity is desirable so that participants may buy and sell their goods and/or services rapidly, at a price reflecting the supply and demand. The costs of transferring ownership and middleman commissions should be low. Finally, the prevailing price should reflect all available information.

2. This is a good discussion question for class because you could explore with students what are some of the alternatives that are used by investors with regards to other assets such as art and antiques. Some possibilities are ads in the paper of your local community or large cities. Another obvious alternative is an auction. With an ad you would have to specify a price or be ready to negotiate with a buyer. With an auction you would be very uncertain of what you would receive. In all cases, there would be a substantial time problem.

3. Liquidity is the ability to sell an asset quickly at a price not substantially different from the current market assuming no new information is available. A share of AT&T is very liquid, while an antique would be a fairly illiquid asset. A share of AT&T is highly liquid since an investor could convert it into cash within 1/8 of a point of the current market price. An antique is illiquid since it is relatively difficult to find a buyer and then you are uncertain as to what price the prospective buyer would offer.

4. The primary market in securities is where new issues are sold by corporations to acquire new capital via the sale of bonds, preferred stock or common stock. The sale typically takes place through an investment banker.

   The secondary market is simply trading in outstanding securities. It involves transactions between owners after the issue has been sold to the public by the company. Consequently, the proceeds from the sale do not go to the company, as is the case with a primary offering. Thus, the price of the security is important to the buyer and seller.

   The functioning of the primary market would be seriously hampered in the absence of a good secondary market. A good secondary market provides liquidity to an investor if he

Harcourt, Inc.

or she wants to alter the composition of his or her portfolio from securities to other assets (i.e., house, etc.). Thus, investors would be reluctant to acquire securities in the primary market if they felt they would not subsequently have the ability to sell the securities quickly at a known price.

5. An example of an initial public offering (IPO) would be a small company selling company stock to the public for the first time. By contrast, a seasoned equity refers to an established company, such as IBM, offering a new issue of common stock to an existing market for the stock. The IPO involves greater risk for the buyer because there is not an established secondary market for the small firm. Without an established secondary market the buyer incurs additional liquidity risk associated with the IPO.

6. Student Exercise

7. In competitive bid the issuer is responsible for specifying the type of security to be offered, the timing, etc. and then soliciting competitive bids from investment banking firms wishing to act as an underwriter. The high bids will be awarded the contracts. Negotiated relationships are contractual arrangements between an underwriter and the issuer wherein the underwriter helps the issuer prepare the bond issue with the understanding that they have the exclusive right to sell the issue.

8. The difference in the price of membership between the two exchanges can be explained by differences in volume and in type of instruments traded. The premium price paid for membership on the NYSE is because the NYSE is the dominant domestic market trading equity shares. Rather than engage in direct competition with the NYSE, the AMEX has become an innovative market with a strong emphasis on foreign stocks and options.

9. One reason for the existence of regional exchanges is that they provide trading facilities for geographically local companies that do not qualify for listing on a national exchange. Second, they list national firms thus providing small local brokerage firms that are not members of a national exchange the opportunity to trade in securities that are listed on a national exchange.

The essential difference between the national and regional exchanges is that the regional exchanges have less stringent listing requirements, thus allowing small firms to obtain listing.

10. The OTC market is larger than the listed exchanges in terms of the number of issues traded, almost 7,000 issues are traded on the OTC market compared to 3,670 stock issues (common and preferred) for the NYSE and 829 stock issues listed on the AMEX. In sharp contrast, the NYSE has a larger total value of trading—in 1997, NYSE value of equity trading was about $4,300 billion and NASDAQ was about $3,500 billion.

11. Level 1 provides a current quote on NASDAQ stocks for brokerage firms that are not regular OTC customers. It is a median quote that is representative of the quotes of the several market makers in the particular security. Level 2 is for serious traders who desire not only current trends but specific quotes of different market makers. This enables the

broker to make a deal with the market maker offering the best price. Level 3 is for investment firms who desire all the information provided in Level 2 but also need the ability to enter their own quotes or change them relative to other market makers. NASDAQ is an electronic quotation system that serves the OTC market. It enables all quotes by all market makers to be immediately available.

12(a). The third market is the OTC trading of exchange listed securities. It enables the non-members of the exchange to trade in exchange listed securities. Most of the large institutional favorites are traded on the third market—e.g., IBM, Xerox, General Motors.

12(b). The fourth market is the direct trading between two parties without a broker intermediary. Institutions trade in the fourth market since these trades are large volume and consequently substantial savings can be made by trading directly with a buyer, thus avoiding commissions.

13(a). A market order is an order to buy/sell a stock at the most profitable ask/bid prices prevailing at the time the order hits the exchange floor. A market order implies the investor wants the transaction completed quickly at the prevailing price. Example: I read good reports about AT&T and I'm certain the stock will go up in value. When I call my broker and submit a market buy order for 100 shares of AT&T, the prevailing asking price is 60. Total cost for my shares will be $6,000 + commission.

13(b). A limit order specifies a maximum price that the individual will pay to purchase the stock or the minimum he will accept to sell it. Example: AT&T is selling for $60—I would put in a limit buy order for one week to buy 100 shares at $59.

13(c). A short sale is the sale of stock that is not currently owned by the seller with the intent of purchasing it later at a lower price. This is done by borrowing the stock from another investor through a broker. Example: I expect AT&T to go to $48—I would sell it short at $60 and expect to replace it when it gets to $55.

13(d). A stop-loss order is a conditional order whereby the investor indicates that he wants to sell the stock if the price drops to a specified price, thus protecting himself from a large and rapid decline in price. Example: I buy AT&T at $60 and put in a stop loss at $57 that protects me from a major loss if it starts to decline.

14. The specialist acts as a broker in handling limit orders placed with member brokers. Being constantly in touch with current prices, he is in a better position to execute limit orders since it is entered in his books and executed as soon as appropriate. Second, he maintains a fair and orderly market by trading on his own account when there is inadequate supply or demand. If the spread between the bid and ask is substantial, he can place his own bid or ask in order to narrow the spread. This helps provide a continuous market with orderly price changes.

The specialist obtains income from both his functions: commissions as a broker, and outperforming the market in his dealer function using the monopolistic information he has on limit orders.

15. The Saitori members are referred to as intermediary clerks. Similar to the U.S. specialists, the Saitori members do not deal with public customers. Their duties entail matching buy and sell orders for the regular members of the Tokyo Exchange and they maintain the book for regular limit orders. Unlike the U.S. exchange specialist, the Saitori are not allowed to buy and sell for their own account and, thus, they do not have the duty or capability to ensure an orderly market.

16. Much of the change experienced on the secondary equity market can be attributed to changes occurring within the financial industry as a whole. As banks, insurance companies, investment companies and other financial service firms enter the capital markets, the volume and size of transactions continues to grow. This dominance by large institutions in the marketplace caused the following changes in the markets:
(1) the imposition of negotiated (competitive) commission rates
(2) the influence of block trades
(3) the impact of stock price volatility
(4) the development of a national market system

These changes have increased the competition among firms that trade large institutional stocks. However, there is some concern that the individual investor is being "crowded out" and that the equity market for smaller firms will also suffer. The evolving globalization of markets will also have an impact.

17. A "give-up" is the practice of the brokerage firm executing the trade paying part of the commission to other brokerage or research firms designated by the institution. Typically, these other brokerage firms provided research or sales services to the institution. These commission transfers were referred to as "soft dollars." "Give-ups" existed in the fixed commission world because brokers realized that institutions were charged more for large trades than justified by the cost.

18. The Exchange requires that the specialist has enough capital to acquire 15,000 shares of each stock assigned or $1 million, whichever is greater. Even when the specialist has the capital he might be unwilling to commit himself to a large position. Holding 15,000 shares in a stock is fairly risky particularly when the market for the underlying stock is thin. The third "c," contacts, could seriously hamper the specialist especially in the light of Rule 113, which prohibits specialists from dealing directly with customers. The specialist is often compelled to contact another institution interested in buying a block of the stock. When he can't contact other potential customers he does not want to take a position in the stock.

19. A block house is a brokerage firm, either member or non-member of an exchange, which stands ready to buy or sell a block for institutions. Block houses evolved because institutions were not getting what they needed from the specialist and, hence, asked institutional brokerage firms to locate other institutions with an interest in buying or selling given blocks.

When an institution wishes to sell a stock it typically contacts a block house, who contacts prospective institutional buyers. If the block house does not find buyers for the entire block, it buys the remainder (thus taking a position) with the hope of selling it later. Naturally, the block house assumes substantial risk on this position because of the uncertainty of subsequent price changes.

20(a). Though, the exact form of the National Market System (NMS) remains nebulous, major features of such a market are:

(1) **Centralized reporting** of all transactions regardless of where the trade took place. Currently, this exists for all NYSE stocks.

(2) **Centralized quotation system** that would list quotes for a given stock from all market-makers on the national exchanges, the regional exchanges, and the OTC. This increased information is beneficial to the investor.

(3) **Central limit order book (CLOB)** that contains all limit orders from all exchanges.

(4) **Competition among market-makers** which would force dealers to offer better bids and asks, thus narrowing the bid-ask spread.

20(b). The Inter-Market Trading System (ITS) is a centralized quotation system, currently available, consisting of a central computer facility with interconnected terminals in the participating market centers. Brokers and market-makers in each market center can indicate to those in other centers specific buying and selling commitments by way of a composite quotation display. A broker or market-maker in any market center can thus exercise his own best judgment in determining, on the basis of current quotations, where to execute a customer's orders. While ITS provides the centralized quotation system that is necessary for a National Market System (NMS), it does not have the capability for automatic execution at the best market; it is necessary to contact the market-maker and indicate that you want to buy or sell at his bid or ask. Also, it is not mandatory that a broker go to the best market to execute a customer's orders.

The data in Table 4.9 indicate significant growth in the number of issues on the system, the volume of shares traded and the size of the trades.

21. Student Exercise

# CHAPTER 4

## Answers to Problems

1(a). Assume you pay cash for the stock: Number of shares you could purchase = $40,000/$80 = 500 shares.

    (1)    If the stock is later sold at $100 a share, the total shares proceeds would be $100 x 500 shares = $50,000. Therefore, the rate of return from investing in the stock is as follows:

$$= \frac{\$50,000 - \$40,000}{\$40,000} = 25.00\%$$

    (2)    If stock is later sold at $40 a share, the total shares proceeds would be $40 x $500 shares = $20,000. Therefore, the rate of return from investing in the stock would be:

$$= \frac{\$20,000 - \$40,000}{\$40,000} = -50.00\%$$

1(b). Assuming you use the maximum amount of leverage in buying the stock, the leverage factor for a 60 percent margin requirement is = 1/percentage margin requirement = 1/.60 = 5/3. Thus, the rate of return on the stock if it is later sold at $100 a share = 25.00% x 5/3 = 41.67%. In contrast, the rate of return on the stock if it is sold for $40 a share = -50.00% x 5/3 = -83.33%.

2(a). Since the margin is 40 percent and Lauren currently has $50,000 on deposit in her margin account, if Lauren uses the maximum allowable margin her $50,000 deposit must represent 40% of her total investment. Thus, $50,000 = .4x then x = $125,000. Since the shares are priced at $35 each, Lauren can purchase $125,000 − $35 = 3,571 shares (rounded).

2(b). Total Profit = Total Return - Total Investment
    (1)    If stock rises to $45/share, Lauren's total return is:
        3,571 shares x $45 = $160,695.
        Total profit = $160,695 - $125,000 = $35,695

    (2)    If stock falls to $25/share, Lauren's total return is:
        3,571 shares x $25 = $89,275.
        Total loss = $89,275 - $125,000 = -$35,725.

2(c)

$$\text{Margin} = \frac{\text{Market Value - Debit Balance}}{\text{Market Value}}$$

where Market Value = Price per share x Number of shares.

Initial Loan Value = Total Investment - Initial Margin.
$$= \$125,000 - \$50,000 = \$75,000$$

Therefore, if maintenance margin is 30 percent:

$$.30 = \frac{(3,571 \text{ shares x Price}) - \$75,000}{(3,571 \text{ shares x Price}}$$

$.30 (3,571 \text{ x Price}) = (3,571 \text{ x Price}) - \$75,000.$
$\quad 1,071.3 \text{ x Price} = (3,571 \text{ x Price}) - \$75,000$
$\quad -2,499.7 \text{ x Price} = -\$75,000$
$\quad\quad\quad\quad \text{Price} = \$30.00$

3.  Profit = Ending Value - Beginning Value + Dividends - Transaction Costs - Interest

Beginning Value of Investment = $20 x 100 shares = $2,000

Your Investment = margin requirement + commission.
$$= (.55 \text{ x } \$2,000) + (.03 \text{ x } \$2,000)$$
$$= \$1,100 + \$60$$
$$= \$1,160$$

Ending Value of Investment = $27 x 100 shares
$$= \$2,700$$

Dividends = $.50 x 100 shares = $50.00

Transaction Costs = (.03 x $2,000) + (.03 x $2,700)
(Commission)    = $60 + $81
$$= \$141$$

Interest = .10 x (.45 x $2,000) = $90.00

Therefore:

Profit = $2,700 - $2,000 + $50 - $141 - $90
$$= \$519$$

The rate of return on your investment of $1,160 is:

$$\$519/\$1,160 = 44.74\%$$

4.  Profit on a Short Sale = Begin.Value -Ending Value -Dividends –Trans. Costs - Interest

Beginning Value of Investment = $56.00 x 100 shares = $5,600
(sold under a short sale arrangement)

4 - 7

Your investment = margin requirement + commission
$$= (.45 \times \$5,600) + \$155$$
$$= \$2,520 + \$155$$
$$= \$2,675$$

Ending Value of Investment = $45.00 x 100 = $4,500
(Cost of closing out position)

Dividends = $2.50 x 100 shares = $250.00

Transaction Costs = $155 + $145 = $300.00

Interest = .08 x (.55 x $5,600) = $246.40

Therefore:

Profit = $5,600 - $4,500 - $250 - $300 - $246.40
= $303.60

The rate of return on your investment of $2,675 is:

$$\$303.60/\$2,675 = 11.35\%$$

5(a). I am satisfied with the profit resulting from the sale of the 200 shares at $40.

5(b). With the stop loss: ($40 - $25)/$25 = 60%
Without the stop loss: ($30 - $25)/$25 = 20%

6(a). Assuming that you pay cash for the stock:

$$\text{Rate of Return} = \frac{(\$45 \times 300) - (\$30 \times 300)}{(\$30 \times 300)} = \frac{13,500 - 9000}{9000} = 50\%$$

6(b). Assuming that you used the maximum leverage in buying the stock, the leverage factor for a 60 percent margin requirement is = 1/margin requirement = 1/.60 = 1.67. Thus, the rate of return on the stock if it is later sold at $45 a share = 50% x 1.67 = 83.33%.

7. Limit order @ $24: When market declined to $20, your limit order was executed $24 (buy), then the price went to $36.
Rate of return = ($36 - $24)/$24 = 50%.

Assuming market order @ $28: Buy at $28, price goes to $36
Rate of return = ($36 - $28)/$28 = 28.57%.

Limit order @ $18: Since the market did not decline to $18 (lowest price was $20) the limit order was never executed.

4 - 8

# CHAPTER 5

# SECURITY-MARKET INDICATOR SERIES

## Answers to Questions

1.  The purpose of market indicator series is to provide a general indication of the aggregate market changes or market movements. More specifically, the indicator series are used to derive market returns for a period of interest and then used as a benchmark for evaluating the performance of alternative portfolios. A second use is in examining the factors that influence aggregate stock price movements by forming relationships between market (series) movements and changes in the relevant variables in order to illustrate how these variables influence market movements. A further use is by technicians who use past aggregate market movements to predict future price patterns. Finally, a very important use is in portfolio theory, where the systematic risk of an individual security is determined by the relationship of the rates of return for the individual security to rates of return for a market portfolio of risky assets. Here, a representative market indicator series is used as a proxy for the market portfolio of risky assets.

2.  A characteristic that differentiates alternative market indicator series is the sample--the size of the sample (how representative of the total market it is) and the source (whether securities are of a particular type or a given segment of the population (NYSE, TSE). The weight given to each member plays a discriminatory role--with diverse members in a sample, it would make a difference whether the series is price-weighted, value-weighted, or unweighted. Finally, the computational procedure used for calculating return--i.e., whether arithmetic mean, geometric mean, etc.

3.  A price-weighted series is an unweighted arithmetic average of current prices of the securities included in the sample--i.e., closing prices of all securities are summed and divided by the number of securities in the sample.

    A $100 security will have a greater influence on the series than a $25 security because a 10 percent increase in the former increases the numerator by $10 while it takes a 40 percent increase in the price of the latter to have the same effect.

4.  A value-weighted index begins by deriving the initial total market value of all stocks used in the series (market value equals number of shares outstanding times current market price). The initial value is typically established as the base value and assigned an index value of 100. Subsequently, a new market value is computed for all securities in the sample and this new value is compared to the initial value to derive the percent change which is then applied to the beginning index value of 100.

5.  Given a four security series and a 2-for-1 split for security A and a 3-for-1 split for security B, the divisor would change from 4 to 2.8 for a price-weighted series.

Harcourt, Inc.

| Stock | Before Split Price | After Split Prices |
|-------|--------------------|--------------------|
| A | $20 | $10 |
| B | 30 | 10 |
| C | 20 | 20 |
| D | 30 | 30 |
| Total | 100/4 = 25 | 70/x = 25 |
|  |  | x = 2.8 |

The price-weighted series adjusts for a stock split by deriving a new divisor that will ensure that the new value for the series is the same as it would have been without the split. The adjustment for a value-weighted series due to a stock split is automatic. The decrease in stock price is offset by an increase in the number of shares outstanding.

**Before Split**

| Stock | Price/Share | # of Shares | Market Value |
|-------|-------------|-------------|--------------|
| A | $20 | 1,000,000 | $20,000,000 |
| B | 30 | 500,000 | 15,000,000 |
| C | 20 | 2,000,000 | 40,000,000 |
| D | 30 | 3,500,000 | 105,000,000 |
| Total |  |  | $180,000,000 |

The $180,000,000 base value is set equal to an index value of 100.

**After Split**

| Stock | Price/Share | # of Shares | Market Value |
|-------|-------------|-------------|--------------|
| A | $10 | 2,000,000 | $20,000,000 |
| B | 10 | 1,500,000 | 15,000,000 |
| C | 20 | 2,000,000 | 40,000,000 |
| D | 30 | 3,500,000 | 105,000,000 |
| Total |  |  | $180,000,000 |

$$\text{New Index Value} = \frac{\text{Current Market Value}}{\text{Base Value}} \times \text{Beginning Index Value}$$

$$= \frac{180,000,000}{180,000,000} \times 100$$

$$= 100$$

which is precisely what one would expect since there has been no change in prices other than the split.

6.  In an unweighted price indicator series, all stocks carry equal weight irrespective of their price and/or their value. One way to visualize an unweighted series is to assume that equal dollar amounts are invested in each stock in the portfolio, for example, an equal amount of $1,000 is assumed to be invested in each stock. Therefore, the investor would own 25 shares of GM ($40/share) and 40 shares of Coors Brewing ($25/share). a $100 stock. An unweighted price index that consists of the above three stocks would be constructed as follows:

5 - 2

| Stock | Price/Share | # of Shares | Market Value |
|-------|-------------|-------------|--------------|
| GM | $ 40 | 25 | $1,000 |
| Coors | 25 | 40 | 1,000 |
| Total | | | $2,000 |

**A 20% price increase in GM:**

| Stock | Price/Share | # of Shares | Market Value |
|-------|-------------|-------------|--------------|
| GM | $ 48 | 25 | $1,200 |
| Coors | 25 | 40 | 1,000 |
| Total | | | $2,200 |

**A 20% price increase in Coors:**

| Stock | Price/Share | # of Shares | Market Value |
|-------|-------------|-------------|--------------|
| GM | $ 40 | 25 | $1,000 |
| Coors | 30 | 40 | 1,200 |
| Total | | | $2,200 |

Therefore, a 20% increase in either stock would have the same impact on the total value of the index (i.e., in all cases the index increases by 10%. An alternative treatment is to compute percentage changes for each stock and derive the average of these percentage changes. In this case, the average would be 10% (20% - 0%)). So in the case of an unweighted price-indicator series, a 20% price increase in GM would have the same impact on the index as a 20% price increase of Coors Brewing.

7. Based upon the sample from which it is derived and the fact that is a value-weighted index, the Wilshire 5000 Equity Index is a weighted composite of the NYSE composite index, the AMEX market value series, and the NASDAQ composite index. We would expect it to have the highest correlation with the NYSE Composite Index because the NYSE has the highest market value. The AMEX index would have the lowest correlation with the Wilshire Index.

8. The high correlations between returns for alternative NYSE price indicator series can be attributed to the **source** of the sample (i.e. stock traded on the NYSE). The four series differ in sample size, that is, the DJIA has 30 securities, the S&P 400 has 400 securities, the S&P 500 has 500 securities, and the NYSE Composite about 2330 stocks. The DJIA differs in computation from the other series, that is, the DJIA is a price-weighted series where the other three series are value-weighted. Even so, there is strong correlation between the series because of similarity of types of companies (see Table 5.11).

9. Using the DJIA as a measure of the NYSE, AMEX Value Index for the AMEX and NASDAQ Composite for the OTC, Table 5.13 shows that the NASDAQ achieved the highest average annual return while the AMEX had the greatest amount of variability (measured by standard deviation). Economic theory would suggest that the larger

5 - 3

companies in the DJIA (all NYSE stocks) would tend to have less risk (the smallest standard deviation of the three U.S. equity market segments) and thus a smaller return (lowest average annual price change). However, examining the coefficient of variation for the DJIA (1.66), it was actually higher than for the NASDAQ (1.49).

10. The two stock price indexes (Tokyo SE and Nikkei) for the Tokyo Stock Exchange listed in Table 5.11 show a high positive correlation (.872). However, the two indexes represent substantially different sample sizes and weighting schemes. The Nikkei-Dow Jones Average consists of 225 companies and is a price-weighted series. Alternatively, the Tokyo SE encompasses a much large set of 1800 companies and is a value-weighted series.

   Although the NYSE is the only index listed in Table 5.11 that includes just NYSE stocks, the S&P 500 has a high concentration of NYSE stocks. Both indexes are value-weighted but are different in sample size. However, the two indexes are highly correlated (.919).

   The correlation between the TSE indexes (Tokyo SE and Nikkei) and NYSE series (S&P 500 and NYSE) are substantially lower (between .30 and .35). These results support the argument for diversification among countries.

11. Since the equal-weighted series implies that all stocks carry the same weight, irrespective of price or value, the results indicate that on average all stocks in the index increased by 23 percent. On the other hand, the percentage change in the value of a large company has a greater impact than the same percentage change for a small company in the value weighted index. Therefore, the difference in results indicates that for this given period, the smaller companies in the index outperformed the larger companies.

12. The bond-market series are more difficult to construct due to the wide diversity of bonds available. Also bonds are hard to standardize because their maturities and market yields are constantly changing. In order to better segment the market, you could construct five possible subindexes based on coupon, quality, industry, maturity, and special features (such as call features, warrants, convertibility, etc.).

13. Since the Merrill Lynch-Wilshire Capital Markets index is composed of a distribution of bonds as well as stocks, the fact that this index increased by 15 percent, compared to a 5 percent gain in the Wilshire 5000 Index indicates that bonds outperformed stocks over this period of time.

14. The Russell 1000, and Russell 2000 represent two different population sample of stocks, segmented by size. The fact that the Russell 2000 (which is composed of the smallest 2,000 stocks in the Russell 3000) increased more than the Russell 1000 (composed of the 1000 largest capitalization U.S. stocks) indicates that small stocks performed better during this time period.

15. One would expect that the level of correlation between the various world indexes should be relatively high. These indexes tend to include the same countries and the largest capitalization stocks within each country.

# CHAPTER 5

## Answers to Problems

1(a). Given a three security series and a price change from period T to T+1, the percentage change in the series would be 42.85 percent.

|   | **Period T** | **Period T+1** |
|---|---|---|
| A | $ 60 | $ 80 |
| B | 20 | 35 |
| C | 18 | 25 |
| Sum | $ 98 | $140 |
| Divisor | 3 | 3 |
| Average | 32.67 | 46.67 |

$$\text{Percentage change} = \frac{46.67 - 32.67}{32.67} = \frac{14.00}{32.67} = 42.85\%$$

1(b).

**Period T**

| Stock | Price/Share | # of Shares | Market Value |
|---|---|---|---|
| A | $60 | 1,000,000 | $ 60,000,000 |
| B | 20 | 10,000,000 | 200,000,000 |
| C | 18 | 30,000,000 | 540,000,000 |
| Total | | | $800,000,000 |

**Period T+1**

| Stock | Price/Share | # of Shares | Market Value |
|---|---|---|---|
| A | $80 | 1,000,000 | $ 80,000,000 |
| B | 35 | 10,000,000 | 350,000,000 |
| C | 25 | 30,000,000 | 750,000,000 |
| Total | | | $800,000,000 |

$$\text{Percentage change} = \frac{1,180 - 800}{800} = \frac{380}{800} = 47.50\%$$

1(c). The percentage change for the price-weighted series is a simple average of the differences in price from one period to the next. Equal weights are applied to each price change.

The percentage change for the value-weighted series is a weighted average of the differences in price from one period T to T+1. These weights are the relative market values for each stock. Thus, Stock C carries the greatest weight followed by B and then A. Because Stock C had the greatest percentage increase and the largest weight, it is easy to see that the percentage change would be larger for this series than the price-weighted series.

Harcourt, Inc.

2(a).

**Period T**

| Stock | Price/Share | # of Shares | Market Value |
|-------|-------------|-------------|--------------|
| A | $60 | 16.67 | $ 1,000,000 |
| B | 20 | 50.00 | 1,000,000 |
| C | 18 | 55.56 | 1,000,000 |
| Total | | | $3,000,000 |

**Period T+1**

| Stock | Price/Share | # of Shares | Market Value |
|-------|-------------|-------------|--------------|
| A | $80 | 16.67 | $ 1,333.60 |
| B | 35 | 50.00 | 1,750.00 |
| C | 25 | 55.56 | 1,389.00 |
| Total | | | $4,470.60 |

$$\text{Percentage change} = \frac{4,472.60 - 3,000}{3,000} = \frac{1,472.60}{3,000} = 49.09\%$$

2(b).

$$\text{Stock A} = \frac{80-60}{60} = \frac{20}{60} = 33.33\%$$

$$\text{Stock B} = \frac{35-20}{20} = \frac{15}{20} = 75.00\%$$

$$\text{Stock C} = \frac{25-18}{18} = \frac{7}{18} = 38.89\%$$

$$\text{Arithmetic average} = \frac{33.33\% + 75.00\% + 38.89\%}{3}$$

$$= \frac{147.22\%}{3} = 49.07\%$$

The answers are the same (slight difference due to rounding). This is what you would expect since Part A represents the percentage change of an equal-weighted series and Part B applies an equal weight to the separate stocks in calculating the arithmetic average.

2(c). Geometric average is the nth root of the product of n items.

$$\begin{aligned}
\text{Geometric average} &= [(1.3333)(1.75)(1.3889)]^{1/3} - 1 \\
&= [3.2407]^{1/3} - 1 \\
&= 1.4798 - 1 \\
&= .4798 \text{ or } 47.98\%
\end{aligned}$$

The geometric average is less than the arithmetic average. This is because variability of return has a greater affect on the arithmetic average than the geometric average.

3.   Student Exercise

4(a).

$$DJIA = \sum_{i=1}^{30} P_{it} / D_{adj}$$

**Day 1**

| Company | Price/Share |
|---------|-------------|
| A | 12 |
| B | 23 |
| C | 52 |

$$DJIA = \frac{12 + 23 + 52}{3} = \frac{87}{3} = 29$$

**Day 2**

| | (Before Split) |
|---------|-------------|
| Company | Price/Share |
| A | 10 |
| B | 22 |
| C | 55 |

$$DJIA = \frac{10 + 22 + 55}{3}$$

$$= \frac{87}{3} = 29$$

| | (After Split) |
|---------|-------------|
| | Price/Share |
| | 10 |
| | 44 |
| | 55 |

$$DJIA = \frac{10 + 44 + 55}{X}$$

$$29 = \frac{109}{X}$$

$$X = 3.7586 \text{ (new divisor)}$$

**Day 3**

| | (Before Split) |
|---------|-------------|
| Company | Price/Share |
| A | 14 |
| B | 46 |
| C | 52 |

$$DJIA = \frac{14 + 46 + 52}{3.7586} = 29.798$$

$$= \frac{112}{3.7586}$$

| | (After Split) |
|---------|-------------|
| | Price/Share |
| | 14 |
| | 46 |
| | 26 |

$$DJIA = \frac{14 + 46 + 26}{Y}$$

$$29.798 = \frac{86}{Y}$$

$$Y = 2.8861 \text{ (new divisor)}$$

Harcourt, Inc.

**Day 4**

| Company | Price/Share |
|---------|-------------|
| A | 13 |
| B | 47 |
| C | 25 |

$$\text{DJIA} = \frac{13 + 47 + 25}{2.8861}$$

$$= \frac{85}{2.8861} = 29.452$$

**Day 5**

| Company | Price/Share |
|---------|-------------|
| A | 12 |
| B | 45 |
| C | 26 |

$$\text{DJIA} = \frac{12 + 45 + 26}{2.8861}$$

$$= \frac{83}{2.8861} = 28.759$$

4(b).   Since the index is a price-weighted average, the higher priced stocks carry more weight. But when a split occurs, the new divisor ensures that the new value for the series is the same as it would have been without the split. Hence, the main effect of a split is just a repositioning of the relative weight that a particular stock carries in determining the index. For example, a 10% price change for company B would carry more weight in determining the percent change in the index in Day 3 after the reverse split that increased its price, than its weight on Day 2.

4(c).   Student Exercise

5(a).   Base   = ($12 x 500) + ($23 x 350) + ($52 x 250)
        = $6,000 + $8,050 + $13,000 = $27,050

Day 1  = ($12 x 500) + ($23 x 350) + ($52 x 250)
        = $6,000 + $8,050 + $13,000 = $27,050

$\text{Index}_1 = (\$27,050/\$27,050) \times 10 = 10$

Day 2  = ($10 x 500) + ($22 x 350) + ($55 x 250)
        = $5,000 + $7,700 + $13,750 = $26,450

$\text{Index}_2 = (\$26,450/\$27,050) \times 10 = 9.778$

Day 3  = ($14 x 500) + ($46 x 175) + ($52 x 250)
        = $7,000 + $8,050 + $13,000 = $28,050

$\text{Index}_3 = (\$28,050/\$27,050) \times 10 = 10.370$

5 - 8

Day 4 $= (\$13 \times 500) + (\$47 \times 175) + (\$25 \times 500)$
$= \$6,500 + \$8,225 + \$12,500 = \$27,225$

$Index_4 = (\$27,225/\$27,050) \times 10 = 10.065$

Day 5 $= (\$12 \times 500) + (\$45 \times 175) + (\$26 \times 500)$
$= \$6,000 + \$7,875 + \$13,000 = \$26,875$

$Index_5 = (\$26,875/\$27,050) \times 10 = 9.935$

5(b).  The market values are unchanged due to splits and thus stock splits have no effect. The index, however, is weighted by the relative market values.

6.  Price-weighted index$(PWI)_{1998} = (20 + 80 + 40)/3 = 46.67$

To accounted for stock split, a new divisor must be calculated:
$(20 + 40 + 40)/X = 46.67$
$X = 2.143$ (new divisor after stock split)

Price-weighted index$_{1999} = (32 + 45 + 42)/2.143 = 55.53$

$VWI_{1998} = 20(100,000,000) + 80(2,000,000) + 40(25,000,000)$
$= 2,000,000,000 + 160,000,000 + 1,000,000,000$
$= 3,160,000,000$

assuming a base value of 100 and 1998 as base period, then $3,160,000,000/3,160,000,000 \times 100 = 100$

$VWI_{1999} = 32(100,000,000) + 45(4,000,000) + 42(25,000,000)$
$= 3,200,000,000 + 180,000,000 + 1,050,000,000$
$= 4,430,000,000$

assuming a base value of 100 and 1998 as period, then $4,430,000,000/3,160,000,000 \times 100 = 1.4019 \times 100 = 140.19$

6(a).  Percentage change in PWI $= (55.53 - 46.67)/46.67 = 18.99\%$

Percentage change in VWI $= (140.19 - 100)/100 = 40.19\%$

6(b).  The percentage change in VWI was much greater than the change in the PWI because the stock with the largest market value (K) had the greater percentage gain in price (60% increase).

6(c).

**December 31, 1999**

| Stock | Price/Share | # of Shares | Market Value |
|-------|-------------|-------------|--------------|
| K | $20 | 50.0 | $1,000.00 |
| M | 80 | 12.5 | 1,000.00 |
| R | 40 | 25.0 | 1,000.00 |
| Total | | | $3,000.00 |

**December 31, 2000**

| Stock | Price/Share | # of Shares | Market Value |
|-------|-------------|-------------|--------------|
| K | $32 | 50.0 | $1,600.00 |
| M | 45 | 25.5* | 1,125.00 |
| R | 42 | 25.0 | 1,050.00 |
| Total | | | $3,775.00 |

(*Stock-split two-for-one during the year)

$$\text{Percentage change} = \frac{3,775.00 - 3,000}{3,000} = \frac{775.00}{3,000} = 25.83\%$$

$$\begin{aligned}
\text{(As a geometric average} &= [(1.60)(1.125)(1.05)]^{1/3} - 1 \\
&= [1.89]^{1/3} - 1 \\
&= 1.2364 - 1 \\
&= .2364 \text{ or } 23.64\%
\end{aligned}$$

Unweighted averages are not impacted by large changes in stocks prices (i.e. price-weighted series) or in market values (i.e. value-weighted series).

7(a).   Using the geometric mean from Table 5.13 for the Nikkei Index:

$$100 \times (1.0697)^{25} = 100 \times 5.3895 = 538.95$$

7(b).   For 1972 = 100/200 = .50
For 1997 = 538.95/125 = 4.3116

$$\begin{aligned}
\text{Return in \$} &= (4.3116/.50)^{1/25} - 1 \\
&= (8.6232)^{1/25} - 1 \\
&= 1.09 - 1 = .09 = 9\%
\end{aligned}$$

5 - 10

# CHAPTER 6

# SOURCES OF INFORMATION ON GLOBAL INVESTMENTS

## Answers to Questions

1.  Past data on Gross Domestic Product can be readily obtained from the *Federal Reserve Bulletin*, *Survey of Current Business*, and *Economic Indicators* among several other sources.

2.  Data on rates of exchange with foreign countries is available from the *Federal Reserve Bulletin* and *The Wall Street Journal* under the section "Foreign Exchange."

3.  The relationship between industry and aggregate industrial production can be estimated by a regression equation - i.e., how sensitive the particular industry is to changes in the aggregate economy and its relative performance in expansions and recessions. Also, the analyst would be interested in whether the industry's output as a percent of industrial production is constant, increasing, or decreasing. Finally, you should analyze factors unique to the industry - sources of raw materials, expansion and retooling requirements, foreign demand, etc.

    Past data for the steel industry and the outlook for the future can be obtained from the Standard & Poor's *Industry Surveys* and trade association publications such as that of the Iron and Steel Institute. Similarly, relevant information on the automobile industry can be readily derived from the *S &P Industry Surveys* and industry magazines like *Automotive News*. The individual industry data can then be compared with national industrial production data, the latter published widely in several government publications such as the *Federal Reserve Bulletin* and the *Survey of Current Business*.

4.  Data on money supply can be obtained from one of several government sources such as the *Federal Reserve Bulletin, Business Conditions Digest, Economic Indicators,* etc. Again, there are numerous sources for data on aggregate stock market prices, depending upon what market indicator series is being employed - i.e., *S & P Trade and Security Statistics* for S&P series, NADAQ-AMEX *Fact Book* for OTC-AMEX market, etc. Other general sources could include the *Wall Street Journal* for daily values and *Barron's* which include daily data reported on a weekly basis.

5.  Information on a company listed over the counter can be obtained from company generated reports such as the annual report, prospectus, and required SEC reports (e.g., 10-K reports); commercial publications such as *Value Line* (limited to large, widely-traded OTC companies), *S & P Stock Reports* or *S & P Stock Guide*, and *Moody's OTC Industrial Manual* (limited to OTC industrials).

Harcourt, Inc.

6.    There are numerous sources from which to obtain macroeconomic data for various countries. One very broad publications source would be *The Economic Intelligence Unit*, which publishes 83 separate quarterly reviews and an annual supplement covering the economic and business conditions and outlook for 160 countries. The review considers the economy, trade and finance, trends in investment and consumer spending, along with information pertaining to the political environment. Another good source would be the US *Institutional Trade Administration, International Economic Indicators*. This quarterly publication of the US Government Printing Office contains comparative economic indicators and trends in the U.S. and its seven principal industrial competitors. Information includes trade indicators, price indicators, finance indicators, labor indicators, and general indicators. The primary sources of data are also listed if more information is needed.

Two sources of industry information could include (1) bank publications within a specific country that contain economic and industry reviews for that country, and (2) specific industry publications that will include up-to-date global information on the particular industry. The best source for company data would be the specific company's annual report. Among other information, this source provides the name of a contact person from which you can get additional information. Another good source would be *Moody's International Manual* that provides financial information on about 3,000 major foreign corporations.

7.    *Barron's* would be a good publication to have. It is a weekly publication that typically contains four articles on topics of interest to investors. In addition, it has the most complete weekly listing of prices and quotes for all financial markets. It provides weekly data on individual stocks and the latest information on earnings and dividends. Finally, there is an extensive statistical section with detailed information on stock market behavior for the past week. *The Outlook is* another publication to which investors could subscribe. It contains advice on the general market environment and also has features on specific groups of stocks or industries. Additionally, it contains weekly figures for 88 industry groups and other market statistics. With regard to international markets, *The Financial Times* provides information similar to *The Wall Street Journal*. However, it goes much further in that it includes a true world perspective on the financial news. Also, *Equities International* emphasizes major trends and events in countries around the world. It includes a complete listing of stock market indicator series for major global markets.

8.    *S&P Trade and Securities Statistics is* a service of Standard & Poor's which includes a basic set of historical data on various economic and security price series and a monthly supplement that updates the series for the recent period. There are two major sets of data: (1) the business and financial section, which includes long-term statistics on trade, banking, industry, prices, agriculture, and financial trends; and (2) the security price index record that contains historical data for all of the Standard & Poor's indexes. The *S&P Industry Survey is* the major publication containing information on a number of industries. Coverage for all the industries is divided into a basic analysis and a current analysis.

Two publications contain substantial information about individual stocks. *Moody's Industrial Manual* covers industrial companies listed on the NYSE, AMEX, and regional exchanges. There is also a section on international industrial firms. The second one is *The Value Line Investment Survey*, which is published in two parts. Part one contains basic historical information on about 1,700 companies, as well as a number of analytical measures of earnings stability, growth rates, a common stock safety factor and a timing factor rating. It also includes extensive two-year projections for each firm and three-year estimates of performance. The second volume is a weekly service that provides general investment advice and recommends individual stocks for purchase or sale.

9.    Student Exercise

# CHAPTER 7

# EFFICIENT CAPITAL MARKETS

## Answers to Questions

1.  There are several reasons why one would expect capital markets to be efficient, the foremost being that there are a large number of independent, profit-maximizing investors engaged in the analysis and valuation of securities. A second assumption is that new information comes to the market in a random fashion; and the numerous profit-maximizing investors adjust security prices rapidly to reflect this new information. Thus, price changes would be independent and random. Finally, because stock prices reflect all information, one would expect prevailing prices to reflect "true" current value.

    Capital markets as a whole are generally expected to be efficient, but the markets for some securities might not be as efficient as others. Recall that markets are expected to be efficient because there are a large number of investors who receive new information and analyze its effect on security values. If there is a difference in the number of analysts following a stock and the volume of trading, one could conceive of differences in the efficiency of the markets. For example, new information regarding actively traded stocks such as IBM and Exxon is well publicized and numerous analysts evaluate the effect. Therefore, one should expect the prices for these stocks to adjust rapidly and fully reflect the new information. On the other hand, new information regarding a stock with a small number of stockholders and low trading volume will not be as well publicized and few analysts follow such firms. Therefore, prices may not adjust as rapidly to new information and the possibility of finding a temporarily undervalued stock are also greater. Some also argue that the size of the firms is another factor to differentiate the efficiency of stocks. Specifically, it is believed that the markets for stocks of small firms are less efficient than that of large firms.

2.  The weak-form efficient market hypothesis contends that current stock prices reflect all available security-market information including the historical sequence of prices, price changes, and any volume information. The implication is that there should be no relationship between past price changes and future price changes. Therefore, any trading rule that uses past market data alone should be of little value.

    The two groups of tests of the weak-form EMH are (1) statistical tests of independence and (2) tests of trading rules. Statistical tests of independence can be divided further into two groups: the autocorrelation tests and the runs tests. The autocorrelation tests are used to test the existence of significant correlation, whether positive or negative, of price changes on a particular day with a series of consecutive previous days. The runs tests examine the sequence of positive and negative changes in a series and attempt to determine the existence of a pattern. For a random series one would expect $1/3(2n - 1)$ runs, where n is the number of observations. If there are too few runs (i.e., long sequences of positive changes or long sequences of negative changes), the series is not random, i.e., you would not expect a positive change to consistently follow a positive change and a negative change consistently after a negative change. Alternatively, if there are too many runs (+-+-+-+- etc.), again the series is not random since you would not expect a negative change to consistently follow a positive change.

In the trading rule studies, the second major set of tests, investigators attempted to examine alternative technical trading rules through simulation. The trading rule studies compared the risk-return results derived from the simulations, including transaction costs, to results obtained from a simple buy-and-hold policy.

3.      The semistrong-form efficient market hypothesis contends that security prices adjust rapidly to the release of all new public information and that stock prices reflect all public information. The semistrong-form goes beyond the weak-form because it includes all market and also all nonmarket public information such as stock splits, economic news, political news, etc.

Using the organization developed by Fama, studies of the semistrong-form EMH can be divided into two groups: (1) Studies which attempt to predict futures rates of return using publicly available information (goes beyond weak-form EMH). These studies involve either time-series analysis of returns or the cross-section distribution of returns. (2) Event studies examine abnormal rates of return surrounding specific event or item of public information. These studies determine whether it is possible to make average risk-adjusted profits by acting after the information is made public.

4.      Abnormal rate of return is the amount by which a security's return differs from the expected rate of return based upon the market's rate of return and the security's relationship with the market.

5.      The CAPM is grounded in the theory that investors demand higher returns for higher risks. As a result of risks specific to each individual security, the announcement of a significant economic event will tend to affect individual stock prices in either a greater or less direction than the market as a whole. Fama, Fisher, Jensen, and Roll portrayed this unique relationship of stock returns and market return for a period prior to and subsequent to a significant economic event as follows:

$$R_{it} = a_i + B_i R_{mt} + e$$

where

$R_{it}$  =  the rate of return on security i during period t
$a_i$  =  the intercept or constant for security in the regression
$B_i$  =  the regression slope coefficient for security I equal to $cov_{im}/\sigma_m^2$
$R_{mt}$  =  the rate of return on a market index during period t
$e$  =  a random error that sums to zero

As an example of how one would derive abnormal risk-adjusted returns for a stock during a specific period, assume the following values for a firm:

$$a_i = .01 \text{ and } B_i = 1.40$$

If the market return ($R_{mt}$) during the specified period was 8 percent, the expected return for stock i would be:

$$E(R_{it}) \;=\; .01 + 1.4(.08)$$
$$=\; .01 + .112$$
$$=\; .122$$

The fact that this is the expected value, implies that the actual value will tend to deviate around the expected value. We will define the abnormal return ($AR_{it}$) as the actual return minus the expected return. In keeping with our example, if the actual return for the stock during this period were 10 percent, the abnormal return for the stock during the period would be

$$Ar_{it} \;=\; .10 - .122$$
$$=\; -.022$$

Thus, the stock price reacted to the economic event in a manner that was 2.2 percent less than expected where expectations were based upon what the aggregate market did and the stock's relationship with the market. This abnormal return surrounding an economic event can be used to determine the effect of the event on the individual security.

6.  First, only use information or data that is publicly available at the time of the decision. As an example, if you use information that is typically not available until six weeks after a period and you assume you have it four weeks after, your investment results should be superior because you implicitly have prior information. Second, take account for all transactions costs for the trading rule. This is important because almost all trading rules involve more transactions than a buy-and-hold policy and if you don't consider this, it will bias the results against buy-and-hold. Third, be sure to adjust all results for the risk involved because many trading rules will tend to select high risk stocks that will have higher returns.

7.  A number of studies have examined the adjustment of stock prices to major world events. These studies analyzed the effect of several unexpected world events on stock prices—namely, whether prices adjusted before or during the announcement or after it. The results consistently showed that the adjustments took place between the close of the previous day and the opening of the subsequent day. Notably, an investor could not derive above average profits from transacting after the news became public, thus supporting the semistrong-form EMH.

8.  In the early 1970s, several studies were performed that examined quarterly earnings reports. The results of the studies provided evidence against the semistrong-form EMH. Specifically, buying a stock after a report of unexpected higher quarterly earnings was profitable. Generally, the abnormal return for the stock occurred 13 or 26 weeks following the earnings announcement and reflected the size of the unanticipated earnings change.

9.  Studies on market efficiency are considered to be dual tests of the EMH and the CAPM. These tests involve a joint hypothesis because they consider not only the efficiency of the market, but also are dependent on the asset pricing model that provides the measure of risk used in the test. For example, if a test determines that it is possible to predict future differential risk-adjusted returns, the results could either have been caused by the market being inefficient or because the risk measure is bad thereby providing an incorrect risk-adjusted return.

10. The strong-form efficient market hypothesis asserts that stock prices fully reflect all information, whether public or otherwise. It goes beyond the semistrong-form because it requires that no group of investors have a monopolistic access to any information. Thus, the strong-form efficient market hypothesis calls for perfect markets in which all information is available to everyone at the same time.

11. The strong-form efficient market hypothesis goes beyond the semistrong-form in that it calls for perfect markets --i.e., no group of investors have a monopolistic access to information. Thus, tests for the strong-form efficient market hypothesis would center around examining whether any group has a monopolistic access to information and can consistently obtain above average profits by using it. Four groups of investors have been featured in these tests-- corporate insiders, the stock exchange specialist, security analysts and professional money managers.

12. In the early 1970s, a study by the Securities and Exchange Commission found that by having access to the limit order books as his source of monopolistic information, coupled with low transaction costs, the stock market specialist consistently obtains above average returns. This is evidence against the strong-form hypothesis because this group apparently has a monopoly source of information and uses it to derive above normal returns.

13. Studies by several authors examined the risk-adjusted performance of professional money managers for various periods and found support for the strong-form efficient market hypothesis. For example, a historical study of mutual fund money managers found that on a risk adjusted basis, only about one-third of the funds outperformed the market. More recent studies have also generally provided similar results on performance.

14. The basic premise of technical analysis is that the information dissemination process is slow--thus the adjustment of prices is not immediate but forms a pattern. This view is diametrically opposed to the concept of efficient capital markets, which contends that there is a rapid dissemination process and, therefore, prices reflect all information. Thus, there would be no value to technical analysis because technicians act after the news is made public which would negate its value in an efficient market.

15. The proponents of fundamental analysis advocate that at one point in time there is a basic intrinsic value for the aggregate stock market, alternative industries, and individual securities and if this intrinsic value is substantially different from the prevailing market value, the investor should make the appropriate investment decision. In the context of the efficient market hypothesis, however, if the determination of the basic intrinsic value is based solely on historical data, it will be of little value in providing above average returns. Alternatively, if the fundamental analyst makes superior projections of the relevant variables influencing stock prices then, in accordance with the efficient market hypothesis, he could expect to outperform the market. The implication is that even with an excellent valuation model, if you rely solely, on past data, you cannot expect to do better than a buy-and-hold policy.

16. To be superior in an efficient market the analyst must be aware of the relevant variables influencing stock prices, and be able to consistently project these accurately. If the analyst

does not have access to inside information and lacks superior analytical ability, there is little likelihood of obtaining above average returns consistently.

To establish the superiority of an analyst it is appropriate to examine the performance of numerous buy and sell recommendations by the analyst over a period of time relative to a randomly selected sample of stocks in the same risk class. To be superior the analyst must consistently perform better than the random selection. Consistency is emphasized because on average you would expect random selection to outperform the market about half the time.

17.  Superior analysts should concentrate their efforts in the second tier of stocks, because they do not receive the attention given the top-tier stocks. Also these analysts should pay attention to BV/MV ratios and the size of the firms. Analysts should concentrate their efforts on these securities, since they are more likely to yield abnormal returns.

18.  The major efforts of the portfolio manager should be directed toward determining the risk preferences of his clients and offering, accordingly, a portfolio approximating the risk and return desires of the clientele. Given evidence of the stationarity of beta for a portfolio, this would not be a difficult task. Further, the level of risk can be controlled by committing a portion of the portfolio to a risk free asset and changing this proportion from time to time in accordance with the client's risk preferences.

Second, the portfolio manager should attempt to achieve complete diversification--eliminate all unsystematic risk. Thus, the portfolio should be highly correlated with the market portfolio of risky assets.

Finally, it is important to minimize transactions costs--minimize taxes for the client, minimize commissions by reducing trading turnover, and minimizing liquidity costs by only trading currently liquid stocks.

19.  Index funds are security portfolios specially designed to duplicate the performance of the overall security market as represented by some selected market index series. The first group of index funds was created in the early 1970s because people started realizing that capital markets are efficient and it is extremely difficult to be a superior analyst. Thus, instead of trying to outperform the market, a large amount of money should be managed "passively" so that the investment performance simply matches that achieved by the aggregate market and costs are minimized so as not to drop returns below the market.

An abundance of research has revealed that the performance of professional money managers is not superior to the market, and often has been inferior. This is precisely what one would expect in an efficient capital market. Thus, rather than expending a lot of effort in selecting a portfolio, the performance of which may turn out to be inferior to the market, it is contended by some that portfolios should be designed to simply match the market. If you match the market and minimize transactions costs you will beat two-thirds of the institutional portfolio managers on average. The index funds are intended to match the market and minimize costs as suggested above. Thus, they are consistent with the EMH.

20.  The portfolio manager should continue to allow his two superior analysts to make investment recommendations for some proportion of the portfolio, making sure that their recommendations are implemented in a way that would conform to the risk preference of the

Harcourt, Inc.

client. They should also be encouraged to concentrate their efforts in the second tier of stocks, because the second tier is probably not as efficient as the top tier (because of lower trading volume) and the possibility of finding a temporarily undervalued security are greater. On the other hand, the portfolio manager should encourage the average and inferior analysts to direct their efforts to matching the performance of the aggregate market. As a result, the overall performance of the portfolio should be superior to the average market performance.

21.    Despite Hawawini's acknowledgment that the European markets are smaller and less active than U.S. markets, one should not be surprised by the finding that European and U.S. markets have a similar level of efficiency. Two trends that tend to promote efficiency are the increasing size of the European equity market as a percentage of the world equity market, and the tendency for portfolio managers to increase the global diversification of their portfolios through investing in various countries' securities. Each of these trends implies that there are a large number of independent, profit-maximizing investors in the European equity markets, promoting efficiency through continuous analyses of new information.

22.    Both autocorrelation tests and "runs" tests can be used as tests of the weak-form EMH for the Japanese stock market. Each of these tests checks for independence between stock price changes over time. *The Wall Street Journal* lists stock prices for the Tokyo market on a daily basis, and serves as an easy source from which to get the required data. It is also possible to do this analysis for individual stocks using prices for Japanese stocks listed in the *WSJ* or for some ADRs listed on the NYSE or AMEX.

23.    CFA Examination I (1992)

23(a).  The notion that stock prices already reflect all available information is referred to as the efficient market hypothesis (EMH). It is common to distinguish among three versions of the EMH: the weak, semi-strong, and strong forms. These versions differ by their treatment of what is meant by "all available information."

The weak-form hypothesis asserts that stock prices already reflect all information that can be derived from studying past market trading data. Therefore, "technical analysis" and trend analysis, etc., are fruitless pursuits. Past stock prices are publicly available and virtually costless to obtain. If such data ever conveyed reliable signals about future stock performance, all investors would have learned to exploit such signals.

The semi-strong form hypothesis states that all publicly available information about the prospects of a firm must be reflected already in the stock's price. Such information includes, in addition to past prices, all fundamental data on the firm, its product, its management, its finances, its earnings, etc., that can be found in public information sources.

The strong-form hypothesis states that stock prices reflect all information relevant to the firm, even including information available to company "insiders." This version is an extreme one. Obviously, some "insiders" do have access to pertinent information long enough for hem to profit from trading on that information before the public obtains it. Indeed, such trading--not only the "insiders" themselves, but also relatives and/or associates--is illegal under rules of SEC.

For weak-form or the semi-strong forms of the hypothesis to be valid does not require the strong-form version to hold. If the strong-form version was valid, however, both the semi-strong and the weak-form versions of efficiency would also be valid.

23(b). Even in an efficient market, a portfolio manager would have the important role of constructing and implementing an integrated set of steps to create and maintain appropriate combinations of investment assets. Listed below are the necessary steps in the portfolio management process.

1. Counseling the client to help the client to determine appropriate objectives and identify and evaluate constraints. The portfolio manager together with the client should specify and quantify risk tolerance, required rate of return, time horizon, taxes considerations, the form of income needs, liquidity, legal and regulatory constraints, and any unique circumstances that will impact or modify normal management procedures/goals.

2. Monitoring and evaluating capital market expectations. Relevant considerations, such as economic, social, and political conditions/expectations are factored into the decision making process in terms of the expected risk/reward relationship for the various asset categories. Different expectations may lead the portfolio manager to adjust a client's systematic risk level even if markets are efficient.

3. The above steps are decisions derived from/implemented through portfolio policy and strategy setting. Investment policies are set and implemented through the choice of optimal combinations of financial and real assets in the marketplace -- i.e., asset allocation. Under the assumption of a perfectly efficient market, stocks would be priced fairly, eliminating any added value by specific security selection. It might be argued that an investment policy which stresses diversification is even more important in an efficient market, context because the elimination of specific risk becomes extremely important.

4. Market conditions, relative asset category percentages, and the investor's circumstances are monitored.

5. Portfolio adjustments are made as a result of significant changes in any or all relevant variables.

24. CFA Examination II (1993)

24(a). The fundamental impact of the Fama and French research is to challenge the validity of the Capital Asset Pricing Model (CAPM). Specifically, they found little relation between beta and average stock returns over the 50 year period 1941-1990 (although there were some sub-periods when a positive relationship was indicated).

To isolate the "pure" impact of beta, Fama and French evaluated the joint roles of beta, size, earnings/price, leverage, and book-to-market over a broad range of large and small-capitalization stocks from 1963-1990. They found no relation between beta and average return over this period; on the other hand, a combination of book-to-market and size factors did explain differences in those average returns.

Harcourt, Inc.

Max's attractive results for his low price/cash flow strategy might have arisen from (1) a bias toward small stocks-as a result of equal-weighting the stocks in the portfolio--and (2) a value bias, which might more realistically be reflecting low price/book relationships.

If asset pricing is rational and the Fama and French research is valid, performance (i.e., returns) should be evaluated by comparing average returns for a portfolio to a benchmark comprised of similar size and book-to-market characteristics, not by reference to beta.

Also, Abel points out that an extension to the CAPM, the consumption CAPM, predicts a much lower equity risk premium compare to what has actually occurred. This suggests that the predictive ability of CAPM, and hence the validity of beta, is questionable.

24(b). Many studies have been done on single-factor models, including such factors as size, price/earnings, beta, "neglect," day-of-the-week, etc., all of which have been referred to as "naive" anomalies. Often, the results have been taken as strong evidence of market inefficiencies and the opportunity to create attractive investment management products. However, these simple variable effects are not independent; rather there may be a complex web of interrelationships underlying a host of different variables.

As computer power has become more available and databases more extensive, researches have been able to test several variables simultaneously, rather than just one variable in isolation, often using a multiple regression framework. Using such techniques, they have been able to disentangle the observed effects and to isolate the "pure" and independent impacts of each variable. Jacobs and Levy, for example, studied a total of 25 separate anomaly measures, together with industry effects, and did so simultaneously.

As a single-factor study, Max's price/cash flow results merely indicate a naive anomaly, one that may simply be a proxy for other, more significant underlying factors. To make them credible would require further research using a more robust model design to see if the results hold up. An example of a similar situation is found in the Jacobs and Levy work, where a simple price/cash flow screen is found to produce an illusory anomaly: its naive results were completely dissipated in the pure form test.

24(c). A number of problems exist with respect to Max's test design including:

1. Survivorship Bias - Max used the current list of S&P 500 Index companies rather than the list as it existed at the start of each test year. Thus, he failed to account for companies that may have left the list during the backtest period due to bankruptcy (affecting his negative returns) or that may have been merged out of existence (affecting his positive returns).

2. Look-Ahead Bias - It is not clear that Max used only that information that was available to all investors at the time that the ranking process implied it was. For example, a company's 1983 cash flow would not have been known until many weeks or several months after the end of 1983, not at actual year end when price data was available.

3. Improper Reference Portfolio - Max compared an equal-weighted stock portfolio to the capitalization-weighted S&P 500 Index.

4. <u>Ignoring the Real World</u> - There is no indication that Max took account of such real-world factors tending to reduce realized returns as turnover, commissions, market impact, implementation shortfalls or fees. In combination, these cost-producing factors could well have significantly lowered-or even eliminated-the potential for excess returns.

5. <u>Time Period</u> - Five years may be too short of a time o have back tested the model.

6. <u>Holdout Sample</u> - Max apparently found the anomaly by looking over the past five years of data. He should use a different time period as a holdout sample to test his model.

7. <u>Inappropriate Sampling</u> - TMP's investment philosophy is to utilize small capitalization stocks. The occurrence of an anomaly across the S&P 500 may be irrelevant to TMP because it may not occur in their investment universe.

8. <u>Market efficiency</u> - Although the anomaly occurred in the past, it may not occur in the future. Buying activity by TMP and other money managers who have discovered this anomaly may drive the price of low price-to-cash-flow stocks up, causing the abnormal returns to dissipate.

9. <u>Data Mining</u> - Max may have investigated hundreds of potential anomalies and found a few that worked. Hence, Max might be guilty of "data mining." To prevent this, Max should start out with a theory of why an anomaly might occur and use the data to test theory.

25. CFA Examination II (1995)

25(a). Efficient market hypothesis (EMH) states that a market is efficient if security prices immediately and fully reflect all available relevant information. Efficient means informationally efficient, not operationally efficient. Operational efficiency deals with the cost of transferring funds. If the market fully reflects information, the knowledge that information would not allow anyone to profit from it because stock prices already incorporate the information.

1. **Weak** form asserts that stock prices already reflect all information that can be derived by examining market trading data such as the history of past prices and trading volume.

*Empirical evidence supports the weak-form.*
A strong body of evidence supports weak-form efficiency in the major U.S. securities markets. For example, test results suggest that technical trading rules do not produce superior returns after adjusting for transaction costs and taxes.

2. **Semi-strong** form says that a firm's stock price already reflects all publicly available information about a firm's prospects. Examples of publicly available information are annual reports of companies and investment data.

*Empirical evidence mostly support the semi-strong form.*
Evidence strongly supports the notion of semi-strong efficiency, but occasional studies (e.g., those identifying market anomalies including the small-firm effect and the January effect)

7 - 9

and events (e.g., stock market crash of October 1987) are inconsistent with this form of market efficiency. Black suggests that most so-called "anomalies" result from data mining.

3. **Strong form** of EMH holds that current market prices reflect all information, whether publicly available or privately held, that is relevant to the firm.

*Empirical evidence does not support the strong form.*
Empirical evidence suggests that strong-form efficiency does not hold. If this form were correct, prices would fully reflect all information, although a corporate insider might exclusively hold such information. Therefore, insiders could not earn excess returns. Research evidence shows that corporate officers have access to pertinent information long enough before public release to enable them to profit from trading on this information.

25(b). Technical analysis in the form of charting involves the search for recurrent and predictable patterns in stock prices to enhance returns. Th EMH implies that this type of technical analysis is without value. If past prices contain no useful information for predicting future prices, there is no point in following any technical trading rule for timing the purchases and sales of securities. According to weak-form efficiency, no investor can earn excess returns by developing trading rules based on historical price and return information. A simple policy of buying and holding will be at least as good as any technical procedure. Tests generally show that technical trading rules do not produce superior returns after making adjustments for transactions costs and taxes.

Fundamental analysis uses earnings and dividend prospects of the firm, expectations of future interest rates, and risk evaluation of the firm to determine proper stock prices. The EMH predicts that most fundamental analysis is doomed to failure. According to semi-strong form efficiency, no investor can earn excess returns from trading rules based on any publicly available information. Only analysts with unique insight receive superior returns. Fundamental analysis is no better than technical analysis in enabling investors to capture above-average returns. However, the presence of many analysts contributes to market efficiency.

In summary, the EMH holds that the market appears to adjust so quickly to information about individual stocks and the economy as a whole that no technique of selecting a portfolio-using either technical or fundamental analysis-can consistently outperform a strategy of simply buying and holding a diversified group of securities, such as those making up the popular market averages.

25(c). Portfolio managers have several roles or responsibilities even in perfectly efficient markets. The most important responsibility is to:

1. Identify the risk/return objectives for the portfolio given the investor's constraints. In an efficient market, portfolio managers are responsible for tailoring the portfolio to meet the investor's needs rather than requirements and risk tolerance. Rational portfolio management also requires examining the investor's constraints, such as liquidity, time horizon, laws and regulations, taxes, and such unique preferences and circumstances as age and employment.

Other roles and responsibilities include:

2. Developing a well-diversified portfolio with the selected risk level. Although an efficient market prices securities fairly, each security still has firm-specific risk that portfolio managers can eliminate through diversification. Therefore, rational security selection requires selecting a well-diversified portfolio that provides the level of systematic risk that matches the investor's risk tolerance.

3. Reducing transaction costs with a buy-and-hold strategy. Proponents of the EMH advocate a passive investment strategy that does not try to find under-or overvalued stocks. A buy-and-hold strategy is consistent with passive management. Because the efficient market theory suggests that securities are fairly priced, frequently buying and selling securities, which generate large brokerage fees without increasing expected performance, makes little sense. One common strategy for passive management is to create an index fund that is designed to replicate the performance of a broad-based index of stocks.

4. Developing capital market expectations. As part of the asset-allocation decision, portfolio managers need to consider their expectations for the relative returns of the various capital markets to choose an appropriate asset allocation.

5. Implement the chosen investment strategy and review it regularly for any needed adjustments. Under the EMH, portfolio managers have the responsibility of implementing and updating the previously determined investment strategy of each client.

25(d). Whether active asset allocation among countries could consistently outperform a world market index depends on the degree of international market efficiency and the skill of the portfolio manager. Investment professionals often view the basic issue of international market efficiency in terms of cross-border financial market integration or segmentation. An integrated world financial market would achieve international efficiency in the sense that arbitrage across markets would take advantage of any new information throughout the world. In an efficient integrated international market, prices of all assets would be in line with their relative investment values.

Some claim that international markets are not integrated, but segmented. Each national market might be efficient, but actors might prevent international capital flows from taking advantage of relative mispricing among countries. These factors include psychological barriers, legal restrictions, transaction costs, discriminatory taxation, political risks, and exchange risks.

Markets do not appear fully integrated or fully segmented. Markets may or may not become more correlated as they become more integrated since other factors help to determine correlation. Therefore, the degree of international market efficiency is an empirical question that has not yet been answered.

# CHAPTER 7

## Answers to Problems

1.     $AR_{it} = R_{it} - R_{mt}$

      $AR_{Bt} = 11.5 - 4.0 = 7.5$

      $AR_{Ft} = 10.0 - 8.5 = 1.5$

      $AR_{Tt} = 14.0 - 9.6 = 4.4$

      $AR_{Ct} = 12.0 - 15.3 = -3.3$

      $AR_{Et} = 15.9 - 12.4 = 3.5$

2.     $AR_{it} = R_{it} - (BETA)(R_{mt})$

      $AR_{Bt} = 11.5 - .95(4.0) = 7.7$

      $AR_{Ft} = 10.0 - 1.25(8.5) = -.625$

      $AR_{Tt} = 14.0 - 1.45(9.6) = .08$

      $AR_{Ct} = 12.0 - .75(15.3) = .525$

      $AR_{Et} = 15.9 - (-.3)(12.4) = 19.62$

3.     The reason for the difference in each case is due to the implications of BETA. BETA determines how the stock will move in relation to movements in the market.

      Considering stock C, a one percent change in the market return will result in a .75 percent change in stock C's return. Therefore, comparing the abnormal return for stock C, the value becomes positive in Problem 2. Conversely, the 1.25 percent change expected by stock F, for every 1 percent change in the market, resulted in the abnormal return moving from positive to negative.

      Stock E should move opposite the market because of the negative beta value. Thus, stock E has a very large abnormal return.

      For stocks B and T, the positive abnormal returns remain positive but do change in value.

4.

$$\text{Stock C} = \frac{47 - 43 + 1.50}{43} = 12.79\%$$

$$\text{C - match} = \frac{24 - 22 + 1.00}{22} = 13.64\%$$

$$\text{Stock R} = \frac{73 - 75 + 2.00}{75} = 0\%$$

$$\text{R - Match} = \frac{38 - 42 + 1.00}{42} = -7.14\%$$

$$\text{Stock L} = \frac{34 - 28 + 1.25}{28} = 25.89\%$$

$$\text{L - Match} = \frac{16 - 18 + 1.00}{18} = -5.55\%$$

$$\text{Stock W} = \frac{57 - 52 + 2.00}{52} = 13.46\%$$

$$\text{W - Match} = \frac{44 - 38 + 1.50}{38} = 19.74\%$$

$$\text{Stock S} = \frac{68 - 63 + 1.75}{63} = 10.71\%$$

$$\text{S - Match} = \frac{34 - 32 + 1.00}{32} = 9.37\%$$

Yes, this individual would be considered a superior analyst on balance. He has outperformed three of the five randomly selected stocks and his average return for the five stocks was 12.57% versus 6.01% for the five randomly selected stocks of equal risk. A wider selection of stocks would create a more accurate picture.

5.     Student Exercise

Harcourt, Inc.

# CHAPTER 8

# AN INTRODUCTION TO PORTFOLIO MANAGEMENT

## Answers to Questions

1.  Investors hold diversified portfolios in order to reduce the variance of the portfolio, which is considered a measure of risk of the portfolio. A diversified portfolio should accomplish this because the returns for the alternative assets should not be correlated so the variance of the total portfolio will be reduced.

2.  The covariance is equal to $E[(R_i - E(R_i))(R_j - E(R_j))]$ and indicates the absolute amount of comovement between two series. If they constantly move in the same direction, it will be a large positive value and vice versa. Covariance is important in portfolio theory because the variance of a portfolio is a combination of individual variances and the covariances among all assets in the portfolio. It is also shown that in a portfolio with a large number of securities the variance of the portfolio becomes the average of all the covariances.

3.  Similar assets like common stock or stock for companies in the same industry (e.g., auto industry) will have high positive covariances because the sales and profits for the firms are being influenced by common factors since their customers and suppliers are the same. Because their profits and risk factors move together you should expect the stock returns to likewise move together and have high covariance. The returns from different assets will not have as much covariance because the returns will not be as correlated. This is even more so for investments in different countries where the returns and risk factors are very unique.

4.  The covariance between the returns of asset i and j is affected by the variability of these two returns. Therefore, it is difficult to interpret the covariance figures without taking into account the variability of each return series. In contrast, the correlation coefficient is obtained by standardizing the covariance for the individual variability of the two return series, that is: $r_{ij} = cov_{ij}/(\sigma_i\sigma_j)$

    Thus, the correlation coefficient can only vary in the range of -1 to +1. A value of +1 would indicate a perfect linear positive relationship between $R_i$ and $R_j$.

5.  The efficient frontier has a curvilinear shape because if the set of possible portfolios of assets is not perfectly correlated the set of relations will not be a straight line, but is curved depending on the correlation. The lower the correlation the more curved.

6.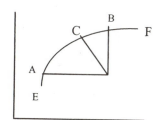

Harcourt, Inc.

A portfolio dominates another portfolio if: 1) it has a higher expected return than another portfolio with the same level of risk. 2) a lower level of expected risk than another portfolio with equal expected return, or 3) a higher expected return and lower expected risk than another portfolio. For example, portfolio B dominates D by the first criteria. A dominates D by the second, and C dominates D by the third.

The Markowitz efficient frontier is simply a set of portfolios that is not dominated by any other portfolio, namely those lying along the segment E-F.

7. The necessary information for the program would be:
   1) the expected rate of return
   2) the expected variance of return
   3) the expected covariance of return with every other feasible stock under consideration.

8. Investor's utility curves are important because they indicate the desired tradeoff by investors between risk and return. Given the efficient frontier, they indicate which portfolio is preferable for the given investor. Notably, because utility curves differ one should expect different investors to select different portfolios on the efficient frontier.

9. The optimal portfolio for a given investor is the point of tangency between his set of utility curves and the efficient frontier. This will most likely be a diversified portfolio because almost all the portfolios on the frontier are diversified except for the two end points--the minimum variance portfolio and the maximum return portfolio. These two could be significant.

10. The utility curves for an individual specify the trade-offs he/she is willing to make between expected return and risk. These utility curves are used in conjunction with the efficient frontier to determine which particular efficient portfolio is the best for a particular investor. Two investors will not choose the same portfolio from the efficient set unless their utility curves are identical.

11. Student Exercise

12. The portfolio constructed containing stocks L and M would have the lowest standard deviation. As demonstrated in the chapter, combining assets with equal risk and return but with low positive or negative correlations will reduce the risk level of the portfolio.

Harcourt, Inc.

# CHAPTER 8

## Answers to Problems

1.  [E($R_i$)] for Lauren Labs

| Probability | Possible Returns | Expected Return |
|---|---|---|
| 0.10 | -0.20 | -0.0200 |
| 0.15 | -0.05 | -0.0075 |
| 0.20 | 0.10 | 0.0200 |
| 0.25 | 0.15 | 0.0375 |
| 0.20 | 0.20 | 0.0400 |
| 0.10 | 0.40 | 0.0400 |
| | E($R_i$) = | 0.1100 |

2.

| Stock | Market Value | Weight ($W_i$) | Expected Security Return ($R_i$) | Expected Portfolio Return $W_i \times R_i$ |
|---|---|---|---|---|
| Phillips | $15,000 | .16 | 0.14 | .0224 |
| Starbucks | 17,000 | .18 | -0.04 | -.0072 |
| Inter. Paper | 32,000 | .34 | 0.18 | .0612 |
| Intel | 23,000 | .24 | 0.16 | .0384 |
| Walgreens | 7,000 | .08 | 0.05 | .0040 |
| | $94,000 | | E($R_{port}$) = | .1188 |

3.

| Month | Madison($R_i$) | General Electric($R_j$) | $R_i$-E($R_i$) | $R_j$-E($R_j$) | [$R_i$-E($R_i$)] x [$R_j$-E($R_j$)] |
|---|---|---|---|---|---|
| 1 | -.04 | .07 | -.057 | .06 | -.0034 |
| 2 | .06 | -.02 | .043 | -.03 | -.0013 |
| 3 | -.07 | -.10 | -.087 | -.11 | .0096 |
| 4 | .12 | .15 | .103 | .14 | .0144 |
| 5 | -.02 | -.06 | -.037 | -.07 | .0026 |
| 6 | .05 | .02 | .033 | .01 | .0003 |
| Sum | .10 | .06 | | | .0222 |

3(a).  E($R_i$) = .10/6 = .0167 $\qquad$ E($R_j$) = .06/6 = .01

3(b).

$$\sigma_i = \sqrt{.0257/6} = \sqrt{.0043} = .06549$$

$$\sigma_j = \sqrt{.04120/6} = \sqrt{.006867} = .08287$$

Harcourt, Inc.

3(c).     $COV_{ij} = 1/6 (.0222) = .0037$

3(d).

$$r_{ij} = \frac{.0037}{(.06549)(.08287)}$$

$$= \frac{.0037}{.005427}$$

$$= .682$$

One should have expected a positive correlation between the two stocks, since they tend to move in the same direction(s). Risk can be reduced by combining assets that have low positive or negative correlations, which is not the case for Madison and General Electric.

4.     $E(R_1) = .15$     $E(\sigma_1) = .10$     $W_1 = .5$

$E(R_2) = .20$     $E(\sigma_2) = .20$     $W_2 = .5$

$E(R_{port}) = .5(.15) + .5(.20) = .175$

If $r_{1,2} = .40$

$$\sigma_p = \sqrt{(.5)^2(.10)^2 + (.5)^2(.20)^2 + 2(.5)(.5)(.10)(.20)(.40)}$$

$$= \sqrt{.0025 + .01 + .004}$$

$$= \sqrt{.0165}$$

$$= 0.12845$$

If $r_{1,2} = -.60$

$$\sigma_p = \sqrt{(.5)^2(.10)^2 + (.5)^2(.20)^2 + 2(.5)(.5)(.10)(.20)(-.60)}$$

$$= \sqrt{.0025 + .01 + (-.006)}$$

$$= \sqrt{.0065}$$

$$= .08062$$

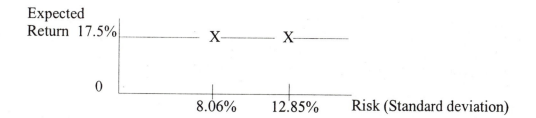

The negative correlation coefficient reduces risk without sacrificing return.

5.  For all values of $r_{1,2}$:

$$E(R_{port}) = (.6 \times .10) + (.4 \times .15) = .12$$

$$\sigma_{port} = \sqrt{(.6)^2(.03)^2 + (.4)^2(.05)^2 + 2(.6)(.4)(.03)(.05)(r_{1,2})}$$

$$= \sqrt{.000324 + .0004 + .00072(r_{1,2})}$$

$$= \sqrt{.000724 + .00072(r_{1,2})}$$

5(a).
$$\sqrt{.000724 + .00072(1.0)} = \sqrt{.001444} = .0380$$

5(b).
$$\sqrt{.000724 + .00072(.75)} = \sqrt{.001264} = .0356$$

5(c).
$$\sqrt{.000724 + .00072(.25)} = \sqrt{.000904} = .0301$$

5(d).
$$\sqrt{.000724 + .00072(.00)} = \sqrt{.000724} = .0269$$

5(e).
$$\sqrt{.000724 + .00072(-.25)} = \sqrt{.000544} = .0233$$

5(f).
$$\sqrt{.000724 + .00072(-.7)} = \sqrt{.000184} = .0136$$

5(g).
$$\sqrt{.000724 + .00072(-1.0)} = \sqrt{.000004} = .0020$$

8 - 5

6(a). $E(R_p) = (1.00 \times .12) + (.00 \times .16) = .12$

$$\sigma_p = \sqrt{(1.00)^2(.04)^2 + (.00)^2(.06)^2 + 2(1.00)(.00)(.04)(.06)(.70)}$$

$$= \sqrt{.0016 + 0 + 0} = \sqrt{.0016} = .04$$

6(b). $E(R_p) = (.75 \times .12) + (.25 \times .16) = .13$

$$\sigma_p = \sqrt{(.75)^2(.04)^2 + (.25)^2(.06)^2 + 2(.75)(.25)(.04)(.06)(.70)}$$

$$= \sqrt{.0009 + .000225 + .00063} = \sqrt{.001755} = .0419$$

6(c). $E(R_p) = (.50 \times .12) + (.50 \times .16) = .14$

$$\sigma_p = \sqrt{(.50)^2(.04)^2 + (.50)^2(.06)^2 + 2(.50)(.50)(.04)(.06)(.70)}$$

$$= \sqrt{.0004 + .0009 + .00084} = \sqrt{.00214} = .0463$$

6(d). $E(R_p) = (.25 \times .12) + (.75 \times .16) = .15$

$$\sigma_p = \sqrt{(.25)^2(.04)^2 + (.75)^2(.06)^2 + 2(.25)(.75)(.04)(.06)(.70)}$$

$$= \sqrt{.0001 + .002025 + .00063} = \sqrt{.002755} = .0525$$

6(e). $E(R_p) = (.05 \times .12) + (.95 \times .16) = .158$

$$\sigma_p = \sqrt{(.50)^2(.04)^2 + (.95)^2(.06)^2 + 2(.05)(.95)(.04)(.06)(.70)}$$

$$= \sqrt{.000004 + .003249 + .00015960} = \sqrt{.0034126} = .0584$$

7.

| Month | DJIA $(R_1)$ | S&P $(R_2)$ | AMEX $(R_3)$ | Nikkei $(R_4)$ | $R_1-E(R_1)$ | $R_2-E(R_2)$ | $R_3-E(R_3)$ | $R_4-E(R_4)$ |
|-------|------|------|------|------|-----------|-----------|-----------|-----------|
| 1 | .03 | .02 | .04 | .04 | .01667 | .00333 | .01333 | .00833 |
| 2 | .07 | .06 | .10 | -.02 | .05667 | .04333 | .07333 | -.05167 |
| 3 | -.02 | -.01 | -.04 | .07 | -.03333 | -.02667 | -.06667 | .03883 |
| 4 | .01 | .03 | .03 | .02 | -.00333 | .01333 | .00333 | -.01167 |
| 5 | .05 | .04 | .11 | .02 | .03667 | .02333 | .08333 | -.01167 |
| 6 | -.06 | -.04 | -.08 | .06 | -.07333 | -.05667 | -.10667 | .02833 |
| Sum | .08 | .10 | .16 | .19 | | | | |

7(a).

$$E(R_1) = \frac{.08}{6} = .01333 \qquad\qquad E(R_2) = \frac{.10}{6} = .01667$$

$$E(R_3) = \frac{.16}{6} = .02667 \qquad\qquad E(R_4) = \frac{.19}{6} = .03167$$

7(b). $\Sigma_1 = (.01667)^2 + (.05667)^2 + (-.03333)^2 + (-.00333)^2 + (.03667)^2 + (-.07333)^2$

$= .00028 + .00321 + .00111 + .00001 + .00134 + .00538 = .01133$

$\sigma_1^2 = .01133/6 = .00189$

$\sigma_1 = (.00189)^{1/2} = .04345$

$\Sigma_2 = (-.00333)^2 + (.04333)^2 + (-.02667)^2 + (.01333)^2 + (.02333)^2 + (-.05667)^2$

$= .00001 + .00188 + .00071 + .00018 + .00054 + .00321 = .00653$

$\sigma_2^2 = .00653/6 = .00109$

$\sigma_2 = (.00109)^{1/2} = .03299$

$\Sigma_3 = (.01333)^2 + (.07333)^2 + (-.06667)^2 + (.00333)^2 + (.08333)^2 + (-.10667)^2$

$= .00018 + .00538 + .00444 + .00001 + .00694 + .01138 = .02833$

$\sigma_3^2 = .02833/6 = .00472$

$\sigma_3 = (.00472)^{1/2} = .06870$

$\Sigma_4 = (.00833)^2 + (-.05167)^2 + (.03833)^2 + (-.01167)^2 + (-.01167)^2 + (.02833)^2$

$= .00007 + .00267 + .00147 + .00014 + .00014 .00080 = .00529$

$\sigma_4^2 = .00529/6 = .00088$

$\sigma_4 = (.00088)^{1/2} = .02970$

Harcourt, Inc.

7(c).

$$COV_{1,2} = \frac{.00006 + .00246 + .00089 - .00004 + .00086 + .00416}{6}$$

$$= .00839/6 = .00140$$

$$COV_{2,3} = \frac{.00004 + .00318 + .00178 + .00004 + .00194 + .00604}{6}$$

$$= .01302/6 = .00217$$

$$COV_{2,4} = \frac{.00003 - .00224 - .00102 - .00016 - .00027 - .00161}{6}$$

$$= -.00527/6 = -.00088$$

$$COV_{3,4} = \frac{.00011 - .00379 - .00256 - .00004 - .00097 - .00302}{6}$$

$$= -.01027/6 = -.00171$$

7(d).

$$R_{1,2} = \frac{.00140}{(.04345)(.03299)} = .98$$

$$R_{2,3} = \frac{.00217}{(.03299)(.06870)} = .96$$

$$R_{2,4} = \frac{.00088}{(.03299)(.02970)} = -.90$$

$$R_{3,4} = \frac{-.00171}{(.06870)(.02970)} = -.84$$

7(e)

$$\sigma_{2,3} = \sqrt{(.5)^2(.03299)^2 + (.5)^2(.06870)^2 + 2(.5)(.5)(.00217)}$$

$$= \sqrt{.00027 + .00118 + .00109} = \sqrt{.00254} = .0504$$

$$E(R)_{2,3} = (.5)(.01667) + (.5)(.02667) = .02167$$

$$\sigma_{2,4} = \sqrt{(.5)^2(.03299)^2 + (.5)^2(.02970)^2 + 2(.5)(.5)(-.00088)}$$

$$= \sqrt{.00027 + .00022 - .00044} = \sqrt{.00005} = .00707$$

$$E(R)_{2,4} = (.5)(.01667) + (.5)(.03167) = .02417$$

The resulting correlation coefficients suggest a strong positive correlation in returns for the S&P 400 and the AMEX combinations (.96), preventing any meaningful reduction in risk (.0504) when they are combined. Since the S&P 400 and Nikkei have a negative correlation (-.90), their combination results in a lower standard deviation (.00707).

8.

$$r_{i,j} = \frac{Cov_{i,j}}{\sigma_i \sigma_j} = \frac{100}{19 \times 14} = \frac{100}{266} = 0.3759$$

# APPENDIX 8

## Answers to Problems

Appendix A

1(a).  When $E(\sigma_1) = E(\sigma_2)$, the problem can be solved by substitution,

$$W_1 = \frac{E(\sigma_1)^2 - r_{1,2}\, E(\sigma_1)\, E(\sigma_1)}{E(\sigma_1)^2 + E(\sigma_1)^2 - 2\, r_{1,2}\, E(\sigma_1)\, E(\sigma_1)}$$

so that

$$W_1 = \frac{E(\sigma_1)^2\, [1 - r_{1,2}]}{2\, E(\sigma_1)^2 - 2\, r_{1,2}\, E(\sigma_1)^2}$$

$$= \frac{E(\sigma_1)^2\, [1 - r_{1,2}]}{2\, E(\sigma_1)^2\, [1 - r_{1,2}]}$$

$$= 1/2 = .5$$

1(b).

$$W_1 = \frac{(.06)^2 - (.5)(.04)(.06)}{(.04)^2 + (.06)^2 - 2(.5)(.04)(.06)}$$

$$= \frac{.0036 - .0012}{.0016 + .0036 - .0024}$$

$$= \frac{.0024}{.0028} = .8571 \ \ (\text{or } 6/7)$$

Appendix B

Variance of the portfolio is zero when:

$$w_1 = \frac{E(\sigma_2)}{E(\sigma_1) + E(\sigma_2)} = \frac{.06}{.04 + .06} = .6 \qquad\qquad w_2 = 1 - w_1 = 1 - .6 = .4$$

# CHAPTER 9

# AN INTRODUCTION TO ASSET PRICING MODELS

## Answers to Questions

1.    It can be shown that the expected return function is a weighted average of the individual returns. In addition, it is shown that combining any portfolio with the risk-free asset, that the standard deviation of the combination is only a function of the weight for the risky asset portfolio. Therefore, since both the expected return and the variance are simple weighted averages, the combination will lie along a straight line.

2.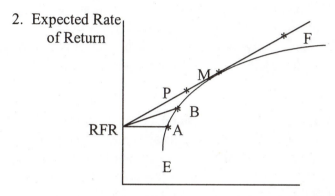

The existence of a risk-free asset excludes the E-A segment of the efficient frontier because any point below A is dominated by the RFR. In fact, the entire efficient frontier below M is dominated by points on the RFR-M Line (combinations obtained by investing a part of the portfolio in the risk-free asset and the remainder in M), e.g., the point P dominates the previously efficient B because it has lower risk for the same level of return. As shown, M is at the point where the ray from RFR is tangent to the efficient frontier. The new efficient frontier thus becomes RFR-M-F.

3.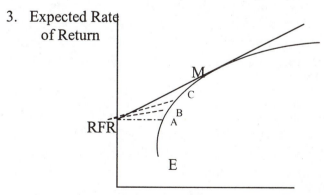

This figure indicates what happens as a risk-free asset is combined with risky portfolios higher and higher on the efficient frontier. In each case, as you combine with the higher return portfolio, the new line will dominate all portfolios below this line. This program continues until you combine with the portfolio at the point of tangency and this line becomes dominant over all prior lines. It is not possible to do any better because there are no further risky asset portfolios at a higher point.

4.  The "M" or "market" portfolio contains all risky assets available. If a risky asset, be it an obscure bond or a rare stamp, was not included in the market portfolio, then there would be no demand for this asset, and consequently, its price would fall. Notably, the price decline would continue to the point where the return would make the asset desirable such that it would be part of the M portfolio--e.g., if the bonds of ABC Corporation were selling for 100 and had a coupon of 8 percent, the investor's return would be 8 percent; however, if there was no demand for ABC bonds the price would fall, say to 80, at which point the 10 percent (80/800) return might make it a desirable investment. Conversely, if the demand for ABC bonds was greater than supply, prices would be bid up to the point where the return would be in equilibrium. In either case, ABC bonds would be included in the market portfolio.

5.  Leverage indicates the ability to borrow funds and invest these added funds in the market portfolio of risky assets. The idea is to increase the risk of the portfolio (because of the leverage), and also the expected return from the portfolio. It is shown that if you can borrow at the RFR then the set of leveraged portfolios is simply a linear extension of the set of portfolios along the line from the RFR to the market portfolio. Therefore, the full CML becomes a line from the RFR to the M portfolio and continuing upward.

6.  You can measure how well diversified a portfolio is by computing the extent of correlation between the portfolio in question and a completely diversified portfolio--i.e., the market portfolio. The idea is that, if a portfolio is completely diversified and, therefore, only has systematic risk, it should be perfectly correlated with another portfolio that only has systematic risk.

7.  Standard deviation would be expected to decrease with an increase in stocks in the portfolio because an increase in number will increase the probability of having more inversely correlated stocks. There will be a major decline from 4 to 10 stocks, a continued decline from 10 to 20 but at a slower rate. Finally, from 50 to 100 stocks, there is a further decline but at a very slow rate because almost all unsystematic risk is eliminated by about 18 stocks.

8.  Given the existence of the CML, everyone should invest in the same risky asset portfolio, the market portfolio. The only difference among individual investors should be in the financing decision they make, which depends upon their risk preference. Specifically, investors initially make investment decisions to invest in the market portfolio, M. Subsequently, based upon their risk preferences, they make financing decisions as to whether to borrow or lend to attain the preferred point on the CML.

9 - 2

9.	It may be recalled that the relevant risk variable for an individual security in a portfolio is its average covariance with all other risky assets in the portfolio. Given the CML, however, there is only one relevant portfolio and this portfolio is the market portfolio that contains all risky assets. Therefore, the relevant risk measure for an individual risky asset is its covariance with all other assets, namely the market portfolio.

10.	Systematic risk refers to that portion of total variability of returns caused by factors affecting the prices of all securities, e.g., economic, political and sociological changes--factors that are uncontrollable, external, and broad in their effect on all securities.

	Unsystematic risk refers to factors that are internal and "unique" to the industry or company, e.g., management capability, consumer preferences, labor strikes, etc. Notably, it is not possible to get rid of the overall systematic risk, but it is possible to eliminate the "unique" risk for an individual asset in a diversified portfolio.

11.	In a capital asset pricing model (CAPM) world the relevant risk variable is the security's systematic risk--its covariance of return with all other risky assets in the market. This risk cannot be eliminated. The unsystematic risk is not relevant because it can be eliminated through diversification--for instance, when you hold a large number of securities, the poor management capability, etc., of some companies will be offset by the above average capability of others.

12.	For plotting, the SML the vertical axis measures the rate of return while the horizontal axis measures normalized systematic risk (the security's covariance of return with the market portfolio divided by the variance of the market portfolio). By definition, the beta (normalized systematic risk) for the market portfolio is 1.0 and is zero for the risk-free asset. It differs from the CML where the measure of risk is the standard deviation of return (referred to as total risk).

13.	CFA Examination I (1993)

	Any three of the following are criticisms of beta as used in CAPM.

	1. Theory does not measure up to practice. In theory, a security with a zero beta should give a return exactly equal to the risk-free rate. But actual results do not come out that way, implying that the market values something besides a beta measure of risk.

	2. Beta is a fickle short-term performer. Some short-term studies have shown risk and return to be negatively related. For example, Black, Jensen and Scholes found that from April 1957 through December 1965, securities with higher risk produced lower returns than less risky securities. This result suggests that (1) in some short periods, investors may be penalized for taking on more risk, (2) in the long run, investors are not rewarded enough for high risk and are overcompensated for buying securities with low risk, and (3) in all periods, some unsystematic risk is being valued by the market.

	3. Estimated betas are unstable. Major changes in a company affecting the character of the stock or some unforeseen event not reflected in past returns may decisively affect the security's future returns.

9 - 3

Harcourt, Inc.

4. Beta is easily rolled over. Richard Roll has demonstrated that by changing the market index against which betas are measured, one can obtain quite different measures of the risk level of individual stocks and portfolios. As a result, one would make different predictions about the expected returns, and by changing indexes, one could change the risk-adjusted performance ranking of a manager.

14.     CFA Examination I (1993)

Under CAPM, the only risk that investors should be compensated for bearing is the risk that cannot be diversified away (systematic risk). Because systematic risk (measured by beta) is equal to one for both portfolios, an investor would expect the same return for Portfolio I and II.

Since both portfolios are fully diversified, it doesn't matter if the specified risk for each individual security is high or low. The specific risk has been diversified away for both portfolios.

15.     CFA Examination II (1994)

15(a). The concepts are explained as follows:
The Foundation's portfolio currently holds a number of securities from two asset classes. Each of the individual securities has its own risk (and return) characteristics, described as specific risk. By including a sufficiently large number of holdings, the specific risk of the individual holdings offset each other, diversifying away much of the overall specific risk and leaving mostly nondiversifiable or market-related risk.

Systematic risk in this market-related risk that cannot be diversified away. Because systematic risk cannot be diversified away, investors are rewarded for assuming this risk.

The variance of an individual security is the sum of the probability-weighted average of the squared differences between the security's expected return and its man return. The standard deviation is the square root of the variance. Both variance and standard deviation measure total risk, including both systematic and specific risk. Assuming the rates of return are normally distributed, the likelihood for a range of rates may be expressed using standard deviations. For example, 68 percent of returns may be expressed using standard deviations. For example, 68 percent of returns can be expected to fall within + or -1 standard deviation of the mean, and 95 percent within 2 standard deviations of the mean.

Covariance measures the extent to which two securities tend to move, or not move, together. The level of covariance is heavily influenced by the degree of correlation between the securities (the correlation coefficient) as well as by each security's standard deviation. As long as the correlation coefficient is less than 1, the portfolio standard deviation is less than the weighted average of the individual securities' standard deviations. The lower the correlation, the lower the covariance and the greater the diversification benefits (negative correlations provide more diversification benefits than positive correlations).

9 - 4

The capital asset pricing model (CAPM) asserts that investors will hold only full diversified portfolios. Hence, total risk as measured by the standard deviation is not relevant because it includes specific risk (which can be diversified away).

Under the CAPM, beta measures the systematic risk of an individual security or portfolio. Beta is the slope of the characteristic line that relates a security's returns to the returns of the market portfolio. By definition, the market itself has a beta of 1.0. The beta of a portfolio is the weighted average of the betas of each security contained in the portfolio. Portfolios with betas greater than 1.0 have systematic risk higher than that of the market; portfolios with betas less than 1.0 have lower systematic risk. By adding securities with betas that are higher (lower), the systematic risk (beta) of the portfolio can be increased (decreased) as desired.

15(b). Without performing the calculations, one can see that the portfolio return would increase because: (1) Real estate has an expected return equal to that of stocks. (2) Its expected return is higher than the return on bonds.

The addition of real estate would result in a reduction of risk because: (1) the standard deviation of real estate is less than that of both stocks and bonds. (2)The covariance of real estate with both stocks and bonds is negative.

The addition of an asset class that is not perfectly correlated with existing assets will reduce variance. The fact that real estate has a negative covariance with the existing asset classes will reduce risk even more.

15(c). Capital market theory holds that efficient markets prevent mispricing of assets and that expected return is proportionate to the level of risk taken. In this instance, real estate is expected to provide the same return as stocks and a higher return than bonds. Yet, it is expected to provide this return at a lower level of risk than both bonds and stocks. If these expectations were realistic, investors would sell the other asset classes and buy real estate, pushing down its return until it was proportionate to the level of risk.

Appraised values differ from transaction prices, reducing the accuracy of return and volatility measures for real estate. Capital market theory was developed and applied to the stock market, which is a very liquid market with relatively small transaction costs. In contrast to the stock market, real estate markets are very thin and lack liquidity.

16.     CFA Examination II (1998)

16(a).  APT vs. the CAPM
        Arbitrage pricing theory does not include any of the following three assumptions incorporated in the capital asset pricing model (CAPM): noted as parts i, ii, and iii:

   i. *Investor utility function or quadratic utility function.* Capital market theory assumes investors want to maximize utility in terms of risk and return preferences; maximum return per unit of risk or minimum risk per unit of return. From the Markowitz model forward, relevant risk has been measured by variance of returns or standard deviation.

APT makes no assumptions regarding investor preferences; the multifactor model commonly used in APT does not include any exponents higher than 1.

ii. *Normally distributed returns.* The probability distribution of expected returns of an investment and the associated dispersion or variability of those returns form the basis of Markowitz portfolio theory and the CAPM. Normal or symmetrically distributed security returns enable estimation of a variance term. In the CAPM, all investors have identical estimates for the probability distributions of future returns (homogeneous expectations).

APT does not describe or specify or require an assumption about security return distributions of any kind.

iii. *The market portfolio.* The CAPM assumes that pricing, valuation, risk, and return are solely functions of an asset's relationship to a market portfolio of all risky assets. In practice, the market portfolio is difficult to specify, so a mistakenly specified market portfolio might result. Roll called this misspecification "benchmark error."

APT does not consider or include an assumption of a market portfolio. APT is predicated on a common set of several (macroeconomic) factors.

16(b). Conceptual Difference between APT and the CAPM
Conceptually, in APT, return is a function of a set of common factors. In the CAPM, return is a function of a market portfolio of all risky assets. Thus, one difference between APT and the CAPM can be described by the fact that APT is a multifactor model that attempts to capture several non-market influences that cause securities or assets to change in price whereas the CAPM is a single-index model that assumes securities or assets change in price because of a common co-movement with one market portfolio of all risky assets.

Another conceptual difference between APT and the CAPM is that, in application of the theory, the market portfolio (or "factor") required by the CAPM is specified. In APT, the common factors are not identified, but the common factors in APT are often described or accepted as including inflation or unanticipated deflation; default risk, government corporate security spread, risk premiums or interest rate spreads; changes in the term structure of interest rates; changes in real final sales, GDP growth or a similar proxy for long-run profits on an economywide basis; major political upheavals; and exchange rates.

A third difference between APT and the CAPM lies in the incorporation of sensitivity coefficients to measure or describe the risk of assets or securities. APT incorporates a number of sensitivity coefficients. These coefficients determine how each independent variable or macroeconomic factor affects each asset. Different assets are affected to different degrees or extents by the common factors. In the CAPM, the only sensitivity factor is beta, an asset's sensitivity to the changes in the market portfolio (often called an asset's "systematic risk").

# CHAPTER 9

## Answers to Problems

1.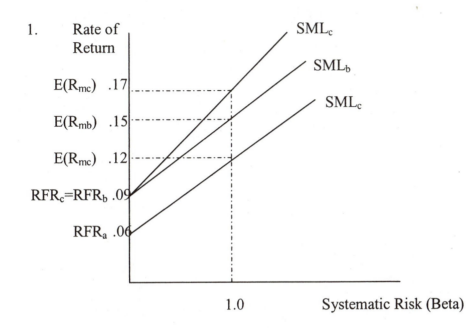

In (b), a change in risk-free rate, with other things being equal, would result in a new $SML_b$, which would intercept with the vertical axis at the new risk-free rate (.09) and would be parallel in the original $SML_a$.

In (c), this indicates that not only did the risk-free rate change from .06 to .09, but the market risk premium per unit of risk $[E(R_m) - R_f]$ also changed from .06 (.12 - .06) to .08 (.17 - .09). Therefore, the new $SML_c$ will have an intercept at .09 and a different slope so it will no longer be parallel to $SML_a$.

2. $E(R_i) = RFR + B_i(R_M - RFR)$

$= .10 + B_i(.14 - .10)$

$= .10 + .04B_i$

| Stock | Beta | (Required Return) $E(R_i) = .10 + .04B_i$ |
|-------|------|-------------------------------------------|
| U | 85 | $.10 + .04(.85) = .10 + .034 = .134$ |
| N | 1.25 | $.10 + .04(1.25) = .10 + .05 = .150$ |
| D | -.20 | $.10 + .04(-.20) = .10 - .008 = .092$ |

Harcourt, Inc.

3.

| Stock | Current Price | Expected Price | Expected Dividend | Estimated Return |
|-------|--------------|----------------|-------------------|------------------|
| U | 22 | 24 | 0.75 | $\dfrac{24-22+0.75}{22}=.1250$ |
| N | 48 | 51 | 2.00 | $\dfrac{51-48+2.00}{48}=.1042$ |
| D | 37 | 40 | 1.25 | $\dfrac{40-37+1.25}{37}=.1149$ |

| Stock | Beta | Required | Estimated | Evaluation |
|-------|------|----------|-----------|------------|
| U | .85 | .134 | .1250 | Overvalued |
| N | 1.25 | .150 | .1042 | Overvalued |
| D | -.20 | .092 | .1149 | Undervalued |

If you believe the appropriateness of these estimated returns, you would buy stocks D and sell stocks U and N.

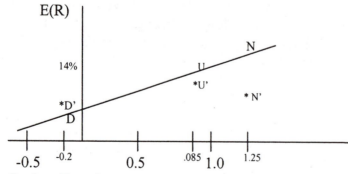

4.  Student Exercise

5.  Student Exercise

6.  Student Exercise

7.  Student Exercise

Harcourt, Inc.

8.　　Student Exercise

9.　　Student Exercise

10.　　Student Exercise

11(a).

$$B_i = \frac{COV_{i,m}}{\sigma_m^2} \text{ and } r_{i,m} = \frac{COV_{i,m}}{(\sigma_i)(\sigma_m)}$$

then $COV_{i,m} = (r_{i,m})(\sigma_i)(\sigma_m)$

**For Intel:**

$COV_{i,m} = (.72)(.1210)(.0550) = .00479$

$$Beta = \frac{.00479}{(.055)^2} = \frac{.00479}{.0030} = 1.597$$

**For Ford:**

$COV_{i,m} = (.33)(.1460)(.0550) = .00265$

$$Beta = \frac{.00265}{.0030} = .883$$

**For Anheuser Busch:**

$COV_{i,m} = (.55)(.0760)(.0550) = .00230$

$$Beta = \frac{.00230}{.0030} = .767$$

**For Merck:**

$COV_{i,m} = (.60)(.1020)(.0550) = .00337$

$$Beta = \frac{.00337}{.0030} = 1.123$$

11(b).　$E(R_i) = RFR + B_i(R_M - RFR)$

$= .08 + B_i(.15 - .08)$

$= .08 + .07B_i$

9 - 9

| Stock | Beta | $E(R_i) = .08 + .07B_i$ |
|---|---|---|
| Intel | 1.597 | .08 + .1118 = .1918 |
| Ford | .883 | .08 + .0618 = .1418 |
| Anheuser Busch | .767 | .08 + .0537 = .1337 |
| Merck | 1.123 | .08 + .0786 = .1586 |

11(c).

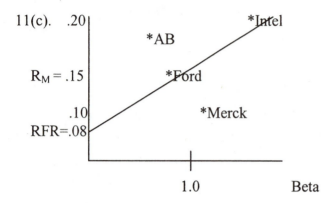

12.     $E(R_i) = RFR + B_i (R_M - RFR)$

$= .068 + B_i (.14 - .08)$

$= .08 + .06B_i$

12(a).  $E(R_A) = .08 + .06(1.72) = .08 + .1050 = .1850 = 18.50\%\%$

12(b).  $E(R_B) = .08 + .06(1.14) = .08 + .0684 = .1484 = 14.84\%$

12(c).  $E(R_C) = .08 + .06(0.76) = .08 + .0456 = .1256 = 12.56\%$

12(d).  $E(R_D) = .08 + .06(0.44) = .08 + .0264 = .1064 = 10.64\%$

12(e).  $E(R_E) = .08 + .06(0.03) = .08 + .0018 = .0818 = 8.18\%$

12(f).  $E(R_F) = .08 + .06(-0.79) = .08 - .0474 = .0326 = 3.26\%$

13.

| Year | Anita $(R_1)$ | General Index $(R_M)$ | $R_1 - E(R_1)$ | $R_M - E(R_M)$ | $(R_1 - E(R_1)) \times R_M - E(R_M)$ |
|---|---|---|---|---|---|
| 1 | 37 | 15 | 27.33 | 6 | 163.98 |
| 2 | 9 | 13 | -.67 | 4 | -2.68 |
| 3 | -11 | 14 | -20.67 | 5 | -103.35 |
| 4 | 8 | -9 | -1.67 | -18 | 30.06 |
| 5 | 11 | 12 | 1.33 | 3 | 3.99 |
| 6 | 4 | 9 | -5.67 | 0 | 0.00 |
|  | $\Sigma = 58$ | $\Sigma = 54$ |  |  | $\Sigma = 92.00$ |

$$E(R_1) = 9.67 \qquad\qquad E(R_M) = 9$$

$$Var_1 = \frac{1211.33}{6} = 201.89 \qquad\qquad Var_M = \frac{410}{6} = 68.33$$

$$\sigma_1 = \sqrt{201.89} = 14.21 \qquad\qquad \sigma_M = \sqrt{68.33} = 8.27$$

$$COV_{1,M} = \frac{92.00}{6} = 15.33$$

13(a).  The correlation coefficient can be computed as follows:

$$r_{1,M} = \frac{COV_{1,M}}{\sigma_1 \sigma_M} = \frac{15.33}{(14.21)(8.27)} = \frac{15.33}{117.52} = .13$$

13(b).  The standard deviations are: 14.21% for Anita Computer and 8.27% for index, respectively.

13(c).  Beta for Anita Computer is computed as follows:

$$B_1 = \frac{COV_{1,M}}{Var_M} = \frac{15.33}{68.33} = .2244$$

14.  CFA Examination II (1995)

14(a).  The security market line (SML) shows the required return for a given level of systematic risk.  The SML is described by a line drawn from the risk-free rate: expected return is 5 percent, where beta equals 0 through the market return; expected return is 10 percent, where beta equal 1.0.

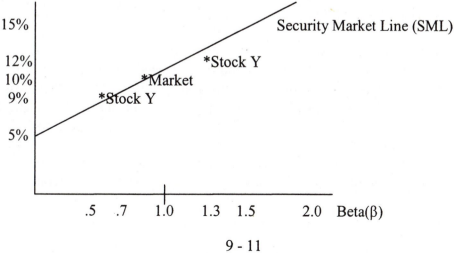

Harcourt, Inc.

14(b). The expected risk-return relationship of individual securities may deviate from that suggested by the SML, and that difference is the asset's alpha. Alpha is the difference between the expected (estimated) rate of return for a stock and its required rate of return based on its systematic risk  Alpha is computed as

$$\text{ALPHA } (\alpha) = E(r_i) - [r_f + B(E(r_M) - r_f)]$$

where

$E(r_i)$ = expected return on Security I
$r_f$ = risk-free rate
$B_i$ = beta for Security I
$E(r_M)$ = expected return on the market

Calculation of alphas:

Stock X:  = 12% - [5% + 1.3% (10% - 5%)] = 0.5%
Stock Y:  = 9% - [5% + 0.7%(10% - 5%)] = 0.5%

In this instance, the alphas are equal and both are positive, so one does not dominate the other.

Another approach is to calculate a required return for each stock and then subtract that required return from a given expected return. The formula for required return (k) is

$$k = r_f + B_i(r_M - r_f).$$

Calculations of required returns:

Stock X: k = 5% + 1.3(10% - 5%) = 11.5%
           = 12% - 11.5% = 0.5%

Stock Y: k = 5% + 0.7(10% - 5%) = 8.5%
           = 9% - 8.5% = 0.5%

14(c). By increasing the risk-free rate from 5 percent to 7 percent and leaving all other factors unchanged, the slope of the SML flattens and the expected return per unit of incremental risk becomes less. Using the formula for alpha, the alpha of Stock X increases to 1.1 percent and the alpha of Stock Y falls to -0.1 percent. In this situation, the expected return (12.0 percent) of Stock X exceeds its required return (10.9 percent) based on the CAPM. Therefore, Stock X's alpha (1.1 percent) is positive. For Stock Y, its expected return (9.0 percent) is below it's required return (9.1 percent) based on the CAPM. Therefore, Stock Y's alpha (-0.1 percent) is negative. Stock X is preferable to Stock Y under these circumstances.

Calculations of revised alphas:

Stock X = 12% - [7% + 1.3 (10% - 7%]
= 12% - 10.95% = 1.1%

Stock Y = 9% - [7% + 0.7(10% - 7%)]
= 9% - 9.1% = -00.1%

15. CFA Examination II (1998)

15(a). Security Market Line

    i.    *Fair-value plot.* The following template shows, using the CAPM, the expected return, ER, of Stock A and Stock B on the SML. The points are consistent with the following equations:

ER on stock = Risk-free rate + Beta x (Market return – Risk-free rate)

ER for A = 4.5% + 1.2(14.5% - 4.5%)

= 16.5%

ER for B = 4.5% + 0.8(14.5% - 4.5%)

= 12.5%

    ii.    *Analyst estimate plot.* Using the analyst's estimates, Stock A plots below the SML and Stock B, above the SML.

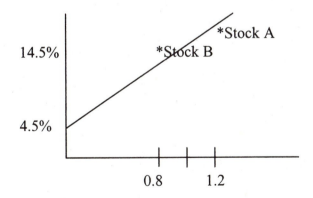

15(b). Over vs. Undervalue

**Stock A is overvalued** because it should provide a 16.5% return according to the CAPM whereas the analyst has estimated only a 16.5% return.

**Stock B is undervalued** because it should provide a 12.5% return according to the CAPM whereas the analyst has estimated a 14% return.

9 - 13

Harcourt, Inc.

# CHAPTER 10

# EXTENSIONS AND TESTING OF ASSET PRICING THEORIES

## Answers to Questions

1.  First, the stability of beta: It is important to know whether it is possible to use past betas as estimates of future betas. Second, is there a relationship between beta and rates of return? This would indicate whether the CAPM is a relevant pricing model that can explain rates of return on risky assets.

2.  Given that beta is the principal risk measure, stable betas make it easier to forecast future beta measures of systematic risk - i.e., can betas measured from past data be used in making investment decisions?

3.  The results of the stability of beta studies indicate that betas for individual stocks are generally not stable, but portfolios of stocks have stable betas.

4.  Is there a positive linear relationship between the systematic risk of risky assets and the rates of return on these assets? Are the coefficients positive and significant? Is the intercept close to the risk-free rate of return?

5.

    In the empirical line, low risk securities did better than expected, while high risk securities did not do as well as predicted.

6.  The "market" portfolio contains all risky assets available. If a risky asset, be it an obscure bond or rare stamp, was not included in the market portfolio, then there would be no demand for this asset and, consequently, its price would fall. Notably, the price decline would continue to the point where the return would make the asset desirable such that it would be part of the "market" portfolio. The weights for all risky assets are equal to their relative market value.

Harcourt, Inc.

While the concept of a market portfolio is reasonable in theory, it is difficult, if not impossible, to implement when testing or using the CAPM. As a result, the majority of studies have used the S&P 500 Index as a proxy for the market portfolio.

7.  According to Roll, a mistakenly specified proxy for the market portfolio can have two effects. First, the beta computed for alternative portfolios would be wrong because the market portfolio is inappropriate. Second, the SML derived would be wrong because it goes from the RFR through the improperly specified market portfolio. In general, when comparing the performance of a portfolio manager to the "benchmark" portfolio, these errors will tend to **overestimate** the performance of portfolio managers because the proxy market portfolio employed is probably not as efficient as the true market portfolio, so the slope of the SML will be underestimated.

8.  Studies of the efficient markets hypothesis suggest that additional factors affecting estimates of expected returns include firm size, the price-earnings ratio, and financial leverage. These variables have been shown to have predictive ability with respect to security returns.

9.  Fama and French found that size, leverage, earnings-price ratios, and book value to market value of equity all have a significant impact on univariate tests on average return. In multivariate tests, size and book to market equity value are the major explanatory factors.

10. Three major assumptions of APT:
    (1). Capital markets are perfectly competitive.
    (2). Investors always prefer more wealth to less wealth with certainty.
    (3) The stochastic process generating asset returns can be represented as a $k$ factor model. This theory does not require that investors have a quadratic utility function, that security returns be normally distributed, nor that there be a market portfolio which contains all risky assets that are mean-variance efficient.

11. Various studies have been performed to test specific hypotheses implicit in the theory. One such hypothesis was that the APT theory would be able to account for the differences in average returns between small firms and large firms. A study by Reinganum concluded that the APT does not explain these returns. Even after taking account of all risk as specified by the APT, the small firms have superior risk-adjusted returns. A subsequent study by Chen provided evidence related to the small firm effect contrary to Reinganum. After adjusting for risk by APT factor loadings, Chen concluded that firm size had no explanatory power.

12. Shanken contends that because the APT is unable to identify the relevant factor structure that affects the asset returns of various securities, the theory is rendered incapable of explaining differential returns between securities. He feels that the APT is not testable because the relevant factor structure must be identified before you can test the APT.

13. CFA Exam III (June 1986)

13(a). The basic Capital Asset Pricing Model (CAPM) assumes that investors care only about portfolio risk and expected return; i.e., they are risk averse. From this assumption comes the conclusion that a portfolio's expected return will be related to only one attribute - its beta (sensitivity) relative to the broadly based market portfolio.

Arbitrage Price Theory (APT) takes a different approach: it is not much concerned about investor preferences, and it assumes that returns are generated by a multi-factor model. APT reflects the fact that several major (systematic) economic factors may effect a given asset in varying degrees. Further, unlike the CAPM, whose single factor is unchanging, APT recognizes that these key factors can change over time (as can investor preferences).

Summarizing, APT 1) identifies several key systematic macroeconomic factors as part of the process that generates security returns vs. only one factor recognized by the CAPM, 2) recognizes that these key factors can change over time, whereas the CAPM's single factor is unchanging, 3) makes fewer assumptions about investor preferences than the CAPM, and 4) recognizes that these preferences can change over time.

13(b). The four systematic factors identified by Roll and Ross are unanticipated changes in: 1) inflation, 2) industrial production, 3) risk premiums, and 4) the slope of the term structure of interest rates.

The APT asserts that an asset's riskiness and, hence, the average long-term return, is directly related to its sensitivities in unanticipated changes in these four economic variables. This relationship may be expressed in equation form as follows:

$$R_i = R_o + b_{i1} F_1 + b_{i2} F_2 + \ldots + b_{in} F_n$$

This means the return ($R_i$) that a certain asset (i) will produce is a combination of some "base" return ($R_o$) plus returns occasioned by the influences or sensitivities ($b_n$) of some systematic external factors ($F_n$).

Harcourt, Inc.

# CHAPTER 10

## Answers to Problems

1.  The results indicate that the betas for Stock E will be smaller relative to the market proxy (1.25) than when compared to the true market (1.72). The reason for the differences in the measured beta stems from the fact that the market proxy does not contain all possible risky assets represented by the true market portfolio. This is a very reasonable relationship because it illustrates the smaller variances in return experienced by the true market portfolio as a result of greater diversification.

2.  Use Graph for both problem 2 and problem 3.

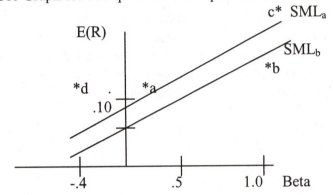

Condition B, with the SML line estimated with the true market portfolio, will present a more difficult scenario for the portfolio manager. The SML for the true market portfolio requires higher returns associated with a given amount of risk in order to outperform the market.

3.  The student should superimpose the given portfolios on the graph used for problem 2. The graph indicates that no matter which SML line is used, portfolios A, C and D will achieve superior results, while portfolio B will tend to be overvalued.

4.  (a). The student should draw SML graphs based on the stated conditions and the following calculations:

| Period | Return of Radius | Proxy Index Return | True Index Return | $(R_{radius} - R_{radius})$ $\times (R_{proxy} - R_{proxy})$ | $(R_{radius} - R_{radius})$ $\times (R_{true} - R_{true})$ |
|---|---|---|---|---|---|
| 1 | 29 | 12 | 15 | 94.0 | 75.2 |
| 2 | 12 | 10 | 13 | 5.4 | 3.6 |
| 3 | -12 | -9 | -8 | 355.2 | 421.8 |
| 4 | 17 | 14 | 18 | 47.6 | 47.6 |
| 5 | 20 | 25 | 28 | 176.4 | 166.6 |
| 6 | -5 | -10 | 0 | 258.4 | 167.2 |
|  | R=10.2 | 7 | 11 | 937.0 | 882.0 |

10 - 4

4(b).    $COV_{radius, proxy} = 937/6 = 156.2$

$COV_{radius, true} = 882/6 = 147.0$

Variance of Proxy Index $= 952/6 = 158.667$

Variance of True Index $= 840/6 = 140$

$\beta$ (using proxy index) $= 156.2/158.667 = .984$

$\beta$ (using true index) $= 147.0/140 = 1.050$

4(c).    $E(R_i) = RFR + B_i (Rm - RFR)$
$= .08 + .984(.12 - .08)$
$= .08 + .039$
$= .119$

$E(R_i) = RFR + B_i (Rm(true) - RFR)$
$= .06 + 1.050(.15 - .06)$
$= .06 + .095$
$= .155$

Since the 11 percent actually earned is less than the expected 11.9 percent using the market proxy, the manager has not done a superior job.

5.    $E(J) = .05 + .02(.80) + .04(1.4) = .12$

$E(L) = .05 + .02(1.6) + .04 (2.25) = .172$

Harcourt, Inc.

# CHAPTER 11

# AN INTRODUCTION TO DERIVATIVE MARKETS AND SECURITIES

## Answers to Questions

1.  Since call values are positively related to stock prices while put values are negatively related, any action that causes a decline in stock price (e.g., a dividend) will have a differential impact on calls and puts. Specifically, an impending dividend will boost put values and depress call values.

    Another way to consider the situation is to represent the difference between the theoretical price of a call option (C) and the theoretical price of a put option (P) as C-P. This is the same as a portfolio that is long a call option and short a put option. For a firm that pays dividends, we expect that the price of its stock will decline by the amount of the dividend on the last day before the stock goes ax-dividend. A decline in stock price makes a call less valuable and a put more valuable, so C-P will decrease.

    This portfolio has the same payoff as being long a forward contract with a contract price equal to the strike price. Since there is no guarantee that the strike price is the forward price, this forward contract will typically have a non-zero value (i.e. the call and put will have different prices). A dividend will decrease the up-front premium for a long position in a forward contract because the expected stock price at expiration decreases. Consequently, C-P is decreased by dividends.

2.  It is generally true that futures contracts are traded on exchanges whereas forward contracts are done directly with a financial institution. Consequently, there is a liquid market for most exchange traded futures whereas there is no guarantee of closing-out a forward position quickly or cheaply. The liquidity of futures comes at a price, though. Because the futures contracts are exchange traded, they are standardized with set delivery dates and contract sizes.

    If having a delivery date or contract size that is not easily accommodated by exchange traded contracts are important to a future/forward end user then the forward may be more appealing. If liquidity is an important factor then the user may prefer the futures contract.

    Another consideration is the mark-to-market property of futures. If a firm is hedging an exposure that is not marked-to-market, it may prefer to not have any intervening cash flows, hence it win prefer forwards.

3.  For forwards, calls and puts, what the long position gains, the short position loses, and vice versa. However, while payoffs to forward positions are symmetric, payoffs to call and put positions are asymmetric. That is to say, long and short forwards can gain as much as they can lose, whereas long calls and puts have a gain potential dramatically greater than their loss potential. Conversely, short calls and puts have gains limited to the option premium but have unlimited liability.

11 - 1

For example, if the price of wheat declines by 10%, the losses to a long position in a futures contract on wheat would be the same as the gains if the price were to increase by 10%. For an at-the-money call option, there would be an asymmetric change in value. A long position in an at-the-money call option on wheat would decline in value less for a 10% fall in wheat prices than it would increase from a 10% rise in wheat prices.

| Position | Loss Potential | Gain Potential | Symmetry |
|---|---|---|---|
| Long Forward | -K | unlimited | symmetric |
| Short Forward | unlimited | K | symmetric |
| Long Call | Call premium | unlimited | asymmetric |
| Short Call | unlimited | Call premium | asymmetric |
| Long Put | Put premium | K | asymmetric |
| Short Put | K | Put Premium | asymmetric |

4.    CFA Examination III (1993)

4(a).   Derivatives can be used in an attempt to bridge the 90-day time gap in the following three ways:

(1) The foundation could buy don") calls on an equity index such as the SUP 500 Index and on Treasury bonds, notes, or bills. This strategy would require the foundation to make an immediate cash outlay for the "premiums" on the calls. If the foundation were to buy calls on the entire $45 million, the cost of these calls could be substantial, particularly if their strike prices were close to current stock and bond prices (i.e., the calls were close to being "in the money").

(2). The foundation could write or sell (short) puts on an equity index and on Treasury bonds, notes, or bills. By writing puts, the foundation would receive an immediate cash inflow equal to the "premiums" on the puts (less brokerage commissions). If stock and bond prices rise as the committee expects, the puts would expire worthless, and the foundation would keep the premiums, thus hedging part or all of the market increase. If the prices fall, however, the foundation loses the difference between the strike price and the current market price, less the value of the premiums.

(3). The foundation could buy (long) equity and fixed-income futures. This is probably the most practical way for the foundation to hedge its expected gift. Futures are available on the S&P 500 Index and on Treasury bonds, notes, and bills. No cash outlay would be required. Instead, the foundation could use some of its current portfolio as a good faith deposit or "margin" to take the long positions. The market value of the futures contracts will, in general, mirror changes in the underlying market values of the S&P BOO Index and Treasuries. Although no immediate cash outlay is required, any gains (losses) in the value of the contracts will be added (subtracted) from the margin deposit daily. Hence, if markets advance as the committee expects, the balances in the foundation's futures account should reflect the market increase.

4(b).   There are both positive and negative factors to be considered in hedging the 90 day gap before the expected receipt of the Franklin gift.

*Positive factors*

(1). The foundation could establish its position in stock and bond markets using derivatives today, and benefit in any subsequent increases in market values in the S&P Index and Treasury instruments in the 90day period. In effect, the foundation would have a synthetic position in those markets beginning today.

(2). The cost of establishing the synthetic position is relatively low, depending on the derivative strategy used. If calls are used, the cost is limited to the premiums paid. If futures are used, the losses on the futures contracts would be similar to the amounts that would be lost if the foundation invested the gift today. Writing the puts is the riskiest strategy because there is an open ended loss if the market declines, but here again the losses would be similar if the foundation invested today and stock and bond markets declined.

(3). Derivative markets (for the types of contracts under consideration here) are liquid.

*Negative factors*

(1). The Franklin gift could be delayed or not received at all. This would create a situation in which the foundation would have to unwind its position and could experience losses, depending on market movements in the underlying assets.

(2). The committee might be wrong in its expectation that stock and bond prices will rise in the 90 day period. If prices decline on stocks and bonds, the foundation would lose part or all of the premium on the calls and have losses on the futures contracts and the puts written. The risk of loss of capital is a serious concern. (Given that the current investment is primarily bonds and cash, the foundation may not be knowledgeable enough to forecast stock prices over the next 90 days.)

(3). Because there is a limited choice of option and futures derivative contract compared to the universe that the committee might wish to invest in, there could be a mismatch between the specific equities and bonds the foundation wishes to invest in and the contracts available in size for $45 million. Unless the 90 day period exactly matches the 90 day period before expiration dates on the contracts, there may be a timing mismatch.

(4). The cost of the derivatives is Potentially) high. For example, if the market in general shares the committee's optimistic outlook, the premiums paid for calls would be expensive and the premiums received on puts would be lean. The opportunity cost on all derivative strategies discussed would be large if the committee is wrong on the outlook for one or both markets.

(5). There may exist regulatory restrictions on the use of derivatives by endowment funds.

11 - 3

*Evaluation*

The negative factors appear to outweigh the positive factors if the outlook for the market is neutral; therefore, the committee's decision on using derivatives to bridge the gap for 90 days will have to be related to the strength of its conviction that stock and bond prices will rise in that period. The certainty of receiving the gift in 90 days is also a factor. The committee should certainly beware that there is a cost to establish the derivative positions, especially if its expectations do not work out. The committee might want to consider a partial hedge of the $45 million.

5.   CFA Examination II (June 1991)

Because Chen is considering adding either short index futures or long index options (a form of protective put) to an existing well-diversified equity portfolio, he evidently intends to create a hedged position for the existing portfolio. Both the short futures and the long options positions will reduce the risk of the resulting combined portfolios, but in different ways.

Assuming that the short futures contract is perfectly negatively correlated with the existing equity portfolio, and that the size of the futures position is sufficient to hedge the risk of the entire equity portfolio, any movement up or down in the level of stock market prices will result in offsetting gains and losses in the combined portfolio's two segments (the equity portfolio itself and the short futures position). Thus, Chen is effectively removing the portfolio from exposure to market movements by eliminating all systematic (market) risk (unsystematic (specific) risk has already been minimized because the equity portfolio is a well-diversified one). Once the equity portfolio has been perfectly hedged, no risk remains, and Chen can expect to receive the risk-free rate of return on the combined portfolio. If the hedge is less than perfect, some risk and some potential for return beyond the risk-free rate are present, but only in proportion to the completeness of the hedge.

If, on the other hand, Chen hedges the portfolio by purchasing stock index puts, he will be placing a floor price on the equity portfolio. If the market declines and the index value drops below the strike price of the puts, the value of the puts increases, offsetting the loss in the equity portfolio. Conversely, if the stock market rises, the value of the put options will decline, and they may expire worthless; however, the potential return to the combined portfolio is unlimited and reduced only by the cot of the puts. As with the short futures, if the long options hedge is less than perfect, downside risk remains in the combined portfolio in proportion to the amount not covered by the puts.

In summary, either short futures or long options (puts) can be used to reduce or eliminate risk in the equity portfolio. Use of the options (put) strategy, however, permits unlimited potential returns to be realized (less the cost of the options) while use of the short futures strategy effectively guarantees the risk-free rate but reduces or eliminates potential returns above that level. Neither strategy dominates the other; each offers a different risk/return profile and involves different costs. Arbitrage ensures that, on a risk-adjusted basis, neither approach is superior.

11 - 4

6.    CFA Examination II (May 1997)

Three prominent pricing inconsistencies are apparent in the table for the Furniture City call options:

1.  The June call option at a strike price of $110 is undervalued. A call option that is in the money should be worth at least as much as its intrinsic value. The intrinsic value of a call option is the maximum of either zero or the difference between the security price and the exercise price (S - E). The June $110 option, therefore, should be worth at least $119.50 - $1 10.00, or $9.50. The current price of $8 7/8 implies that the option is undervalued.

2.  The August call option at a strike price of $120 is undervalued. Call options having the same strike price but with longer maturities are more valuable than those with shorter maturities because the stock has more time in which to rise above the strike price; that is, the time value increases with maturity. The August $120 option of $3 is below the July $120 option of $3 3/4; therefore, the August $120 option is undervalued. Alternatively, the July $120 option could be said to be overvalued.

3.  The September call option at a strike price of $130 is overvalued. Call options having the same maturity but with higher strike prices that are more out of the money are worth less because a larger and less likely move in the stock price will be needed for the option to pay off. The September $130 option is priced higher than the September $120 option; therefore, the September $130 option is overvalued. Alternatively, the September $120 option could be said to be undervalued.

(Note: Candidates receive full credit for identifying other, less prominent, pricing inconsistencies.)

7.    The important distinction is whether the option is a covered or uncovered position. If the option is added to a portfolio that already contains the underlying asset (or something highly correlated), then the option will frequently be a covered position and, consequently, lower overall risk. For example, selling a call without owning the underlying asset leaves the seller open to unlimited liability and (probably) increases portfolio price fluctuation (risk). But if the seller of the call owns the underlying asset, then selling the call neutralizes the portfolio from price changes above the strike price and (probably) decreases risk.

Because options are bets that an asset's price will be above or below some level (the strike price), they represent a way of leveraging one's subjective view on the asset's future price. Options always cost less than the underlying asset and consequently can change in price more (on a percentage basis) than the underlying asset does. This provides the same effect as borrowing money to buy the asset or selling the asset short and investing the proceeds in bonds. (in fact, this is how option pricing theory values options, by replicating the price of an option using the underlying asset and bonds.)

8.      Call options differ from forward contracts in that calls have unlimited upside potential and limited downside potential, whereas the gains and losses from a forward contract are both unlimited. Therefore, since call options do not have the downside potential of forwards, they represent only the "good half" (the upside potential) of the forward contract. The "bad half" of the long forward position is the unlimited downside potential that is equivalent to being short a put. This is consistent with put-call parity where being long a call and short a put yields the same payoff as a forward contract.

9.      Since options have nonlinear (kinked) payoffs, broad market movements may have different relative effects on the value of a portfolio with options depending on whether the market moves up or down. For example, a portfolio that is put-protected may not move down much if the market declines 10% but may move up nearly 10% if the market rises 10%.     Consequently, the returns are asymmetric or skewed. This makes standard deviation a less informative statistic because it reveals information only about the degree of variation and not the "direction" of the variation. Since investors usually care about downside risk (standard deviation), investors probably will not care as much if all of the variation is in the upside return.  The standard deviation statistic could be modified to only measure the variation in negative returns (the so-called semi-variance) so that it was a measure of downside risk only.

10.     A synthetic off-market forward contract with a forward price of $25 could be created using put-call parity. Buying a call struck at $25 and selling a put struck at $25 assures the investor of buying the stock at the expiration date for $25. This portfolio then has the same requirements as the off-market forward at $25. C-P is one-half of the put-call parity relationship, and we know it has to equal S-PV(K).  Since S = $32 and the risk free-rate can be calculated as (35-32)/32 = 9.375%, we can calculate that the off-market forward is worth S-P($25) = $32-$25 / (1 + .09375) = $9.14.

# CHAPTER 11

## Answers to Problems

1(a).

(i). A long position in a forward with a contract price of $50.

| Expiration Date Tando Stock Price (S) | Long Forward (K=$50) Payoff=S-50 | Initial Long Forward Premium | Net Profit |
|---|---|---|---|
| 25 | ($25.00) | $0.00 | ($25.00) |
| 30 | ($20.00) | $0.00 | ($20.00) |
| 35 | ($15.00) | $0.00 | ($15.00) |
| 40 | ($10.00) | $0.00 | ($10.00) |
| 45 | ($5.00) | $0.00 | ($5.00) |
| 50 | $0.00 | $0.00 | $0.00 |
| 55 | $5.00 | $0.00 | $5.00 |
| 60 | $10.00 | $0.00 | $10.00 |
| 65 | $15.00 | $0.00 | $15.00 |
| 70 | $20.00 | $0.00 | $20 00 |
| 75 | $25.00 | $0.00 | $25.00 |

(ii). A long position in a call option with a exercise price of $50 and a front-end premium expense of $5.20.

| Expiration Date Tando Stock Price (S) | Long Call (K=$50) Payoff = max (0,S-50) | Initial Long Call Premium | Net Profit |
|---|---|---|---|
| 25 | $0.00 | ($5.20) | ($5.20) |
| 30 | $0.00 | ($5.20) | ($5.20) |
| 35 | $0 00 | ($5.20) | ($5.20) |
| 40 | $0.00 | ($5.20) | ($5.20) |
| 45 | $0 00 | ($5.20) | ($5.20) |
| 50 | $0.00 | ($5 20) | ($5 20) |
| 55 | $5.00 | ($5 20) | ($0.20) |
| 60 | $10.00 | ($5.20) | $4.80 |
| 65 | $15.00 | ($5.20) | $9.80 |
| 70 | $20.00 | ($5.20) | $14.80 |
| 75 | $25.00 | ($5.20) | $19.80 |

Harcourt, Inc.

(iii). A short position in a call option with an exercise price of $50 and a front-end premium receipt of $5.20.

| Expiration Date Tando Stock Price (S) | Short Call (K=$50) Payoff = -max (0,S-50) | Initial Short Call Premium | Net Profit |
|---|---|---|---|
| 25 | $0.00 | $5.20 | $5.20 |
| 30 | $0.00 | $5.20 | $5.20 |
| 35 | $0.00 | $5.20 | $5.20 |
| 40 | $0.00 | $5.20 | $5.20 |
| 45 | $0.00 | $5.20 | $5.20 |
| 50 | $0.00 | $5.20 | $5.20 |
| 55 | ($5.00) | $5.20 | $0.20 |
| 60 | ($10.00) | $5.20 | ($4.80) |
| 65 | ($15.00) | $5.20 | ($9.80) |
| 70 | ($20.00) | $5.20 | ($14.80) |
| 75 | ($25.00) | $5.20 | ($19.80) |

l(b). (i). A long position in a forward with a contract price of $50.

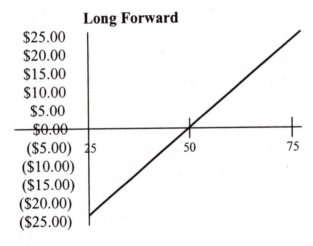

(ii.) A long position in a call option with an exercise price of $50 and a frontend premium expense of $5.20:

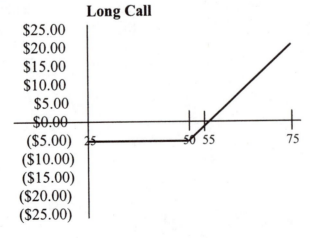

11 - 8

Harcourt, Inc.

(iii.) A short position in a call option with an exercise price of $50 and a front-end premium receipt of $5.20

**Short Call**

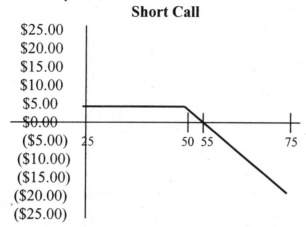

THE BREAKEVEN POINT FOR THE CALL OPTIONS IS $55.20.

l(c). The long position in a forward with a contract price of $50: The purchaser believes that the price of Tando stock will be <u>above $50</u>.

The long position in a call option with an exercise price of $50 and a frontend premium expense of $5.20: The purchaser believes the price will be <u>above $55.20.</u>

The short position in a call option with an exercise price of $50 and a front-end premium receipt of $5.20: The seller believes the price of Tando stock will be <u>below $55.20.</u>

2(a).

(i). A short position in a forward with a contract price of $50.

| Expiration Date Tando Stock Price (S) | Short Forward (K=$50) Payoff= S-50 | Initial Short Forward Premium | Net Profit |
|---|---|---|---|
| 25 | $25.00 | $0.00 | $25 00 |
| 30 | $20.00 | $0.00 | $20.00 |
| 35 | $15.00 | $0.00 | $15.00 |
| 40 | $10.00 | $0.00 | $10.00 |
| 45 | $5.00 | $0.00 | $5.00 |
| 50 | $0.00 | $0.00 | $0.00 |
| 55 | ($5.00) | $0.00 | ($5.00) |
| 60 | ($10.00) | $0.00 | ($10.00) |
| 65 | ($15.00) | $0.00 | ($15.00) |
| 70 | ($20.00) | $0.00 | ($20.00) |
| 75 | ($25.00) | $0.00 | ($25.00) |

11 - 9

Harcourt, Inc.

(ii). A long position in a put option with a exercise price of $50 and a front-end premium expense of $3.23.

| Expiration Date Tando Stock Price (S) | Long Put (K=$50) Payoff= max (0,50-S) | Initial Long Put Premium | Net Profit |
|---|---|---|---|
| 25 | $25.00 | ($3.23) | $21.77 |
| 30 | $20.00 | ($3.23) | $16.77 |
| 35 | $15.00 | ($3.23) | $11.77 |
| 40 | $10.00 | ($3.23) | $6.77 |
| 45 | $5.00 | ($3.23) | $1.77 |
| 50 | $0.00 | ($3.23) | ($3.23) |
| 55 | $0.00 | ($3.23) | ($3.23) |
| 60 | $0.00 | ($3.23) | ($3.23) |
| 65 | $0.00 | ($3.23) | ($3.23) |
| 70 | $0.00 | ($3.23) | ($3.23) |
| 75 | $0.00 | ($3.23) | ($3.23) |

(iii.) A short position in a put option with an exercise price of $50 and a front-end premium receipt of $3.23.

| Expiration Date Tando Stock Price (S) | Short Put (K=$50) Payoff= -max (0,50-S) | Initial Short Put Premium | Net Profit |
|---|---|---|---|
| 25 | ($25.00) | $3.23 | ($21.77) |
| 30 | ($20.00) | $3.23 | ($16.77) |
| 35 | ($15.00) | $3.23 | ($11.77) |
| 40 | ($10.00) | $3.23 | ($6.77) |
| 45 | ($5.00) | $3.23 | ($1.77) |
| 50 | $0.00 | $3.23 | $3.23 |
| 55 | $0.00 | $3.23 | $3.23 |
| 60 | $0.00 | $3.23 | $3.23 |
| 65 | $0.00 | $3.23 | $3.23 |
| 70 | $0.00 | $3.23 | $3.23 |
| 75 | $0.00 | $3.23 | $3.23 |

2(b). (i). A short position in a forward with a contract price of $50:

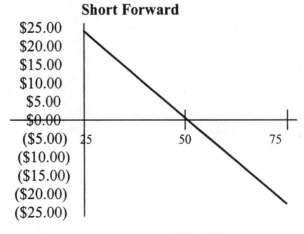

**Short Forward**

11 - 10

Harcourt, Inc.

(ii). A long position in put option with an exercise price of $50 and front-end premium expenses of $3.23:

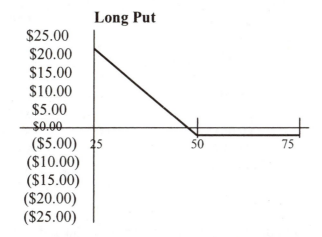

(iii). A short position in a put option with an exercise price of $50 and a front-end premium receipt of $3.23:

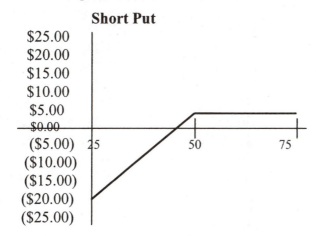

THE BREAKEVEN POINT FOR BOTH PUT OPTIONS IS $46.77.

2(c). A short position in a forward with a contract price of $50: The seller believes the price of Tando will be <u>below $50.</u>

A long position inch put option with an exercise price of $50 and front-end premium expense of $3.23: The buyer of the put believes the price will be <u>below $46.77</u>.

A short position in a put option with an exercise price of $50 and a front-end premium receipt of $3.23: The seller of the put believes the price will be <u>above $46.77.</u>

3(a).   (i). A short position in a forward option with a exercise price of $50.

| Expiration Date Tando Stock Price (S) | Short Forward (K=$50) Payoff =max (0, S-50) | Initial Short Forward Premium | Net Profit |
|---|---|---|---|
| 25 | $25.00 | $0.00 | $50.00 |
| 30 | $20.00 | $0.00 | $50.00 |
| 35 | $15.00 | $0.00 | $50.00 |
| 40 | $10.00 | $0.00 | $50.00 |
| 45 | $5.00 | $0.00 | $50.00 |
| 50 | $0.00 | $0.00 | $50.00 |
| 55 | ($5.00) | $0.00 | $50.00 |
| 60 | ($10.00) | $0.00 | $50.00 |
| 65 | ($15.00) | $0.00 | $50.00 |
| 70 | ($20.00) | $0.00 | $50.00 |
| 75 | ($25.00) | $0.00 | $50.00 |

(ii). A long position in a put option with a exercise price of $50 and a front-end premium expense of $3.23.

| Expiration Date Tando Stock Price (S) | Long Put (K=$50) Payoff = max (0,50-S) | Initial Long Put Put Premium | Net Profit |
|---|---|---|---|
| 25 | $25 00 | ($3 23) | $46.77 |
| 30 | $20.00 | ($3.23) | $46.77 |
| 35 | $15.00 | ($3.23) | $46.77 |
| 40 | $10.00 | ($3 23) | $46.77 |
| 45 | $5.00 | ($3 23) | $46.77 |
| 50 | $0.00 | ($3.23) | $46.77 |
| 55 | $0.00 | ($3 23) | $51.77 |
| 60 | $0.00 | ($3.23) | $56.77 |
| 65 | $0.00 | ($3 23) | $61.77 |
| 70 | $0.00 | ($3.23) | $66.77 |
| 75 | $0.00 | ($3.23) | $71.77 |

(iii). A short position in a call option with an exercise price of $50 and a front-end premium receipt of $5.20.

| Expiration Date Tando Stock Price (S) | Short Call (K=$50) Payoff = -max (0,S-50) | Initial Short Call Premium | Net Profit |
|---|---|---|---|
| 25 | $0.00 | $5.20 | $30.20 |
| 30 | $0.00 | $5.20 | $35.20 |
| 35 | $0.00 | $5.20 | $40.20 |
| 40 | $0.00 | $5.20 | $15.20 |
| 45 | $0.00 | $5.20 | $50.20 |
| 50 | $0.00 | $5.20 | $55.20 |
| 55 | ($5.00) | $5.20 | $55.20 |
| 60 | ($10.00) | $5.20 | $55.20 |
| 65 | ($15.00) | $5.20 | $55.20 |
| 70 | ($20.00) | $5.20 | $55.20 |
| 75 | ($25.00) | $5.20 | $55.20 |

11 - 12

3(b). (i). A short position in a forward with a contract price of $50:

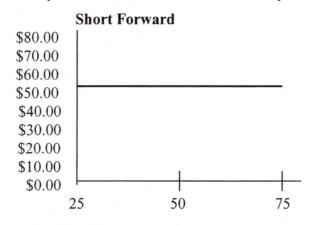

(ii). A long position in a put option with an exercise price of $50 and a front-end premium expense of $3.23:

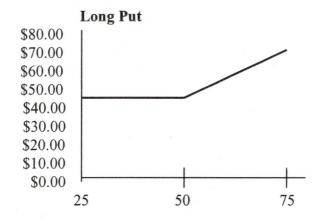

(iii). A short position in a call option with an exercise price of $50 and a front-end premium expense of $5.20:

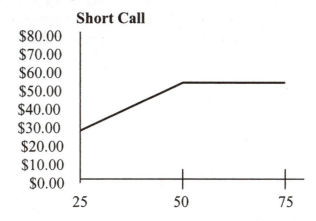

3(c).　　　$F_{0,T} = $ Call - Put + PV(Strike)

$50.00 = 5.20 - 3.23 + PV(\$50)$

$48.03 = PV(\$50)$

$PV = 1.041$

11 - 13

Harcourt, Inc.

$$S = F/(PV\ Factor)$$
$$\$50 = F / 1.041$$
$$\$50 \times 1.041 = F$$
$$\$52.05 = F$$

The zero value contract price, $52.05, differs from the $50 contract price because the put and the call prices are not the same. If they were, the combination of the two would yield a zero-value forward price.

4(a).    With $13,700 to spend, one could:
(1) Purchase 100 shares of Breener Inc. stock (@ $137 per share)or
(2) Purchase 1370 call options with exercise price of $140
Potential payoff is unlimited in both cases, however the leverage that options provide will translate into a higher percentage gain than purely purchasing stock.  However, leverage works both ways.

4(b).    (1) Stock price increases to $155
    a.   Stock return = ($155 - $137)/$137 = 13.14%
    b.   Option return: Exercise option @ $140, sell stock at $155

| | |
|---|---|
| Sell Stock@ $155 x 1370 = | $212,350 |
| Cost of stock @ $140 | (191,800) |
| Option purchase @ $10 | ( 13,700) |
| Profit | $    6,850 |

Rate of return = $6850/$13,700 = 50%

(2) Stock price decreases to $135
    a.   Stock return = ($135 - $137)/$137 = -1.5%
    b.   Option return: Option would not be exercised, lose entire option purchase price (-100%)

4(c).    Breakeven on this call option is $150.  In other words, the writer of the call option will receive the premium of $10, that is, the maximum amount the seller will receive.  If the seller does not currently own the stock, his/her loss is potentially unlimited.

5(a). Givens:
Current Price of XYZ = $42
Put ($40) = $1.45
Call ($40) = $3.90
RFR = 8% (annual); 4% (semiannual)

(i). Buy one call option

| Expiration Date XYZ Stock Price (S) | Long Call (K=$40) Payoff = max (0,S-40) | Initial Long Call Premium | Net Profit |
|---|---|---|---|
| 20 | $0.00 | ($3.90) | ($3.90) |
| 25 | $0.00 | ($3.90) | ($3.90) |
| 30 | $0.00 | ($3.90) | ($3.90) |
| 35 | $0.00 | ($3.90) | ($3.90) |
| 40 | $0.00 | ($3.90) | ($3.90) |
| 45 | $5.00 | ($3.90) | $1.10 |
| 50 | $10.00 | ($3 90) | $6.10 |
| 55 | $15.00 | ($3.90) | $11.10 |
| 60 | $20.00 | ($3.90) | $16.10 |

**Long Call**

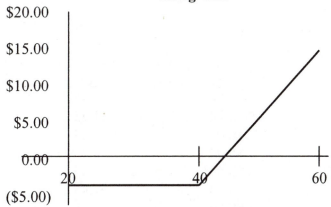

(ii). Short one call option

| Expiration Date XYZ Stock Price (S) | Short Call (K=$40) Payoff =-max (0,S-40) | Initial Short Call Premium | Net Profit |
|---|---|---|---|
| 20 | $0.00 | $3.90 | $3.90 |
| 25 | $0.00 | $3.90 | $3.90 |
| 30 | $0.00 | $3.90 | $3.90 |
| 35 | $0.00 | $3.90 | $3.90 |
| 40 | $0.00 | $3.90 | $3.90 |
| 45 | ($5.00) | $3.90 | ($1.10) |
| 50 | ($10.00) | $3.90 | ($6.10) |
| 55 | ($15.00) | $3.90 | ($11.10) |
| 60 | ($20.00) | $3.90 | ($16.10) |

Harcourt, Inc.

**Short Call.**

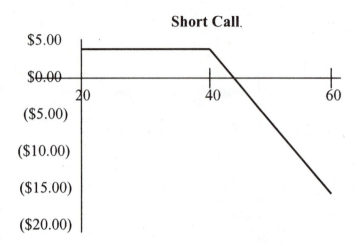

Both call positions will break even at a stock price of $43.90.

5(b). (i). Buy one put option

| Expiration Date XYZ Stock Price (S) | Long Put (K=$40) Payoff =max (0,40-S) | Initial Long Put Premium | Net Profit |
|---|---|---|---|
| 20 | $20.00 | $1.45 | $18.55 |
| 25 | $15.00 | $1.45 | $13.55 |
| 30 | $10.00 | $1.45 | $8.55 |
| 35 | $5.00 | $1.45 | $3.55 |
| 40 | $0.00 | $1.45 | ($1.45) |
| 45 | $0.00 | $1.45 | ($1.45) |
| 50 | $0.00 | $1.45 | ($1.45) |
| 55 | $0.00 | $1.45 | ($1.45) |
| 60 | $0.00 | $1.45 | ($1.45) |

**Long Put**

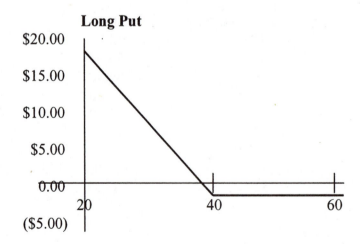

(ii). Short one put option

| Expiration Date XYZ Stock Price (S) | Long Put (K=$40) Payoff =-max (0,40-S) | Initial Long Put Premium | Net Profit |
|---|---|---|---|
| 20 | ($20.00) | $1.45 | ($18.55) |
| 25 | ($15.00) | $1.45 | ($13.55) |
| 30 | ($10.00) | $1.45 | ($8.55) |
| 35 | ($5.00) | $1.45 | ($3.55) |
| 40 | $0.00 | $1.45 | $1.45 |
| 45 | $0.00 | $1.45 | $1.45 |
| 50 | $0.00 | $1.45 | $1.45 |
| 55 | $0.00 | $1.45 | $1.45 |
| 60 | $0.00 | $1.45 | $1.45 |

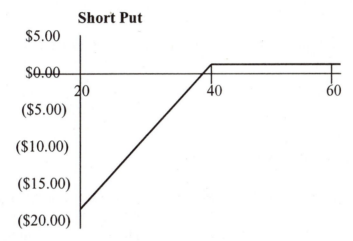

**Short Put**

Both put positions will break even at a stock price of $38.55.

5(c). Does Call - Put = S - PV(K)?

$3.90 - $1.45 ≠ $42 - 40/(1.04)

$2.45 ≠ $3.53

NO! Put-call parity does not hold for this European-style contract.

6. CFA Examination III (1987)

6(a). The manager wishes to be protected from any decline in the government bonds' price (any rise in rates) while maintaining a participation in a price advance, should it occur. The manager also wishes to hold the existing bond position over the next six months. The option strategy best suited for this goal is a protected put strategy.

The manager should purchase the put options in size sufficient to protect the $1.0 million portfolio. The manager should purchase 10 put contracts. In this strategy, the bond portfolio will be protected against any price decline below 98, (the put strike price - the put premium) yet will participate with any price advance on the bond less 2.00 (the put premium).

6(b). The manager is now willing to sell the existing bonds in order to create a portfolio structure that achieves the goal. Two strategic options structures equivalent to the structure in Part A above can be designed as follows:

Alternative 1

- Sell the government 8% bonds
- Invest the proceeds in the T-bills and buy the appropriate amount of 8% bond futures
- Buy the put options to protect against price declines while participating in price advances.

Buying T-bills and futures is equivalent to holding the bonds. The manager could purchase $1.0 million in T-bills and 10 futures contracts.

The manager would complete the option strategy alternative 1 by buying 10 put options.

Alternative 2

- Sell the government 8% bonds
- Invest the proceeds in the T-bills
- Buy the appropriate amount of call options

A T-bill plus call option position is equivalent in structure to a bond plus put option position. The bill plus call options provides protection against bond price declines since the investor can only lose the premium on the call option. Participation in any bond price advance is achieved since the call option premium will increase.

Specifically, the manager could purchase $1.0 million in T-bills and 10 call options.

6(c). Given the put-call parity pricing relationship, the put options and call options appear misvalued versus each other.

If the call is correctly priced at 4.00, the put should be priced at:

$$put = 4.00 - bond\ price + present\ value\ of\ strike$$
$$= 4.00 - 100 + 100/1.03$$
$$= 4.00 - 100 + 97.09$$
$$= 1.09$$

If the put is correctly priced at 2.00, the call should be priced at:

$$call = 2.00 + 100 - 100/1.03$$
$$= 2.00 + 100 - 97.09$$
$$= 4.91$$

Harcourt, Inc.

The put is <u>overpriced</u> versus the call. Therefore:

(1) in the put buying strategies the put premium appears very fully priced.
(2) in the future buying- put buying strategy, similar comments hold. Also the future appears overvalued.
(3) in the buy bills/buy calls strategy, the call option price appears attractive.

In addition, the price of the future at 101 appears high; however, a fair price for the future would be:

price future = price bond + (bill income - bond income) price
$$= 100 + (-1) = 99$$

The option strategy involving buying T-bills and the call options is recommended.

7(a). To solve this problem, express put call parity in the following form:

$$C(K) - P(K) - S + PV(K) = 0$$

Now we can equate put-call parity for two different options:

$$C(40) - P(40) - S + PV(40) = C(50) - P(50) - S + PV(50)$$

Note that the S on each side cancels.

Then the only unknown is P(50). Solving for P(50) yields:

$P(50) = C(50) + PV(50) - C(40) + P(40) - PV(40)$
$P(50) = 2.47 + 50/1.03 - 8.73 + .59 - 40/1.03$
$P(50) = \$4.03$

The same can be done to find the value of C(45):

$C(40) - P(40) - S + PV(40) = C(45) - P(45) - S P PV(45)$
$C(45) = C(40) - P(40) + PV(40) + P(45) - PV(45)$
$C(45) = 8.73 - .59 + 40/1.03 + 1.93 - 45/1.03$
$C(45) = \$5.21$

7(b). If the future price of Commodity Z is \$48, then the spot price (S) should be
$S = PV(\$48) = 48/1.03 = \$46.60$.

Then solving for the theoretical price differential between calls and puts (K=\$40) gives:
$C(40) - P(40) = S - PV(40)$
$C(40) - P(40) = \$46.60 - 4/1.03$
$C(40) - P(40) = \$7.77$ which is less than the \$8.14 difference observed in the market.

By selling the "overpriced" portfolio C(40) - P(40) = $8.14 and buying the "underpriced" portfolio S - PV(40) = $7.77, we can obtain an arbitrage profit of $8.14 - $7.77 = $.37 since we know by put-call parity that these two portfolios must have the same payoff at expiration.

This total portfolio position is:

- short the call
- long the put
- long the stock
- borrow PV(40)

8. CFA Examination III (1988)

8(a). Distribution of returns:
Portfolio 1 holds stock index put options on $1 million of /stocks, which is a protective put strategy. The protective put strategy has an asymmetric impact on return distributions, by reducing downside risk while allowing upside returns.

Portfolio 2 has sold $2 million of stock index futures, which hedges both downside and upside returns and has a symmetrical impact on return distributions.

Systematic and specific risk:
Both stock index put options and stock index futures modify systematic risk, but not specific risk. Since the stock portfolio is broadly diversified, but not an index fund, neither hedge is diskless, but are cross hedges. Both Portfolios 1 and 2 continue to have specific risk on the entire $9 million stock portfolio.

8(b). Mispricing of futures and options:
Portfolio 1 is subject to mispricing of options when the puts are initially purchased or when they expire and must be rolled over. Mispricing represents a cost or risk when the puts are purchased at a price different from a theoretical value determined by a model, such as Black-Scholes.

Portfolio 3, which uses a dynamic hedging process, may require frequent trading of futures to maintain the appropriate hedge ratio. Frequent trading subjects the portfolio to the risk that the futures must be purchased or sold at prices different from fair value.

Unexpected change in stock volatility:
For put options already owned, unexpected changes in volatility do not affect the put's cost or ability to hedge downside risk. Changes in volatility will impact the prices of subsequent option transactions. Thus, Portfolio 1 is not subject to the risk of unexpected changes in stock volatility until the puts expire and are rolled over at then prevailing prices.

Unexpected increases in stock volatility results in more frequent trading of futures and a higher hedging cost in Portfolio 3. Increases in stock volatility together with futures mispricing may produce significantly higher costs in a dynamic asset allocation process.

8(c). Constructing Portfolio 1 requires buying $1 million of at-the-money index puts, which are normally fairly liquid, but their cost may be somewhat unpredictable due to the impact of stock volatility on option prices. Portfolio 1 requires revision when the puts expire, at which time they must be rolled over, again at somewhat unpredictable prices. The $950,000 of cash plus the puts on $1 million of the stock portfolio eliminates the downside risk on about $2 million of Portfolio 1. A withdrawal of $3 million would risk realizing a loss on $1 million of the stock portfolio. Since Portfolio 1 requires revision only at the expiration of the puts, it is as practical for Mr. Selbst as Portfolio 2 and more practical than Portfolio 3.

Constructing Portfolio 2 requires selling $2 million of stock index futures, which are normally fairly liquid and normally priced close to fair value. Portfolio 2 requires revision when the futures expire, at which time they must be rolled over. The $1 million of cash plus the $2 million futures hedge on the stock portfolio eliminates the systematic risk on $3 million of Portfolio 2, making it possible to withdraw $3 million without the risk of loss. Since Portfolio 2 requires revision only at the expiration of the futures, it is as practical for Mr. Selbst as Portfolio 1 and more practical than Portfolio 3.

Portfolio 3 requires the use of some type of option model (binomial, Black-Scholes, etc.) to determine the appropriate hedge ratio. Constructing and revising Portfolio 3 requires nearly constant monitoring and sometimes frequent trading of futures to maintain the hedge ratio. The $1 million of cash plus the dynamic hedge on $1 million of the stock portfolio eliminates the downside risk on about $2 million of Portfolio 3. A withdrawal of $3 million would risk realizing a loss on $1 million of the stock portfolio. Since Portfolio 3 may require frequent revision, it is not as practical for Mr. Selbst as Portfolios 1 or 2. Among the three alternative portfolios, Portfolio 2 is recommended for Mr. Selbst. Portfolio 2 is easy to construct and revise, has no risk of loss on the withdrawal of $3 million, and is practical for Mr. Selbst.

8(d). For Approaches 1 and 2 the protection against loss due to a decline in stock price is identical. At any stock price for X or Y below their current levels, the minimum value of the put, either on the stock or on the index, exactly matches the decline in value of the stocks. For example:

|   | New Stock Price | New Stock Value | Option Price | Option Value |
|---|---|---|---|---|
| X | 50 | 5000 | 10 | 1000 |
| Y | 30 | 3000 | 10 | 1000 |
|   |   | 8000 |   | 2000 |

Portfolio Value $10,000

| New Index Price | New Index Value | Index Option Price | Index Option Value |
|---|---|---|---|
| 40 | 4000 | 10 | 2000 |

Portfolio Value $10,000

11 - 21

The second approach costs less than the first because the volatility (variance) of the index is less. The variance of the index is less because the variance of the index portfolio (50% X and 50% Y) is not the sum of the variances of X and Y. Instead, portfolio variance recognizes the covariance (or correlation) of the stocks in the portfolio. In almost every case, the variance of a portfolio is less than the sum of the variances of the stocks.

A portfolio of puts insures against the risks of each stock. This strategy is unnecessarily expensive because the investor wants a put on the portfolio as a whole to protect against the risk of that portfolio.

9. CFA Examination III (1990)

9(a). Alternative 1 (Buy Puts)

- Buy S&P 500 put options with market exposure equal to equity holdings to protect these holdings.
- Buy Government bond put options with market exposure equal to the bond holdings to protect these holdings.

This could be done by (1) buying $150 million of S&P 500 put options. Since each option is equivalent to $35,000 market exposure, this could be done by buying:

$150,000,00/($35,000/option) = 4,286 S&P 500 put options

and (2) buying $150 million of Government bond put options. Since each option is equivalent to $ 100,000 market exposure, this could be done by buying:

$150,000,000/($100,000/option) =1,500 Government bond put options

By buying 4,286 S&P 500 put options and 1,500 Government bond put options, the portfolio is protected and upside participation is achieved.

Alternative 2 (Sell Futures/Buy Calls)

- Sell S&P stock index futures equal to the equity exposure in the portfolio and buy S&P 500 call options equal to the exposure.
- Sell Government bond futures equal to the bond exposure in the portfolio and buy bond call options equal to the exposure.

This could be done by:

(1) Selling $150 million of S&P futures. Since each future is equivalent to $ 175,000 of equity exposure, this could be done by selling:

$150,000,000/($175,000/future) = 857 S&P futures

Buying $150 million of S& P 500 call options or 4,286 call options (see above calculation).

11 - 22

(2) Selling $ 150 million of Government bond futures contracts. Since each bond future is equivalent to $100,000 of bond exposure, this could be done by selling:

$150,000,000/($100,000/future) = 1,500 bond futures .

Buying $150 million of Government bond call options or 1,500 call options (see above calculation).

By selling 857 S&P futures and 1,500 bond futures, and buying 4,286 S&P call options and 1,500 bond options, the portfolio is protected from loss and upside participation is achieved.

9(b). Given the put-call parity relationship, the put options appear misvalued compared to the call options.

Given the S&P 500 call price, the put should be priced at:

put = 8.00 - index price + present value of (strike + income)
    = 8.00 - 350 + (.01) x (350)
    = 8.00 - 350 + 1.015
    = 6.28

Given the bond call price, the bond put option should be priced at:

put = 2.50 - bond price + present value of (strike + income)
    = 2.50 - 100 + (.02) x (100)
    = 2.50 - 100 + 1.015
    = 2.99

For both the S&P 500 options and the Government bond options, the put options appear overvalued compared to the prices of the calls.

The prices of the futures also appear high. A fair price for the S&P 500 future would be:

S& P 500 future = index price + (bill income - dividend income)
        = 350 + [(.015 - .01) x (350)]
        = 351.75

A fair price for the bond future would be:

Bond future price = bond price + (bill income - bond income)
        = 100 + [(.015 - .02) x (100)]
        = 99.5

From this analysis the futures are somewhat overvalued and the put options are relatively overpriced compared o the call options.

11 - 23

Alternative 1 involves buying relatively expensive assets (the put options).
Alternative 2 involves selling expensive assets (the futures contracts) and buying relatively inexpensive assets (the call options).

Alternative 2 where protection is gained by selling futures and buying call options. is recommended.

10(a). A synthetic put can be created by shorting the stock, buying a call, and lending PV(x) - S.

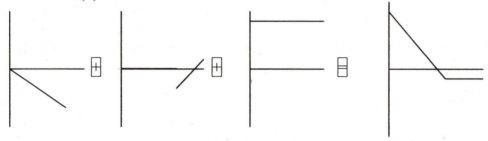

Since the synthetic put and an actual put have the same payoff at maturity, they must have the same price today or there would be an arbitrage opportunity. The arbitrage would be to sell the more expensive "put" and buy the less expensive 'put" netting the difference in price.

10(b). Buying a call and selling a put gives the same payoff as a long forward:

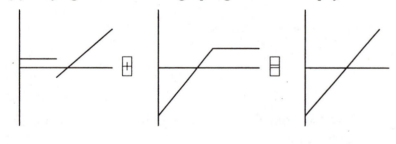

11(a).

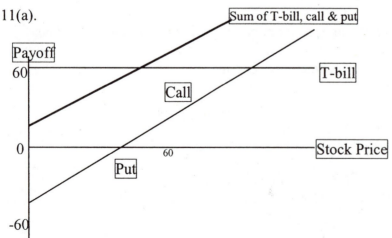

11(b). Using put-call parity the "no arbitrage price" is
  $$S = PV(K) + C - P$$
  $$S = 0.6*97 + 3.18 - 3.38$$
  $$S = \$58.00$$

11(c). Since put-call parity indicates the "no arbitrage" price of the stock is $58 and the stock selling at $60, the arbitrage would be to sell the over-valued portfolio (the stock) and use the proceeds ($60) to buy the undervalued portfolio (.6 t-bills, long 1 call, short 1 put). This set of trades yields $2 in arbitrage profits. Since by put-call parity we know that the two portfolios will have exactly offsetting terminal payoffs, the trade is Diskless.

12(a).

| Expiration Date Stock Price(S) | Long Put (K=$55) Payoff = max(0,55-S) | Initial Long Put Premium | Net Profit |
|---|---|---|---|
| 35 | $20.00 | ($1.32) | $53.68 |
| 40 | $15.00 | ($1.32) | $53.68 |
| 45 | $10.00 | ($1.32) | $53.68 |
| 50 | $5.00 | ($1.32) | $53.68 |
| 55 | $0.00 | ($1.32) | $53.68 |
| 60 | $0.00 | ($1.32) | $58.68 |
| 65 | $0.00 | ($1.32) | $63.68 |
| 70 | $0.00 | ($1.32) | $68.68 |
| 75 | $0.00 | ($1.32) | $73.68 |

12(b).

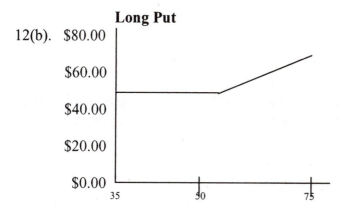

**Long Put**

Using put-call parity, the position could have been replicated by selling the portfolio, buying the call option at the ask price, and investing the balance in T-bills yielding 7%.

12(c).

| Expiration Date Stock Price(S) | Short Call (K=$55) Payoff = max(0,S-55) | Initial Short Call Premium | Net Profit |
|---|---|---|---|
| 35 | $0.00 | $2.55 | $37.55 |
| 40 | $0.00 | $2.55 | $42.55 |
| 45 | $0.00 | $2.55 | $47.55 |
| 50 | $0.00 | $2.55 | $52.55 |
| 55 | $0.00 | $2.55 | $57.55 |
| 60 | ($5.00) | $2.55 | $57.55 |
| 65 | ($10.00) | $2.55 | $57.55 |
| 70 | ($15.00) | $2.55 | $57.55 |
| 75 | ($20.00) | $2.55 | $57.55 |

11 - 25

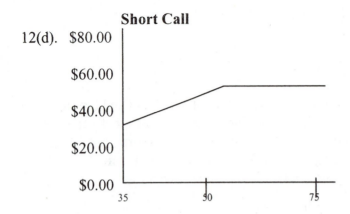

**Short Call**

12(d).

Using put-call parity, the position could have replicated by selling the portfolio, selling the put option at the bid price, and then investing the balance in T-bills yielding 7%.

13(a). Since the forward price is the same as the strike price, going long a call and short a put is the same as a zero-value forward contract. Hence, the call price must equal the put price, so C =3.22 for the "no arbitrage" price. Rounding to the nearest eighth yields:

|  | bid | ask |
|---|---|---|
| Call | $3.125 | $3.250 |

13(b). Using put-call parity: $S = C - P + PI$
from part (a): C-P=O,
so $S = 45/(1.065^{.75})$
   $S = 42.92$

13(c). To make an arbitrage profit you want to sell the overvalued portfolio (short 0.45 t-bills, short call, long put) and use the proceeds to buy the undervalued portfolio (the stock). The arbitrage profit would be:
Profit $= 45/(1.065^{.75}) + 3.125 - 3.25 - 41$
Profit $= \$1.80$

13(d). The present value of the dividend would have to be equal to the difference in theoretical and actual prices:
PV(div) $= 42.92 - 41.00$
   div $= (1.065^{.75})*1.92$
   div $= \$2.01$

Harcourt, Inc.

# CHAPTER 12

# ANALYSIS OF FINANCIAL STATEMENTS

## Answers to Questions

1.  The kind of decisions that require the analysis of financial statements include whether to lend money to a firm, whether to invest in the preferred or the common stock of a firm, and whether to acquire a firm. To properly make such decisions, it is necessary to understand what financial statements are available, what information is included in the different types of statements, and how to analyze this financial information to arrive at a rational decision.

2.  Analysts employ financial ratios simply because numbers in isolation are typically of little value. For example, a net income of $100,000 has little meaning unless analysts know the sales figure that generated the income and the assets or capital employed in generating these sales or this income. Therefore, ratios are used to provide meaningful relationships between individual values in the financial statements.

3.  A major problem with comparing a firm to its industry is that you may not feel comfortable with the measure of central tendency for the industry. Specifically, you may feel that the average value is not a very useful measure because of the wide dispersion of values for the individual firms within the industry. Alternatively, you might feel that the firm being analyzed is not "typical," that it has a strong "unique" component. In either case, it might be preferable to compare the firm to one or several other individual firms within the industry that are considered comparable to the firm being analyzed in terms of size or clientele. For example, within the computer industry it might be optimal to compare IBM to Burroughs and/or Control Data rather than to some total industry data that might include numerous small firms.

4.  In general, jewelry stores have very high profit margins but low asset turnover. It could take them months to sell a 1-carat diamond ring, but once it is sold, the profit could be tremendous. On the other hand, grocery stores usually have very low profit margins but very high asset turnover. Assuming both business risk and financial risk of the firms are equal, the ROE's should likewise be equal.

5.  Business risk is measured by the relative variability (i.e., the coefficient of variation) of operating earnings for a firm over time. In turn, the variability of operating earnings is caused by sales volatility and the amount of operating leverage employed by the firm. Sales variability is the prime determinant of earnings volatility because operating earnings variability cannot be lower than sales variability. In addition, the greater the firms operating leverage, the more variable the operating earnings series will be relative to the sales variability.

12 - 1

6.     The steel company would be expected to have greater business risk. As discussed in question #5, sales variability and operating leverage are the two components of business risk. While both the steel and the retail food chain will have high operating leverage, the steel firm is more sensitive to the business cycle than the retail food chain. That is, the steel firm will have a very volatile sales pattern over the business cycle. Therefore, the steel firm should have higher business risk than the retail food chain.

7.     When examining a firm's financial structure, we would also be concerned with its business risk. Since financial risk is the additional uncertainty of returns faced by equity holders because the firm uses fixed-obligation debt securities, the acceptable level of financial risk usually depends on the firm's business risk. For a firm with low business risks, investors are willing to accept higher financial risk. On the other hand, if the firm has very high business risk, investors probably would not feel comfortable with high financial risk also.

8.     The total debt/total asset ratio is a balance sheet ratio that indicates the stock of debt as compared to the stock of equity. While the total debt/total asset ratio is a common measure of financial risk, many analysts prefer to employ the fixed charge coverage ratio, which reflects the flow of funds from earnings that are available to meet fixed-payment debt obligations.

9.     A cash flow ratio represents the cash available to service the debt issue, whereas a proportion of debt ratio simply indicates the amount of debt outstanding. For example, a large amount of debt (i.e. high proportion of debt indicating greater financial risk) could be issued with a low coupon rate, thereby requiring only a small amount of cash to service the debt. Generally, when these two types of debt ratios diverge, one should concentrate on the cash flow ratios since they represent the firm's ability to make its debt obligations.

10.    Growth analysis is important to common stockholders because the future value of the firm is heavily dependent on future growth in earnings and dividends. The present value of a firm with perpetual dividends payment is:

$$V = \frac{\text{Dividend Next Period}}{\text{Required Rate of Return - Growth Rate}}$$

Therefore, an estimation of expected growth of earnings and dividends on the basis of the variables that influence growth is obviously crucial. Growth analysis is also important to debt-investors because the major determinant of the firm's ability to pay an obligation is the firm's future success which, in turn, is influenced by its growth.

11.    The rate of growth of any economic unit depends on the amount of resources retained and reinvested in the entity and the rate of return earned on the resources retained. The more reinvested, the greater the potential for growth.

Harcourt, Inc.

12. Assuming the risk of the firm is not abnormally high, a 24% ROE is quite high and probably exceeds the return that the equity investor could earn on the funds. Therefore, the firm should retain their earnings and invest them at this rate.

13. This does not mean that Orange Company is better than Blue Company. In order to make this judgment, we have to know what factors (components) caused the extra four points of ROE. If it comes from either the profit margin or the total asset turnover component of the ROE, we can comfortably claim that equity holders of Orange Company are better off than equity holders of Blue Company. On the other hand, it would not be so if the extra four points is because the Orange Company has higher financial leverage, since this extra return is simply a compensation to its equity holders for the higher financial risk they bear. Finally, we are not told anything about the business risks of the two firms.

14. External market liquidity is the ability to buy or sell an asset quickly with little change in price (from prior transaction), assuming no new information has been obtained. The two components of external market liquidity are: (1) the time it takes to sell (or buy) the asset, (2) the selling (or buying) price as compared to recent selling (buying) prices.

    Real estate is considered an illiquid asset because it can take months to find a buyer (or seller), and the price can vary substantially from the last transaction or comparable transactions.

15. Some internal corporate variables such as the total market value of outstanding securities and the number of security owners are good indicators of market liquidity. If the firm has a fairly large number of stockholders, it would be very likely that, at any point in time, some of these investors will be buying or selling for a variety of purposes. Therefore, the firm's security would enjoy a liquid secondary market. On the other hand, a small number of security holders would probably indicate an illiquid secondary market. The ultimate indicator is the volume of trading in the security either in absolute terms or relative turnover (shares traded as a percent of outstanding shares).

16. Student Exercise

# CHAPTER 12

## Answers to Problems

1(a).

$$\text{Return on Total Equity} = \frac{\text{Net Income}}{\text{Equity}} = \frac{400,000}{1,160,000} = 34.5\% \text{ based on the 3 components}:$$

$$\text{ROE} = \frac{\text{Sales}}{\text{Total Assets}} \times \frac{\text{Total Assets}}{\text{Equity}} \times \frac{\text{Net Income}}{\text{Sales}}$$

$$= \frac{6,000,000}{4,000,000} \times \frac{4,000,000}{1,160,000} \times \frac{400,000}{6,000,000}$$

$$= 1.5 \times 3.45 \times .067$$

$$= 34.7\% \text{ (slight difference is due to rounding)}$$

1(b).   Growth Rate = (retention rate) x (return on equity)
= (1 - 160,000/400,000) x .345
= (1 - .40) x .345
= .60 x .345
= 20.7%

1(c)

$$\text{ROE} = \frac{240,000}{1,160,000} = 20.7\%$$

ROE = 1.5 x 3.45 x .04 = 20.7%

1(d).   Growth Rate = .60 x .207 = 12.42%

If dividends were $40,000, then RR = (1 - $40,000/400,000)
= 1 - .10 = .90

Then growth rate = .90 x .207 = 18.63%

2(a).   ROE = Total asset turnover  x  Total assets/equity  x  Net profit margin
Company K:  ROE = 2.2 x 2.4 x .04 = .21
Company L:  ROE = 2.0 x 2.2 x .06 = .26
Company M:  ROE = 1.4 x 1.5 x .10 = .21

2(b).   Growth Rate = Retention Rate x ROE
= (1 - Payout Rate) x ROE

Harcourt, Inc.

Company K:  Growth Rate $= (1 - 1.25/2.75) \times .21$
$= .55 \times .21 = .1155$

Company L:  Growth Rate $= (1 - 1.00/3.00) \times .26$
$= .67 \times .26 = .1742$

Company M:  Growth Rate $= (1 - 1.00/4.50) \times .21$
$= .78 \times .21 = .1638$

3.  Current ratio $= 650/350 = 1.857$

Quick ratio $= 320/350 = 0.914$

Receivable turnover $= 3500/195 = 17.95x$

Average collection period $= 365/17.95 = 20.33$ days

Total asset turnover $= 3500/2182.5 = 1.60x$

Inventory turnover $= 2135/280 = 7.625x$

Fixed asset turnover $= 3500/1462.5 = 2.39x$

Equity turnover $= 3500/1035 = 3.382x$

Gross profit margin $= (3500 - 2135)/3500 = .39$

Operating profit margin $= 258/3500 = .074$

Return on capital $(129 + 62)/2182.5 = .088$

Return on equity $= 129/1185 = .109$

Return on common equity $= 114/1035 = .110$

Debt/equity ratio $= 625/1225 = .51$

Debt/total capital ratio $= 625/1850 = .338$

Interest coverage $= 258/62 = 4.16x$

Fixed charge coverage $= 258/[62 + (15/.66)] = 3.045x$

Cash flow/long-term debt $= (129 + 125 + 20)/625 = .438$

Cash flow/total debt $= (129 + 125 + 20)/975 = .281$

Retention rate $= 1 - (40/114) = .65$

Eddie's current performance appears in line with its historical performance and the industry average except in the areas of profitability (measured by return on capital and return on equity) and leverage (debt/equity and debt/total capital ratios).

Harcourt, Inc.

4.   CFA Examination I (1990)

|                                                    | 1985 | 1989 |

4(a).   Operating Margin = (Operating Income – Depreciation)/Sales

$$= (38 - 3)/542 = 6.46\% \qquad\qquad = (76 - 9)/979 = 6.84\%$$

Asset Turnover = Sales/Total Assets

$$= 542/245 = 2.21x \qquad\qquad = 979/291 = 3.36x$$

Interest Burden = Interest Expense/Total Assets

$$= 3/245 = 1.22\% \qquad\qquad = 0/291 = 0\%$$

Financial Leverage = Total Assets/Common Shareholders Equity

$$= 245/159 = 1.54x \qquad\qquad = 291/220 = 1.32x$$

Tax Rate = Income Taxes/Pre-tax Income

$$= 13/32 = 40.63\% \qquad\qquad = 37/67 = 55.22\%$$

The recommended formula is:

Return on (ROE) = [(Op. Margin x Asset Turnover) - Int. Burden] x Equity Financial Leverage x (100% - Income Tax Rate)

1985   = [(6.46% x 2.21x) - 1.22%] x 1.54 x (100% - 40.63%)
       = 13.05 x 1.54 x .5937 = 11.93%

1989   = [(6.84% x 3.36x) - 0%] x 1.32 x (100% - 55.22%)
       = 22.98 x 1.32 x .4478 = 13.58%

Two alternative approaches are also correct.

ROE = [(Op. Margin - (Int. Burden/Asset Turnover)] x Financial Leverage x Asset Turnover x (100% - Income Tax Rate)

ROE = [(Financial Leverage x Asset Turnover x Operating Margin) - (Financial Leverage x Interest Burden)] x (100% - Income Tax Rate)

4(b).   Asset turnover measures the ability of a company to minimize the level of assets (current and fixed) to support its level of sales. The asset turnover increased substantially over the period thus contributing to an increase in the ROE.

Financial leverage measures the amount of financing outside of equity including short and long-term debt. Financial leverage declined over the period thus adversely affected the ROE. Since asset turnover rose substantially more than financial leverage declined, the net effect was an increase in ROE.

# CHAPTER 13

# AN INTRODUCTION TO SECURITY VALUATION

## Answers to Questions

1.  The top-down valuation process begins by examining the influence of the general economy on all firms and the security markets. The next step is to analyze the various industries insight of the economic environment. The final step is to select and analyze the individual firms within the superior industries and the common stocks of these firms. The top-down approach thus assumes that the first two steps (economy-market and industry) have a significant influence on the individual firm and its stock (the third step). In contrast, the bottom-up approach assumes that it is possible to select investments (i.e. firms) without considering the aggregate market and industry influences.

2.  It is intuitively logical that aggregate market analysis precede industry and company analysis because the government and federal agencies can exert influence on the aggregate economy via fiscal (changes in government spending, taxes, etc.) and monetary (changing money supply, interest rates, etc.) policy. Further, inflation, another aggregate economic variable, must be considered because of its major impact on interest rates and the spending and saving/investment of consumers and corporations. Therefore, a major division is the asset allocation among countries based upon the differential economic outlook including exchange rates (the outlook for the currency).

    Again, industry analysis should precede individual security analysis since there are several factors that are generally national in scope but have a pervasive effect on some industries--e.g., industry-wide strikes, import/ export quotas, etc. In addition, alternative industries feel the impact of economic change at different points in the business cycle-- e.g., industries may lead or lag an expansion. Further, some industries are cyclical (e.g., steel, auto), some are stable (utilities, food chains, etc.).

    The thrust of the argument is that very few, if any industries perform well in a recession, and a "good" company in a "poor" industry may be difficult to find.

3.  All industries would not react identically to changes in the economy simply because of the different nature of business. The auto industry for instance tends to do much better than the economy during expansions but also tends to do far worse during contractions as consumers' consumption patterns change. In contrast, the earnings of utilities undergo modest changes during either expansion or recession since they serve a necessity and thus their sales are somewhat immune to fluctuations. Also, some industries "lead" the economy while others only react late in the cycle (e.g., construction).

4.  Estimating the value for a bond is easier than estimating the value for common stock since the size and the time pattern of returns from the bond over its life are known amounts. Specifically, a bond promises to make interest payments during the life of the

Harcourt, Inc.

bond (usually every 6 months) plus payment of principal on the bond's maturity date. With common stock, there are no such guarantees.

5.  The required rate of return on an investment is primarily determined by three major factors: (1) the economy's real risk-free rate (RFR), (2) the expected rate of inflation (I), and (3) a risk premium (RP). While this basic framework will apply no matter what country you choose to invest in, there will be significant differences in these factors among different countries over time. Among the specific reasons why an investor may have different required returns for U.S. and Japanese stocks are:

    The real risk-free rate: For all countries, this rate should be an approximation of the economy's real growth rate. However, the real growth rate among countries might be significantly different due to differences in the growth rate of the labor force, growth rate in the average number of hours worked, and differences in the growth rate of labor productivity.

    The expected rate of inflation: Again, there are differences between the U.S. and Japanese inflation rate that are bound to imply a difference between the required return between the two countries.

    The risk premium: The risk premium is derived from business risk, financial risk, liquidity risk, exchange rate risk, and country risk. Each of these components are influenced by differences in general economic variability, political conditions, trade relations, and operating leverage employed within the countries. It is necessary to evaluate these differences in risk factors and assign a unique risk premium for each country.

6.  The nominal risk-free rate (RFR) is composed of two factors: (1) real risk-free rate and (2) expected rate of inflation. As mentioned in the answer to question #5, the real risk-free rate for all countries is an approximation of the economy's real growth rate. It is highly unlikely that two countries will have the same real risk-free rate due to differences in the growth rates. Also, the expected rate of inflation will vary from country to country. Taking these factors into account, one would not expect the U.S. nominal risk-free rate to be the same as that in Germany. As Table 10.4 illustrates, Germany's nominal risk-free rate is expected to be lower than that of the U.S. in 1999.

7.  No, the Indonesian and United Kingdom stocks should have significantly different risk premiums. Specifically, Indonesian stocks should have much larger risk premiums because they are relatively new securities, lack liquidity, and in many cases the underlying firms are involved in highly risky ventures (i.e. business risk). On the other hand, United Kingdom stocks typically are issued by established firms, quite liquid, and the underlying firms are typically engaged in less speculative activities.

8.  No, the Singapore stock should be more risky than the United States stock based upon similar reasoning as presented in question #7.

9.   Student Exercise

10.  Student Exercise

11.  The relative valuation ratios to evaluate a stock should be used in cases where:
     (1) a good set of comparable entities (e.g., industries or similar companies) is available, or
     (2) when the aggregate market is not at a valuation extreme (e.g., a seriously overvalued or undervalued market).

12.  The discounted cash-flow valuation approaches can be used for stocks that pay dividends, particularly in the case of a stable, mature firm where the assumption of relatively constant growth for the long term is appropriate.

     The present value of operating cash flow technique can be used when comparing firms that have diverse capital structures.

     The present value of free cash flow to equity is important to an equity holder since this approach measures the amount of cash flow available to the equity holder after debt payments and expenditures to maintain the firm's asset base.

13.  The two valuation approaches should **not** be considered to be competitive approaches, rather the text suggests that both approaches should be used in the valuation of common stock. The discounted cash flow techniques reflect how we describe value, that is, the present value of expected cash flows. However, these techniques could generate values that are substantially difference from the prevailing prices in the marketplace. On the other hand, the relative valuation techniques provide information on how the market is **currently** valuing the stock. These techniques should be used together in determining equity valuation, that is, the approaches should be considered complementary.

# CHAPTER 13

## Answers to Problems

1. Assume semiannual compounding

| | |
|---|---|
| Par value | $10,000 |
| Coupon Payment (every six months) | $450 |
| Number of periods | 20 |
| Required return | 3.5% |

 Therefore,

| | |
|---|---|
| Present value of interest payments | $ 6,395.58 |
| Present value of principal payment | 5,025.66 |
| Present value of bond | $11,421.24 |

2. If the required return rises to 11 percent then,

| | |
|---|---|
| Number of periods | 20 |
| Required return | 5.5% |

 Therefore,

| | |
|---|---|
| Present value of interest payments | $5,377.67 |
| Present value of principal payment | 3,427.29 |
| | $8,804.96 |

3. Annual dividend $9.00
  Required return  11%

Therefore, the value of the preferred stock = $9.00/.11 = $81.82

At a market price of $96.00, the promised yield would be $9.00/$96.00 = 9.375%, which is less than your required rate of return of 11%. Therefore, you would decide against a purchase at this price. The maximum price you will be willing to pay is $81.82.

4.

| | |
|---|---|
| Earnings per share: last year | $10.00 |
| Dividends per share: last year | $6.00 |
| Estimated earnings per share: this year | $11.00 |
| Required rate of return | 12% |
| Expected sales price at end of year | $132.00 |

Since the last dividend payout ratio = $6.00/$10.00 = 60%, and assuming you maintain the same payout ratio, then dividends per share at the end of the year is:
EPS x Payout = $11.00 x 60% = $6.60.

Therefore, the present value of BBC's share is:

$$Value = \frac{\$6.60}{(1+.12)} + \frac{\$132.00}{(1+.12)} = \$5.89 + \$117.86 = \$123.75$$

This ($123.75) is the maximum price you would be willing to pay for BBC's stock.

5.  
| | |
|---|---:|
| Earnings per share: last year | $10.00 |
| Dividends per share: last year | $6.00 |
| Required rate of return | 8% |
| Expected sell price | $110.00 |

$$Value = \frac{\$6.60}{(1+.08)} + \frac{\$110.00}{(1+.08)} = \$6.11 + \$101.85 = \$107.96$$

This ($107.96) is the maximum price you would be willing to pay for BBC's stock.

6.  
| | |
|---|---|
| Dividends at the end of this year: | $6 x 1.08 = $6.48 |
| Required rate of return | 11% |
| Growth rate of dividends | 8% |

$$Value = \frac{\$6.48}{.11 - .08} = \$216.00$$

Thus, you would be willing to pay up to $216.00 for BBC's stock.

7.  
| | |
|---|---:|
| Estimated earnings per share | $11.00 |
| Dividend payout ratio | 60% |
| Required rate of return | 12% |
| Growth rate of dividends | 9% |

$$P/E \text{ of BBC Company} = \frac{.60}{.12 - .09} = 20x$$

Thus, the maximum price you would be willing to pay for BBC's stock is:  20 x $11 = $220.00

8.  
| | |
|---|---|
| Dividend payout ratio | 40% |
| Return on equity | 16% |

Growth rate = (Retention rate) x (Return on equity)
$$\begin{aligned} &= (1 - payout\ ratio) \times (Return\ on\ equity) \\ &= (1 - .40) \times (.16) \\ &= .60 \times .16 \\ &= 9.6\% \end{aligned}$$

9. Dividend payout ratio    40%
   Dividend growth rate      9.6%
   Required rate of return   13%

$$P/E \text{ of SDC Company} = \frac{.40}{.13 - .096} = 11.76x$$

10. Dividend payout ratio    50%
    Required rate of return   13%

$$\begin{aligned} \text{Growth rate} &= (1 - .50) \times (.16) \\ \text{(new)} &= .50 \times .16 \\ &= .08 \end{aligned}$$

$$P/E \text{ of SDC Company} = \frac{.50}{.13 - .08} = 10.00x$$
(new)

11.

$$ROE = \frac{\text{Net Income}}{\text{Sales}} \times \frac{\text{Sales}}{\text{Total Assets}} \times \frac{\text{Total Assets}}{\text{Equity}}$$

$$= \text{Profit Margin} \times \text{Total Asset Turnover} \times \text{Leverage}$$

As the above equation illustrates, ROE can be increased through increases in profit margin, total asset turnover, or leverage. As an example of each, suppose ABC company saw an increase in demand for their product, knowing that they have a clearly superior product to others in the industry and their customers are extremely loyal, they will raise prices, thus generating more net income per sale, and have greater profit margin. As can be seen from the formula, holding other things constant, ABC will achieve a greater ROE.

Likewise, suppose demand for the product has increased on an industry wide basis. ABC knows if they raise their prices they may lose sales to the competition. As a result they decide to increase their leverage to increase ROE.

The final method of increasing ROE is by increasing overall efficiency and thus increasing the dollar value of sales to assets on hand.

The student should provide a numerical example of each of these effects.

12. Although grocery chains realize a very low profit margin because of heavy competition (around 1%), they do enjoy a very high asset turnover ratio, thereby enabling them to achieve a ROE of about 12%.

13.    Student Exercise

14.    Required rate of return (k)        14%
       Return on equity (ROE)           30%
       Retention rate (RR)              90%
       Earnings per share (EPS)         $5.00

       Then growth rate  =  RR x ROE
                          =  .90 x .30 = .27

$$P/E = \frac{D/E}{k-g} = \frac{.10}{.14-.27}$$

Since the required rate of return (k) is less than the growth rate (g), the earnings multiplier cannot be used (the answer is meaningless).

However, if ROE = .19 and RR = .60,
then growth rate = .60 x .19 = .114

$$P/E = \frac{.40}{.14-.114} = \frac{.40}{.026} = 15.38 = 15.38x$$

If next year's earnings are expected to be:  $5.57 = $5.00 x (1 + .114)

Applying the P/E:  Price = (15.38) x ($5.57) = $85.69
Thus, you would be willing to pay up to $85.69 for Maddy Computer Company stock.

15(a).  Projected dividends next 3 years:

              Year 1 ($1.25 x 1.08) = $1.35
              Year 2 ($1.35 x 1.08) = $1.46
              Year 3 ($1.46 x 1.08) = $1.58

       Required rate of return    12%
       Growth rate of dividends    8%

       The present value of the stock is:

$$V = \frac{1.35}{1.12} + \frac{1.46}{(1.12)^2} + \frac{1.58}{(1.12)^3} + \frac{40}{(1.12)^3}$$

$$= \frac{1.35}{1.12} + \frac{1.45}{1.2544} + \frac{1.58}{1.4049} + \frac{40}{1.5735}$$

$$= 1.21 + 1.16 + 1.12 + 25.42 = \$28.91$$

15(b). Growth rate                  8%
       Required rate of return     12%

$$V = \frac{1.35}{.12 - .08} = \frac{1.35}{.04} = \$33.75$$

15(c). Assuming all the above assumptions remain the same, the price at end of year 3 will be:

$$P_3 = \frac{D_4}{k - g} = \frac{1.25 \ \times \ (1.08)^4}{.12 - .08} = \frac{1.25 \times 1.3605}{.04} = \$42.52$$

16.     Student Exercise

# CHAPTER 14

# THE ANALYSIS OF ALTERNATIVE ECONOMIES AND SECURITY MARKETS: THE GLOBAL ASSET ALLOCATION DECISION

## Answers to Questions

1.  The reason for the strong relationship between the aggregate economy and the stock market is obvious if one considers that stock prices reflect changes in expectations for firms and the results for individual firms are affected by the overall performance of the economy. In essence, you would expect earnings of firms to increase in an expansion. Then, if the PIE ratio remains constant or increases because of higher expectations and there is no reason why it should not, you would expect an increase in stock prices.

2.  Stock prices turn before the economy for two reasons: First, investors attempt to estimate future earnings and thus current stock prices are based upon future earnings and dividends, which in turn are determined by expectations of future economic activity. The second possible reason is that the stock market reacts to various economic series that are leading indicators of the economy - e.g., corporate earnings, profit margins, and money supply.

3.  A diffusion index specifies the percent of reporting units experiencing a given result, indicates how pervasive a given movement is in a series. Leading indicators usually reach peaks or toughs before corresponding peaks or toughs in aggregate economic activity. Evidence strongly indicates that stock prices usually turn before the economy does (i.e., leading indicator). Therefore, a diffusion index of leading indicator series could help predict stock market movement by reporting the percentage of indicator with a certain characteristic (e.g., upward or downward movements).

4.  Virtually all research has shown the existence of a strong relationship between money supply and stock prices as is evident from high $R^2$s when money supply is used to explain stock price changes. However, it is not possible to use money supply changes to predict changes in stock prices, and this is not contradictory, since the stock market apparently reacts immediately to changes in money supply or investors attempt to predict this important variable. As a result, it is impossible to derive excess profits from watching current or recent past changes in the growth rate of the money supply.

5.  Excess liquidity is the year-to-year percentage change in the M2 money supply less the year-to-year percentage change in nominal GNP. The economy's need for liquidity is given by its nominal growth. Any growth in M2 greater than that indicates excess liquidity that is available for buying securities, which would drive up prices.

6.    The excess liquidity argument in question #5 suggests that stock prices should rise. On the other hand, monetary growth in excess of GNP growth may lead to expected inflation. The rise in expected inflation should cause the nominal RFR to rise, in turn, causing the required return to rise. This should lead to a decline in stock prices.

7.    If the market fully anticipates the rise in inflation, the long bond rate should rise to 10%. If we assume annual coupons, the 16-year 8% bond will go from a price of $1,091.03 to $847.89.

8.    Most of the inputs in determining the price of a bond are known – for instance, the promised coupon payments, the principal amount, and the dates on which those payments will be received. The one variable to be estimated is the required return, which can be found easily by comparing the bond in questions to a similar existing bond.

      In contrast, the payments on common stock are not known, nor the dates on which they might be received. Further, the required return is more difficult to estimate.

9.    Based on the economic projections, there will be a low correlation of stock prices among the various countries. As a result, the investor can reduce risk by diversifying his holdings among various countries. The relationships between the various countries' economic variables are reinforced in Table 14.9. This table shows a fairly high correlation of stock returns between the United States and Canada and one of the lowest relationships between the United States and Japan, although this correlation has tended to increase over time as the two economies become more interdependent.

10.   Assuming a $1,000 investment, a return of 10 percent would amount to $1,100, whereas returns in the German market would amount to DM 1,695. If the exchange rate goes to 1.30 over the year, the dollar equivalent would be $1,303.84. Thus, the investor should invest in Germany. An appreciation of the dollar to 2.00 DM/$ would reduce the dollar-equivalent return of investing in West Germany to 1,824 DM/$2.0 = $912; thus, it would be more advantageous to invest in the United States.

Harcourt, Inc.

# CHAPTER 14

## Answers to Problems

1. Student Exercise

2. CFA Examination I (June 1983)

2(a).1. The National Bureau of Economic Research has conducted extensive analysis of leading, coincident, and lagging indicators of general economic activity. *Business Conditions Digest* classifies economic indicators by their participation in the stage of the economic process and their relationship to business cycle movements.

The leading indicators include those economic time series that usually reach peaks or troughs before the corresponding points in aggregate economic activity. The group includes 12 series. One of the 12 leading series is common stock prices, which has a median lead of nine months at peaks and four months at troughs. Another leading series is the money supply in constant dollars which has a median lead of ten months at peaks and eight months at toughs.

2(a).2. Leading indicators have historically been a good tool for anticipating the economy. Investment managers should be aware of this information and, where possible, investment decisions might reflect projected trends. However, these indicators are by no means infallible. They often generate false signals. A downturn in leading indicators might precede only a retardation of growth rather than a full blown recession if the downturn is shallow or brief One of the most consistent leading indicators is stock prices represented by the S & P 500 Stock Composite Index. Thus, we are dealing with indicators that are roughly coincident with the most significant determinant of stock returns and price changes. An efficient market should already reflect this information. Thus, the attainment of above-average returns using only these series is questionable.

2(b). Interest rate forecasts are usually important in investment management for the following reasons:
Interest rates help determine the relative competitiveness of stocks versus bonds;

They have an effect on the stock returns from interest rate sensitive industries;

They help determine the maturity structure of bond portfolios;

They significantly effect investment in interest futures;

They affect the discount rate used in various equity valuation models.

2(c). Three economic time series, indicators, or data items that might be of key relevance to an auto analyst would be disposable personal income, consumer interest rate series, and consumer confidence survey results. An increase in disposable personal income might mean more discretionary income is available with which to purchase consumer durables such as automobiles. A decline in consumer interest rates might make the effective price

14 - 3

of a car, including borrowing charges, more affordable. Survey results that showed a high and growing level of consumer confidence about the future of the economy would likely have a positive psychological effect on consumer willingness to commit to new, large-ticket purchases.

In summary, the following variables constitute likely indicators of profits and performance in the automobile industry:

Real disposable personal income per capita - to indicate affordability of automobiles;

Installment debt as a percent of disposable income - to indicate ability of consumer to finance new car purchases;

The replacement cycle - indicating the average age of cars on the road, suggesting the inclination of consumers to consider new car purchases;

Trends in the cost of major components of auto production, including the prices charged by major suppliers.

3.      CFA Examination III  (June 1985)

3(a).   Overall, both managers added value by mitigating the currency effects present in the Index. Both exhibited an ability to "pick stocks" in the markets they chose to be in (Manager B in particular). Manager B used his opportunities not to be in stocks quite effectively (via the cash/bond contribution to return), but neither of them matched the passive index in picking the country markets in which to be invested (Manager B in particular).

|  | Manager A | Manager B |
|---|---|---|
| Strengths | Currency Management | Currency Management<br>Stock Selection<br>Use of Cash/Bond Flexibility |
| Weaknesses | Country Selection<br>(to a limited degree) | Country Selection |

3(b).   The column reveals the effect on performance in local currency terms after adjustment for movements in the U.S. dollar and, therefore, the effect on the portfolio. Currency gains/ losses arise from translating changes in currency exchange rates versus the U.S. dollar over the measuring period (three years in this case) into U.S. dollars for the U.S. pension plan. The Index mix lost 12.9% to the dollar, reducing what would otherwise have been a very favorable return from the various country markets of 19.9% to a net return of only 7.0%.

4.      Student Exercise

5.      Student Exercise

6.      Student Exercise

# CHAPTER 15

# BOND FUNDAMENTALS

### Answers to Questions

1.  A bond is said to be "called" when the issuer, at its own discretion, "calls" in the bond, and purchases it from the holder at a price stipulated in the bond indenture. When a bond is "refunded," it is called, but the firm reissues bonds for the same amount with a lower coupon rate. On a pure call (without refunding), the issue is usually retired.

2.  The three factors affecting the price of a bond are coupon, yield, and term to maturity. The relationship between price and coupon is a direct one--the higher the coupon, the higher the price. The relationship between price and yield is an inverse one--the higher the yield the lower the price, all other factors held constant. The relationship between price and maturity is not so clearly evident. Price changes resulting from changes in yields will be more pronounced, the longer the term to maturity.

3.  For a given change in the level of interest rates, two factors that will influence the relative change in bond prices are the **coupon** and **maturity** of the issues. Bonds with longer maturity and/or lower coupons will respond most vigorously in a given change in interest rates. Other factors likewise cause differences in price volatility, including the call features, but these factors are typically much less important.

4.  A call feature and a sinking fund are bond indenture provisions that can affect the maturity of the bond issue. Specifically there are three alternative call features: (1) freely callable provision that allows the issuer to retire the bond at any time during the life of the bond issue, (2) noncallable provision that does not allow the issuer to retire the bond prior to its maturity, and (3) deferred call provision that allows the issuer to retire the bond after a designated period of time. A sinking fund requires that a bond be paid off during the life of the issue rather than at maturity.

5.  Interest income from municipal bonds is normally not taxable by the federal government or by the state or city in which it is issued. Interest income on U.S. Treasury bonds is taxable at the federal level, but not by state or local governments. Corporate bond interest is taxable at all levels, as are capital gains from any of the bonds.

6.  Several institutions who participate in the market are life insurance companies, commercial banks, property and liability insurance companies, private and governmental retirement and pension funds, and mutual funds. They participate in the market because of restrictions on equity purchases (banks), the need for predictable cash flows (insurance companies), the tax exposure of the institutions, and the nature of the institutions' liabilities. Commercial banks are subject to normal tax exposure and have fairly short-term liability structures, so they tend to favor intermediate term municipals. Pension funds and life insurance companies are virtually tax-free institutions with long-term commitments, so they generally prefer high yielding long-term corporate bonds.

7.  An investor should be aware of the trading volume for a particular bond because a lack of sufficient trading volume may make selling the bond in a timely manner impossible. As a result, prices may vary widely while the investor is trying to change his position in the bond.

8.  Bond ratings provide a very important service in the market for fixed income securities because they provide the fundamental analysis for thousands of issues. The rating agencies conduct extensive analyses of the intrinsic characteristics of the issue to determine the default risk for the investor and inform the market of the analyses through their ratings.

9.  Based on the data presented in Table 15.1, the United States bond market share has shown the largest percentage increase, that is, 1.8% increase from 1993 to 1997 (46.0% in 1993 to 47.8% in 1997). Other countries that have shown an increase in market share are the United Kingdom, German and Italian. The Japanese bond market has shown the largest decline in market share during the period, 21.2% in 1993 to 17.8% in 1997. Other countries that have shown a decline in bond market share are Canada, Sweden, Denmark, Switzerland, Netherlands, and Belgium. The market share for the remaining countries listed in Table 15.1, either remained the same or the increase was very small (e.g., .1% for Australia).

10. While approximately 50% of the U.S. bond market is made up of government and agency issues, these issues only account for approximately 26.2% of the German market. By contrast, approximately 36-38% of domestic deutschemark bonds are issued by the major commercial banks. The capital market in Germany is dominated by these commercial banks because there is no formal distinction between investment, merchant, or commercial banks as there is in the United States. As a result, German banks continuously raise capital through bond issues to finance various industrial operations. Since these industrial corporations rely on the banks for loans, outstanding bonds of these domestic corporations is minimal (only about 0.1%).

11. In the United States, government agency issues although not direct issues of the Treasury, carry the full faith and credit of the U.S. government. The rate of interest on these securities is higher than the rate of interest on straight Treasury bond issues. However, some of the government agency issues are subject to state and local income tax, whereas interest received on Treasury issues is exempt from state and local levies.

12. The difference between a foreign bond and a Eurobond can be broken down as a difference in issuer and the market in which they are issued. For example, a foreign bond in Japan (e.g., a Samurai) is denominated in the domestic currency (yen) and is sold in the domestic market (Japan), but it is sold by non-Japanese issuers. On the other hand, a Eurobond (e.g., an Euro-DM) is denominated in the domestic currency (deutschemark) but it is sold outside the domestic country in a number of national markets. These bonds are typically underwritten by international syndicates. The relative size of these two markets varies by country.

Harcourt, Inc.

13. CFA Examination I (1993)

The following differences exist between Eurodollar and Yankee bonds:

| Differences in: | Eurodollar | Yankee |
|---|---|---|
| Primary market trading | Outside of U.S. | U.S. |
| Major secondary market trading | Outside of U.S. | U.S. |
| Registration | None | S.E.C. |
| Underwriter | International syndicate | U.S. syndicate |
| Issuer | Any entity | Non-U.S. entity |
| Coupon | Usually annually | Semiannually |

# CHAPTER 15

## Answers to Problems

1.

$$\text{ETY} = \frac{i}{1-t} = \frac{.055}{1-.28} = \frac{.055}{.72} = .07639$$

Assuming all other relevant factors are equal, the corporate bond carrying an 8 percent coupon and selling at par offers a better return than a 5 1/2 percent municipal bond (with an equivalent tax yield of 7.639 percent).

2(a).   Present Value = Future Value x Present Value Factor

PV = $1,000 x .17411 = $174.11
where .17411 is the present value factor for 6% interest (12% annually/2 interest payments per year) for 30 semi-annual periods (15 years x 2 interest payments per year)

2(b).   PV = $1,000 x .14205 = $142.05
where .14205 is the present value factor for 5% interest (semi-annually) for 40 semi-annual periods.

3.

$$\text{ETY} = \frac{i}{1-t}$$

3(a).   For the 15% tax bracket

$$\text{ETY} = \frac{.084}{1-.15} = \frac{.084}{.85} = .0988$$

3(b).   For the 25% tax bracket

$$\text{ETY} = \frac{.084}{1-.25} = \frac{.084}{.75} = .1120$$

3(c).   For the 35% tax bracket

$$\text{ETY} = \frac{.084}{1-.35} = \frac{.084}{.64} = .1292$$

4(a). Present Value = Future Value x Present Value Factor

PV = 1,000 x .30832 = $308.32
where .30832 is the present value factor for 4% interest (8% annually/2 interest payments per year) for 30 semi-annual periods (15 years x 2 interest payments per year)

4(b). PV = $1,000 x 0.39012 = $390.12
where .39012 is the present value factor for 4% interest for 24 semi-annual periods.

4(c). PV = $1,000 x .31007 = $310.07
where .31007 is the present value factor for 5% interest for 24 semi-annual periods.

5(a). PV  =  FV x PV factor
=  1,000 x .09722 = $97.22
where .09722 is the present value factor for 6% interest for 40 semi-annual periods.

5(b). PV = FV x PV factor
$601 = $1,000 x PV factor for 4% and 2N periods
Solving for the unknown (4%, 2N PV factor) = .601
Using the PV table, the solution is 13 semi-annual periods, or 6 1/2 years (time to maturity).

5(c). PV = FV x PV factor
$350 = $1,000 x PV factor for N/2% and 18 semi-annual periods
Solving for the unknown (N/2%, 18 periods PV factor)= .350
Using the PV table, the solution is 6% semi-annual or 12% annual interest.

Harcourt, Inc.

# CHAPTER 16

# THE ANALYSIS AND VALUATION OF BONDS

## Answers to Questions

1. The present value equation is more useful for the bond investor largely because the bond investor has fewer uncertainties regarding future cash flows than does the common stock investor. By investing in bonds with relatively no default risk (i.e., government securities) the investor can value a bond based primarily on expected cash flows (coupon rate and par value), required return (market yield), and the number of periods in the investment horizon (maturity date). Each of these factors can be incorporated into the present value equation.

   By contrast, common stocks have no stated maturity date and the valuation process is predominantly an estimate of future earnings. Although the present value method can be used for common stock analysis by estimating dividend payments and change in price over a given time frame, the uncertainties involved are much greater.

2. The most crucial assumption the investor makes is the assumption that cash flows will be reinvested at the promised yield. This assumption is crucial because it is implicit in the mathematical equation that solves for promised yield. If the assumption is not valid, an alternative method must be used, or the calculations will yield invalid solutions.

3(a). RFR is the riskless rate of interest, I is the factor for expected inflation, and RP is the risk premium for the individual firm.

3(b). The model considers the firm's business conditions. The risk of not breaking even would be reflected in the model through changes in the variable RP. This uncertainty would change the nature of the frequency distribution for earnings.

4. The *expectations hypothesis* imagines a yield curve that reflects what bond investors expect to earn on successive investments in short-term bonds during the term to maturity of the long-term bond. The *liquidity preference hypothesis* envisions an upward-sloping yield curve owing to the fact that investors prefer the liquidity of short-term loans but will lend long if the yields are higher. The *segmented market hypothesis* contends that the yield curve mirrors the investment policies of institutional investors who have different maturity preferences.

5. CFA Examination I (June 1982)

5(a). The term structure of interest rates refers to the relationship between yields and maturities for fixed income securities of the same or similar issuer. Expectations regarding future interest rate levels give rise to differing supply and demand pressures in the various maturity sectors of the bond market. These pressures are reflected in differences in the yield movements of bonds of different maturity.

The "term structure of interest rates," or "yield curve," will normally be upward sloping in a period of relatively stable expectations. The theoretical basis for the upward sloping curve is the fact that investors generally demand a premium, the longer the maturity of the issue, to cover the risk through time, and also to compensate for the greater price volatility of longer maturity bonds.

5(b).   According to the expectations theory of yield curve determination, if borrowers prefer to sell short maturity issues at the time lenders prefer to invest in longs, which happens when interest rates are expected to fall, longer maturity issues will tend to yield less than shorter maturity issues. The yield curve will be downward sloping. This generally occurs in periods when restrictive monetary policy by the Federal Reserve System, in an attempt to control inflation and inflation expectations causes very high short-term interest rates. In these circumstances, demand for short-term maturities is severely dampened.

5(c).   The "real" rate of interest is simply the difference between nominal interest rates and some measure of inflation, such as the current consumer price index or GNP deflator. In other words, it is an inflation-adjusted interest rate.

5(d).   The market for U.S. Treasury securities is very large and highly liquid as a result of the huge cumulative debt of the United States Government over time. Features of treasury securities tend to be fairly standardized and, by definition, all from one issuer. AAA corporate bonds, on the other hand, are issued by hundreds of different corporations and there are unique features to every different issue even from the same corporation. Thus, the market for these corporate bonds is much more complex in terms of assessing individual securities.

Some corporate issues are large and trade in very liquid markets. Others, however, are much smaller and tend to have restricted marketability. With so many issuers as well as issues, there is more room for inefficiencies to exist for short periods of time, given the diversity of the marketplace.

Any market that is less than efficient offers arbitrage opportunities. Because of these inefficiencies, issues of comparable quality, maturity, and other features can be priced differently, offering swap opportunities for bond traders or portfolio managers. Also, bonds that may appear identical for various reasons, could have better trading characteristics and may warrant a certain premium because of the superior liquidity.

5(e).   Over the past several years, fairly wide spreads have existed between AAA-corporates and Treasuries. Investor preference for Treasuries stems from several factors. Treasury securities typically are extremely liquid and provide investors with more flexibility. Secondly, Treasury securities typically do not have restrictive call features generally encountered with high-grade corporates. Thus, in a period of high interest rates, investors purchasing long-term securities anticipate an eventual decline in inflation and interest rates and thus prefer to lock in higher long-term yields.

6.    CFA Examination III (June 1982)

The mini-coupon bonds would be preferable to the current coupon bond for three reasons:

1.    A mini-coupon bond will have a **longer duration** than the current bond because of the smaller coupon. Its price will be **more volatile** for a given change in market interest rates and this is a plus under the assumption of a decline in interest rates over the next three years.

2.    The mini-coupon bonds have **less reinvestment risk** because more of the return comes from the price change over time, which is assumed to increase at the YTM rate. In contrast, the total coupon for the 14 percent bond must be reinvested at the 13.75 percent rate; this could be difficult if rates are declining during this period.

3.    The mini-coupon bonds have **greater call protection,** as they are callable at 103, or more than double the current market. In contrast, if rates decline about 2 percent, the current coupon bond could be called at 114 (against the current market of about 102). Between the two mini-coupon bonds, the large pension fund would buy the original issue discount bond with its lower price and higher yield to maturity. This price discrepancy between the two bonds that are otherwise similar reflects the fact that an investor subject to income taxes has to pay a capital gain each year of the OID. It is possible to also make an argument for the other mini-coupon bond on the basis of its longer duration because it has a lower yield to maturity, all else the same. The point is, because you expect lower rates, you want the longest duration security.

7(a).    Given that you expect interest rates to decline during the next six months, you should choose bonds that will have the largest price increase, that is, bonds with long durations.

7(b).    Case 1: Given a choice between bonds A and B, you should select bond B, since duration is inversely related to both coupon and yield to maturity.

Case 2: Given a choice between bonds C and D, you should select bond C, since duration is positively related to maturity and inversely related to coupon.

Case 3: Given a choice between bonds E and F, you should select bond F, since duration is positively related to maturity and inversely related to yield to maturity.

8.    You should select portfolio A because it has a longer duration (5.7 versus 4.9 years) and greater convexity (125.18 versus 40.30), thereby offering greater price appreciation. Portfolio A is also noncallable, therefore there is no danger of the bonds being called in by the issuer when interest rates decline (as you expect they will).

9(a). Call-adjusted duration takes into account the probability of a call and its impact on the actual duration of a bond. If a bond is noncallable, duration is based on all cash flows up to and including maturity. If interest rates drop and a call becomes likely, then duration should be calculated based on the time to call, which can be substantially sooner than maturity.

The range for duration now is 8.2 to 2.1 years. Because the bond is trading at par, its duration should be near 8.2 years.

9(b). If rates increase, then duration will drop (recall that duration is inversely related to yield to maturity.) However, call is now very unlikely, so call-adjusted duration will stay near the high end of the range.

9(c). If rates fall to 4%, call becomes highly probable, so call-adjusted duration will drop to the low end. (Remember here that duration to call is now greater than 2.1 years because of the inverse relationship between duration and yield to maturity).

9(d). Negative convexity refers to slow price increases of callable bonds as interest rates fall. Indeed, at some point the price change will be zero. This is due to the call price placing a ceiling on the price of a callable bond.

10. CFA Examination I (1990)

The two methods are **modified** and **Macaulay** duration.

Macaulay duration measures the average life of a bond, ignoring any options embedded in the security. Modified duration measures the price sensitivity of a bond to the change in yield to maturity.

Modified duration is the more widely used method particularly for corporate and mortgage backed issues.

11. CFA Examination II (1995)

**Option-adjusted duration:** Option-adjusted duration (OAD) is the duration of a callable bond after adjusting for the call option. The formula for OAD is:

$OAD = ( Price_{NCB}/Price_{CB})$ x $Dur_{NCB}$ x $(1 - Delta)$

where

$Price_{NCB}$ = price of noncallable bond
$Price_{CB}$ = price of callable bond
$Dur_{NCB}$ = modified duration of the noncallable bond
Delta = delta of the call option

As the equation shows, OAD depends on three elements:

1.  The ratio of the price of the noncallable bond to the price of the callable bond. The difference between the price of a noncallable bond and a callable bond is equal to the price of the call option. The higher dower) the price of the call option, the greater (smaller) the ratio. The OAD will depend on the price of the call option.

2.  The modified duration of the corresponding noncallable (option-free) bond.

3.  The delta of the call option. The delta, which varies between 0 and 1, measures the change in the price of the call option when the price of the underlying bond changes.

OAD permits the analyst to evaluate different fixed-income securities with embedded options (such as a callable bond) by analyzing each of these above components. For a callable bond, for example, using modified duration is inappropriate because the expected cash flow changes as the yield changes. OAD covers the call option component, which is important in assessing callable bonds. Unlike modified duration, which calculates duration risk for option-free bonds, OAD also considers the value and price sensitivity of the option. The OAD of a callable bond win be less than the modified duration of a noncallable bond anywhere between a deep-discount bond and a premium bond with a high coupon rate relative to the prevailing market yield.

**Effective duration.** Modified duration is a measure of the sensitivity of a bond's price to interest rate changes, if the expected cash flow does not change with interest rates. Effective duration allows for changes in the cash flow if interest rates chance. The formula for effective duration is:

**Effective duration** $= (P_- - P_+)/[(P_0)(y_+ - y_-)]$
where
$P_0$ = initial price (per \$100 of par value)
$P_-$ = price if yield is decreased by x basis points
$P_+$ = price if yield is increased by x basis points
$y_-$ = initial yield minus x basis points
$y_+$ = initial yield plus x basis points

Effective duration can be used to analyze mortgaged-backed securities for changing prepayment rates of cash flows as interest rates change. Effective duration also allows investors to compare the risk (duration) and return (cash flow) between a bond with embedded options and one without any options. Other applications of effective duration include the analysis of assetbacked securities and bonds having call/put options and sinking-fund provisions.

16 - 5

12.    CFA Examination II (1995)

12(a).   Description of Adjustment

1. **Historical real interest rate.** The historical real interest rate should be adjusted to remove distortion caused by the U.S. government's "pegging" of interest rates at artificially low levels in the 1940s and early 1950s, when Treasury-bill rates averaged a 0.53 percent return (1941-50). If the government had not pegged interest rates during this period, the rate probably would have been higher than observed, and the "true" long-term average rates would be higher. This situation suggests an upward adjustment to historical real interest rates.

2. **Bond maturity premium.** The observed bond maturity premium should be adjusted to remove bias caused by the pronounced upward trend in inflation and nominal interest rates during the period 1926-87, when investors systematically experienced capital losses on long-term bond holdings. Arnott-Sorenson estimated the loss on long-term bonds at 0.8 percent a year. Therefore, an upward adjustment to the long-term bond maturity premium is also indicated to remove the trend.

**Justification:** The justification for each of these adjustments is that the data contain systematic, long-lasting artificial biases. Such biases must be removed if these data items are to be useful for forming valid expectations.

12(b).   Adjustments are justified when existing or prospective circumstances relating to the economic or market factors to be considered differ from those reflected in the historical data. Key circumstances to consider when forming expectations about future returns are:

1. **Current yield curve and rate of inflation.** In deriving expected returns, an investor might adjust the historical returns of different asset classes to consider the current yield curve and inflation rate. Over time, prospective returns may converge on historical experience, but the expectations embedded in current data must also be considered in deriving best expectations of the future.

2. **"Halo" or markdown effect.** A halo effect may develop around an asset class that has done unusually well over a prolonged period, resulting in a historical record needing adjustment. Market participants do not easily forget bad investment experience with a particular asset class. Therefore, investors might want to adjust historical returns on an asset class that has done badly over a prolonged period to eliminate any embedded bias.

3. **Distinct period.** The historical return data since 1926 include many distinct eras with different capital market and inflation experiences. An investor might want to reflect the possibility that the forecast period might differ substantially from the historical norm or might closely resemble a subperiod.

4. **New dimensions in environment.** The environment of today's capital markets has dimensions to it such that history may be of little use. These dimensions include the savings/investment and import export disequilibria in the U.S. economy, the globalization and integration of capital markets, and rapid innovation in financial instruments. An investor may want to consider these dimensions in forecasting future returns.

5. **Different growth prospects.** If the economic growth prospects today differ from history, an investor should consider this circumstance when forming expectations about future returns.

6. **Unavailability of complete or comparable data.** The lack of availability of complete or comparable data on a given asset class (e.g., real estate, venture capital, and non-U.S. investments) does not justify ignoring them. An investor might use available results plus knowledge of the risk/return characteristics of that asset class to derive useful expected return data and, thus, include that class in the universe of available asset classes.

7. **Link between risk tolerance and value of capital assets.** Sharpe points out that a direct link exists between the collective risk tolerance of investors and the per capita value of capital assets. An increase in this measure should cause risk premia (maturity, default, equity) to decline, and vice versa. An investor who believes market participants have not considered this may want to adjust historical risk premia appropriately.

13.  CFA Examination I (1992)

Two alternative interpretations of this question are possible.

Alternative 1
In this alternative, the yields shown in the table in the question are assumed to be current yields to maturity and except for the 30 year bonds, all of the Treasury Zeros have higher yields to maturity than equivalent maturity Treasury Coupons. One explanation of the higher yield to maturity on the Zeros is that they have significantly higher durations, and hence higher risk, than equivalent maturity Coupon bonds. Secondly, investors who are subject to income taxes must pay annual income taxes on the imputed income on the Zeros even though they receive no current income. Thus Zeros have higher "promised yields" because they have higher risk and tax disadvantages.

Alternative 2
In this alternative, the yields shown in the table in the question are assumed to be the returns actually realized by the investor at maturity. One explanation of the higher realized return on the Zero is that interest rates declined in the holding period, and there was no reinvestment rate risk on the Zeros (i.e., no coupons to reinvest), while the coupon payments on the other Treasuries were reinvested at the lower interest rates. A second explanation of higher realized yields on the Zeros is that even though transactions costs are usually higher on the initial purchase on Zeros as compared to Coupon Treasuries, the periodic brokerage commissions on the reinvested semi-annual coupons may have reduced the realized yield.

14.  CFA Examination II (1993)

14(a).  The call provision generally causes the offering yield of a bond to be higher, all other things being equal. The call is an option, exercisable by the issuer. From the issuer's viewpoint, the call feature is valuable when prevailing market rates drop below the coupon rate on the existing bonds. Refinancing at a lower rate would lower interest costs

16 - 7

to the company. Between the first call date and maturity the company has this right and, therefore, the call is valuable to the company. Investors are willing to grant this valuable option to the issuer, but only for a price that reflects the likelihood the bond will be called. Therefore, callable bonds sell for a higher offering yield and lower price by the value of the option.

14(b). Duration
Adding a call feature to a proposed bond issue will shorten the duration of the bond.

Duration may be lowered because the call feature can potentially accelerate the payments, dependent on what happens to interest rates. When interest rates are high and the option is deep out-of-the-money, a call is unlikely, and the call-adjusted duration of the callable bond will be slightly lower than the duration of the noncallable bond. With decreasing rates, the likelihood of call increases, and the callable bond's duration decreases, relative to the duration of the noncallable bonds.

The resulting duration measure will be greater than duration to call and less than duration to maturity.

An additional impact is that the call feature increases the uncertainty of duration relative to a non-callable bond (NCB).

Convexity
Relative to a NOB, the call feature reduces the convexity (call-adjusted convexity) of the callable bond.

The call feature reduces the convexity across all interest rates, but the reduction is minimal at high rates when the call is out of the money and is greatest as the market price approaches the strike price and the call becomes more likely.

In fact, the call feature may induce negative convexity as the market price approaches and exceeds the strike price. When the call is more likely to be exercised, the market price won't appreciate much above the call price.

14(c). To use callable bonds and still maintain duration and convexity targets, the value and price sensitivity of the option must be taken into account. The managers will need to calculate call-adjusted duration and convexity for callable bonds and modified duration and convexity for option-free (noncallable) bonds to use them both in the same strategy.

14(d). Some advantages of including callable bonds are as follows:

- Callable bonds have higher offering yields (or more income or more cash flow) than comparable non-callable bonds.
- The larger supply of callable bonds make it easier to maintain duration and convexity targets.

Some disadvantages are:

- The reinvestment risk of having the bonds called away and having to invest at lower rates.
- Management time needed to rebalance when securities called or when rates change.
- Uncertainty about cash flows.

15.   CFA Examination II (1996)

15(a). The significance is to show the downward slope of the yield curve in the first year, coinciding with the 50 bp change in six months and 50 bp in one year.

**Discussion**
The yield curve is steeply inverted (downward sloping), at least through the first year to reflect the two 50 bp adjustments, then becomes slightly inverted through the 2 ½-year mark, and is basically flat by three years.

15(b). The shape of the yield curve is explained by the Expectations Theory or the Liquidity Preference Theory. Expectations Theory postulates that the shape of the term structure is determined by market participants' expectations of future interest rates, which allow the accurate prediction of future spot rates from the current term structure.

The liquidity Preference Theory postulates that whatever risk-averse investors' expectations are about rates, because they prefer to hold short-term maturity bonds, they require a yield premium to buy longer term bonds. When the market anticipates lower rates, the liquidity premium will dampen the downward slope of the yield curve.

**Alternative approach to the answer**: Spot rates area geometric average of forward rates. When rates are expected to fall, investors will require higher yields to hold shorter maturities (because of the lower yields expected when the short maturities must be reinvested), and the term structure will slope downward. The small term premiums will modify the slope of the curve but not enough to make the shape of the curve upward sloping in the early years.

Forward rates and spot rates are related according to the following formula:

$$(1 + R_t)^t = (1 + R_{t-j})^{t-j}(1 + f_{j,t-j})^j$$

Under the Liquidity Preference Theory, the relationship between spot and forward rates is somewhat different:

$$(1 + R_t)^t = (1 + R_{t-j})^{t-j}(1 + E(R_{j,t-j}) + L)^j$$

15(c). Assume that the expected 50 bp declines in Federal Funds rates in 6 and 12 months are both delayed by 6 months and that the Federal Funds rate is now expected to increase by 100 bp in 2 ½ years (when no increase was previously expected).

If you agree with the new interest rate forecast, you should select the two-year benchmark U.S. Treasury (bullet) instead of the cash/three-year U.S. Treasury barbell.

16 - 9

The delayed 50 bp drops in future rates and the 100 bp increase both cause current cash or spot rates to increase, implying an upward shift of the yield curve, which will occur in two weeks. Both investments have the same duration, but the barbell, which has the greater convexity, might be expected to have the smaller decline in value in two weeks when the market shares your view. However, the yield curve shift is nonparallel. A steepening occurs, where the three-year rate increases more than the two-year rate. Such a steepening increases the value of a bullet relative to a barbell. In this example, he steepening is sufficient for the bullet to experience a lower decline in value than the barbell.

**Alternative justification.** Given the new expectations about future interest rates, the two-year interest rate will increase approximately 25 bp and the three-year rate will increase approximately 33 bp. Given prevailing U.S. Treasury rates, increases of this size will cause the three-year Treasury to decline much more than the two-year (the three-year falls roughly twice as much). Even though the barbell invests only about two-thirds of its value in the three-year (and the rest in cash), the total dollar decline in the barbell will be more than the total dollar decline in the two-year bullet.

16.    CFA Examination II (1997)

16(a). **Why Pricing Spread Is Not Appropriate for ABS**
In traditional yield-spread analysis, an investor compares the yield to maturity of a bond with the yield to maturity of an on-the-run Treasury security of similar maturity. Such a comparison makes little sense because the cash flow characteristics of the two corporate bonds will not be the same as that of the benchmark security.

The proper way to compare non-Treasury bonds of the same maturity but with different coupon rates is to compare them to a portfolio of Treasury securities that have the same cash flow characteristics.

The pricing spread also uses only one point along the yield curve, whereas more recent methods use points all along the yield curve (e.g., the forward rates) for the assumed reinvestment rate.

16(b). **Description of Concepts**

i. **Zero-volatility (ZV) spread** has emerged as one of the best methods for addressing the relative valuation of amortizing securities. The ZV spread is the one spread that, when added to each cash flow's discrete discount rate, produces a total present value of all cash flows that is equal to the bond's price. In other words, it measures the average spread to the entire discount curve over the period in which cash flows are projected for a particular security. This method uses only one interest rate path in determining the zero-volatility spread. The ZV calculation involves three steps:

   - Project all cash flows for the security, including scheduled amortization, coupon, and prepayments, using an assumed prepayment rate or series of prepayment rates.

- Determine the present value of each cash flow using the appropriate Treasury based rate (same maturity as the cash flow) plus a constant spread. Use the same spread for all maturities.
- Add the present values of all cash flows. If the total equals the price of the security, the spread chosen is the ZV spread. If not, try other constant spreads until the present value equals the price.

ii. **Option-adjusted spread** analysis is used for bonds with embedded interest-rate-sensitive options, such as the option held by mortgagees to prepay their mortgages. Automobile asset-backed securities are not sensitive to interest rate movements, but mortgage-backed securities are. Therefore, for mortgage-backed securities, the analyst should create a large number of interest rate paths (and thus a large number of prepayment schedules) derived from a random number generator. Creation of the new paths will be heavily influenced by the assumptions regarding interest rate volatility.

16(c). **Why OAS Is Appropriate for Second Mortgage ABS**

Second mortgage prepayments are sensitive to changes in interest rates. Consequently, option-adjusted spread, which allows cash flows to be path dependent (e.g., allows for the possibility of prepayment in response to interest rate declines), is the correct measure of value.

17. CFA Examination II (1998)

17(a). **Letter of Credit (LOC)** - LOCs are a type of external credit support (also known as third-party credit enhancement) for credit card securities. They are issued by third-party banks and guarantee a specified amount of funds available to the issuer in case of cash shortfalls from the collateral.

LOCs expose the investor to the credit risk of the third-party bank providing the enhancement. The rating downgrade of an LOC-provider bank could affect the rating of the ABS, thus causing the ABS to trade at a wider spread than before.

17(b). **Early Amortization** - Early amortization is another credit enhancement for credit card securities. Early amortization begins if certain characteristics of the collateral pool deteriorate to some preset (trigger) level. If early amortization is triggered, the security's revolving period immediately ends and the investor certificate's share of all further repayments is passed through to investors until the certificate is retired.

Early amortization means that principal is returned at par at unanticipated times. When such returns occur in a low-interest-rate environment, the principal will have to be reinvested at lower rates. And if the security was bought at a premium, this event will result in the loss of the premium. The indicator used to judge a security's potential for early amortization is its current *excess spread,* also called its *protection level.*

18. CFA Examination II (1998)

18(a). **Change in MBS Principle Cash Flows**

The principal cash flows increase during the first year because of increased principal prepayments and decrease in the next year because of decreased principal prepayments. Principal prepayments increase in the first year because mortgagees react to the decrease in interest rates by refinancing their existing mortgages into new, lower-interest-rate mortgages. The "instantaneous" decline strengthens the idea that mortgagees react quickly rather than wait to refinance their mortgages. Principal prepayments decrease in the second year as interest rates increase because mortgagees have little incentive to refinance their mortgages into what are by then higher mortgage interest rates.

18(b). **Duration Measure**

Rachel Morgan should use **effective duration** to evaluate the price sensitivity of her MBS Effective duration takes into account changes in expected cash flows because of changes in interest rates when determining price sensitivity, whereas modified duration does not. Because modified duration does not take into account changing cash flows caused by changing interest rates, it overstates price sensitivity in a declining-interest-rate environment and understates price sensitivity in a rising-interest-rate environment. The effective duration of the MBS will be less than its modified duration and will decrease more as rates decline and increase more as rates rise. As effective duration decreases, MBS price sensitivity decreases; as effective duration increases, MBS price sensitivity increases.

18(c). **Change in IO**

The price of Morgan's Interest-Only-Security (IO) will act quite differently from her pass through MBS in the first year of her interest rate scenario. If interest rates decline by 250 basis points (a large decline), the IO's price will *decline* whereas the pass-through MBS price will increase as normally expected. The IO entitles the holder to receive, only interest cash flows generated by the security's underlying mortgages. As interest rates decline and prepayments accelerate, the interest cash flows that were expected to be generated by outstanding mortgage principal balances *are not generated* The principal has been prepaid, it cannot pay interest. Because the IO price is the present value of the interest-only cash flows, its price must decline as investors realize that there are less and less interest-only cash flows in the future to present value to obtain a fair market price.

19. CFA Examination III (1996)

19(a). An informed manager will recommend purchase of Aaa bonds over Aa bonds for an investment with a one-year horizon. Although the Aa bonds show the largest *indicated incremental return,* based on -the initial spreads of expected return over governments, the Aaa bonds can be expected to produce the largest *realized incremental return,* as shown by the following calculation:

| Incremental return | = | Initial spread - (Change in Spread x Duration) |
|---|---|---|
| Aaa bonds | = | 31 bp - (0 bp x 3.1 years) = 31 bp |
| Aa bonds | = | 40 bp - (10 bp x 3.1 years) = 9 bp |

16 - 12

Realized spreads are dependent on the interaction of the three elements (initial spread, horizon spread, and horizon duration) and can differ substantially from initial indications of relative return and relative attractiveness.

19(b). While many economic, issue-specific and market-related variables can and do influence realized incremental returns, several are of primary importance. Initial spreads, call provisions, and expected changes in interest rates and/or the shape of the yield curve are all examples of variables that a thorough analysis will consider before arriving at an investment decision. Other fundamental variables that must be weighed and evaluated include the following:

*Changes in issue-specific credit quality*. Changes in credit quality can cause realized incremental returns to differ from initial indicated spreads. Improving (deteriorating) credit quality will typically cause spreads to narrow (widen) impacting incremental returns. Example: Aa-rated bond currently trading at 40 bp over a comparable treasury widens to 60 bp because of perceived deterioration of credit quality. This could be caused by such factors as additional issuance of debt, changes in accounting policy, or mergers and acquisitions *without* an accompanying change in bond rating.

*Changes in credit rating*. Improving (deteriorating) credit rating can cause realized incremental returns to differ from initial spreads. Improving (deteriorating) quality will typically cause spreads to tighten (widen), impacting incremental returns. For example, bond credit rating upgrade from Baa to A will realize higher incremental returns than those indicated by initial yield spreads.

Changes in relative bond rating category spreads. A general change in quality spreads because of changes in either economic conditions or investors' required risk premiums will impact realized incremental returns. Example: A general improvement in the economy will likely lead to strong corporate earnings and improved balance sheets, decreasing the risk of default. This in turn would cause the yield spread of corporate bonds to narrow relative to treasuries increasing realized incremental returns.

**Rolling down the credit quality curve**. As bonds roll down the credit quality curve, spreads will tend to tighten, impacting realized incremental returns. The impact can be either positive or negative among differing bond rating categories. For example, lower-grade bonds can tighten (relative to treasuries) more than their higher grade counterparts as the bonds approach maturity, causing realized incremental returns to increase.

20. CFA Examination III (1998)

20(a). **Effect of Changes in U.S. Dollar**
The difference between the hedged and unhedged returns is a function of fluctuations in the currency return over the time period studied. Over the five-year period, the U.S. dollar was relatively weak against other currencies, causing the unhedged index to outperform the hedged by 8.7 percentage points. For the recent one-year period, the U.S. dollar strengthened against other currencies. The index returns hedged into U.S. dollars increased by 5.5 percentage points because of the relative dollar strength.

16 - 13

**20(b).** **Transferability of Duration and Sector Management**

*Duration Management* is more difficult in international fixed-income investing because few non U.S. bond markets have liquid issues with maturities greater than 10 years. Most non U.S. bond markets also lack the broad range of instruments, such as strips and repos, that allow low-cost duration management in the U.S. market. Although interest rate futures are available in most non U.S. markets and offer a low-cost vehicle, they are limited typically to the short end of the term structure. Swap markets are liquid and generally available but pose challenges in counterparty credit and technical and operational barriers. A U.S. bond portfolio's duration, benchmarked to the U.S. yield curve, is managed in the aggregate. Managing the durations of international portfolios against an aggregate benchmark can be difficult because of the differing volatility and correlation characteristics among the markets composing the index.

*Sector management* is also difficult outside the United States. A scarcity of corporate bonds often exists outside the United States because of policies favoring the raising of capital through bank financing and equity issuance. Market anomalies can arise from differing tax treatments among markets. Implementing some sector management strategies may be difficult because mortgage markets and the derivative instruments produced by that sector may not exist to the extent available in the United States.

**21.** CFA Examination II (1999)

**21(a).** As interest rates decline, the price of both bonds would increase. However, the price appreciation of Colina will be limited by the call price of 102.00. As interest rates declines, the probability of the issuer calling the bonds increases, as the company will consider issuing new bonds at lower interest rates. On the other hand, the price appreciation of Sentinel bond would not be limited, as the bond is not callable. Therefore, Sentinel bond would be the preferred investment if you expect interest rates to decrease by more than 100 basis points.

**21(b).** Kerr would prefer the Colina bond in *either a rising or a stable* interest rate scenario. The Colina bond has an embedded option, which is sold by the investor to the issuer of the bond. The higher yield compensates Kerr for the risk of being short the embedded call option. If rates are stable or increase, the investor earns the extra income without having to worry about having the bond called from them. Additionally, if rates increase, Colina bond price should decrease less relative to Sentinel bond because of Colina's shorter effective duration due to the embedded call option.

**21(c)(i)** Since the Sentinel bond is noncallable, increased interest rate volatility would not impact its directional price change.

    **(ii)** Callable bond value = Non-callable bond value - Call option value

The level and volatility of interest rates are key factors in determining the value of a bond with an embedded call option. The greater the variance or uncertainty of interest rates, the greater the value of the embedded call option. As the embedded option value increases, it causes the value of Colina's callable bond to decrease.

16 - 14

# CHAPTER 16

## Answers to Problems

1(a). Assuming annual compounding

$$AYC = \frac{70 + \dfrac{1{,}100 - 1{,}000}{4}}{\dfrac{1{,}100 + 1{,}000}{2}} = \frac{70 + 25}{1050} = \frac{95}{1050} = 9.05\%$$

1(b). Assuming annual compounding, AYC = 9.18% nominal yield

$$
\begin{aligned}
\$1{,}000 &= 70 \times (3.2270) + 1{,}100 \times (.7038) \\
&= 225.89 + 774.18 \\
&= \$1{,}000.07 \text{ (rounding)}
\end{aligned}
$$

where 3.2270 is the present value of annuity factor and .7038 is the present value factor (both calculated for 4 periods at a 9.18 percent interest rate per period).

Since compounding is annual, nominal and effective annual yields are the same.

1(c). Assuming annual compounding, 5% interest, 21 years remaining

$$
\begin{aligned}
\text{Price} &= [70 \times (12.82115)] + [1{,}000 \times (.35894)] \\
&= 897.48 + 358.94 \\
&= \$1{,}256.42
\end{aligned}
$$

where 12.82115 is the present value of annuity factor and .35894 is the present value factor (both calculated for 21 periods at a 5 percent interest rate per period).

2(a). Assuming semiannual compounding

$$AYC = \frac{40 + \dfrac{1{,}000 - 1{,}012.50}{24}}{\dfrac{1{,}000 + 1{,}012.50}{2}} = \frac{40 - .52}{1006.25} = \frac{39.48}{1006.25} = 3.92\% \text{ (semiannual)}$$

3.92% x 2 = 7.84% annual

2(b). Assuming semiannual compounding, ARY = 7.84% (= 2 x 3.92%) (nominal yield)

$$
\begin{aligned}
\$1{,}012.50 &= [40 \times (15.37262)] + [1{,}000 \times (.39739)] \\
&= 614.90 + 397.39 \\
&= \$1{,}012.29 \text{ (rounding)}
\end{aligned}
$$

where 15.37262 is the present value of annuity factor and .39739 is the present value factor (both calculated for 24 periods at a 3.92 percent interest rate per period).

Effective yield = $(1 + .0392)^2 - 1 = .07993 = 7.99\%$

16 - 15

2(c). Assuming semiannual compounding, callable in 3 years with 8% premium, AYC = 9.86% (2 x 4.93%)

$$\$1,012.50 = 40 \times (5.08707) + 1,080 \times (.74921)$$
$$= 203.48 + 809.15$$
$$= \$1,012.63 \text{ (rounding)}$$

where 5.08707 is the present value of annuity factor and .74921 is the present value factor (both calculated for 6 periods at a 4.93 percent interest rate per period).

3.

| (1) | (2) | (3) | (4) | (5) | (6) |
|---|---|---|---|---|---|
| | Cash | PV | PV | PV as % | |
| Period | Flow | at 5% | of Flow | of Price | (1) x (5) |
| 1 | $ 40 | .9524 | $ 38.10 | .04014 | .04014 |
| 2 | 40 | .9070 | 36.28 | .03822 | .07644 |
| 3 | 40 | .8638 | 34.55 | .03640 | .10920 |
| 4 | 40 | .8227 | 32.91 | .03467 | .13868 |
| 5 | 40 | .7835 | 31.34 | .03302 | .16510 |
| 6 | 1,040 | .7462 | 776.05 | .81756 | 4.90536 |
| | | | $949.23 | 1.00000 | 5.43492 |

The duration equals 5.43492 semiannual periods or 2.71746 years.

3(a).

$$\text{Modified duration} = \frac{2.71746}{1 + (.10/2)} = \frac{2.71746}{1.05} = 2.588 \text{ years}$$

3(b). Percentage change in price $= -D_{mod} \times \Delta i$
$$= -(2.588) \times (-50/100)$$
$$= 1.294 \text{ percent}$$

The bond price should increase by 1.294% in response to a drop in the bonds YTM from 10% to 9.5%. If the price of the bond before the decline was $949.23, the price after the decline in the YTM should be approximately $949.23 x 1.01294 = $961.51.

4. Assuming semiannual compounding, 10 years, zero coupon, $1,000 par value, 12% YTM

Purchase Price = $1,000 (.31180) = $311.80
where .31180 is the present value factor for 6% interest
(12% annually/2 interest payments per year) for 20 semi-annual periods (10 years x 2 interest payments per year)
After two years, assuming semiannual compounding, 8 years remaining, zero coupon, $1,000 par value, 8% YTM

Selling Price = $1,000 (.53391) = $533.91
where .53391 is the present value factor for 4% interest
(8% annually/2 interest payments per year) for 16 semi-annual periods (8 years remaining x 2 interest payments per year)

16 - 16

Assuming you bought the bond for \$311.80 and sold it after two years for \$533.91, the ARY = 28.78% annual (14.39% semiannual)

$$\$311.80 \ = \ 533.91 \text{ x } (.58405)$$
$$= \ \$311.83 \text{ (rounding)}$$

where .58405 is the present value factor (calculated for 4 semiannual periods (2 years) at a 14.39% interest rate per period.

5(a).   Assuming semiannual interest payments

$$\text{Modified duration} \ = \ \frac{5.7}{1 + (.095/2)} = \frac{5.7}{1.0475} = 5.442 \text{ years}$$

$$\text{Percentage change in price} \ = \ -D_{mod} \text{ x } \Delta i$$
$$= \ -(5.442) \text{ x } (+150/100)$$
$$= \ -8.163 \text{ percent}$$

A misestimate of the price change will arise because the modified-duration line is a linear estimate of a curvilinear function. That is, convexity measures the rate of change in modified duration as yields change. The effect of convexity on price should be added to the effect of duration on price in order to obtain an improved approximation of the change in price given a change in yield.

5(b).  Percentage change in price = -5.442 x -3%  = +16.33%

The 3% decline in rates may not elevate the bond price by 16.33% if the bond's call price is violated and protection against a call has elapsed.

6.      CFA Examination I (1992)

There are three components of return for international (German) bonds: coupon income, capital appreciation (or loss) as resulting from interest rate movements, and profits (or loss) from changes in currency exchange rates; in contrast, only the first two components of return (coupon income and capital appreciation, or loss) apply to domestic (U.S. government) bonds.

Since both bonds were selling at par on 1/1/91 (in both cases, the market yields on the bonds equaled their coupons), the contribution from coupon income is simply the coupon rate indicated in the table. Given we're dealing with holding period return here, its appropriate to use the beginning price of the issue to measure the current yield (coupon) component of return. Price change resulting from interest rate movements can be calculated using the change in yield times the modified duration, with the sign changed:

16 - 17

Harcourt, Inc.

Percent price change = - modified duration x yield change x 100

German government bond: -0.50 x -7.0 = +3.50%

U.S. Government Bond: -1.25 x -6.5 = +8.13%

The percentage change from currency movements can be approximated by taking the reciprocal of the DM/U.S. exchange rate (to express the exchange rate in dollar terms) and finding the percentage change:

$$(1/1.50) / (1 /1.55) = .6667/.6452 = 1.033 = +3.3\% \text{ change}$$

Thus, the contribution to total return for the two bonds can be summarized as follows:

|  | Domestic Coupon Income | + | Domestic Capital Gain | + | Currency Movements | = | Total Return |
|---|---|---|---|---|---|---|---|
| German Govt. Bond | 8.5% | + | 3.5% | + | 3.7% * | = | 15.7% |
| or approximated as | 8.5% | + | 3.5% | + | 3.3% | = | 15.3% |
| U.S. Govt. Bond | 8.0% | + | 8.1% | + | 0.0% | = | 16.1% |

As indicated in the table above, the U.S. government bond offered the superior return relative to the German government bond.

*A more accurate formula to reflect currency movements is:
[(100% + coupon income + capital change) x (currency change)]
=[(100% + 8.5% + 3.5%) x (.033)] = 3.7%

7.   CFA Examination I (1993)

7(a).  Modified duration is Macaulay duration divided by 1 plus the yield to maturity divided by the number of coupons per year:

$$\text{Modified duration} = \frac{\text{Macaulay duration}}{1 + \dfrac{\text{Yield}}{k}}$$

Where k is the number of coupons per year. If the Macaulay duration is 10 years and the yield to maturity is 8 percent, then modified duration equals 10/(1+ (.08/2)) = 9.62.

7(b).  For option-free coupon bonds, modified duration is a better measure of the bond's sensitivity to changes in interest rates. Maturity considers only the final cash flow, while modified duration includes other factors. These factors are he size of coupon payments, the timing of coupon payments, and the level of interest rates (yield-to-maturity).

7(c).  Modified duration increases as the coupon decreases. Modified duration decreases as maturity decreases.

7(d). Convexity measures the rate of change in modified duration as yields change. Convexity refers to the shape of the price-yield relationship and can be used to refine the modified duration approximation of the sensitivity of prices to interest rate changes. Convexity shows the extent to which bond prices rise at a greater rate (as yields fall) than they fall (as yields rise). The effect of duration on price and the effect of convexity on price should be added together to obtain an improved approximation of the change in price for a given change in yield.

8. CFA Examination I (1993)

To compare the German bond performance versus the U.S. bond performance, one must first compute the return over the six-month period for each security. The return for each security is: Return = Income + forward discount or premium + change in bond price.
Return on German Bond = 7.5/2 + (-.75) + Change in German Bond Price
Return on U.S. Bond = 6.5/2 + 0 + 0 = 3.25

If Return on German Bond = Return on U.S. Bond, then:

3.75 + (-.75) + Change in German Bond Price = 3.25
Change in German Bond Price = **.25%** = an increase in price of 1/4 point

9. CFA Examination II (1990)

9(a). The forward rate is the expected yield during some future period - e.g., the forward rate for year three is the one year rate expected to prevail in year three (three years from now). To calculate the forward rate for a three year bond two years from now, you would use the following formula:

$$(1+_{t+m}r_{n-m,t})^{n-m} = (1+_tR_n)^n \big/ (1+_tR_m)^m$$

where: r = the forward rate for the period n-m
$R_n$ = the observable yield for a security with maturity n
$R_m$ = the observable yield for a security with maturity m

In this case, we are looking for the forward rate for a three year bond, two years from now (i.e., the forward three year rate for the period from two to five years). Therefore, the computation would be as follows:

$$= (1+_tR_5)^5/(1+_tR_2)^2 \quad \text{which in this example would be:}$$

$$= (1+.077)^5/(1+.079)^2 = 7.566\%$$

9(b). The January 19XX term structure indicates an upward sloping yield curve. The **pure expectations hypothesis** would contend that investors are expecting higher short-term rates in the future and, therefore, the forward rate curve would be even steeper than the currently prevailing yield curve which is the geometric average of these future short-term rates. The market segmentation hypothesis would contend that there is greater demand for short-term securities by those who have an interest in this segment of the market. Put another way, those institutions that tend to invest in the short-term segment of the yield curve have greater funds at the present time compared to those who have an interest in long-term securities. The liquidity hypothesis would imply that this upward sloping yield curve is a natural by-product of risk averse investors who require a higher yield to invest in longer term securities because of the higher risk involved - i.e., the greater volatility of longer maturity securities.

9(c). The term structure over this period experienced what is referred to as a "snap down" in that the short-term rates went up, but the long-term rates went down substantially. As a result, a portfolio with a maturity of two years (and a duration of less than two) would have experienced a fairly small price decline because the yields for one and two year bonds went up. Therefore, this portfolio would have had a small decrease in value during this transition. In sharp contrast, the long-term rates went down substantially and, therefore, a portfolio with a maturity of 10 years (which would have a duration of about 6 years) would have experienced greater volatility than the two year maturity portfolio, but also positive price changes during this period because all the long maturity bonds experienced a decrease in yields. Therefore, this portfolio would have experienced an increase in value.

9(d). In January 19XX, the spread between short-term and long-term was about 135 basis points compared to the normal spread of 170 basis points. Under these conditions, you would expect this spread to increase during the ensuing period, and this could happen in several ways. Assuming no change in the general level of rates, you could either expect short rates to decline or long rates to increase. Alternatively, if you expected an increase in rates, you would envision that long rates would experience a larger increase in order to reestablish the normal spread. Finally, if you expected a decline in rates, you would expect long rates to decline by less than short rates to reestablish the norm. The point is, in all scenarios, you would expect the change in long rates to be less than optimal. Put another way, this set of expectations would discourage you from aggressively investing in long-term securities. Obviously, this portfolio decision would have been suboptimal based upon what happened because the long bonds had the very best performance because of the "snap down" in the yield curve. This example reflects the point made in the Meyer article that when making a decision with regard to yield spreads, it is also necessary to have some expectations regarding the future level of interest rates. If you really expected that interest rates would decline substantially in the future, you would have possibly anticipated the change in the shape of the yield curve or been willing to invest in long bonds simply because of the greater volatility during a period of declining interest rates.

10. CFA Examination II (1992)

10(a). If yield-to-maturity (Y-T-M) on Bond B falls 75 basis points:

-75 basis points = -75/100 = -.75 $\Delta$ in Y-T-M

Pro. Price $\Delta$ = (-modified duration) ($\Delta$ in Y-T-M)+ (1/2)(convexity)($\Delta$ in Y-T-M)$^2$
     = (-6.8)(-.75) + (1/2)(.6)(.75)$^2$
     = 5.1+.16875
     = 5.27

So the projected price will rise to $105.27 from its current $100 price.

16 - 20

10(b). For Bond A, the callable bond, neither maturity nor cash flow is certain. The analysis of callable bonds can take one of four approaches. The first is to ignore the call feature and analyze on a "to maturity basis." All calculations for yield, duration, and convexity are distorted. Durations are too long and yields are too high.

A second approach is to treat the premium bond selling above the call price on a "to call" basis. The duration is unrealistically short and yields too low.

The most effective approach is to use an option evaluation approach. The callable bond can be decomposed into two separate securities - a non-call bond and an option.

Price of callable Bond = Price of non-callable Bond - Price of Option

Since the option will always have some positive value, the callable bond will always have a price that is less than the non-callable security.

An alternative, but less rigorous approach, is to use horizon analysis. The horizon approach considers the three sources of potential dollar return in analyzing a callable bond. The investor is required to estimate an investment holding period, a reinvestment rate, and a call date.

11. CFA Examination II (1992)

11(a). Final Spot Rate:

$$1000 = \frac{70}{(1+y_1)^1} + \frac{70}{(1+Y_2)^2} + \frac{70}{(1+y_3)^3} + \frac{70}{(1+y_4)^4} + \frac{1070}{(1+y_5)^5}$$

$$1000 = \frac{70}{(1.05)^1} + \frac{70}{(1.0521)^2} + \frac{70}{(1.0605)^3} + \frac{70}{(1.0716)^4} + \frac{1070}{(1+y_5)^5}$$

$$1000 = 66.67 + 63.24 + 58.69 + 53.08 + 1070/(1+y_5)^5$$

$$1000 - 241.68 = 1070/(1+y_5)^5$$

$$758.32 = 1070/(1+y_5)^5$$

$$(1+y_5)^5 = 1070/758.32$$

$$y_5 = (1.411)^{1/5} - 1 = 7.13\%$$

Final Forward Rate:

$$(1.0713)^5/(1.0716)^4 - 1 = 1.411/1.3187 - 1 = 1.0699 - 1 = 7.00\%$$

11(b). Yield-to-maturity is a single discounting rate for a series of cash flows to equate these flows to a current price. It is the internal rate of return.

Spot rates are the unique set of individual discounting rates for each period. They are used to discount each cash flow to equate to a current price. Spot rates are the theoretical rates for zero coupon bonds.

16 - 21

Spot rates can be determined from a series of yields-to-maturity in an internally consistent method such that the cash flows from coupons and principal will be discounted individually to equate to the series of yield-to-maturity rates.

Yield-to-maturity is not unique for any particular maturity, whereas spot rates and forward rates are unique.

Forward rates are the implicit rates that link any two spot rates. They are a unique set of rates that represent the marginal interest rate in a future period. They are directly related to spot rates, and therefore yield-to-maturity. Some would argue (expectations theory) that forward rates are the market expectations of future interest rates. Regardless, forward rates represent a break-even or rate of indifference that link two spot rates. It is important to note that forward rates link spot rates, not yield-to-maturity rates.

11(c). The spot rate at 4 years is 7.16%. Therefore, 7.16 is the theoretical yield to maturity for the zero coupon U.S. Treasury note. The price of the zero coupon at 7.16% is the present value of $1000 to be received in 4 years.

Annual compounding: PV = 758.35 also can be approximated from
"Present Value of $1 Table"

Semi-annual compounding: PV = 754.73

12. CFA Examination III (1992)

Duration is a weighted average term-to-maturity of a security's cash flows, where the weights are the present value of each cash flow as a percentage of the present value of all cash flows. Compared to a bond with a higher coupon, a bond with a lower coupon provides a larger proportion of its total cash flows at maturity. Hence, it has a longer duration, and exhibits greater percentage price volatility in the face of interest rate changes. Thus the US$-pay SLMA, with its lower coupon, will have a longer duration and increase more in value if rates fall by 100 basis points. Currency fluctuations do not affect directly measures of volatility; the price increases would be in local currency terms.

13. CFA Examination II (1993)

13(a). Calculation of One-Year Forward Rate for January 1, 1996:

$$(1+ R_4)^4 = (1+ R_3)^3(1+ f_{1,3})$$
$$(1+.055)^4 = (1.05)^3 (1 + f_{1,3})$$
$$f_{1,3} = (1 + .055)^4/(1.05)^3 - 1$$
$$f_{1,3} = 1.2388/1.1576 - 1$$
$$f_{1,3} = 0.701 \text{ or } 7.01\%$$

OR

Harcourt, Inc.

| Date | Calculation of Forward Rate (Linking Method) |
|------|------------------------------------------------|
| 1/1/93 | 3.5% |
| 1/1/94 | $(1.045)^2 = (1.035)(1 + f)$<br>$f = 0.0551$ or 5.51% |
| 1/1/95 | $(1.05)^3 = (1.035) \times (1.0551) \times (1 + f)$<br>$f = 0.0601$ or 6.01% |
| 1/1/96 | $(1.055)^4 = (1.035) \times (1.0551) \times (1.0601) \times (1 + f)$<br>$f = 0.0701$ or 7.01% |

13(b). The conditions would be those that underlie the pure expectations theory of the term structure: (1) risk neutral market participants who are willing to (2) substitute among maturities solely on the basis of yield differentials. This behavior would rule out liquidity or term premia relating to risk as well as market segmentation based on maturity preferences.

13(c). Under the expectations hypothesis, lower implied forward rates would indicate lower expected future spot rates for the corresponding period. Since the lower expected future rates embodied in the term structure are nominal rates, either lower expected future real rates or lower expected future inflation rates would be consistent with the specified change in the observed (implied) forward rate.

13(d). Multiple scenario forecasting is a technique for developing a set of expectations that reflects the effects that different realizations of key economic variables will have on capital market returns. By providing a mechanism that reveals information about market participants expectations for future interest rate levels (and about changes in these expectations), the term structure can be a useful source of inputs in the process of assembling scenario forecast.

The decline in anticipated futures short-term nominal rates could be depicted either by revising the scenario outcome, (the states) to reflect the possibility of lower future rates or by reweighting the probabilities attached to the scenarios to increase the odds associated with lower future rates.

To maintain consistency, it would also be necessary to take into account changes in other variables that might be induced by lower future interest rates.

The contrast in effects between lower anticipated inflation and a lower real rate of interest will have implications for the development of scenarios.

14. CFA Examination III (1993)

14(a). The calculations necessary for obtaining the expected returns are shown below:

Bill:   Coupon = 12.5/4 = 3.125% for the period
        1500 * 1.03125 = 1546.875
        With currency effect: 1546.875/1526 = 1.01368 - 1 = 1.368%

Note: Coupon = 10/4 = 2.5% for the period
With duration effect:
100bp * 6 mod dur = 6%
1500 (1.025 + .06) = 1627.50
With currency effect: 1627.50/1526 = 1.06651 - 1 = 6.651%

An alternate approach for obtaining the expected returns is:

| | |
|---|---:|
| Bill: Yield 12.5%/4 = | 3.125% |
| Currency (1500/15261) – 1 | - 1.704 |
| Return = | 1.421% |

| | |
|---|---:|
| Note: Yield 10.0%/4 = | 2.500% |
| 100 basis point change in expected return over | |
| 3-month horizon x 6.00 modified duration = | 6.000 |
| Currency (1500/15261) - 1 = | - 1.704 |
| Return = | 6.796% |

15.    CFA Examination I (1994)

15(a).  Current yield = Annual dollar coupon interest / Price = 70/960 = 7.3%.

The annual yield to maturity (YTM) is

$$P = \sum_{t=1}^{n} \frac{C}{(1 + y)^t} + \frac{M}{(1 + y)^n}$$

where: P = price of the bond
       C = semiannual coupon
       M = maturity value
       n = number of periods, and
       y = semiannual yield to maturity.

That is,

$$960 = \sum_{t=1}^{10} \frac{35}{(1 + y)^t} + \frac{1000}{(1 + y)^{10}}$$

y = 4.0% semiannual return, YTM=8% per year.

Horizon yield (also called total return) accounts for coupon interest, interest on interest, and proceeds from sale of the bond.

1. Coupon interest + interest on interest

$$= C \left[ \frac{(1 + r)^n - 1}{T} \right]$$

where: C = semiannual coupon

r = semiannual reinvestment rate, and

n = number of periods

That is,

$$= 35 \left[ \frac{(1.03)^6 - 1}{0.03} \right] = 226.39$$

2. Projected sale price at the end of three years is $1,000 because bonds that yield the required rate of return always sell at par

3. Sum the results of Steps 1 and 2 to obtain $1.226.39.

4. Semiannual total return

$$= \left[ \frac{1226.39}{960} \right]^{1/6} -1 = 4.166\%$$

5. Double the interest rate found in Step 4 for the annual total rate of return of 8.33 percent.

15(b). The shortcomings of the yield measures are as follows: (1) Current yield does not account for interest on interest (compounding) or changes in bond price during the holding period. It also does not allow for a gain or loss from a bond purchased at a discount or premium. (2) Yield to maturity assumes that the bond is held to maturity and that all coupon interest can be reinvested at the yield-to-maturity rate. Because yields change constantly, that assumption is incorrect. However, yield to maturity is the industry standard for comparing one bond with another. (3) Total return (as calculated) assumes that all coupons can be invested at a constant reinvestment rate and requires assumptions about holding period, reinvestment rate, and yield on the bond at the end of the investor's holding period. Although it is a more complete measure of return, it is only as accurate as its inputs.

16.  CFA Examination I (1994)

16(a).  In U.S. dollars, one share of Euro Disney sells for 86.80 x 0.1761 = $15.29. The exchange value is 19.651 x 15.29 = $300.37.

16(b). Disadvantages to Disney resulting from redeeming the zero-coupon note and replacing some of the funds with proceeds from the issue of 100-year bonds include: (1) Notes with a yield to maturity of 6 percent are replaced with bonds at a higher yield to maturity, 7.55 percent. (2) No annual cash payment is required for the zero-coupon note, but annual cash payments are required for the 100-year bond. (3) The new bonds are not callable until the year 2023 (30 years of call protection for a holder of the bond), whereas the zero-coupon note has no call protection. (4) Only with the zero-coupon note does Disney get a cash tax savings from a deduction for interest without an associated cash outflow for interest. (5) Of lesser importance, transaction costs (investment banking fees, etc.) associated with the replacement may be significant.

17. CFA Examination II (1994)

The essence of the answer is to price each bond's cash flows using the spot curve (Table 2).

The nonarbitrage price of bond A is

$$\frac{10}{1.05} + \frac{10}{(1.08)^2} + \frac{110}{(1.11)^3} = 98.53$$

The market price of Bond A is 98.40, which is 13 cents (13.2 basis points of market price) less than the nonarbitrage price.

The nonarbitrage price of Bond B is

$$\frac{6}{1.05} + \frac{6}{(1.08)^2} + \frac{106}{(1.11)^3} = 88.36$$

The market price of Bond B is 88.34, only 2 cents (2.3 basis points of market price) less than the nonarbitrage price.

*Conclusion:* Despite having the lower yield to maturity (10.65 percent versus 10.75 percent), Bond A is the better value because the excess of its nonarbitrage price over market price is greater than for Bond B.

18. CFA Examination II (1996)

18(a). Because modified duration measures percentage price changes for small yield changes, the price change can be computed as:

Modified duration x Yield change = Percentage change in bond price
= 7.0 x 0.50 = 3.5%.

Alternatively, duration can be used with yield change and the price value of a basis point (PVBP) as follows:

0.0001 x 50 x 7 = .035 or 3.50% or 350 basis points.

18(b). The calculation used to answer Part A must be modified because both the duration of the KC bond and the yield change for the KC bond are different. Adjusting for these changes, the computation becomes

Modified duration x Yield change = Percentage change in bond price
= 6.93 x (1.22 x 0.50) = 6.93 x .61 = 4.23%.

16 - 26

Answering Part B requires knowing that yield change must first be calculated and then the percentage price change using the duration formula. Two separate formulas are needed: (1) yield change and (2) percentage price change.

In addition to using a single formula, a dual formula method can be used assuming an interest rate and then a 50-basis-point change.

Assuming an interest rate and then a 50-basis-point change:
Beginning yield      = 0.54 + 1.22(7.00) = 9.08
Ending yield         = 0.54 + 1.22(7.50) = 9.69
Ending yield         = 0.54 + 1.22 (6.50) = 8.47

Ending yield - Beginning yield = 61 basis points if rates increase
Ending yield - Beginning yield = -61 basis points if rates decrease

Duration formula: [-Modified duration x Yield change = Percentage price change]
If rates decrease, then: -6.93 x -0.61 = 4.23% or 423 basis points price change
If rates increase, then: -6.93 x 0.61 = -4.23% or -423 basis points price change

Alternatively, two other methods may be used to calculate percentage price change using duration:

1. One method is to raise (1 + the yield change) to the power of the bond's modified duration:

   Percentage price change = Modified duration x Yield change
                                 = Modified duration x ln (I + Yield change)

   Taking the analog of the far right hand side of the equation, the above then solves to:

   Percentage price change = (1 + Yield change)^Modified duration

2. Another method is to use the slope of the regression formula multiplied by U.S. Treasury percentage price change, times the ratio of the KC bond duration to the U.S. Treasury bond duration:

   1.22 x (3.50% or 350 basis points) x (6.93/7.00) = (4.23% or 423 basis points).

19. CFA Examination II (1997)

19(a). **Effective Duration of Tranche T-3**

Effective duration = $(P_{[-]} - P_{[+]})/[P_{[0]} \times (Y_{[+]} - Y_{[-]})]$

where:

        $P_{[-]}$ = price at the next lower yield
        $P_{[+]}$ = price at the next higher yield
        $P_{[0]}$ = price at the current yield
        $Y_{[-]}$ = next lower yield
        $Y_{[+]}$ = next higher yield

16 - 27

Therefore,

        TrancheT-1:     (105.5-95.0)/[100 x (0.075-0.065)]=10.5

        TrancheT-2:     (104.0-95.5)/[100 x (0.075-0.065)]=8.5

        **Tranche T-3:   (105.5 - 95.5)/[100 x (0.075 - 0.065)] = 10**

        TrancheT-4:     (102.0-98.5)/[100 x (0.075-0.065))=3.5

## 19(b). Calculation of Negative Convexity

As interest rates fall from 8 percent to 6 percent, the price changes for Tranche T-2 show a pattern of declining price increases: +5.0, +4.5, +4.0, +3.5. These decelerating price changes show negative convexity. For the other tranches, accelerating price changes show positive convexity:

        Tranche T-1:  +4.5, +5, +5.5, and +6

        Tranche T-3:  +3.5, +4.5, +5.5, and +6.5

        Tranche T-4:  +1, +1.5, +2, and +2.5

Effective convexity is $(P_{[+]} + P_{[-]} - 2 P_{[0]})/\{P_{[0]} \times [0.5 \times (Y_{[+]} - Y_{[-]})]^2\}$

Therefore,

      T- 1:  $(95.0 + 105.5 - 2 \times 100)/\{100[0.5(0.075 - 0.065)]^2\} = 200$

      **T-2:  $(95.5 + 104.0 - 2 \times 100)/\{100[0.5(0.075 - 0.065)]^2\} = -200$**

      T-3:  $(95.5 + 105.5 - 2 \times 100)/\{100[0.5(0.075 - 0.065)]^2\} = 400$

      T-4:  $(98.5 + 102.0 - 2 \times 100)/(100[0.5(0.075 - 0.065)]^2\} = 200$

*(Note:* In calculating effective convexity, the candidate readings give alternative approaches - Candidates receive credit for either approach.)

## 19(c). Plausible Spread at 12 Percent Volatility

Pattern A is the only pattern that is plausible if volatility of 12 percent is assumed. Option-adjusted spreads will decline for mortgage pass-throughs as volatility increases. Option-adjusted spread measures the spread over U.S. Treasuries after explicitly accounting for any options embedded in the bonds. For mortgages, the most important option is the borrower's right to prepay--a call option. As volatility increases, so does the chance that interest rates will decline enough for the borrower to prepay. The prepayment option, therefore, becomes more valuable as volatility increases. Because total spread equals option value (measured in yield) plus option-adjusted spread, as volatility increases (and option values increase), more of the (constant) total spread is option value and the option-adjusted spread is correspondingly lower.

## 20.   CFA Examination II (1998)

## 20(a). Bonds' Price Changes

Percentage price change = -Duration x (Yield change) x 100:

CIC:   -7.35 x (-0.005) = 3.675%.

PTR:   -5.40 x (-0.005) = 2.70%.

## 20(b).  Horizontal Return Calculation

$$\text{Horizon Return} = \left[ \frac{\text{Total coupon Payment + Reinvestment income + Price at end}}{\text{Initial Price}} \right] - 1$$

CIC:  $= (31.25 + 1055.5/1017.5) - 1 = 0.068058$, or $6.8058\%$.
PTR:  $= (36.75 + 1041.5/1017.5) - 1 = 0.059705$, or $5.970\%$.

Because there is no reinvestment (interest on interest), the internal rate of return framework can also be used for the computation.

## 20(c).  Explanation of Difference in Price Changes

The actual price change for the CIC bond will be greater than forecasted by effective duration alone because the CIC noncallable bond has positive convexity. Duration is a linear approximation of bond price change that follows a curvilinear or convex function. Noncallable bonds have positive convexity, which indicates that as interest rates decline, the rate at which the bond price increases becomes faster.

The actual price change for the PTR bond will be lower than forecasted by effective duration alone because the PTR bond has negative convexity stemming from the call feature. As interest rates decline, it becomes increasingly likely that the issuer will call the bond to refinance at lower interest rates. So, as interest rates fall, the price of a callable bond will not initially increase as fast as a noncallable bond and, eventually, will not increase at all as the market price approaches the call price.

21.  CFA Examination II (1999)

21(a)(i) Pure Expectations (Unbiased)- according to the pure expectation theory, the expected one-period rate of return on investment is the same, regardless of the maturity of security in which one invests. Hence, the expected holding period return at the time of initial investment would be the same for all possible maturity strategies. Under this theory forward rates exclusively represent expected future rates, thus the entire term structure at a given time reflects the market's expectations of the compilation of future short-term rates. Under this theory, an upward sloping yield curve would signify the market expects short-term rates to rise through the relevant future.

(ii) Uncertainty and Term Premiums- according to this theory the pure expectations theory applies but is modified for a risk or term premium. The longer the maturity of the security, the greater is said to be the risk of fluctuation in value of principal to the investor. In order to induce investors to invest in long-term securities, a risk, or term premium must be offered. An upward sloping yield curve may reflect expectations that future interest rates either will rise, be flat or even fall, but with a liquidity premium increasing fast enough with maturity so as to produce an upward sloping yield curve.

(iii) <u>Market Segmentation-</u> this theory suggests that the segmented market behavior of lenders and borrowers basically determine the shape of the yield curve. A market segmentation theory implies that the rate of interest for a particular maturity is determined solely by demand and supply factors for that maturity, with no reference to conditions for other maturities. Borrowers and lenders have rigid maturity preferences and do not deviate from those preferences no matter how attractive the yields are for other maturities. The upward sloping yield curve would signify the greater demand/smaller supply for short-term securities or a greater supply of long term debt/lesser demand for long-term securities.

21(b).

$$_nf_t = [(1 + y_{n+t})^{n+t} / (1 + y_n)^n]^{1/t} - 1$$

$$_3f_2 = [(1 + 0.0651)^5 / (1 + 0.0619)^3]^{1/2} - 1$$

$$_3f_2 = 6.99\%$$

The assumption underlying the calculation of the implied forward rate is risk neutrality among investors. Regardless of the expected holding period, the expected return would be the same for all maturity strategies. That is it would not matter whether an investor would purchase a one year investment or purchase a two year investment and sell it at the and of one year, the return would be the same for any strategy.

# CHAPTER 17

# BOND PORTFOLIO MANAGEMENT STRATEGIES

## Answers to Questions

1.  An indexing portfolio strategy is one in which the investor selects a bond portfolio that matches the performance of some bond-market index. The basic justification for this strategy is that many empirical studies have shown that portfolio managers on average can't match the risk-return performance in the bond market using active portfolio management.

2.  *A pure yield pickup swap is* selling a bond and buying another one with a higher coupon. Normally, both current yield and yield-to-maturity are enhanced. *A substitution swap is* the swapping of one bond for another between which a yield spread imbalance exists. The investor expects the imbalance to disappear through the mechanism of having the yield on the purchased bond drop (through a price increase) to the level of the swapped bond, leading to attractive capital gains. *A tax swap* is simply a bond swap that enables an investor to realize capital losses on one bond to offset capital gains that she has realized on some other investment.

3.  These active management strategies include interest rate anticipation, credit analysis, and spread analysis. *Interest rate anticipation is* the riskiest strategy because it relies on forecasting uncertain future interest rate behavior. The strategy involves altering the maturity (duration) structure of the portfolio to preserve capital when an increase in interest rates is anticipated and achieve capital gains when they are expected to decline. A *credit analysis* strategy involves attempting to project changes in quality ratings assigned to bonds. It is necessary to analyze internal changes in the firm and external changes in the environment to project rating changes prior to the actual announcement by rating agencies. *Spread analysis* involves monitoring the yield relationships between various bond sectors to take advantage of abnormal relationships by executing various sector swaps. Liquidity is a key factor in this strategy, as abnormal relationships are only believed to be temporary.

4.  Two important variables when analyzing junk bonds include: 1) the use of cash flows in relation to debit obligations, and 2) a detailed analysis of potential asset sales. The *cash flow analysis is* important in determining the firm's ability to make interest payments, as well as maintain cash for research and growth in periods of economic decline. Cash flow can also affect the firm's borrowing capacity to provide flexibility and needed working capital. In many cases, asset sales are a critical part of the strategy for a leveraged buyout. In order to analyze the market value of these assets it is necessary to determine whether there are any prior liens against the assets, as well as the true liquidation value and a reasonable time period for the sale.

Harcourt, Inc.

5.     High-yield bonds have been described as having characteristics of common stocks, such as, higher yields and more risks. The higher yield on high-yield bonds (just like common stocks) compensate the investor for assuming various risks such as risk of default, price volatility. liquidity, or uncertainty regarding maturity. Since the characteristics of high-yield bonds are similar to those of common stocks, it is not surprising that high-yield bond returns are more correlated to common stocks returns than to investment-grade bond returns.

6.     The advantage of the cash-matched portfolio is that it is a relatively conservative strategy in which cash flows generated from the portfolio are designed to exactly match liability schedules in both timing and amount. Such a portfolio is often difficult to construct as a result of certain call features often associated with the higher-yielding deep discount bonds. On the other hand, if the portfolio manager limits himself to only Treasury bonds, he will likely forego significant added returns that could be achieved with other investments, thus adding to the net cost of funding the liability stream.

7.     Interest rate risk comprises two risks - a price risk and a coupon reinvestment risk. Price risk represents the change that interest rates will differ from the rates the manager expects to prevail between purchase and target date. Such a change causes the market price for the bond (i.e., the realized price) to differ from the expected price. Obviously, if interest rates increase, the realized price for the bond in the secondary market will be below expectations, while if interest rates decline, the realized price will exceed expectations.

    Reinvestment risk arises because interest rates at which coupon payments can be reinvested are unknown. If interest rates change after the bond is purchased, coupon payments will be reinvested at rates different than that prevailing at the time of the purchase. As an example, if interest rates decline, coupon payments will be reinvested at lower rates than at the time of purchase and their contribution to the ending wealth position of the investor will be below expectations. Alternatively, if interest rates increase, there will be a positive impact as coupon payments will be reinvested at rates above expectations.

8.     A portfolio of investments in bonds is *immunized* for a holding period if the value of the portfolio at the end of the holding period, regardless of the course of interest rates during the holding period, is at least as large as it would have been had the interest rate function been constant throughout the holding period. Put another way, if the realized return on an investment in bonds is sure to be at least as large as the computed yield to the investment horizon, then that investment is immunized. As an example, if an investor acquired a portfolio bond when prevailing interest rates were 10% and had an investment horizon of four years, then the investor would expect the value of the portfolio at the end of four years to be 1.4641 times the beginning value. This particular value is equal to 10% compounded for four years.

    A bond manager would want to immunize the portfolio in the instance where he/she had a specified investment horizon and had a definite required or promised yield for the bond portfolio. In the case where this required or expected yield was below current prevailing market rates, it would be worthwhile for the bond managers to immunize the portfolio and therefore "lock in" the prevailing market yield for this period. Put another way, it is used when the bond portfolio manager is willing to engage in non-active bond portfolio management and accept the current prevailing rate during the investment horizon.

9.  As mentioned, the purpose of immunization is to mitigate the price risk and reinvestment risk associated with changes in interest rates over the investment horizon. Assuming a constant flat yield curve over the investment horizon, there is no need to immunize the portfolio. The investor can obtain investment objectives by simply purchasing bonds scheduled to mature at the end of his investment horizon. With no change in interest rates, the stated yield-to-maturity at the time of purchase should equal the realized yield at the time the bonds mature.

10. Investment horizon a year later = 3
    Duration of portfolio a year later = 3.2

    While the term-to-maturity has declined by a year, the duration has only declined by .8 years. This means that, assuming **no changes in market rates,** the portfolio manager must rebalance the portfolio to reduce its duration to three years.

11. The objective of immunization centers around mitigating the two components of interest rate risk-price risk and coupon reinvestment risk. Keeping this in mind, many feel that a zero coupon bond is the ideal financial instrument to use for immunization because it eliminates these risks, and thus eliminates the need to rebalance the portfolio. Reinvestment risk is eliminated because it is assumed the value of the bond will grow at the stated discount rate, and price risk is eliminated because if you set the duration equal to your time horizon, you will receive the face value of your bond at maturity.

12. Several characteristics of duration make it impossible to set a duration equal to the initial time horizon of a portfolio and ignore it thereafter. First, because duration declines more slowly than term-to-maturity, even if one assumes no changes in interest rates, the portfolio manager must periodically rebalance the portfolio. Second, if there is a change in market rates, the duration of the portfolio will change. If the deviation becomes large compared to original duration of the portfolio, the manager will again have to rebalance. Third, the technique assumes that when market rates change, they will change by the same amount and in the same direction. Since this is not true of the real world, the manager must assure that the portfolio is composed of various bonds with durations that bunch around the desired duration of the portfolio. Finally, developing the portfolio can be a problem since there can always be a problem of acquiring the desired bonds in the market.

13. A contingent immunization strategy allows the investor an opportunity to obtain a higher return on his portfolio if he is willing to accept greater uncertainty and a possibly lower ending wealth value. By specifying a floor return lower than the current market rate, the

investor gives up the certainty involved with immunizing the portfolio at the current rate. However, the investor gains the benefit of his portfolio being actively managed in such a way as that *potential returns* may be achieved over the investment horizon that are above the then-current market rate at the beginning of the horizon.

14. CFA Examination III (1983)

14(a).  Interest rate risk comprises two risks - a price risk and a coupon reinvestment risk. *Price risk* represents the chance that interest rates will differ from the rates the manager expects to prevail between purchase and target date. Such a change causes the market price for the bond (i.e., the realized price) to differ from the expected price. Obviously, if interest rates increase, the realized price for the bond in the secondary market will be below expectations, while if interest rates decline, the realized price will exceed expectations.

*Reinvestment risk* arises because interest rates at which coupon payments can be reinvested are unknown. If interest rates change after the bond is purchased, coupon payments will be reinvested at rates different than that prevailing at the time of the purchase. As an example, if interest rates decline, coupon payments will be reinvested at lower rates than at the time of purchase and their contribution to the ending wealth position of the investor will be below expectations. Contrariwise, if interest rates increase there will be a positive impact as coupon payments will be reinvested at rates above expectations.

14(b). A portfolio of investments in bonds is immunized for a holding period if the value of the portfolio at the end of the holding period, regardless of the course of interest rates during the holding period, is at least as large as it would have been had the interest rate function been constant throughout the holding period. Put another way, if the realized return on an investment in bonds is sure to be at least as large as the computed yield to the investment horizon, then that investment is immunized. As an example, if an investor acquired a portfolio bond when prevailing interest rates were 10% and had an investment horizon of four years, then the investor would expect the value of the portfolio at the end of four years to be 1.4641 x the beginning value. This particular value is equal to 10% compounded for four years.

A bond manager would want to immunize the portfolio in the instance where he/she had a specified investment horizon and had a definite required or promised yield for the bond portfolio. In the case where this required or expected yield was below current prevailing market rates, it would be worthwhile for the bond managers to immunize the portfolio and therefore "lock in" the prevailing market yield for this period. Put another way, it is when the bond portfolio manager is willing to engage in non-active bond portfolio management and accept the current prevailing rate during the investment horizon.

14(c). As set forth by a number of authors, the technique used to immunize a portfolio is to set the duration of the portfolio equal to the investment horizon for the portfolio. It has been proven that this technique will work because during the life of the portfolio, the two

17 - 4

major interest rate risks (price risk and reinvestment risk) offset each other at this point in time. The zero coupon bond is an ideal immunization instrument because, by its very nature, it accomplishes these two purposes when the maturity of the zero coupon bond equals the investment horizon because the duration of a zero coupon bond is equal to its maturity period. In contrast, when you match the maturity of the bond to the investment horizon, you are only taking account of the price risk whereby you will receive the par value of the bond at the maturity of the bond. The problem is that you are not sure of how the investment risk will work out. If rates rise, you will receive more in reinvestment than expected. Alternatively, if rates decline, you will not benefit from the price advantage and, in fact, will lose in terms of the reinvestment assumptions.

14(d). The zero coupon bond is a superior immunization security because it eliminates both interest rate risks-price and reinvestment.

A zero coupon bond is a perfect immunizer when its duration (or maturity, as they are the same) is equal to the liability or planning horizon of the portfolio. Given adequate availability, the portfolio manager would match these elements and no further activity is necessary to the end of the horizon.

The zero coupon bond is superior to a coupon paying instrument because the lack of cash flow prior to maturity eliminates any coupon reinvestment and, therefore, the risk of realized return changes due to uncertainty of these levels. Price risk is also nonexistent regardless of the timing or nature of yield curve shifts.

14(e). The primary difference between contingent and classical immunization is the role of active management. Classical immunization precisely matches the duration of the portfolio with the horizon of the particular liability. Management of such a portfolio is limited to periodic rebalancing necessitated by yield curve shifts, yield changes, and time effects on duration. Contingent immunization is an active form of management, initially, and can continue in this mode until the manager's results are unfavorable to the extent that a predetermined target return is unlikely to be achieved. At this point, the active mode is triggered to a classical passive immunization to "lock-in" the minimum desired return.

Contingent immunization achieves its risk control by establishing two parameters: (1) The minimum return target for more specifically the difference between the minimum return target and the immunization return than available in the market, and (2) the acceptable range for the terminal horizon date of the program. The chart below illustrates the potential rewards from contingent immunization based on possible moves in interest rates. It is interesting to note the similarity of this curve to that of option strategies.

Harcourt, Inc.

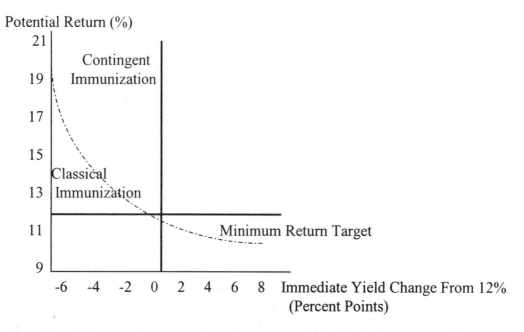

Careful monitoring of the value achieved by the manager in the portfolio is important. A return or portfolio value line can be established, initially which traces the required dollar value of the portfolio at any given point in time and would be a minimum level necessary for the portfolio to reach its minimum return target. If the return or value falls to this, the "safety net" is activated.

A key facet of contingent immunization is the benefit from flexibility or loosening of rigid conditions. Substantial flexibility is granted the portfolio's manager if either the horizon time is widened to a range rather than a single point or if the minimum return is meaningfully below that available currently through classical immunization.

By granting this flexibility and being willing to accept a slightly lower than current market return, the plan sponsor or portfolio manager has the opportunity to achieve much greater returns through interest rate anticipation, swapping and other facets of active management.

This approach is attractive to a portfolio manager who believes his/her skills will provide "excess returns" yet establishes a downside risk control that assures achievement of a minimum target return.

15.   CFA Examination III (1986)

15(a).   With an immunized portfolio the goal is to provide a minimum dollar amount of assets at a single horizon.

*Contingent immunization is* primarily an active strategy. However, a minimum return is required. Should the portfolio deteriorate to the point where this return is threatened, there is a switch to full immunization of the portfolio.

17 - 6

The purpose of a *cash-matched dedicated portfolio is* to have a portfolio that will generate cash flows that specifically match the required *stream* of cash outflows. Therefore, it is necessary to match maturities and amounts over a time period, not a single time period. This is accomplished by planning maturities and interim cash flows from the portfolio.

The purpose of a *duration-matched dedication portfolio is* likewise to match the cash flows from the portfolio to the required cash outflows over time. The major difference from the cash-matched dedication is that you recognize that you do this by matching the weighted average duration of the obligations with the duration of your investment portfolio.

15(b). When managing an *immunized* portfolio, it is necessary to maintain the duration of the portfolio equal to the investment horizon. The problem is that this requires *rebalancing* because (1) duration declines slower than term to maturity, and (2) duration is affected by changes in market yields - i.e., there is an inverse relationship between yield and duration.

15(c). With a cash-matched dedication portfolio it is necessary to make several major decisions:

(1). Timing of initiation. Usually, the client wants to initiate the portfolio immediately. Let the client prevail unless the portfolio manager considers a delay advisable.

(2). Payments time intervals. Specify when the required payments are to be made - yearly, semiannually, or quarterly.

(3). How to avoid call risk. Is this accomplished by having deep-discount bonds or non-callable securities?

(4). What is your reinvestment rate assumption for the interim flows? You should be very conservative in your estimate to avoid negative surprises.

15(d). Three basic components should be specified for contingent immunization:

(1). Immunized Base Return - the return which could be earned if the portfolio is immunized at today's rates.

(2). Investment Objective - the return goal which exceeds the Immunized Base Return to be achieved by active management.

(3). Assured Minimum Return - the minimum allowable return consistent with the needs of the client. This is the trigger for full immunization.

Harcourt, Inc.

In addition to the above, the client and manager should agree on the flexibility to be allowed the manager in an active strategy. The agreement should specify *the time horizon* and *duration variance.*

15(e). Once the portfolio is established, the *cash-matched dedicated* portfolio probably requires the least supervision over time. You do not have to rebalance the immunized portfolio or adjust the duration of the duration matched dedicated portfolio.

16.    CFA Examination III (June 1988)

Restructuring opportunities are not a function of time, but rather a result of changing market conditions. Conditions that are generally favorable to restructuring include:

(1). Availability of more efficient issues. When you originally structured the portfolio program, you used the issues that were available. Over time, more issues become available through trading or new issues come to market that do a better job of fitting the requirements of the portfolio. As a result, you can substitute issues that do a better job (i.e., are more efficient) of meeting the goals of the portfolio.

(2). Changes in the shape of the yield curve. If the yield curve changes (e.g., goes from positively sloped to negative), it might be possible to shift out of a pure cash matched policy to one where you receive the cash flows earlier and can invest them at a higher rate of return to exceed expectations. The question becomes: What was the assumed reinvestment rate compared to the current rates, given the prevailing yield curve?

(3). Changes in quality or sector spreads. This would involve changes in the price relationship between quality groups (e.g., agencies versus Treasuries, AAA versus AA) or sectors (e.g., industrials versus utilities). You could envision an instance where the yield spread of AAA corporates to treasuries that were in the portfolio declined and the spread for FNMA issue increased which would allow you to swap the AAA corporate for the FNMA issue. This swap would provide a portfolio of equal quality and probably allow a cash takeout.

17.    CFA Examination III (1988)

17(a). You would generally expect it to be easier to match the performance of a bond index as contrasted to a stock index because of the aggregate homogeneity of the bond market compared to the stock market. As a result you could match the performance of the bond index with substantially fewer issues. As an example, in order to match the performance of the SUP 500 Stock Index, it generally requires anywhere from 300 to 450 issues. In contrast, one could do a fairly good job of tracking a bond index that would include thousands of issues with less than 100 bonds simply because bonds are so heavily influenced by the general movements in interest rates. Therefore, although you might need bonds with different characteristics to match the index (e.g., industry and quality characteristics), it would not be necessary to have numerous issues with each of the desired characteristics.

17(b). While it might be possible to match the bond index with fewer issues, the selection and operational process of running the bond index fund would be more difficult. First, it is

17 - 8

going to **require more characteristics to derive the desired diversification.** While the equity market only requires serious consideration of capitalization and risk docile, bonds have many characteristics that can effect return including maturity, duration, credit quality, capitalization, coupon, industrial classification, sinking fund, and a call features. Thus, it will be necessary to determine the makeup for each of these characteristics and attempt to match it in the portfolio.

A second factor would be the **difficulty of tracing bonds** as opposed to stocks. In the case of a stock index you are typically dealing with very large capitalization stocks traded on an exchange or involved in an active over-the-counter market. In contrast, the secondary corporate bond market is not nearly as liquid and so it is `1ifficult to buy and sell for the bond index fund.

Finally, there is greater difficulty in **reinvestment of the cash flows** from a bond index fund rather than a stock index. Because of heavier cash flows from a bond index fund you are going to have more frequent buying programs. These can be a blessing because it allows you to change the makeup of the fund, but also it could be difficult to avoid changing the fund with small buying programs. The point is, it is going to require balancing cash flow purchases among all relevant bond characteristics to avoid changing the bond index fund portfolio.

18.    CFA Examination III (1988)

18(a).  Assuming that Kaufmann does not take currency hedging into account in his analysis, he would have to project portfolio returns in each country based on (1) coupon, (2) changes in interest rates (bond prices), and (3) changes in currency. Estimated changes in the money supply, GNP/GDP, and inflation are already factored into estimated interest and exchange rates.

One method to determine investment weighting would be to estimate the income from the bond, change in bond price, and foreign currency change.    Assuming a duration of 8 for the bond portfolio, the calculations are as follows:

|  | INCOME | BOND PRICE | CURRENCY | EXPECTED RETURN | RECOMMEND |
|---|---|---|---|---|---|
| U.S. | 8.8% | (1.6%) | N/A | 7.2% | Overweight/Neutral |
| Japan | 6.1 | 0 | 0.8 | 6.9 | Underweight/Neutral |
| W.Germany | 6.1 | (7.2%) | 4.0 | 2.9 | Underweight |
| United Kingdom | 9.8 | 2.4 | (1.7) | 10.5 | Overweight |

In the above solution, the conclusion will vary, depending upon the duration of the portfolio and the coupon income.

Harcourt, Inc.

In a more simplistic analysis, Kaufmann could evaluate whether the factors of real rates, direction of rates, and exchange rates are positive or negative.

Real rates in each country are as follows:

| | |
|---|---|
| United States | 5.2% |
| Japan | 3.1% |
| West Germany | 4.8% |
| United Kingdom | 4.7% |

Real interest rates are highest in the United States and lowest in Japan, with West Germany and the United Kingdom in the middle.

| | REAL RATES | OF RATES | EXCHANGE RATE | RECOMMEND |
|---|---|---|---|---|
| U.S. | + | -/0 | N/A | Overweight/Neutral |
| Japan | - | 0 | +/0 | Underweight |
| W.Germany | 0 | -/0 | N/A | Overweight |
| United Kingdom | 0 | + | 0 | Overweight |

0 = Neutral
+ = Positive
++ = Very Positive
- = Negative
-- = Very Negative

Given all of the above factors, Kaufmann would overweight the United Kingdom. Interest rates are expected to decline, the exchange rate is not expected to change dramatically, and real interest rates are moderate. West Germany would likely be underweighted, since interest rates are anticipated to rise dramatically, offsetting any benefits from currency. Japan and the United States would have rankings between the other two. For the United States, exchange rates are not a factor, so relatively high rates that are not projected to rise dramatically would probably warrant a neutral or slight overweighting. In Japan, rates are anticipated to be stable, and since currency is only a very slight positive factor, this country's bonds should be weighted neutrally or slightly underweighted.

18(b). If hedging is used, then changes in currency will not be part of the return analysis. In this case, the decision would probably not change. The United Kingdom still has the most appealing outlook.

19. CFA Examination III (1988)

19(a). The three issues that Robert and Neil should address are the following:

(1). The starting yield level relative to the U.S. If the spread is positive, this provides a cushion against unfavorable moves in either interest rates in the foreign market or in

Harcourt, Inc.

the value of the foreign currency. If the spread is negative, the foreign market must make up the difference by outperforming in local currency terms or by experiencing an appreciation in its currency (or both).

(2). The prospects for internal price movements relative to the U.S. bond market. In other words, what is the likely trend in yield spreads between the foreign market and the U.S.? Unlike in the U.S., where yields in different sectors will generally move in the same direction, albeit at different rates, yields in foreign markets may move in opposite directions to the U.S., due to differences in economic, social and political factors in those foreign markets.

(3). The prospects for currency gain or loss versus the dollar. The factors Robert and Neil should look at to assess prospects for the Deutschemark and the Australian dollar include:
(a). trends in the balance of payments
(b). inflation and interest rate differentials
(c). the social and political atmosphere, particularly as it relates to foreign investment
(d). the extent of central bank intervention in the currency markets.

19(b). The two reasons for investing in a mixture of international bonds are (1) the opportunity for superior rates of return and (2) diversification. With respect to return, economic and interest rate cycles tend not to move in parallel worldwide. As a result, being able to invest in a host of different markets presents opportunities for above-average return in comparison to having access to only one individual and relatively homogeneous market. Similarly, as regards diversification, foreign bond markets are not perfectly correlated with the U.S. bond market. This means that the volatility of return for a portfolio of global bonds will be less than for a portfolio comprised only of U.S. bonds.

The ERISA account does have a 10% position in Canadian bonds, but the close interrelationship of the Canadian economy and its capital markets makes Canada highly correlated with the U.S. In that sense, the Canadian position does not afford the return and diversification opportunities that other foreign bond markets would offer.

20. CFA Examination 1990 (1990)

20(a). Market liquidity should be a major consideration when investing in high yield bonds. It has been demonstrated on many occasions that high yield bonds possess substantially less liquidity than Treasury securities and high grade corporate bonds. This lack of liquidity has been very evident following credit problems for several individual issues. Apparently tied to some default announcements, there were days when there was almost no trading at all in the high-yield bond market. Even though high-yield bonds are less liquid than Treasury and high-grade corporate bonds, it is important to recognize that they are still more liquid than corporate bank loans or private placement bond issues in the debt continuum.

The pricing of high-yield bonds has likewise come under some scrutiny from those accustomed to the continuous pricing available in equities, the reasonably good pricing available for Treasury issues, and the frequent quotes typically available for high-grade corporate bonds. Even though some high-yield issues have been listed on either the New York or American exchanges, which implies that there should be more pricing available, it is universally recognized that the volume of bond transactions on the exchanges is only a very limited proportion of total trading since almost all of the large, important trades are done over-the-counter, and these transactions are not reported. Also, there are important differences between quoted prices and the actual price that would be received if an attempt to trade a fairly large block of a high-yield issue was made.

Because high-yield bonds are generally less liquid and are more difficult to price, this should enter into the pricing of these securities (i.e., it is necessary to include a liquidity/pricing premium as part of your required rate of return in addition to the credit risk premium). Second, because of the relative illiquidity, when adding these to a portfolio, it must be recognized that they cannot be used for short-term trading. Alternatively, a portfolio manager may decide that he/she wants to invest in high-yield bonds, but will limit investments to the set of high-yield bonds that enjoy fairly active, liquid markets with relatively frequent pricing.

20(b). The reason that Treasury bonds and high-grade corporate bonds are so highly correlated (in excess of .98) is because the major factor causing changes in their rates of return are aggregate market interest rates (i.e., the yield curve for Treasury securities). In terms of the Capital Asset Pricing Model (CAPM, the fact that these rates of return move together means that they possess very high systematic risk (i.e., all rates of return are being driven by one major aggregate market variable which in this case is market interest rates). The rates of return for high-yield bonds are likewise influenced by market interest rates, but they also have a very large unique component that is the performance of the company and the credit quality of the issue. In terms of the CAPM, this unique risk possessed by high-yield bonds would be described as "unsystematic risk." Notably, this unsystematic risk can be diversified away in a large portfolio. This implies that while it is essential to diversify a portfolio of high-yield bonds to eliminate the unsystematic risk, it also means that such bonds are good additions to a portfolio with high systematic risk, as described above.

Because the rates of return for high-yield bonds are not very highly correlated with rates of return for Treasuries and high-grade corporate bonds, they would be an excellent addition to such a portfolio because they would help reduce its overall risk. This would be like adding common stocks to such a bond portfolio. In addition, if the expected rates of return on these securities were higher than those on treasuries and high-grade corporates, you could be in a position of not only reducing the overall risk of the portfolio, but also increasing its average rate of return. The fact is, for most of the years prior to 1989, the total rates of return on high yield bonds was consistently higher than comparable returns on Treasuries or high-grade corporate bonds.

20(c). The duration for high-yield bonds would be much lower than the duration for high-grade corporates because of the impact of all three of the major factors that influence duration: maturity, coupon and market yield. The average maturity of high-yield bonds is shorter than high-grade corporates simply because of the inherent risk which causes investors to demand shorter maturities - e g, l0 to 15 year maturities for high-yield bonds compared to 15 to 25 years for high-grade corporates. The average maturity for high-yield bonds is lower than for high-grade corporates, and duration is positively related to maturity.

Second, because of the risk of high-yield bonds, they have a higher required rate of return that is reflected in a higher coupon for these securities, and there is an inverse relationship between the coupon and the duration of the security.

Third, not only is the coupon high, but the market yield to maturity on these securities would likewise be high. Again, there is an inverse relationship between the discount rate used to compute duration (i.e., the yield to maturity) and the duration of the bond.

21.    CFA Examination II (1990)

21(a).  Concept
To evaluate the uses of convexity and duration. Option theory is not required to answer this question as this is probably a Level m concept at this point. However, many candidates will incorporate it into their answer.

(1).  Kemp should be generally concerned about the ability of the new portfolio structure to outperform the old in a falling interest rate environment. He should ask about the degree of negative convexity being added through use of the callable bonds. Treasury bonds will rise more in price, based on a mathematical model, versus a callable corporate. Since the move forecasted is relatively large, convexity will become quite important.

(2).  Kemp should ask about the yield calculations being used for the corporate bonds. If it is "yield-to-maturity" and the bonds are selling at a premium, he should ask for spreads on a "yield-to-call" basis. Results from a yield-to-maturity basis - both spreads and calculations will be unrealistic.

(3).  Kemp may want to encourage the bond group to state the swap on an option adjusted spread basis. This is the most effective approach to describe the characteristics of callable bonds. Each bond is broken into two portions - the non-callable and the option owned by the issuer.

21(b).  Given the outlook for significantly lower rates, it is important to minimize negative convexity. He should look for non-callable corporates and lower the coupon level of the purchases to accomplish this.

He also should take a close look at the option adjusted spreads received on any corporate to see if it is worth reducing convexity in a bull market. There may be some doubt if this is realistic.

If he does proceed with corporate bonds, they should insist on adhering to the use of utilities where event risk is lower. While maturity is a major determinant of volatility, credit spreads can also add significant risk to the duration. Utility bonds are less likely to be subject to this.

22.    CFA Examination II (1994)

22(a).    *Competition*. In an industry where large firms have pricing power, a small firm could be at a significant disadvantage, particularly if it has higher unit costs than the large firms. A price war to capture market share could drive small competitors out of business. To the extent that a small company can differentiate its product and, therefore, control a segment of the market, this size factor is less important. However, this market niche must be monitored to ensure that it remains under the control of the small company.

Greater competition within the industry could affect the future cash flows of a company because of price wars or market-share-volume declines. Cash flow could also be negatively affected if a company responds to competition by increasing R&D expenses and capital expenditures to retain market share. Whether driven by declining gross revenues or increased expenditures, competition could lead to a compression of margins, declining earnings, and reduced cash flow from operations. This reduction exposes bondholders to the potential of a company being unable to service its debt obligations.

*Liquidation*. The liquidation value of the assets must be determined or approximated. Assets are occasionally spun off to the equity owners of the company. The bondholders could, under those circumstances, experience a sudden and substantial deterioration in the credit quality of the issuer because of the lower asset level. The bondholder should have specific identification of collateral to ensure the bond's value and marketability. The analyst must also be aware of the location of the company assets. Finally, the bondholder must be cognizant of asset protection in the event of a takeover. Assets that originally provided protection for the bondholder could be usurped to secure new debt that is senior to the original bondholder's issue.

*Management.* The management team must be evaluated for depth. Is there a strong financial manager? What is management turnover? What is the managers' experience/track record? Also important is their record of honesty and integrity in dealing with bondholders. How good are the financial controls? Is there a strong marketing manager? Significant ownership by management is generally viewed positively because of the resulting large personal incentive to build a growing, profitable company.

23.    CFA Examination III (1999)

23(a).    The consultant is incorrect. The portfolio duration measure for international bond portfolios is far more limiting than domestic portfolios. While a domestic portfolio's duration can equal the weighted sum of its individual securities' durations when all the yields and corresponding term structures are the same, an international portfolio's total duration will rarely be equal to a simple sum of the duration weighted components. This is because interest rate movements in different countries are not perfectly correlated. Also, differing volatility of interest rates across markets means that the contribution to duration from a given market is not entirely comparable to that of another market. The yield curve structures and yields on the constituent bonds are all different also.

23(b). Excess return can be added through:
- Bond Market Selection/Country Selection. By correctly over- and underweighting the best and worst performing countries/markets, added return can be very large. The component is arguable the largest source of potential excess return.
- Sector/Issue Selection. Corporate and other non-government issues can be invested in to add incremental value. However, these bonds are not as widely available in many countries.
- Security Selection. Credit quality or rating, credit revisions or re-ratings, inefficiently or mis-priced securities provide opportunity to add value.
- Yield Curve Strategy. Shifts or twists in yield curve, barbell or bullet strategy, or butterfly strategy.

# CHAPTER 17

## Answers to Problems

1. Modified duration = 7/1.10 = 6.36 years

   Percentage change in portfolio = +2 x -6.36 = -12.72 percent

   Value of portfolio = $50 million x (1 - .1272) = $43.64 million

2(a). $200 million x $(1.06)^2$ = $224.72 million

2(b). Since modified duration will equal the remaining horizon (5 years), the change in bond price must be +10% or (-5) "times" (-2%). The new value of the portfolio would then be $247.192 million or $224.72 million "times" (1.10).

3(a). **Computation of Duration (assuming 10% market yield)**

| (1)<br>Year | (2)<br>Cash Flow | (3)<br>PV@10% | (4)<br>PV of Flow | (5)<br>PV as % of Price | (6)<br>(1) x (5) |
|---|---|---|---|---|---|
| 1 | 120 | .9091 | 109.09 | .1014 | .1014 |
| 2 | 120 | .8264 | 99.17 | .0922 | .1844 |
| 3 | 120 | .7513 | 90.16 | .0838 | .2514 |
| 4 | 120 | .6830 | 81.96 | .0762 | .3047 |
| 5 | 1120 | .6209 | 695.41 | .6464 | 3.2321 |
|   |   |   | 1075.79 | 1.0000 | 4.0740 |

   Duration = 4.07 years

3(b). **Computation of Duration (assuming 10% market yield)**

| (1)<br>Year | (2)<br>Cash Flow | (3)<br>PV@10% | (4)<br>PV of Flow | (5)<br>PV as % of Price | (6)<br>(1) x (5) |
|---|---|---|---|---|---|
| 1 | 120 | .9091 | 109.09 | .1026 | .1026 |
| 2 | 120 | .8264 | 99.17 | .0933 | .1866 |
| 3 | 120 | .7513 | 90.16 | .0848 | .2544 |
| 4 | 1120 | .6830 | 764.96 | .7194 | 2.8776 |
|   |   |   | 1063.38 | 1.0000 | 3.4212 |

   Duration = 3.42 years

3(c). The duration of the portfolio should always be equal to the remaining time horizon and duration declines slower than term-to-maturity assuming no change in market interest rates as shown in a and b above.

## 4(a). Computation of Duration (assuming 8% market yield)

| (1) Year | (2) Cash Flow | (3) PV@8% | (4) PVof Flow | (5) PV as % of Price | (6) (1) x (5) |
|---|---|---|---|---|---|
| 1 | 100 | .9259 | 92.59 | .0868 | .0868 |
| 2 | 100 | .8573 | 85.73 | .0804 | .1608 |
| 3 | 100 | .7938 | 79.38 | .0745 | .2234 |
| 4 | 1100 | .7350 | 808.50 | .7583 | 3.0332 |
| | | | 1066.24 | 1.0000 | 3.5042 |

Duration = 3.5 years

## 4(b). Computation of Duration (assuming 12% market yield)

| (1) Year | (2) Cash Flow | (3) PV@12% | (4) PV of Flow | (5) PV as % of Price | (6) (1) x (5) |
|---|---|---|---|---|---|
| 1 | 100 | .8929 | 89.29 | .0951 | .0951 |
| 2 | 100 | .7972 | 79.72 | .0849 | .1698 |
| 3 | 100 | .7118 | 71.18 | .0758 | .2274 |
| 4 | 1100 | .6355 | 699.05 | .7442 | 2.9768 |
| | | | 939.24 | 1.0000 | 3.4691 |

Duration = 3.47 years

4(c).   A portfolio of bonds is immunized from interest rate risk if the duration of the portfolio is always equal to the desired investment horizon. In this example, although nothing changes regarding the bond, there is a change in market rates which causes a change in duration which would mean that the portfolio is no longer perfectly immunized.

5(a).   $300 million x $(1.06)^{10}$ = $537,254,310

5(b).   PV of $537.25 million for 4 years @ 12 percent
        537.25 (.627) = $336.86 million

        PV of $537.25 million for 3 years @ 10 percent
        537.25 (.746) = $400.79 million

        PV of $537.25 million for 2 years @ 14 percent
        537.25 (.763) = $409.92 million

5(c).   340 - 336.86  =   $3.14 million safety margin
        375 - 400.79  =   $25.79 million deficiency
        360.2 - 409.92 =  $49.72 million deficiency

6.

|  | CURRENT BOND | CANDIDATE BOND |
|---|---|---|
| Dollar Investment | 839.54 | 961.16 |
| Coupon | 90.00 | 110.00 |
| i on One Coupon | 2.59 | 3.16 |
| Principal Value at Year End | 841.95 | 961.71 |
| Total Accrued | 934.54 | 1,074.87 |
| Realized Compound Yield | 11.0125 | 11.4999 |

Value of swap: 48.6 basis points in one year

$P_0 = 45 \times (16.04612) + 1,000 \times (.11746) = 839.54$
$P_0 = 55 \times (15.53300) + 1,000 \times (.10685) = 961.16$
$P_0 = 45 \times (15.80474) + 1,000 \times (.13074) = 841.95$
$P_0 = 55 \times (15.31315) + 1,000 \times (.11949) = 961.71$

where:

16.04612 is the PVA factor and .11746 is the PV factor, both for 40 periods at 5.5 percent per period.

15.53300 is the PVA factor and .10685 is the PV factor, both for 40 periods at 5.75 percent per period.

15.80474 is the PVA factor and .13074 is the PV factor, both for 38 periods at 5.5 percent per period.

15.31315 is the PVA factor and .11949 is the PV factor, both for 38 periods at 5.75 percent per period.

7.

|  | CURRENT BOND | CANDIDATE BOND |
|---|---|---|
| Dollar Investment | 868.21 | 849.09 |
| Coupon | 90.00 | 90.00 |
| i on One Coupon | 2.36 | 2.36 |
| Principal Value at Year End | 869.40 | 869.40 |
| Total Accrued | 961.76 | 961.76 |
| Total Gain | 93.55 | 112.67 |
| Gain per Invested Dollar | .10775 | .12370 |
| Realized Compound Yield | 10.50 | 12.856 |

Value of swap: 235.7 basis points in one year

$P_0 = 45 \times (17.57281) + 1,000 \times (.07743) = 868.21$
$P_0 = 45 \times (17.24714) + 1,000 \times (.07297) = 849.09$
$P_0 = 45 \times (17.41389) + 1,000 \times (.08577) = 869.40$

17 - 18

Harcourt, Inc.

where:

17.57281 is the PVA factor and .07743 is the PV factor, both for 50 periods at 5.25 percent per period.

17.24714 is the PVA factor and .07297 is the PV factor, both for 50 periods at 5.375 percent per period.

17.41389 is the PVA factor and .08577 is the PV factor, both for 48 periods at 5.25 percent per period.

8.     CFA Examination III (June 1984)

8(a).   *Active management* (or expectations management) seeks the highest return possible (above bond market returns) while not exceeding the desired risk posture. This is done through a process consisting of:

(1).  Formation of expectations about interest rates, credit risk and spread changes.

(2).  Their transformation into return and risk measures via a return simulation process.

(3).  Their implementation via an optimization routine for the actual building of the portfolio.

Reinvestment rate risk is not protected against in any systematic way and is, therefore, of real concern. It must be considered when making all portfolio changes, as it is one of the most important components of the total return that will be achieved.

8(b). *Classical immunization* can be defined by any of the following:

(1).  Any investment strategy designed to minimize the risk of reinvestment over a specific time horizon.
(2).  Being assured that the assets at the end of the horizon period are greater than, or equal to, some minimum level that might have been established.
(3).  Achieving the maximum return possible with minimum reinvestment risk.

The classical immunizer spends a considerable amount of time rebalancing the portfolio to bring the duration of the portfolio back in line with the duration of the liabilities that are being immunized. This is because classical immunization is based on three unrealistic assumptions:

(1). a flat yield curve,
(2). parallel yield curve shifts, and
(3). an instantaneous change in yields.

Reinvestment rate risk is significantly reduced or almost eliminated by matching duration to the time horizon. The price risk is in the opposite direction of the reinvestment risk, and these offsetting risks equal each other when the duration of the portfolio is equal to the investment horizon of the portfolio.

8(c).    *Dedicated portfolios* are used to generate sufficient cash to finance each of a sequence of liability payments as they come due, with virtually no interest rate risk. This is accomplished using one of two techniques:

(1). a cash-matched portfolio or
(2). a duration-matched portfolio.

At least two practical problems introduce some reinvestment risk: (a) the risk that bonds in the portfolio may be called prior to maturity; and (b) in the case of cash-matching, the life of the liabilities may extend beyond the normal maturity range of bonds. If the amount of the liabilities diminishes over time, then the reinvestment risk is further reduced.

Conventionally, a conservative reinvestment rate is chosen to represent that rate at which cash flows are assumed to be reinvested from the date they are received through coupons and maturities until the payment date of the liability being financed.

8(d).    *Contingent immunization* is an active-passive strategy normally having three components:

(1). *Immunized Base Return* - the return that can be currently achieved with little or no active management for a specific time horizon regardless of the future direction of interest rates.
(2). *Investment Objective* - a return goal in excess of the Immunized Base Return to be achieved with active management strategies.
(3). *Assured Minimum Return* - a return set below the immunized base return that can be assured with the future use of immunization if active management decisions are wrong.

Due to the use of a specific time horizon, there is a real element of reinvestment rate-risk that should be addressed regularly by the portfolio manager.

All of the reinvestment rate-risk to which active management is subject exists for the contingent immunizes, unless having failed his performance goals by falling to the Assured Minimum Return. In that case, the portfolio would be immunized and reinvestment rate-risk would be eliminated subject to the same conditions discussed in B.

9.    CFA Examination III (June 1985)

9(a).    The required ending wealth value to equal to:

$300 million x 1.629 (5%fortenperiods) = $488.70 million

17 - 20

9(b). and 9(c).

| YEAR | MARKET VALUE (MIL $) | MARKET YIELD | REQUIRED FLOOR PORTFOLIO (MIL $) | SAFETY MARGIN OF ERROR (MIL $) |
|---|---|---|---|---|
| 1 | 340.09 | 10% | 330.85 | 10.05 |
| 2 | 405.50 | 08% | 386.07 | 19.43 |
| 3 | 395.20 | 12% | 367.05 | 8.15 |

In general, the required floor portfolio is the present value of the required ending value ($88.70 million) at the current market yield.

For Year One -    The required floor portfolio is the present value of $488.70 at 10% for four years (5% for eight periods).

$488.70 X .667 = $330.85

For Year Two -    Lee required floor portfolio is the present value of $488.70 at 8% for three years (4% for six periods).

$488.70 X .790 = $386.07

For Year Three -    The required floor portfolio is the present value of $488.70 at 12% for two years (6% for four periods).

$488.70 X .792 = $387.05

9(d).    If the margin of error at the end of any year had been zero or negative, the portfolio manager would discontinue active management of the portfolio and immunize it. If the margin of error had been negative, the manager would immunize the portfolio and thereby minimize any further losses to the portfolio.

10.    CFA Examination II (1990)

10(a).    Advantages of the three strategies as set forth in Table 2 are as follows.

Active management

1)    Active management incurs greater volatility of returns in exchange for higher potential returns. The best performing active managers in the top docile had the highest return per unit of risk (return/standard deviation) of 83.7% over the past 15 years .

2)    Active managers can attempt to achieve higher returns through security selection by choosing superior securities or by avoiding poor performers. Securities not in the WGB Index can be selected by an active manager.

3)    Active managers can adjust country and currency weights based on expectation of political and economic events.

4)    Durations can be changed to anticipate yield curve movements.

17 - 21

Passive management

1) Passive management has lower expected volatility of returns than active management with a lower management fee.
2) Fewer transactions should also result in lower transaction cost
3) Small duration shifts can be used to make minor adjustments to interest rate movements
4) The historical data indicate that passive management had higher average returns per unit of risk (73.8% versus 69.4%) than active management.
5) Limitations on country allocations keep funds diversified internationally.
6) This strategy would allow the manager some limited flexibility to add value.
7) Compared with active management, PTC's Investment Committee retains more control over investment strategy and the ability to easily monitor the manager's contribution.

Indexing

1) Indexing produces returns that should closely track the returns of the WGB Index.
2) Little risk exists in picking a poor manager, as Table 2 shows little difference between top docile and bottom docile managers.
3) Indexing has the lowest management fees and, except for rebalancing, should have very low transactions costs.
4) Indexing has produced the most favorable average return per unit of risk (75.8%).
5) The value added by the investment advisor through indexing can be measured with relative ease and precision.

10(b). The primary disadvantage of *active management* is the risk of significant under-performance by managers who miss either interest rate, currency, or country trends. Of the three strategies, returns of active manager are the most dependent on manager selection (as shown by the difference between highest and lowest docile returns). Also, active management has the highest fees, the highest standard deviation of returns, and the lowest average return-to-risk ratio.

The *passive management* strategy does not produce returns that differ greatly from the index returns but does have both higher standard deviation of returns and larger difference between highest and lowest docile managers. Also, passive management incurs higher management fees than indexing.

*Indexing* has the highest opportunity costs with little or no ability to outperform the index. Due to transaction costs and fees, the indexed portfolio will frequently underperform the index. The top docile return-to-standard deviation ratio is 80.5% for indexing compared to 83.9% for active managers, and indexing has virtually no flexibility to avoid poor performance in bear markets, to avoid anticipated deteriorating credits, or to invest in assets outside the index.

10(c). *Full replication* is a portfolio construction technique in which all securities represented in an index are owned in proportions identical to their index weights. A key advantage of

17 - 22

Harcourt, Inc.

this approach is that a portfolio so constructed would track the index accurately. However, this approach may not be practical, in that most fixed income indices contain thousands of securities; some of the bonds in the index may not be liquid or attractively priced; and receipt of cash inflows requires periodic portfolio rebalancing.

The *stratified sampling* technique divides the index into cells based on parameters such as country, coupon, term-to-maturity, and duration. If required, the index could be stratified further into subsectors. Stratification is followed by selection of the security or securities to represent each cell; the process of setting up an index fund is complete when all cells in the index have been replicated. An advantage of this approach is the ability to include attractive securities in the portfolio which are not contained in the index. However, the stratified sampling approach, while simple in concept, is labor intensive and relies upon portfolio management expertise to appropriately stratify the index. Unless properly structured, the resulting portfolio may not track the index accurately. Finally, the portfolio may have to be optimized using either linear or quadratic programming to achieve the highest yield and greatest convexity.

10(d). The selection of an appropriate benchmark is a key decision in any indexing strategy. The Salomon Brothers WGB Index does not represent currency exposures that are even close to the liability exposures of Planet Trade's pension plan. For example, 23.3% of PTC's non-U.S. dollar liabilities are in Australia that has only a 2% weighting in the Salomon Index.

| Country | Liabilities | Index |
|---|---|---|
| Australia | 23.3% | 2% |
| Japan | 20.0 | 37 |
| Singapore | 20.0 | 0 |
| Thailand | 13.3 | 0 |
| Spain | 13.3 | 0 |
| Malaysia | 10.0 | 0 |
| Others | 0.0 | 61 |
| | 100.0% | 100% |

Therefore, in an asset-liability management context, the recommendation is inappropriate. If accepted, the proposal would result in a mismatch between the investment assets and the liabilities of the plan.

11. CFA Examination II (1996)

11(a). The total debt to total capital ratio measures the degree of leverage of the firm. Leverage is the relationship of debt owed to the company's total resources as valued on the balance sheet. An analyst would evaluate the absolute leverage and the change in the use of leverage for a firm and compare the level of leverage to that of other companies in the same industry. A firm with a high total debt-total capital ratio will be perceived as having a higher level of credit risk. By comparing this ratio to its competitors' ratio, an analyst can judge the prudence of such leverage for a company it the particular industry. A firm

17 - 23

increases its financial leverage when it takes on more debt in proportion to its total capitalization (resources). The change in financial leverage may indicate a change in the company's attitude towards risk taking. The firm will lose some financial flexibility-financing alternatives and ability to access funds-and will generally pay a higher price to acquire funds than a lower-leveraged company. Higher financial leverage may also reduce the firm's choices for financing future growth and paying dividends. Covenants may restrict the company's ability to use its financial resources as it sees fit when this ratio becomes too high.

The pretax interest coverage ratio measures the annual interest burden (the amount the firm must pay its creditors) placed on a firm relative to its earning capacity. This coverage ratio is important because it looks at the firm's ability to pay its annual interest expense from pretax earnings (EBIT). A high coverage ratio is considered positive; a low coverage ratio may indicate more risk, which is a financial constraint. The ratio also suggests the protection afforded creditors to continue to receive interest income, despite a business downturn or an increase in leverage by the firm. Although this ratio indicates the ability of the company to pay cash to its creditors, the numerator includes noncash earnings and is reduced by noncash expenses. Finally, the comfort level of coverage should be based on the expected consistency of earnings (an industry issue) and with consideration given to the firm's access to cash.

Cash flow as a percent of total debt focuses not only on earnings, but also on the firm's ability to generate the cash needed to service its debt. "Earnings" can be deceptive because of noncash items used to get earnings. Analyzing cash flow is critical because it provides insight into a firm's ability to cover debt with internally generated funds. By relating cash flow to total debt, the analyst can make a judgment about the firm's ability to repay the principal-creditor's original investment and debt service (principal and interest). The ratio suggests the amount of time needed for a firm to pay off the original borrowings from internally generated cash.

11(b). PowerTool's capitalization ratio, after the acquisition, would continue to allow the company to repurchase dividends or buy stock. By increasing this ratio as a result of the acquisition, the company has reduced its financial flexibility. This is because any such payment of dividends or stock repurchase would be more limited than before the acquisition. The firm's ability to pay dividends adds to its flexibility when issuing common or preferred stock and to the value placed on the new stock. Increasing capitalization without adding debt improves the ratio. The company still has flexibility to issue debt--this covenant does not restrict the amount of debt.

With a put option covenant, the bondholders have the option to keep or put the bonds if the rating drops. If, for this definition, "A-" officially falls outside of the "A" category, then the company may already be in this situation. At the very least, the debt rating is so close to being "A-" and on its way to being "BBB+" that further debt issuance is restricted. At this point, the company should have a provision for paying off the debt, if put, such as a line or letter of credit. Such action would add to the company's financial flexibility in two ways. It would give the firm the ability to buy back the debt and indicate to potential investors the willingness of an outside source to lend money to the company.

Whether or not investors choose to exercise the put option after a downgrade depends largely on the current market price of the bonds. If the bonds are trading at a price below 105, exercise of the put is probable. At prices near 105, investors may consider retaining their holding if they perceive that the company is leveraging for the right reasons and that the company will be stronger in the long run.

If the put is exercised by bondholders, the company may have to issue new debt at a lower price and higher interest cost. This action would add to the cost of doing business and reduce the firm's financial flexibility.

### 11(c). Industrial Tool Business

From the perspective of PowerTool bondholders, there are several advantages to the Fenton acquisition with regard to the industrial tool business.

#### *Advantages*

1. The industrial tool market is mature. This business has little growth potential except by acquiring market share or buying share through price competition, which erodes margin and financial strength in the short run. PowerTool is already the largest in this no-growth industry. It can control its market share to provide a "cash cow" for growth outside that market. It should be able to concentrate on the success of the new product. The acquisition of Fenton will provide growth and improve profitability of PowerTool.

2. PowerTool bought a company in a related business, in an industry with significant growth prospects. Fenton's R&D has produced a patented new line that has tested positively. All of these aspects of Fenton are good reasons for the acquisition. The R&D may provide growth opportunities in the industrial tool market by making a new market or "improved" replacement product to sell to existing customers.

3. Although a large company buying a small, innovative company can often result in conflict because of differences in management style, this is not likely to be the case with Fenton. The retirement of Jerry Fenton could ease the transition. The larger company may be able to offer employees benefits that the smaller, highly leveraged company could not, which may inspire employees to stay on.

4. PowerTool has a strong sales force, and Fenton needs a sales force to sell its new product. This also gives the sales force an opportunity to see both its sales and its employee income grow. Income growth will contribute to bondholder protection.

*Disadvantages*

1. The tactics for prospering in a mature market and buying competition require financial flexibility. PowerTool has reduced its financial alternatives through this costly acquisition. The cost includes not only the cost of buying the company but also the resources needed to make Fenton grow.

2. Fenton's retail market may not be compatible with PowerTool's industrial line. PowerTool's new power tools also may not be compatible with Fenton's current line. If the new business detracts from the industrial business, PowerTool could lose important market share, and profits may decline, causing bond rating to decline.

3. The lack of marketing strength of both PowerTool and Fenton makes this a poor match. A strong sales force at PowerTool may be insufficient to satisfy the marketing needs of the industrial tool business. In retail, marketing is even more important than in industrial sales, and, in this area, Fenton is also weak.

4. PowerTool must invest funds in the market areas for both companies and probably in manufacturing facilities for the new power tools. The leveraging up of PowerTool may reduce the financial flexibility necessary to produce, market, and sell the product. Increased leverage may also affect the firm's ability to maintain the dominant position in industrial tools.

## Retail Tool Business

From the perspective of PowerTool bondholders, there are several advantages and disadvantages to acquiring Fenton regarding the retail tool business.

*Advantages*

1. The patent on the new Fenton product gives the company the marketing opportunity of not having a directly competitive product in the market. The uniqueness reduces the competition based on price because there is no duplicate product. Otherwise, pricing can be a strong competitive tool in retail. Price competition comes with products that can be interchanged or substituted for one another with relative indifference. Fenton has created a product that test markets suggest will address customers needs. Thus, the company is buying into a growth market with a new protected product that looks like a winner. Such products inspire investors to provide capital to such a firm, thus adding to financial flexibility. PowerTool has bought new, innovative products that should boost its growth above the industry's growth prospects.

2. PowerTool's distribution system and sales force may help solve the marketing shortcomings regarding the sale of the new product line. This may be accomplished by getting the product to the geographic locations on a timely basis and by providing the people to spread the word about the new products.

3. After the acquisition, the financial position of PowerTool is still much better than Fenton's financial position. PowerTool may not have to spend much money expanding

Harcourt, Inc.

facilities and markets for its industrial tools. Yet, the growth opportunities at Fenton are much better than those of PowerTool.

4. PowerTool's market recognition in the tool business should help market the retail line. The name and size of the company can add credence to the quality of the retail products and influence shelf location.

5. Fenton has proven technological and innovative strengths that PowerTool may lack. Innovation is important for the company to stay competitive in the retail market. Thus, PowerTool is staying in a related business and buying much-needed growth potential through innovation. R&D-intensive firms are likely to have future staying power and a competitive edge.

6. Diversifying the product mix can reduce the volatility of earnings and help insure positive returns. Diversification of product may provide pricing flexibility. For example, one product can compete on price (slim margins) without affecting the profit margins of the other. PowerTool has added a product line that may be able to use the existing production capacity. Diversification will therefore reduce bondholder risk.

### *Disadvantages*

1. Fenton's new product needs marketing expertise, and so does PowerTool's old product. Marketing is critical in the retail business. PowerTool's reduced financial flexibility will limit the potential strength of the new product if it cannot be properly marketed.

2. The growth in the retail market may not be large enough to affect PowerTool's returns because PowerTool is a large company and Fenton is a small company.

3. Fenton's new product has shown promise only in test markets. It has no track record, yet it is projected to account for 50 percent of the business in five years. Any uncertainty about the success of the new product adds uncertainty about the success of the acquisition and increases risk for bondholders.

4. Management of both companies is in transition. If Jerry Fenton were the innovator at Fenton, this transition would affect the value of the company because he has retired. The old Fenton employees are now subject to a more mature management style. Whether the mix works is always uncertain in these situations. The expectation is that the old management style at PowerTool will continue; if it does not, confusion will replace the clear direction this acquisition -needs.

11(d). Reason supporting a *hold* of PowerTool bonds.

1. PowerTool management-has a proven track record, little turnover, and is well respected. Despite its marketing problems, PowerTool has the ability to stay competitive. Management judgment seems to be good. Although the CEO retired,

there seems to be continuity. Management is experienced and can generally make a profit and maintain adequate financial flexibility.

2. In the industrial tools business, it would probably take a technical breakthrough such as Fenton's to grow unless management wanted to compete on price or acquire the competition. Buying Fenton is a logical alternative to fighting in a no-growth business. PowerTool bondholders may benefit by the innovative expertise of Fenton and diversify out of a no-growth business.

3. PowerTool is buying its way into a new segment of its existing business, which adds customer diversification without straying far outside its realm of expertise. The potential for using the existing facilities for the production of retail hand tools (a growing business) adds financial flexibility because PowerTool can transform production for a best use. This also helps ensure customer satisfaction regarding delivery time and the filling of quantity orders.

4. Fenton needs PowerTool's financial flexibility and management expertise to take advantage of its innovative strength. PowerTool will use its strong sales force to market the new product and increase profitability, which will be positive for its bonds.

5. The put option covenant provides downside risk protection to its bondholders in case the acquisition does not succeed and the bond rating declines below A.

6. The dividend covenant imposes discipline on the managers and prevents them from distributing cash to shareholders to the detriment of bondholders.

Reason supporting a *sell* of PowerTool bonds.

1. PowerTool is the largest company in a no-growth industry. Its marketing skills are not up to customer standards already. PowerTool is leveraging itself into a credit downgrade to buy a small company in a different market. Fenton has its own marketing failings, but its "hot new product" will require a successful market introduction.

2. Credit deterioration and stringent new covenants reduce the financial flexibility of the company. The firm needs to overcome its deficiency in the marketing area, including the ability to counteract any offensive moves by competitors in the no-growth industrial tool business. Debt will cost more in the future. It will be harder to draw equity investment with the covenants that now exist. If the covenants in Part B are not attached to the bonds, other bondholders have a superior claim on corporate assets.

3. PowerTool may have paid too big a premium for Fenton.

4. The test marketing for the new product may be a gamble. This is especially true if the marketing is done by a company without marketing resources. PowerTool has a sales

Harcourt, Inc.

force that is seen as strong, yet customers complain about marketing. This is even more important in the retail market. Without good marketing, the new product's success is in jeopardy. It seems that the new product was the reason for the acquisition, given that the product is expected to be 50 percent of Fenton's sales in a mere five years. This product has no track record.

5. PowerTool was between ratings classes before the acquisition and was given the lower rating. The company may receive an A- or lower rating, which would trigger the exercise of the put option by some debt holders. If PowerTool has to refinance the debt at a higher interest rate, this would affects the price of debt and might result in further downgrading. Also, PowerTool might not be able to immediately respond to a sudden exercise of the options, causing a delay in the return of bondholders' principal.

6. The bonds are currently trading as A-rated bonds, which may imply a price that is higher than the underlying credit quality of the company (A-) warrants.

12. CFA Examination II (1997)

**12(a). Ratios Based on Projected 1997 Data**
   i.     Operating income to sales = 8.8%
   ii.    EBIT/Total assets = Earnings before interest and taxes/Total assets = 2.9%
   iii.   Times interest earned = Earnings before interest and taxes/Interest = 1.01x
   iv.    Long-term debt to total assets = 55.5%

**12(b). Effect of 1997 Merger on Ratios and Creditworthiness**
   i.     **Operating income to sales**: The creditworthiness of BRT Corporation, from the standpoint of operating profit margin. Has declined because of the merger. Operating margins for the combined companies have weakened because of their inability to generate higher operating profits on the new combined sales. This ratio should be evaluated over a longer term to determine whether the operating efficiency of the company is improving.

   ii.    **EBIT/Total assets**: The return on assets ratio declined. The firm's productive use of its assets has not improved, causing a continued decline in credit quality. The creation of a large intangible asset can affect this ratio. An analyst must determine whether, over time, management has the ability to generate higher earnings from the intangible asset. This ratio is very weak; it provides insight into possible underutilization of the intangible rights.

   iii.   **Times interest earned**: The interest coverage ratio decreased significantly, creating a credit concern regarding BRT's ability to meet its fixed obligations. The earnings before interest and taxes of the merged company have not grown proportionally to the amount of interest owed per year. A declining interest coverage ratio indicates a lack of excess funds available for other capital expenditures. When a company's times interest earned approaches 1.00, the creditworthiness of the company is dramatically reduced because of its potential inability to pay its fixed obligations.

iv. **Long-term debt to total assets**: The leverage ratio remained flat. Although leverage ratio alone does not indicate a credit problem, the leverage ratio in combination with other ratios does. BRT is unable to generate higher returns with the same amount of leverage, which affects operating performance. The issuance of additional stock allowed the companies to merge without incurring a larger proportion of debt.

## 12(c). Should Clayton Asset Management Hold or Sell the BRT Bonds

Currently, the BRT bonds are trading as BB-rated bonds. Prior to the merger, BRT's ratios approximated a weak BB credit. After the merger, all the ratios declined below those representative of a BB credit except the ratio of debt to total assets, which maintained a BB credit quality.

Several other factors may cause further deterioration in the financial strength of BRT. First, a large portion of assets is now intangible, which introduces the potential for overstating current values. The value of the intangibles is best measured by their ability to generate revenues. Recently, their ability is suspect. Second, BRT is not generating sufficient income to cover interest expenses. The lack of income makes providing for capital expenditures to maintain and build current business difficult. Third, with the weakening financial structure of BRT, the company has further reduced its flexibility to compete in a highly competitive environment.

Additional contributing factors include management's focus on aggressive expansion at the expense of bondholders' interests and the competitive pressures created by government regulation of the industry.

The cumulative effect of declining financial ratios, potentially overvalued assets, reduced ability to meet capital expenditure needs, and reduced financial flexibility to compete in a highly competitive industry will have a negative impact on BRT's creditworthiness. Clayton should *sell* the BRT bonds in anticipation of a widening spread between the bonds and U.S. Treasuries. This widening in spread relative to Treasuries will cause the bonds to underperform as the market adjusts the values of the bonds in line with comparable lower-credit-quality bonds.

13. CFA Examination II (1998)

Jane Berry should buy the **Patriot Manufacturing bond.**

**Table 1 factors.** Table 1 shows that Patriot is less risky than Sturdy Machines. First, the pretax interest coverage of Sturdy Machines is just over one vs. Patriot's at 6.1 times. Second, Patriot's cash flow/total debt is higher than Sturdy Machines and is improving faster. Finally, Patriot's total debt/capital is lower than Sturdy Machines and is decreasing.

**Qualitative factors.** The qualitative factors supporting this recommendation include, first, the fact that Patriot is an improving credit, as evidenced by the recent rating upgrade. Sturdy Machines, on the other hand, is a deteriorating credit, as evidenced by the recent rating downgrade. Second, given that the credit-rating changes were recent, one would expect no change (or continued increases) in the rating of the Patriot bonds and no change (or continued decreases) in the rating of the Sturdy Machines bonds. Finally, Berry can anticipate that the Patriot bonds will fall in yield (rise in price). Sturdy Machines' bonds appear to be riskier than Patriot's bonds.

14. CFA Examination II (1999)

14(a)(i) **Adjusted Interest Coverage** = EBITDA / Interest Expense = **2.81**.
   This is a reduction of 1.91 from the pre-adjustment ratio of 4.72.

| Off-Balance Sheet Item | EBITDA Impact | Interest Expense Impact | Interest Coverage Impact |
|---|---|---|---|
| Pre-adjustment | $4,450,000 | $942,000 | 4.72 |
| - Guarantee of debt (n/a) | $0 | $0 | |
| - Sale of receivables (1) | +$40,000 | +$40,000 | |
| - Operating lease (2) | $0 | +$614,400 | |
| Net Adjustment | +$40,000 | +$654,400 | |
| Post-adjustment | $4,490,000 | $1,596,400 | **2.81** |

(1) Sale of receivables = Interest income (EBITDA) & interest expense
   $500,000 @ 8% = $40,000.
(2) Operating lease = Interest expense: $6,144,000 @ 10% = $614,400.

In adjusting for the sold accounts receivable and treating it as a secured loan, operating income (EBITDA) should be increased by the interest income ($40,000). This is because, presumably, the "loan proceeds" from the financed receivables would be invested to generate interest income (for simplicity sake, the same rate of interest is assumed - an alternative rate could be justified). The financing costs of the loan ($40,000) would be added to interest expense and will not impact EBITDA. (Level I 1998 - White, Sondi, and Fried, 1994, Chapter 10, pp. 715-721.)

In adjusting for the operating lease and treating it as a capital lease, interest expense for the first year of the lease ($614,400) should be added to adjusted interest expense. (Level I 1998 - White, Sondi, and Fried, 1994, Chapter 8, pp. 594-601.)

[Note that this is a new operating lease and therefore there is no adjustment necessary for operating lease expenses since they have not yet been incurred and included in the financials. Had the lease been in effect for the past year, the present value of the lease would now be less than the full amount ($6,144,000) and the principal and interest adjustments would be less. In addition, there would need to be other adjustments made: operating income (EBITDA) would be increased by the amount of the annual lease payment - $1,000,000 for operating lease expense eliminated and, correspondingly, depreciation expense would be increased to cover the first year's write-off of the lease asset.]

(ii) **Adjusted Leverage** = Long-term Debt / Equity = **0.50.**
This is an increase of 0.20 from the pre-adjustment ratio of 0.30.

| Off-Balance Sheet Item | Long-term Debt Impact | Equity Impact | Leverage Impact |
|---|---|---|---|
| Pre-adjustment | $10,000,000 | $33,460,000 | 0.30 |
| - Guarantee of debt (n/a) | +$995,000 | $0 | |
| - Sale of receivables (1) | $0 | $0 | |
| - Operating lease (2) | +$5,758,400 | $0 | |
| Net Adjustment | +$6,753,400 | $0 | |
| Post-adjustment | $16,753,400 | $33,460,000 | **0.50** |

(1) Guarantee of debt = Long-term debt: $995,000.
(2) Operating lease = Long-term debt: $6,144,000 (PV of lease) - $385,600 (current portion) = $5,758,400.

In adjusting for the guarantee of affiliate's debt and treating it as internal long-term debt, long term debt should be increased by the amount of the guarantee ($995,000).

In adjusting for the operating lease and treating it as a capital lease, long-term debt should be increased by the present value of the lease ($6,144,000) less the current or short-term portion - the principal due in the next 12 months ($1,000,000 - $614,400 = $385,600). (Level 1 1998 White, Sondhi, and Fried, 1994, Chapter 8, pp. 594-601.)

(iii). **Adjusted Current Ratio** = Current Assets /Current Liabilities = **0.97**. This is a reduction of 0.08 from the pre-adjustment ratio of 1.05.

| Off-Balance Sheet Item | Current Assets Impact | Current Liabilities Impact | Current Ratio Impact |
|---|---|---|---|
| Pre-adjustment | $4,735,000 | $4,500,000 | 1.05 |
| - Guarantee of debt (n/a) | $0 | $0 | |
| - Sale of receivables (1) | +$500,000 | +$500,000 | |
| - Operating lease (2) | 0 | +$385,600 | |
| Net Adjustment | +$500,000 | +$885,600 | |
| Post-adjustment | $5,235,000 | $5,385,600 | **0.97** |

(1)     Sale of receivables = Accounts receivable (current assets) & notes payable (current liabilities): $500,000.
(2)     Operating lease=Current portion of lease obligation (current liabilities): $1,000,000 (annual payment) - $614,400 (interest expense) = $385,600 (principle payment).

In adjusting for the sold accounts receivable and treating it as a secured loan, accounts receivable (current assets) and notes payable (current liabilities) should both be increased by the amount of the sale ($500,000). (Level I 1998 - White, Sondhi, and Fried, 1994, Chapter 10, pp. 715-721.)

In adjusting for the operating lease and treating it as a capital lease, leases payable (current liabilities) should be increased by the principal due in the next 12 months on the lease. This is equal to the annual lease payment less the first year's interest expense ($1,000,000 - $614,400 $385,600). (Level I 1998 - White, Sondhi, and Fried, 1994, Chapter 8, pp. 594-601.)

14(b). The current rating of the Montrose bond as an "A" does not incorporate the effect of the off-balance-sheet items, and the current credit yield premium of 55 basis points is not sufficient to compensate Smith for the credit risk of the bond. After adjusting for the three off-balance sheet items, all three internal bond-rating criteria indicate that the Montrose bond should have a lower credit rating:

- The lower interest coverage ratio (2.81) indicates that the bond is more risky, should have a lower (BB) rating, and a higher premium (+125 basis points).
- The higher leverage ratio (0.50) indicates that the bond is more risky, should have a lower (BBB) rating, and a higher premium (+100 basis points).
- The lower current ratio (0.97) indicates that the bond is more risky, should have a lower (BBB) rating, and a higher premium (+100 basis points).

Montrose should be rated as a "BBB" instead of an "A" and should be paying a premium of at least 100 basis points. The Montrose bond is more risky than it appears and Smith should not purchase the bond at its current price.

# CHAPTER 18

# STOCK-MARKET ANALYSIS

1.   Although corporate earnings may rise by 12 percent next year, that information by itself is not sufficient to forecast an increase in the stock market. The market level is a product of both corporate earnings and the earnings multiple. The earnings multiple must likewise be projected since it is not stable over time.

2.   Student Exercise

3.   The investor can improve his net profit margin estimate by working from the gross margin down to the net profit margin. By this procedure, the investor explicitly considers each major component that affects the net profit margin. This level of analysis provides insights into the components which do not behave consistently over time. Also, the gross profit margin should be easier to estimate since it has the lowest level of relative variability.

4.   The effect of a decline in capacity utilization should be a decline in the aggregate profit margin, all else the same, because it will mean greater overhead and depreciation per unit of output. Also more fixed financial charges per unit.

5.   In addition to the estimate of the changes in the hourly wage rate, an estimate of the productivity rate change is also needed to forecast the unit labor cost change. The relationship is:

$\% \, \Delta \text{ Hourly Wages} - \% \, \Delta \text{ Productivity} = \% \, \Delta \text{ Unit Labor Cost}$

The unit labor cost is negatively related to the profit margin.

$\% \, \Delta \text{ Hourly Wages} - \% \, \Delta \text{ Productivity} = \% \, \Delta \text{ Unit Labor Cost}$

6.   7.0 - 5.0 = 2.0% increase in the unit labor cost. This increase would, holding other factors constant, decrease the aggregate profit margin.

7.   Because it is a low rate of increase, the effect on the profit margin should be small.

7(a).   An increase in the ROE with no other changes should cause an increase in the multiple because it would imply a higher growth rate. An important question is, how was the increase in ROE accomplished?  If it was due to operating factors (higher asset turnover or profit margin) it is positive.  If it was due to an increase in financial leverage, there could be some offset due to an increase in the required rate of return (k).

Harcourt, Inc.

7(b).   Increase, because this will increase earnings growth by raising equity turnover. It could also cause a decrease because it will increase the financial risk and, therefore, the required k.

7(c).   Decrease, because this will increase growth and therefore raise the real RFR. It could also reduce inflation, which would decrease the nominal RFR, causing the multiplier to rise.

7(d).   Increase, because a decrease in the dividend payout rate increases the retention rate, raising the growth rate. It could also cause a decrease because it reduces the next period's dividends.

8.   Both the present value of cash flow approaches and the relative valuation ratios approach require two factors be estimated: (1) required rate of return on the stock, because this rate becomes the discount rate or is a major component of the discount rate, and (2) growth rate of the variable used in the valuation techniques, such as, dividends, earnings, cash flows or sales.

9.   The DDM assumes that (1) dividends grow at a constant rate, (2) the constant growth rate will continue for an infinite period, and (3) the required rate of return (k) is greater than the infinite growth rate (g).  Therefore, the infinite period DDM cannot be applied to the valuation of stock for growth companies because the high growth of earnings for the growth company is inconsistent with the assumptions of the infinite period constant growth DDM model.  A company cannot permanently maintain a growth rate higher than its required rate of return, because competition will eventually enter this apparently lucrative business, which will reduce the firm's profit margins and therefore its ROE and growth rate.  Therefore, after a few years of exceptional growth (a period of temporary supernormal growth) a firm's growth rate is expected to decline.  Eventually its growth rate is expected to stabilize at a constant level consistent with the assumptions of the infinite period DDM.

# CHAPTER 18

## Answers to Problems

1.   Using only the graph and drawing a line over from ten percent to the line of best fit and down to the horizontal percent change indicates an estimate of slightly under 10% for the S & P series. Alternatively, if you apply the following regression equation:

%  Δ S & P 400 Sales = -.024 + 1.16 (% Δ in Nominal GDP)
$$= -.024 + 1.16 (0.10)$$
$$= -.024 + .116$$
$$= .092 \text{ or } 9.2\%$$

Figure 18.8 was based upon as analysis that encompassed the period: 1975-1997. The overall average GNP percentage changes was 7.6%, with 6.5% change in S&P 400. During the 1990s, the percentage change in GNP has been lower than the average over the period (approximately 5.8%) and lower than the 10% proposed in the problem. Therefore, one could argue that based upon recent observations, % change in S&P 400 Sales should also be lower.

2(a)
$$P/E = \frac{.60}{.13 - .07} = .60/.06 = 10x$$

2(b).
$$P/E = \frac{.50}{.13 - .07} = .50/.06 = 8.3x$$

2(c)
$$P/E = \frac{.60}{.16 - .09} = .60/.07 = 8.57x$$

2(d)
$$P/E = \frac{.60}{.10 - .06} = .60/.04 = 15x$$

3.   CFA Examination I (June 1985)

3(a).   Overall, both managers added value by mitigating the currency effects present in the Index. Both exhibited an ability to "pick stocks" in the markets they chose to be in (Manger B. in particular). Manager B used his opportunities not to be in stocks quite effectively (via the cash/bond contribution to return), but neither of them matched the passive index in picking the country markets in which to be invested (Manger B, in particular).

Harcourt, Inc.

|  | MANAGER A | MANAGER B |
|---|---|---|
| STRENGTHS | Currency Management | Currency Management |
|  |  | Stock Selection |
|  |  | Use of Cash/Bond Flexibility |
| WEAKNESSES | Country Selection | Country Selection |
| (to a limited degree) |  |  |

3(b). The column reveals the effect on performance in local currency terms after adjustment for movements in the U.S. dollar and, therefore, the effect on the portfolio. Currency gains/losses arise from translating changes in currency exchange rates versus the U.S. dollar over the measuring period (3 years in this case) into U.S. dollars for the U.S. pension plan. The Index mix lost 12.9% to the dollar, reducing what would otherwise have been a very favorable return from the various country markets of 19.9% to a net return of only 7.0%.

4(a). Growth = .60 x .12 = .072 = 7.2%

4(b).
$$P/E = \frac{.40}{.10 - .072} = 14.29x$$

4(c). The market price will rise to: Price = 14.29 x $39 = $557.14

4(d). Rate of Return =
$$\frac{557.14 - 700 + 22}{700} = -17.27\%$$

5(a).

| $1020 x .152 | = | $155.04 (operating profit margin) |
|---|---|---|
| $155.04 - $45 | = | $110.04 (depreciation) |
| $110.04 - $18 | = | $ 92.04 (interest) |
| $92.04 x (1-.32) | = | $ 62.59 (Estimated EPS) |

5(b). Optimistic:

| $1020 x .155 | = | $158.10 (operating profit margin) |
|---|---|---|
| $158.10 - $45 | = | $113.10 (depreciation) |
| $113.10 - $18 | = | $ 95.10 (interest) |
| $95.10 x (1 -.32) | = | $ 64.67 (Estimated EPS) |

Pessimistic:

| $1020 x .149 | = | $151.98 (operating profit margin) |
|---|---|---|
| $151.98 - $45 | = | $106.98 (depreciation) |
| $106.98 - $18 | = | $ 88.98 (interest) |
| $88.98 x (1 - .32) | = | $ 60.51 (Estimated EPS) |

18 - 4

6(a).   Growth Rates:                                Required return:
        High    = (1 - 0.45) x 0.16 = .088         High    = 0.08 + 0.03 = 0.11
        Low     = (1 - 0.65) x 0.10 = .035         Low     = 0.10 + 0.05 = 0.15
        Consensus = (1 - 0.55) x 0.13 = .0585      Consensus = 0.09 + 0.04 = 0.13

        P/E Ratios:
        High    = 0.45/(0.11 – 0.088) = 0.45/.022 = 20.4545
        Low     = 0.65/(0.15 – 0.035) = 0.65/.115 = 5.6522
        Consensus = 0.55/(0.13 – 0.0585) = 0.55/.0715 = 7.6923

        Price:
        High    = 52.87 x 20.4545  = $ 1081.43
        Low     = 49.40 x  5.6522  = $  279.22
        Consensus = 51.14 x  7.6923  = $  393.38

6(b).   High         = (1081.43/750) –1  = +.4419
        Low          =  (279.22/750) –1  = -.6277
        Consensus    =  (393.38/750) –1  = -.4755

7.      Student Exercise

Harcourt, Inc.

# CHAPTER 19

# INDUSTRY ANALYSIS

## Answers to Questions

1. The results of empirical studies concluded that there are substantial differences in absolute or relative performance among industries during any given time period. In addition, industry performance differences are found in alternative time periods where the time periods may vary in length. Therefore, the investor must examine alternative industries after he has forecasted market movements because of the wide dispersion of industry performance around the expected market performance.

2. Studies show that relative industry performance is inconsistent over time. When industries are ranked over successive time periods, there is little correlation in the rankings. This result holds for different types of markets and for alternative length time periods. These findings imply that simple extrapolation of past performance is not useful by itself. Therefore, the analyst must put additional effort into his industry analysis by projecting industry performance based upon future expectations of industry conditions. This obviously makes industry analysis more demanding.

3. A greater emphasis must be placed upon industry analysis when the performances of the individual firms cluster about the industry performance. In contrast, once the industry performance is estimated, the need for individual firm analysis is reduced since these results imply that all the firms will behave similar to the industry.

4. Disagree. Although studies have shown a significant dispersion of individual firm performance within a given industry, they also found that the industry component could partially explain individual firm performance. Although the strength of the industry component varies among industries, industry analysis is an important step before proceeding to the company analysis. The important implication is that individual company analysis would be relatively more important for industries where individual company returns are widely dispersed. The point is, the dispersion among companies within industries indicates a need for company analysis after industry analysis.

5. For given time periods, there were significant differences in risk among alternative industries. An analysis of Beta coefficients for the 30 *Barron's* industry groups indicated a wide range of systematic risk. The substantial dispersion in risk for alternative industries implies that the analyst must examine the risk levels for alternative industries.

6. While there is substantial dispersion in industry risk during a given time period, studies indicate reasonably stable beta coefficients over time. This implies that past industry risk analysis may be useful in estimating future risk.

7.      The fourth stage of the industrial life cycle is stabilization and market maturity. During this stage, sales grow in line with the economy. If sales per share for an industry in this stage of the life cycle were predicted to increase by 20 percent, this would imply a growth rate of the aggregate economy of 20 percent. A sales growth rate of 20 percent is high for an industry in the fourth stage of the industrial life cycle.

8.      As an investor, you would like to discover a firm just entering the rapid accelerating growth stage. During this stage, a firm will experience high sales growth, high profit margins, and little competition.

9.      An industry experiencing the kind of explosive growth characteristics of stage two (rapid accelerating growth) is the internet-related industry.

10.     Input-output analysis is one of three popular methods for forecasting industry sales. For autos, industries supplying steel, glass, tires and upholstery fabrics should be scrutinized as well as the spending capabilities/habits of consumers. For computers, the suppliers of critical components would have to be studied along with the spending capabilities/habits of potential users.

11.     A substitute product for steel would limit the prices firms in that industry could charge. The degree of limitation would depend on how closely the substitute product was in price and function to steel.

12.     Both the present value of cash flow approaches and the relative valuation ratios approach require two factors be estimated: (1) required rate of return on the stock, because this rate becomes the discount rate or is a major component of the discount rate, and (2) growth rate of the variable used in the valuation techniques, such as, dividends, earnings, cash flows or sales.

13.     Earnings multiplier (P/E) is determined by:
        (1) the expected dividend payout ratio,
        (2) the estimated required rate of return on the stock (k), and
        (3) the expected growth rate of dividends for the stock (g).
        Within the retail food industry, one would look at a company's fundamental risk (business, financial, liquidity, exchange and country risks). Difference in fundamental risk levels will determine a company's performance within the industry. One could also look at the competitive environment of an industry – rivalry among the existing competitors, threat of new entrants, threat of substitute products, bargaining power of buyers, and bargaining power of suppliers.

14.     The two-stage FCFE model would applied to the valuation of stock for growth companies because the high growth of earnings for the growth company is inconsistent with the assumptions of the infinite period constant growth DDM model. A company cannot permanently maintain a growth rate higher than its required rate of return, because competition will eventually enter this apparently lucrative business, which will reduce the

firm's profit margins and therefore its ROE and growth rate. Therefore, after a few years of exceptional growth (a period of temporary supernormal growth) a firm's growth rate is expected to decline. Eventually its growth rate is expected to stabilize at a constant level consistent with the assumptions of the infinite period DDM.

15. The reason for the difference in the P/CF ratios can be explained by differences in the growth rate of CF per share between the market and industry, and the risk (volatility) of the CF series over time. Therefore, an increase in the growth rate of the industry CF compared to the growth of the market CF, as well as, the industry CF series becoming more consistent in its growth would cause an increase in the industry-market ratio.

16. CFA Examination II (1999)

16(a).

| SUV Model | Identify Current Stage in Product Life Cycle (circle one) and Justify Your Choice |
|-----------|----------------------------------------------------------------------------------|
| Raven | Declining<br><br>The number of Raven SUV units sold has declined since its peak in 1997 and the decline is expected to accelerate in 1999 and 2000. |
| Hawk | Mature<br><br>The rate of increase in the number of Hawk SUV units sold has slowed and the number sold is expected to increase only modestly in 1999 and 2000. |
| Eagle | Expanding<br><br>The number of Eagle SLTV units sold has increased rapidly since its introduction in 1997 and is expected to continue growing rapidly in 1999 and 2000. |

16(b). The statement that Nelson Motors is enjoying increasing SUV profitability is true. SUV Division profits have increased from $45 million in 1990 to $1,311 million in 1998, with additional substantial increases forecast for 1999 and 2000. The SLTV division has grown from approximately 4% of Nelson Motors' profits in 1990 to an estimated 52% of profits in 2000. The Eagle is primarily responsible for this profit growth because of its high unit sales growth and greater profit per vehicle compared to the Raven and the Hawk.

The second part of the statement, that Nelson Motors enjoys declining earnings risk going forward, is not true. Nelson Motors is relying heavily on the Eagle to take the place of the Raven, which is in the declining phase of its life cycle, and the Hawk, which is in the maturity phase of its life cycle. Note that Nelson Motors has no SUV models other than the Eagle in the early phase of their life cycle. The increasing dependence of Nelson on the profitability of the SUV division increases the exposure of the company to developments that would affect that product line.

Harcourt, Inc.

In summary, while Nelson Motors may enjoy increased profitability due to the success of the Eagle, the risk to earnings has actually increased because the company is more dependent on one model in the future. In the existing SUV product portfolio, the Raven and Hawk are aging, and their contribution to Nelson's profits is dropping dramatically.

17.    CFA Examination II (1999)

| Statement | Valid / Not Valid (circle one) | Industry Characteristics (cite two by number for each statement) |
|---|---|---|
| I recommend that we invest in toy companies with a substantial percentage of revenues derived from non-U. S. sales. | Valid | Valid:       1, 2, 4, 5, 6, 15  <br><br>Not Valid:       none |
| Companies selected for the portfolio should derive a large portion of revenues from the largest discount toy retailer. | Not Valid | Valid:       13  <br><br>Not Valid:       13, 14, 15 |
| I am particularly interested in a start-up company that has an exciting new toy coming out based on a very popular television show. | Not Valid | Valid:       12  <br><br>Not Valid:   7, 8, 10, 11, 16 |
| Although MasterToy has the dominant market share, smaller companies will have better opportunities for growth. | Not Valid | Valid:       none  <br><br>Not Valid: 7, 8, 9, 10, 11, 16 |

# CHAPTER 19

## Answers to Problems

1.    Student Exercise

2.    Student Exercise

3.    Student Exercise

4.    Student Exercise

5.    Student Exercise

6.    Student Exercise

7.    Student Exercise

8.    CFA Examination II (1995)

8(a).    Relevant data items from Table 1 that support the conclusion that the retail auto parts industry as a whole is in the stabilization phase of the industry life cycle are:
1.    The population of 18-29 year olds, a major customer base for the industry, is gradually declining.
2.    The number of households with income less than $35,000, another important customer base, is not expanding.
3.    The number of cars 5-15 years old, an important end market, has recorded low annual growth (or actual declines in some years), so the number of units that potentially need parts is not growing.
4.    Automotive aftermarket industry retail sales have been growing slowly for several years.
5.    Consumer expenditures on automotive parts and accessories have grown slowly for several years.
6.    Average operating margins of all retail autoparts companies have steadily declined.

8(b).    Relevant items of data from Table 1 that support the conclusion that Wigwam Autoparts Heaven, Inc. (WAEI) and its major competitors are in the growth stage of their life cycle are:
1.    Sales growth of retail autoparts companies with 100 or more stores have been growing rapidly and at an increasing rate.
2.    Market share of retail autoparts stores with 100 or more stores has been increasing but is still only 19 percent, leaving room for much more growth.
3.    Average operating margins for retail autoparts companies with 100 or more stores are high and rising.

Harcourt, Inc.

Because of industry fragmentation (i.e., most of the market share is distributed among many companies with only a few stores), the retail autoparts industry apparently is undergoing marketing innovation and consolidation. The industry is moving toward the "category killer" format, in which a few major companies control large market shares through the proliferation of outlets. The evidence suggests that a new "industry within an industry" is emerging in the form of the 'category killer" large chain-store company. This industry subgroup is in its growth stage (i.e. rapid growth with high operating profit margins) despite the fact that the industry is in the stabilization stage of its life cycle.

9.    The industry (I) would have a lower P/E than the market (M) because:
(a)    ROE for the industry is lower than the market ROE;
(b)    Growth for the industry is lower than for the market; and
(c)    Beta for the industry is higher (more risk) than for the market

|  | Industry | Market |
|---|---|---|
| $g = RR \times ROE$ | $g = .60 \times .12 = .072$ | $g = .55 \times .16 = .088$ |

Assuming RFR = 6% and 16%, $k = RFR + \beta(R_m - RFR)$

$$k = .06 + 1.05(.16 - .06) \qquad k = .06 + 1.0(.16 - .06)$$
$$= .165 \qquad = .16$$

$$P/E = \frac{D/E}{k - g} \qquad P/E = .40/(.165 - .072) \qquad P/E = .45/(.16 - .088)$$
$$= .40/.093 = 4.3x \qquad = .45/.072 = 6.25x$$

# CHAPTER 20

# COMPANY ANALYSIS AND STOCK SELECTION

## Answers to Questions

1.  Examples of growth companies would include technology firms such as Intel and Microsoft. These firms have experienced very high rates of return on total assets and returns on equity when compared to market values. They retain high percentages of earnings to fund superior investment projects. Stock issues of Intel and Microsoft have been considered growth stocks since their P/E ratios are above the industry average.

2.  A cyclical stock would be any stock with a high beta value. Examples of high beta stock would include stocks of typical growth companies and some investment firms. As to whether the issuing company is a cyclical company will depend on the specific selection.

3.  The biotechnology firm may be considered a growth company because (1) it has a growth rate of 21 percent per year which probably exceeds the growth rate of the overall economy, (2) it has a very high return on equity and (3) it has a relatively high retention rate. However, since a biotechnology firm relies heavily on continuous research and development, the above-average risk will require a high rate of return. Therefore, it is unlikely that the stock would be considered a growth stock due to the extremely high price of the stock relative to its earnings.

4.  Student Exercise

5.  Student Exercise

6.  Student Exercise

7.  Student Exercise

8.  The DDM assumes that (1) dividends grow at a constant rate, (2) the constant growth rate will continue for an infinite period, and (3) the required rate of return (k) is greater than the infinite growth rate (g). Therefore, the infinite period DDM cannot be applied to the valuation of stock for growth companies because the high growth of earnings for the growth company is inconsistent with the assumptions of the infinite period constant growth DDM model. A company cannot permanently maintain a growth rate higher than its required rate of return, because competition will eventually enter this apparently lucrative business, which will reduce the firm's profit margins and therefore its ROE and growth rate. Therefore, after a few years of exceptional growth (a period of temporary supernormal growth) a firm's growth rate is expected to decline. Eventually its growth rate is expected to stabilize at a constant level consistent with the assumptions of the infinite period.

9.  Price/Book Value (P/BV) is used as a measure of relative value because, in theory, market price (P) should reflect book value (BV). In practice, the two can differ dramatically. Some researchers have suggested that firms with low P/BV ratios tend to outperform those with high P/BV ratios.

10. A high P/BV ratio such as 3.0 can result from a large amount of fixed assets being carried at historical cost. A low ratio, such as 0.6, can occur when assets are worth less than book value, for instance, bad real estate loans by banks.

11. The price/cash flow ratio (P/CF) has become more popular because of the increased emphasis on cash by various analysts and because of the increased availability of cash flow numbers. Differences could result from differences in net income or non-cash items.

12. Price/sales ratio varies dramatically by industry. For example, the sales per share for retail firms are typically higher than sales per share for technology firms. The reason for this difference is related to the second consideration, the profit margin on sales. The retail firms have high sales per share, which will cause a low P/S ratio, which is considered good until one realizes that these firms have low net profit margins.

13. The major components of EVA include the firm's net operating profit less adjusted taxes (NOPLAT) and its total cost of capital (in dollars) including the cost of equity. A positive EVA implies that NOPLAT exceeds the cost of capital and that value has been added for stockholders.

14. Absolute EVA makes it difficult to judge whether a firm is succeeding relative to past performance or if the growth rate can support additional capital. To overcome those shortcomings and to facilitate the comparison of firms of different size, it is preferable to compute an EVA return on capital ratio: EVA/Capital.

15. While the EVA measures a firm's internal performance, the MVA reflects the market's judgment of how well the firm performed in terms of the market value of debt and equity vis-a-vis the capital invested in it. Since the latter measure is affected by external factors such as interest rates, it is not surprising that the EVA and MVA share a weak relationship.

16. The two factors that determine a firm's franchise value are (1) the difference between the expected return on new opportunities and the current cost of equity and (2) the size of those new opportunities relative to the firm's current size. In the absence of a franchise value, an equity cost of 11% would translate into a (base) PIE ratio of 9.1 (or 1/.11).

17. Above average earnings growth is a characteristic of a growth company. Additionally, a rather high retention rate of 80 percent implies that the firm will have the resources to take advantage of high-return investment opportunities. These factors lend support to classifying the firm as a growth company. However, as a result of the high retention rate, investors will continue to require a high return on investment. Only if the firm can

20 - 2

continue to achieve returns above its cost of capital will the firm continue to be classified as a growth company.

18. In a perfectly competitive economy, if other companies see a particular firm achieving returns consistently above risk-based expectations, it is expected that these other companies will enter that particular industry or market and eventually drive prices down until the returns are consistent with the inherent risk. In other words, the competition would not allow the continuing existence of excess return investments and so competition would negate such growth. The computer industry is a good example of increased competition resulting in lower profit margins. The theory implies that in truly competitive environments, a true growth company is a temporary classification.

19. Because the dividend model assumes a constant rate of growth for an infinite time period, the point is that a true growth company is earning a rate of return above its cost of capital and this should not be possible in a competitive environment. Therefore, it is impossible for a true growth firm to exist for an infinite time period in a purely competitive environment. Changes in non-competitive factors, as well as changes in technology will tend to cause various growth patterns. Therefore, we will consider special valuation models that allow for finite periods of abnormal growth and for the possibility of different rates of growth.

20. The growth duration model attempts to compute the implied growth duration for a growth firm given differential past growth rates for the market and for the firm and also alternative PIE ratios. These major assumptions of the model are: (1) equal risk between the securities compared; (2) no significant differences in the payout ratio of different firms; and (3) the stock with the higher P/E ratio has the higher growth rate. While the assumption of equal risk may be acceptable when comparing two larger, well-established firms to each other or to a market proxy, it is probably not a valid assumption when comparing a small firm to the aggregate market. Likewise, the assumption of no significant differences in payout ratios could present a problem. For example, many growth firms have low initial payout ratios in order to use retained earnings for future investment projects. It might be inappropriate to compare a well-established company with a new start-up firm on the basis of an equal payout ratio. Finally, while the model assumes that the stock with the higher PIE ratios has the higher growth rate, in many cases you will find that this is not true.

21. The projected growth rate for the company (15%) is above that of the market (8%); however, the growth company also has a lower PIE ratio than the aggregate market. This implies that the stock of the growth company might be undervalued. It would be necessary to investigate the company further to determine if the firm's stock is a growth stock. It is still necessary to estimate the average payout ratio and the ROE and its components for both the firm and the aggregate market in order to make a proper comparison of the growth company to the aggregate market. This should help you determine if it is currently a true growth company and if this performance can be sustained.

Harcourt, Inc.

22. Walgreen seems to illustrate "simple long-run growth" since r>k and b>0. Its failure to observe a constant retention rate precludes "dynamic growth".

23. GM is likely an example of "expansion" since r=k and b>0.

24. In order to use the Mao three-stage growth model, one must make estimates for the retention rate, the required return, the return on growth investments, and the length of time each stage (dynamic growth, simple growth, and declining growth) will last.

25. CFA Examination I (1993)

    The computation of book value is: (assets - liabilities) / # of shares

    Accounting conventions can affect this computation by increasing or decreasing any of the three components: assets, liabilities, or number of shares.

    **Increasing or Decreasing Assets**
    - Accountant's use of historic cost does not recognize the replacement value of assets and is, therefore, not an accurate measurement of an assets value. This is particularly true of real estate assets.
    - Several assets with real economic value are ignored by accountants. Internally developed goodwill, management expertise, market share, and technological innovation are just a few of the assets ignored by accountants.
    - Some assets that are on the balance sheet should not be recognized. Purchased goodwill is an accounting convention that is often placed on or stays on the balance sheet when there is no economic reason for it to exist.
    - Assets can change value for any of the following reasons:
      - Different estimates result in different values (estimates of different asset lives can affect depreciation calculations and then the book value of an asset)
      - Different accounting standards can result in changes in balance sheet values (the decision to adopt SFAS 106 immediately or over 20 years)
      - Adoption of different accounting choices can affect asset values
        - LIFO/FIFO inventory
        - Straight line/accelerated depreciation
        - Short-term/long-term marketable securities
        - Purchase/pooling acquisitions
        - Cost/equity recognition
        - Lower of cost or market
        - Capitalization of costs
        - Pension options
        - Deferral of taxes
        - Foreign currency translations
        - Revenue recognition choices

**Increasing or Decreasing Liabilities**

- Off-balance-sheet liabilities will change book value. Contingent liabilities and off-balance-sheet financing are two such liabilities that sometimes are not included on the balance sheet that should be included.
- Changes in the value of existing liabilities can affect book value. When interest rates change long-term debt which is on the balance sheet does not change even though the economic value of these liabilities do change.

**Increasing or Decreasing # of Shares**

- The existence of warrants or options can increase the number of shares depending upon the decision to include them in the computation of book value or not.
- The purchase or sale of shares at a value different from book value will change book value.

26. CFA Examination II (1995)

26(a). Some arguments for a high dividend payout policy are:

1. **Limited investment opportunities.** If a firm has cash flows greater than those needed to fund projects with positive net present values, it should return the capital to shareholders as higher dividends.

2. **Clientele effect.** Some investors require some income from investments. The higher the dividend, the greater the proportion of investors who will be satisfied with the income of a given investment.

3. **Certainty of dividends versus capital gains.** The "bird in hand" argument says that (a) cash dividends are a definite return whereas capital appreciation is less certain, or (b) investors should apply a lower discount rate to cash dividends versus capital appreciation because dividends are more certain.

4. **Tax effects.** Corporate and tax exempt investors in some tax jurisdictions pay no income tax on dividends.

5. **Informational content.** Management uses the dividend payout policy to communicate the long-term prospects of the corporation.

Some arguments against a high dividend payout policy are:

1. **No effect on value.** A firm's investment decisions determine its profitability. Dividend policy does not affect investment decisions, but it does affect the amount of outside financing needed by a firm.

2. **Less cash available for investments.** Paying high dividends reduces the cash available to finance profitable investment projects. With less internal financing, a firm

Harcourt, Inc.

may resort to external financing to finance projects, which may reduce earnings per share because of greater interest expense or more shares outstanding.

3. **Taxes.** Investors can defer taxes on capital appreciation until realized but pay taxes on dividends (except tax-exempt investors) even if dividends are reinvested. Also, double taxation exists on corporate profits and dividends paid to investors.

4. **Violation of an indenture.** High dividend payouts may violate bond indentures or loan covenants.

5. **Financial distress.** Paying high dividends while financing investment projects may force the firm to increase its leverage ratios and lead to a higher level of risk. This could eventually lead to financial distress.

26(b). The constant growth dividend discount model, $P_0 = D_1/(k - g)$, implies that a stock's value, $P_0$, will be greater

1. the larger its expected dividend per share, $D_1$;
2. the lower the market capitalization rate, k, (also called the required rate of return);
3. the higher the expected growth rate of dividends, g.

The director has ignored the denominator used to convert the dividend to a present value. The denominator consists of two variables, both of which dividend policy could influence. One variable is the market capitalization rate, k, which risk affects. Investors may view a higher dividend payout as increasing risk because a higher payout may lead to an increase in a firm's leverage ratios. The other variable is the expected growth rate of dividends, g, which is likely to be lower if firms pay higher dividends in the short run. In summary, a higher dividend payout may increase k and lower g. Therefore, the statement by the director that the use of dividend discount models by investors is "proof" that "the higher the dividend, the higher the stock p Ace" is potentially misleading and possibly inaccurate.

### 26(c). (i) Internal (implied, normalized, or sustainable) growth rate

The internal-growth rate of dividends, g, is calculated as:

$$g = ROE \times b$$

where: ROE = return on equity
b = plowback or earnings retention ratio (1 -dividend payout ratio).

As the dividend payout ratio increases, the expected growth rate in dividends decreases. If the firm pays out all earnings as dividends, the expected growth rate in dividends would be zero. Valuation would also decrease to the degree investors would pay a lower ratio of price to earnings for the lower growth rate calculated in this manner.

## (ii) Growth in book value

A higher dividend payout ratio would slow the increase in book value (all other factors being equal) because the retained earnings included in stockholders' equity would increase at a slower rate (reflecting the higher dividend payout).

27.  CFA Examination II (1997)

### 27(a). Possible Valuation Decrease

The constant-growth-rate version of the DDM is often expressed as

$$P = \frac{D_1}{K - g} \quad \text{and also} \quad P = \frac{D_0(1 + g)}{K - g} \quad \text{in that} \quad D_1 = D_0(1 + g)$$

in which $D_1$ is next year's dividend per share, $k$ is the required rate of return (sometimes called the internal rate of return), and $g$ is the dividend growth rate.

Soft Corporation's acquisition of a slower-growth competitor might decrease its valuation based on a constant-growth DDM because

- SC's $300 million in new long-term debt and related interest costs decreases the likelihood that the dividend will be increased next year ($D_1$);
- the acquisition of a slower-growth company reduces the acquirer's long-term growth rate for dividends;
- the higher financial leverage resulting from the acquisition will increase the perceived riskiness of SC, raising investors' required rate of return ($k$);
- everything else being equal, these factors (lower dividend growth rate and higher required rate of return) could interact to increase the denominator and decrease the numerator of the DDM.

### 27(b). Possible Increase in P/E Multiple

The acquisition might increase the P/E multiple investors will be willing to pay for SC for the following reasons:

- The acquisition could provide internal sources of growth. *Synergies* (the opportunity for cost cutting, economies of scale, etc.) from the combination might well emerge in time, which would increase the earnings growth rate in the intermediate term. Investors might anticipate this improved growth rate, which would enhance the P/E multiple.
- The acquisition could provide external sources of growth. Particularly if the acquired company is an important direct competitor, investors' perceptions of *reduced competition* and *improved pricing* in the future could lead to a higher multiple on the stock on current earnings.
- The acquisition will add value if returns exceed costs. The use of debt to finance the acquisition will enhance the ROE of SC *if* the incremental profitability exceeds the after-tax cost of debt capital. If investors perceive this higher ROE to be *sustainable,* their expectations for growth and, consequently, the multiple they are willing to pay for the stock are likely to increase.

Harcourt, Inc.

- Investors may decide that the external sources of growth (see above) justify *viewing the riskiness of the combined entity as less than that of SC alone,* which would justify a higher P/E multiple.
- Short-term EPS may drop because of the expenses related to the acquisition, but investors looking beyond this short-term drop may believe that *longer-term earnings growth* prospects have improved. The multiple on current earnings may rise as a result of this expectation.
- If SC is currently underleveraged, the debt load taken on in this acquisition may actually *optimize SC's leverage,* which would produce a lower overall cost of capital and justify a higher P/E multiple.

28.  CFA Examination II (1999)

1    Life of the asset (N). Typically, bonds have a stated maturity. Bond investors will be paid coupons and repaid principal at or before that maturity. The life of the bond is contractually determined and creates an obligation to honor the promised payments. There is no maturity for common stocks; indeed the life of the corporation is assumed to be infinite.

2.   Contractual nature of the cash flows (CF). The contractual nature of bond payments creates an obligation, which makes the estimation of these payments a fairly routine task especially for high quality bonds. Dividend payments on common stocks, on the other hand, are much more difficult to estimate because dividends are discretionary or indeterminate based on factors such as profitability, financial structure, capital expenditures, management discretion, etc.

3.   Appropriate discount rate (k). The discount rate, or required rate of return, reflects the risk of the asset. The required rate of return on a bond is observable and typically determined by comparison with other bonds of similar maturity (as given by the yield curve) and the issuer credit risk (as given by the bond rating). The estimation of the required rate of return for a common stock is more subjective, often relying on an estimated risk proxy such as beta or similar measures of riskiness.

# CHAPTER 20

## Answers to Problems

1.  Student Exercise

2.  Student Exercise

3.  Student Exercise

4(a).  $R_H = .07 + 1.75(.15 - .07) = .07 + .14 = .21$ or 21%

4(b).  $R_H = .07 + 1.75(.10 - .07) = .07 + .0525 = .1225$ or 12.25%

5.  Student Exercise

6.
$$\ln \frac{24}{16} = T \ln \frac{1 + .14 + .02}{1 + .06 + .04}$$

$\ln (1.50) = T \ln (1.16/1.10)$
$\ln (1.50) = T \ln (1.05455)$
$\quad T = \ln (1.50)/\ln (1.05455)$
$\quad T = 0.40547/0.05311$
$\quad T = 7.635$ years

7(a).  $\ln (x) = 10 \ln (1.18/1.08)$
$\ln (x) = 10 \ln (1.09259)$
$\ln (x) = 10 (0.08855)$
$\ln (x) = 0.8855$
$\quad x = 2.424$

Thus, the P/E ratio would be 33.94x (2.424 x 14).

7(b).  $\ln (x) = 5 \ln (1.18/1.08)$
$\ln (x) = 5 \ln (1.09259)$
$\ln (x) = 5 (0.08855)$
$\ln (x) = 0.44275$
$\quad x = 1.55698$

Thus, the P/E ratio would be 21.80x (1.55698 x 14).

Harcourt, Inc.

8(a). <u>Company A</u>

$$\ln \frac{30}{18} = T \ln \frac{1 + .18 + .00}{1 + .07 + .02}$$

ln (1.6667) = T ln (1.18/1.09)
ln (1.6667) = T ln (1.08257)
$\quad$ T = ln (1.667)/ln (1.08257)
$\quad$ T = .51083/.07934
$\quad$ T = 6.44 years

<u>Company B</u>

$$\ln \frac{27}{18} = T \ln \frac{1 + .15 + .01}{1 + .07 + .02}$$

ln (1.50) = T ln (1.16/1.09)
ln (1.50) = T ln (1.06422)
$\quad$ T = ln (1.50)/ln (1.06422)
$\quad$ T = .40547/.06224
$\quad$ T = 6.51 years

8(b).

$$\ln \frac{30}{27} = T \ln \frac{1 + .18 + .00}{1 + .15 + .01}$$

ln (1.11) = T ln (1.18/1.16)
ln (1.11) = T ln (1.01724)
$\quad$ T = ln (1.11)/ln (1.01724)
$\quad$ T = .10536/.01709
$\quad$ T = 6.16 years

8(c). After computing the implied growth durations, the analyst must decide whether the projected growth rates can be sustained over the periods implied in the model. If the implied growth duration is greater than you believe is reasonable, you would likely advise against buying the respective stock.

9. CFA Exam II (June 1981)

9(a). Three factors that must be estimated for any valuation model are:

The expected stream of returns--which is specified for bonds in terms of interest (coupon) and principal payments, but is uncertain for common stocks as dividends are not contractual or precisely predictable.

The time pattern of expected returns--specified for bonds, in terms of semi-annual interest payments and principal payments annually (sinking fund) or at maturity, but is uncertain for common stocks because although dividends may be paid annually, a stock is in effect "perpetual." Maturity value of a bond is known, while the sale price for stock involves an estimate of earnings in that year and P/E that will then prevail, the concept of a terminal P/E is used.

The required rate of return on the investment adjusted for risks is uncertain for both stocks and bonds. For bonds, this generally depends upon the prevailing risk-free rate. For common stocks, given the security market line prevailing at a point in time, and the estimate of the stock's beta with the market portfolio of risky assets, it is possible to derive the return that should be required for the investment.

9(b). The problem in using a dividend valuation model is that growth is a changing phenomenon and cannot be projected to infinity, as indicated in each of the following three types of companies:

1. Constant growth in dividends is unrealistic for a corporation that is subject to cyclical swings in its business.

2. Maturing companies might be experiencing a slowing in the rate of growth of dividends, although some such companies maintain dividend growth by increasing the payout ratio, but this is a short-term phenomenon.

3. Small, rapidly growing companies are not able to sustain above average rates of growth indefinitely.

10. CFA Exam I (June 1985)

The analyst would recommend investing in the lease obligation since, for each dollar invested, the present value of the future cash flows generated by the lease is greater than the present value of the cash flow that will be realized when the stock is sold.

### Present Value of Common Stock

| Year | Cash Flow | PV @ 10% | $ PV |
|------|-----------|----------|------|
| 1 | $0 | .909 | $ 0 |
| 2 | $0 | .826 | 0 |
| 3 | $100,000 x $(1.1)^3$ = $133,100 | .751 | $100,000 |
| | | | $100,000 |

### Present Value of Lease Cash Flow

| Year | Cash Flow | PV @ 10% | $ PV |
|------|-----------|----------|------|
| 1 | $0 | .909 | $ 0 |
| 2 | $15,000 | .826 | 12,390 |
| 3 | $100,000 + $25,000 = $125,000 | .751 | 93,875 |
| | | | $106,265 |

Ratio of common stock PV for $ 1 invested = 1.00
Ratio of lease PV for $1 invested ($106,265/$100,000) = 1.06

11.    CFA Examination I (1990)

11(a). The dividend discount model is

$$P = \frac{d}{k - g}$$

   where:  P = value of the stock today
           d = annual dividend stream
           k = discount rate
           g = constant dividend growth rate

   Solving for k:   (k - g) = d / P
                    k = d/P + g

   So k becomes the estimate for the long-term return of the stock.

   k = ($.60 / $20.00) + 8% = 3% 8% = 11%

11(b).  Many professional investors shy away from the dividend discount framework analysis due to its many inherent complexities.

   1)   The model cannot be used where companies pay very small or no dividends and speculation on the level of future dividends could be futile. (Dividend policy may be arbitrary.)

   2)   The model presumes one can accurately forecast long term growth of earnings (dividends) of a company. Such forecasts become quite tenuous beyond two years out. (A short-term valuation may be more pertinent.)

   3)   For the variable growth models, small differences in g for the first several years produce large differences the valuations.

   4)   The correct k or the discount rate is difficult to estimate for a specific company as an infinite number of factors affect it which are themselves difficult to forecast, e.g., inflation, riskless rate of return, risk premium on stocks and other uncertainties.

   5)   The model is not definable when g > k as with growth companies, so it is not applicable to a large number of companies.

   6)   Where a company has low or negative earnings per share or has a poor balance sheet, the ability to continue the dividend is questionable.

   7)   The components of income can differ substantially, reducing comparability.

11(c). Three alternative methods of valuation would include:
       1) Price/Earnings ratios
       2) Price/Asset value ratios (including market and book asset values)
       3) Price/Sales ratios
       4) Liquidation or breakup value
       5) Price/cash flow ratios

12. CFA Examination I (1992)

12(a). The formula for the constant growth discounted dividend model is shown below:

$$Price = \frac{D_0(1+g)}{k-g} \qquad \text{where } D_0 = \text{current dividend per share}$$

$$\text{For Eastover:} \quad Price = \frac{1.20(1+.08)}{0.11-0.08} = 1.296/.03 = \$43.20$$

This compares with its current stock price of 28. On this basis, it appears that Eastover is undervalued.

12(b). The formula for the two-stage discounted dividend model is as follow:

$$Price = \frac{D_1}{1+k} + \frac{D_2}{(1+k)^2} + \frac{D_3}{(1+k)^3} + \frac{P_3}{(1+k)^3}$$

For Eastover:   $g_1 = .12,$   $g_2 = .08$

| | | | | | | |
|---|---|---|---|---|---|---|
| $D_0$ | = | 1.20 | | | | |
| $D_1$ | = | 1.20 | * | 1.12 | = | 1.34 |
| $D_2$ | = | 1.20 | * | $(1.12)^2$ | = | 1.50 |
| $D_3$ | = | 1.20 | * | $(1.12)^3$ | = | 1.69 |
| $D_4$ | = | $D_3$ | * | (1.08) | = | 1.82 |
| $P_3$ | = | 1.82 / (.11 - .08) | | | = | 60.67 |

$$Price = \frac{1.34}{1.11} + \frac{1.50}{(1.11)^2} + \frac{1.69}{(1.11)^3} + \frac{60.67}{(1.11)^3}$$

$$= 1.2072 + 1.2174 + 1.2357 + 44.3614 = \$48.03$$

This approach indicates that Eastover is even more undervalued than was the case with the constant growth approach.

An alternative solution to the two-stage model is:

$$Price = \frac{D_1}{1+k} + \frac{D_2}{(1+k)^2} + \frac{P_2}{(1+k)^2}$$

| | | | | | | |
|---|---|---|---|---|---|---|
| $D_0$ | = | 1.20 | | | | |
| $D_1$ | = | 1.20 | * | 1.12 | = | 1.34 |
| $D_2$ | = | 1.20 | * | $(1.12)^2$ | = | 1.50 |
| $D_3$ | = | 1.20 | * | $(1.12)^3$ | = | 1.69 |
| $P_2$ | = | 1.69/(.11 - .08) | | | = | 56.33 |

20 - 13

$$\text{Price} = \frac{1.34}{1.11} + \frac{1.50}{(1.11)^2} + \frac{56.33}{(1.11)^2} = 1.21 + 1.22 + 45.72 = \$48.15$$

This answer differs from previous answer because of round off error.

12(c). Constant growth model:

Advantages:
1) logical, theoretical basis
2) simple to compute
3) inputs can be estimated

Disadvantages:
1) very sensitive to inputs of growth
2) g and k difficult to estimate accurately
3) result is meaningless if g > k
4) constant growth is an unrealistic assumption
5) assumes growth will never slow down
6) dividend payout must remain constant
7) not usable for firm not paying dividend
8) assumes stock price will increase at g

Improvements with the two-stage model:
1. The two-stage model is more realistic. It accounts for low, high, or zero growth in the first stage, followed by constant long-term growth in the second stage.
2. The model can solve for stock value when the growth rate in the first stage exceeds the required rate of return.

13.    CFA Examination I (1992)

13(a). In order to determine whether a stock is undervalued or overvalued, analysts often analyze price-earnings ratios (P/Es) and price-book value ratios (P/Bs) as compared to those of the market as represented by the S&P 500 Index. The formulas for these calculations are:

Relative P/E = P/E of specific company /(P/E of S&P500)

Relative P/B = P/B of specific company /(P/B of S&P500)

To evaluate EO and SHC using the relative P/E model, Mulroney should calculate the five year average P/E for each stock, and divide that number by the 5 year average P/E for the S&P 500. This gives the average relative P/E. Mulroney should then compare the average historical relative P/E to the current relative P/E, which is the current P/E on each stock, using 1992 estimated EPS, divided by the current P/E of the market, again using the 1992 estimate.

For the price/book model, Mulroney should make similar calculations, i.e., divide the five year average price/book ratio for a stock into the five year average price/book for the S&P 500, and compare the result to the current relative price/book (using 1991 estimated book value, as that is all that is available).

The results are shown below:

|  |  | EO | SHC | S&P500 |
|---|---|---|---|---|
| P/E Model: | 5 yr. avg. P/E | 16.6x | 11.9x | 15.2x |
|  | Relative B yr. P/E | 1.09x | 0.78x |  |
|  | Current P/E | 17.5x | 16.0x | 20.20x |
|  | Current relative Pie | 0.87x | 0.79x |  |
| Price/Book: | 5 yr. avg. price/book | 1.50x | 1.10x | 2.10x |
|  | Relative 5 yr. p/b | 0.71x | 0.52x |  |
|  | Current price/book | 1.62x | 1.49x | 2.60x |
|  | Current relative p/b | 0.62x | 0.57x |  |

From this analysis, it is evident that EO is trading at a discount to its historical 5 year relative P/E ratio, whereas Southampton is trading right at its historical 5 year relative P/E. With respect to price/book, Eastover is trading at a discount to its historical relative price/book ratio, whereas SHC is trading modestly above its 5 year relative price/book ratio. As noted in the preamble, however, Eastover's book value is understated due to the very low historical cost basis for its timberlands. The fact that Eastover is trading at below its 5 year average relative price to book ratio even though its book value is understated makes Eastover seem especially attractive on a price/book basis.

13(b). Disadvantages of relative P/E model:
1) measures relative, not absolute, value
2) accounting earnings estimate for next fiscal year may not be representative of sustainable earnings
3) no standardization on which earnings to use
4) changing accounting standards may make historical comparisons difficult
5) requires estimating earnings growth for next fiscal year

Disadvantages of relative P/B model:
1) book value may be under or overstated - particularly for a company like Eastover, which has valuable lumberlands on its books carried at low historical cost
2) book value may not be representative of earning power or future growth potential
3) changing accounting standards may make historical comparisons difficult

14. CFA Examination I (1993)

14(a). The formula for a multistage DDM model with two distinct growth stages consisting of a first stage with five years of above-normal constant growth followed by a second stage of normal constant growth is:

$$P = \frac{D_1}{(1+r)^1} + \frac{D_2}{(1+r)^2} + \frac{D_3}{(1+r)^3} + \frac{D_4}{(1+r)^4} + \frac{D_5}{(1+r)^5} + \frac{D_6/(r-g)}{(1+r)^5}$$

$$P = \frac{\$2.29}{(1.10)^1} + \frac{\$2.75}{(1.10)^2} + \frac{\$3.30}{(1.10)^3} + \frac{\$3.96}{(1.10)^4} + \frac{\$4.75}{(1.10)^5} + \frac{\$5.08/(0.10-0.07)}{(1.10)^5}$$

$$P_0 = \$117.62$$

Note: Though referred to as a multistage DDM, the use of the so-called "H-Model" is incorrect in this application. The H-Model assumes that the growth rate declines in a linear fashion from the above-normal growth rate of 20% to the normal growth rate of 7%. The problem as stated, depicts a situation in which the growth rate drops abruptly from 20% to 7% after five years.

14(b). 

| | | | |
|---|---|---|---|
| Philip Morris P/E (12/31/91) = | $80.25 / $4.24 | = | 18.9x |
| S&P500 P/E (12/31/91) = | $417.09 / $16.29 | = | 25.6x |
| Philip Morris relative P/E = | 18.9x / 25.6x | = | 0.74x |

14(c). 

| | | | |
|---|---|---|---|
| Philip Morris book value (12/31/91) = | $12,512 / 920 | = | $13.60 |
| Philip Morris P/B (12/31/95) = | $80.25 / $13.60 | = | 5.90x |
| S&P500 P/B (12/31/95) = | $417.09 / $161.08 | = | 2.59x |
| Philip Morris relative P/B = | 5.90x / 2.59x | = | 2.28x |

15.   CFA Examination I (1993)

15(a). **Multistage Dividend Discount Model**

**Advantages**
1. Excellent for comparing greatly different companies.
2. Solid theoretical framework.
3. Ease in adjusting for risk levels.
4. Dividends relatively easy to project.
5. Dividends not subject to accounting.
6. Flexibility in use and more realistic than constant growth model.

**Disadvantages**
1. Need to forecast well into the future.
2. Problem with non-dividend paying companies.
3. Most investors aren't looking to collect a stream of dividends.
4. Problem with high growth companies (g>k).
5. Problems projecting "forever after" ROE and payout ratio.
6. Small changes in assumptions can have big impact.
7. Need technology for more advanced models.
8. Quality of payouts may differ.

## Absolute and Relative Price/Earnings Ratio

### Advantages
1. Widely used by investors.
2. Easy to compare with market and other companies in specific industries.

### Disadvantages
1. Difficult with volatile companies.
2. Need to determine what is "normal."
3. Difficult to project earnings.
4. Effect of accounting differences.
5. Many factors influence multiples.
6. Can be used only for relative rather than absolute measurement.
7. Point in time "snapshot."
8. Doesn't address quality of earnings.
9. Problem with companies with no income.

## Absolute and Relative Price/Book Ratio

### Advantages
1. Incorporates some concept of asset values.
2. Easy to compute even for companies with volatile or negative earnings.
3. Easy to compare with market and specific industries.

### Disadvantages
1. Subject to differing accounting rules.
2. Effected by non-recurring items and share repurchases.
3. Subject to historical costs.
4. Book may be poor guide to actual asset values.
5. Ignores future earnings prospects and growth potential.

15(b). Support can be given to either position.

Philip Morris is undervalued because:
1. DDM indicates intrinsic value above current market price.
2. Given forecasts of dividends over two stages, DDM is best to use for this situation and should be given more weight.
3. P/E below market despite past growth and forecast of superior future growth.
4. P/E relative below 10-year average.
5. P/B for Philip Morris is high due to share repurchases and FAS 106 having much greater effect than other companies on average.

Philip Morris is overvalued because:
1. P/B considerably higher than market.
2. P/B relative higher than 10-year average.
3. DDM discount rate used should be higher than market's 10% due to large potential risks in cigarette manufacturing business.
4. P/E on Philip Morris should be low relative to market and past growth due to risks inherent in its business.

16. CFA Examination II (1995)

16(a). **Constant growth dividend discount model:** $D_1/(k - g) = P_0$
Litchfield: $\$0.90/(0.10 - 0.08) = \$45.00$
Aminochem: $\$1.60/(0.11 - 0.07) = \$40.00$

16(b). **Expected return:** $R_f + \beta(R_m - R_f) = k$
Litchfield: $5\% + 1.2(20\% - 5\%) = 23\%$
Aminochem: $5\% + 1.4(20\% - 5\%) = 26\%$

16(c). **Internal growth rate:** $[(E- D)/E]\ [E/BV] = g$
Litchfield: $[(\$4.00 - \$0.90)/\$4.00][\$4.00/\$30.00] = 10.3\%$
   $BV = \$300/10 = \$30.00$
Aminochem: $[(\$3.20- \$1.60)/\$3.20][\$3.20/\$16.00] = 10.0\%$
   $BV= \$320/20 = \$16.00$

16(d). **Recommendation:** Aminochem (AOC) is a more attractive investment than Litchfield (LCC) based on the answers to parts A, B, and C, and the information provided in Table 7.

**Justification:** Using the constant growth dividend discount model (DDM) (computed in Part A), the stock price of AOO is more attractive at a price of $30 (well below its DDM value of $40) than LCC at a price of $50 (above the DDM value of $45).

AOC has the higher expected return (computed in Part B) because it has a higher beta and the market (S&P 500) is expected to rise.

LCC's internal growth rate (computed in Part C) is higher than that of AOC, but LCC's higher price-to-earnings ratio of 12.5 ($50/$4) versus 9.4 ($30/$3.20) for AOC is not justified by the small difference in growth rate.

17. CFA Examination II (1997)

17(a). **Ratio Calculation for Jerry's Department Stores (JDS) and Miller Stores (MLS)**

**i. Price-to-book ratio:**

| _Ratio_ | _JDS_ | _MLS_ |
|---|---|---|
| Book value | = $6,000/250 shares | = $7,500/400 shares |
|  | = $24.00 | = $18.75 |
| Price/book value | = $51.50/$24.00 | = $49.50/$18.75 |
|  | = 2.1458x | = 2.6400x |

Harcourt, Inc.

**ii. Total debt to equity for Jerry's Department Stores and Miller Stores**

| Ratio | JDS | MLS |
|---|---|---|
| Total debt to equity | = $0 + $2,700 / $6,000 | = $1,000 + $2,500 / $7,500 |
| | | |
| Total debt = (Short-term debt + Long-term debt) /Equity | = $2,700 / $6,000 = 45.00% | = $3,500 / $7,500 = 46.67% |

**iii.   Fixed-asset utilization (turnover) for Jerry's Department Stores and Miller Stores**

| Ratio | JDS | MLS |
|---|---|---|
| Sales / fixed assets | = $21,250 / $5,700 = 3.7281x | = $18,500 / *$5,500* = 3.3636x |

**17(b).   Investment Choice and Justification Based on Part A**

Based on Westfield's investment criteria for investing in the company with the lowest price-to-book ratio (P/B) and considering solvency and asset utilization ratios, *JDS is the better purchase candidate:*

| Ratio | JDS | MLS | Company Favored |
|---|---|---|---|
| i. Price-to-book ratio (P/B) | 2.14x | 2.64x | JDS: lower P/B |
| ii. Total debt to equity | 45% | 47% | JDS: lower debt or ratios are very similar |
| iii. Asset turnover | 3.73x | 3.36x | JDS: higher turnover |

**17(c).   Balance Sheet Adjustments** (millions)

**Jerry's Department Stores:**
i.   *Leases*-recognition of JDS's present value lease payments will add $1,000 to JDS's property, plant, and equipment (PP&E) and is offset by a $1,000 addition to JDS's long-term debt.

ii.   *Receivables*-recognition of JDS's sale of receivables with recourse will increase assets (accounts receivable) by $800 and short-term debt used to finance accounts receivable by $800.

**Miller's Stores:**
iii.   Inventory -recognition of LIFO inventory reserve will add $700 to assets (inventory) and $700 to owners' equity.

iv.   Pension-recognition of current excess funding for the pension plan will add $1,600 to assets and $1,600 to owners' equity ($3,400 plan assets - $1,800 projected benefit obligation).

Harcourt, Inc.

17(d). **Adjusted Calculations** (millions)

**Jerry's Department Store:**

Needed adjustments:

| Assets | | Liabilities |
|---|---|---|
| (PP&E) | | (Long-term debt [LTD]) |
| +$1,000 | + | $1,000 |
| (Accounts receivable) | | (Short-term debt [STD]) |
| +$800 | | +$800 |

i. *Book value per common share:* No net adjustment to JDS owners' equity of $6,000; thus,

$6,000 / 250 million shares = $24.00 book value per share.

ii. *Adjusted total debt-to-equity ratio:*

| $2,700 | Historical LTD |
|---|---|
| + 1,000 | LTD |
| 800 | STD |
| $4,500 | Adjusted total debt. |

Adjusted debt-to-equity ratio = $4,500 / $6,000 = 75%.

iii. *Fixed-asset utilization* (turnover)

| $5,700 | Historical fixed assets |
|---|---|
| +1,000 | PP&E (JDS leases) |
| $6,700 | JDS adjusted fixed assets |

Adjusted fixed-asset utilization (sales/adjusted fixed assets): $21,250 / $6,700 = 3.17x.

**Miller's Stores:**

Needed adjustments:

| Assets | Owners' Equity |
|---|---|
| (Inventory) | |
| +$700 | +$700 |
| (Pension) | |
| +$1,600 | +$1,600 |

i. *Book value per common share:* $7,500 historical equity + $700 + $1,600 = $9,800 adjusted equity; thus,

$9,800/400 million shares = $24.50 adjusted book value per share

ii.     *Adjusted total debt-to-equity ratio:*

Adjusted debt (no adjustments) / Adjusted equity = Adjusted debt/equity:
$3,500 / $9,800 = 36%

iii.    *Fixed-asset utilization* (turnover):

Sales / Fixed assets (no adjustments): $18,500/$5,500     3.36x

**Summary:**

| Ratio | JDS | MLS |
|---|---|---|
| Adjusted book value | $24.00 | $24.50 |
| Adjusted debt to equity | 75% | 36% |
| Fixed-asset utilization | 3.17x | 3.36x |

### 17(e). **Investment Choice and Justification Based on Part D**

Based on Westfield's investment criteria of investing in the company with the lowest adjusted P/B and considering the adjusted solvency and asset utilization ratios, *MLS is the better purchase candidate:*

| Ratio | JDS | MLS | Company Favored |
|---|---|---|---|
| i. Price to adjusted book | 2.14x[a] | 2.02[b] | MLS - lower adjusted P/B |
| ii. Adjusted debt to equity | 75% | 36% | MLS - lower adjusted debt to equity |
| iii. Fixed-asset utilization | 3.17x | 3.36x | MLS - higher asset utilization |

[a] $51.50/$24.00 = 2.14          [b] $49.50/$24.50 = 2.02

### 18.     CFA Examination II (1998)

### 18(a).  **Conclusion Support**

The following factors from Table 1 support Janet Ludlow's conclusion that the electric toothbrush industry is in the maturity (i.e., late) phase of its industry life cycle:

**Return on equity.** ROE figures for the industry have been generally increasing in the past six years, but the increases are occurring at a decreasing rate.  Therefore, the industry may be in the maturity phase of the industry life cycle.

**Average P/E.**  The price-to-earnings ratio for an industry may be interpreted as a measure of the prospective growth rates in earnings and dividends that are anticipated by the market.  P/Es tend to be quite volatile; therefore, the P/E for an industry should be compared with P/Es for the market as a whole.  As the data in Table 1 indicate, the P/Es for the electric toothbrush industry have been decreasing in the past six years whereas the P/E for the market has nearly doubled.  Investors apparently are becoming less optimistic about the growth prospects for the industry and may be characterizing it as mature.

**Dividend payout ratio.**  Mature industries are characterized by high dividend payout ratios.  Generally, companies pay higher dividends to shareholders when the companies

20 - 21

have fewer opportunities for growth in the market. Dividend payout ratios have been generally increasing in the electric toothbrush industry in the past six years. This characteristic signals an industry in the maturity phase.

*Average dividend yield.* The dividend yield is an important measure because it, and capital gains make up a stock investor's return. There tends to be an inverse relationship between the level of the dividend yield and the anticipated rate of capital gain (growth). The dividend yield for the electric toothbrush industry has been increasing, whereas the market's dividend yield has been declining. Even though the yield for the electric toothbrush industry is still below that of the market, the gap has narrowed substantially. The implication is that investors perceive less growth potential for the industry than in the past and thus are requiring a higher percentage of their return from yield. The evidence is that the electric toothbrush industry is moving toward the maturity phase of the industry life cycle.

### 18(b). Conclusion Refutation
The following factors from Exhibit 1 refute Ludlow's conclusion:

*Growth rate.* An industry growth rate of 10-15% is too high for a mature industry. *Non-U.S. markets.* Some U.S. electric toothbrush companies may be entering fast-growing non-U.S. markets, which remain largely unexploited.
*Mail order sales.* Some manufacturers have created a new niche in the industry by selling electric toothbrushes directly to customers through mail order. Sales for this industry segment are growing at 40% a year.
*Niche markets.* Some electric toothbrush manufacturers continue to develop new, unexploited niche markets in the United States based on company reputation, quality, and service.
*New entrants.* New manufacturers continue to enter the market.

### 19. CFA Examination II (1998)

### 19(a). Criticism of Karen Ludlow's Analysis and Conclusions
QuickBrush has indeed shown higher sales and growth in earnings per share (EPS) than SmileWhite in the past few years; margins are also higher. However, these factors do not make QuickBrush a superior and more profitable company than SmileWhite. Return on equity (ROE) analysis indicates that SmileWhite is more profitable than QuickBrush. SmileWhite has a ROE of 21.4%, which has been stable in the past few years. QuickBrush has a ROE of 11.9%, and the ROE has been declining.

ROE analysis using the DuPont formula shows why SmileWhite is more profitable despite its lower operating margins:

| Component | Definition | QuickBrush | SmileWhite |
|---|---|---|---|
| Tax burden (1 - Tax rate) | Net income/Pretax income | 67.4% | 66.0% |
| Interest burden | Pretax income/EBIT[a] | 1.00x | 0.955x |
| Operating margins | EBIT/Sales | 8.5% | 6.5% |
| Asset turnover | Sales/Assets | 1.42x | 3.55x |
| Leverage | Assets/Equity | 1.47x | 1.48x |
| Return on equity | Net income/Equity | 11.9% | 21.4% |

[a]EBIT = Earnings before interest and taxes

The tax burden, interest burden, and leverage components of ROE are similar for the two companies. Operating margins and asset turnover for the two companies differ significantly. Although SmileWhite's operating margins are lower, it gets far more productivity out of its assets than QuickBrush does; SmileWhite's asset turnover ratio is 3.55x as compared with QuickBrush's asset turnover of 1.42x. Despite QuickBrush's higher operating margins, it does not have better overall profitability because SmileWhite generates higher returns on shareholders' capital.

Sustainable growth evaluation is as important as profitability analysis. Sustainable growth can be defined as Return on equity x Retention rate. Sustainable growth rates for QuickBrush and SmileWhite are as follows:

| | ROE | Retention Rate | Sustainable Growth Rate | | |
|---|---|---|---|---|---|
| QuickBrush | 11.9% x | 100% = | 11.9% | vs. | Ludlow's estimate of 30% |
| SmileWhite | 21.4% x | 0.34% = | 7.4% | vs. | Ludlow's estimate of 10% |

Ludlow has overestimated the sustainable growth rate for both companies. For QuickBrush to grow 30%, its ROE would have to increase substantially from current levels. But QuickBrush is currently retaining all of its earnings and, therefore, cannot improve its sustainable growth rate by adjusting its retention rate.

SmileWhite, on the other hand, has the ability to improve its growth rate by increasing its retention rate.

Ludlow's analysis ignored the impact of payout ratios on sustainable growth. SmileWhite currently pays out 66% of EPS to shareholders as dividends. If SmileWhite retained 100% of earnings and did not pay a dividend, its theoretical sustainable growth rate would increase to 21.4%. Practically, this rate would of course, depend on SmileWhite's ability to reinvest additional retained earnings at its current ROE. SmileWhite may not have the reinvestment opportunities that QuickBrush has, which is why it pays out 66% of its earnings to shareholders. Furthermore, like QuickBrush, SmileWhite can also increase its growth rate by improving its ROE.

In summary, although QuickBrush's current sustainable growth rate is higher than SmileWhite's, changes in SmileWhite's discretionary dividend payout ratio could lead to a higher sustainable growth rate for SmileWhite.

20 - 23

19(b). **Explanation of QuickBrush's ROE**

QuickBrush's EPS growth in the past two years has been by increasing-its book value per share at a high and probably unsustainable rate.

Because EPS equals book value per share times ROE, EPS growth depends on increases in either or both of these variables. In QuickBrush's case, ROE is low and declining but book value per share has increased twofold to threefold in the past two years.

Companies can increase book value per share in two ways: (1) retaining earnings and/or (2) issuing additional stock at a market price greater than book value. QuickBrush has been retaining all of its earnings, but this cannot account for the rapid growth in book value. Rather, the increase in the number of shares outstanding indicates that QuickBrush has raised book value by issuing a substantial amount of stock in the past few years. Furthermore, its high average annual P/E in the past few years indicates that QuickBrush has been able to issue that stock at relatively high prices compared with book value. QuickBrush's 40% EPS growth rate may not be possible in the long run if its P/E continues to decline in line with the industry. Only when new stock is priced above book value is the effect of new stock anti-dilutive (i.e., increases EPS).

20. CFA Examination II (1998)

The following Completed template shows QuickBrush's 1998 projected income statement constructed by the percent-of-sales forecasting method:

QuickBrush
Projected Income Statement for 1998
($ 000 except per share data)

| | | |
|---|---|---|
| Revenues | 10,088 | 30% growth x 1997 revenues |
| Cost of goods sold | 7,893 | 78.24% x 1998 projected revenues |
| Selling, general, and administration | 1,328 | 13.16% x 1998 projected revenues |
| Depreciation and amortization | 69 | 2% of 1997 property, plant, & equipment |
| Operating income | 798 | |
| Interest expense | 0 | Given |
| Income before taxes | 798 | |
| Taxes | 271 | 34% of Income before taxes |
| Income after taxes | 527 | |
| Earnings per share | $1.40 | Income after taxes divided by 376,000 shares |

Harcourt, Inc.

21. CFA Examination II (1998)

21(a). **Required Rate of Return: SmileWhite**

The required rate of return is the risk-free rate + beta x (the market return - the risk-free rate):

$$k = R_f + \beta(Rm - R_f)$$
$$= 0.045 + 1.15(0.145 - 0.045)$$
$$= 16.0\%.$$

21(b). **Intrinsic Value: SmileWhite**

The formula is

$$P_0 = \sum_{t=1}^{N} \frac{D_t}{(1+k)^t} + \frac{D_{N+1}}{k-g} \; X \; \frac{1}{(1+k)^N}$$

where
$D_t$ = Dividend at time t
$k$ = Required rate of return
$g$ = Dividend growth rate

Assumptions:

|  |  | Growth Period 1 | Growth Period 2 |
|---|---|---|---|
| $R_f$ | Risk-free rate | 4.50% | Same |
| $R_m$ | Return for market | 14.50% | Same |
| β | Beta | *1.15* | Same |
| g | Dividend growth rate | 12.00% | 9.00% |
| k | Required rate of return | 16.00% | Same |

According to the two-stage DDM, the intrinsic value of a share of stock is equal to the present value of dividends during the first growth period plus the present value of the stock price at the end of the first growth period.

Estimate of future dividends

| Year | $D_{t-1}$ x (1 + g) | | $D_t$ |
|---|---|---|---|
| 1998 | $1.72 x 1.12 | = | $1.93 |
| 1999 | $1.93 x 1.12 | = | $2.16 |
| 2000 | $2.16 x 1.12 | = | $2.42 |
| 2001 | $2.42 x 1.09 | = | $2.64 |

Present Value of the first three dividends

| Year | $D_t$ | x | Present Value Factor | = | Present Value of Dividends |
|---|---|---|---|---|---|
| 1998 | $1.93 | x | $(1/(1+0.16)^1)$ | = | $1.66 |
| 1999 | $2.16 | x | $(1/(1+0.16)^2)$ | = | $1.61 |
| 2000 | $2.42 | x | $(1/(1+0.16)^3)$ | = | $1.55 |
|  |  |  |  |  | $4.82 |

Price at the end of 2000 $\dfrac{D_{2001}}{k - g} = \dfrac{\$2.64}{(0.16 - 0.09)} = \$37.71$

Present Value of Stock Price at end of 2000 $= \$37.71 \times (1/(1 + 0.16)^3) = \$24.16$

SmileWhite's Intrinsic Value $= \$4.82 + 24.16 = \$28.98$

## 21(c). Recommendation

Janet Ludlow should recommend **QuickBrush** stock for purchase because it is selling below Ludlow's estimate of intrinsic value, whereas SmileWhite is selling above Ludlow's estimate of intrinsic value. QuickBrush has a positive expected return based on the comparison of its intrinsic value with its current market price, whereas SmileWhite has a negative expected return.

### Calculations:

SmileWhite: Intrinsic value $= \$28.98$ vs. current market price $= \$30.00$

Estimated return: $(\$28.98 - \$30.00)/\$30.00 = -3.40\%$

QuickBrush: Intrinsic value $= \$63.00$ vs. current market price $= \$45.00$

Estimated return: $(\$63.00 - \$45.00)/\$45.00 = 40\%$

## 21(d). DDM Strengths and Weaknesses

***Strengths of the two-stage DDM in comparison with the constant-growth DDM.*** The DDM is extremely sensitive to the estimated growth rate, $g$. The two-stage model allows for a separate valuation of two distinct periods in a company's future. As a result, a company such as QuickBrush can be evaluated in light of an anticipated change in sustainable growth. Industries have distinct life cycles in which they typically move from a period of rapid growth, to normal growth, and then to declining growth. The two-stage model has many of the same problems as the constant-growth model, but it is probably a more realistic approach than assuming a constant growth rate for all time.

The use of a two-stage model is a key valuation tool, in that analysts with superior insight into a potential shift in a company's growth rate at a future date can use that expectation to assess the proper valuation of each stage.

***Weaknesses inherent in all DDMS.*** All DDM models are extremely sensitive to input values. For example, small changes in the growth rate estimates, $g$, and/or required rate of return, $k$, lead to large changes in a stock's estimated value. These inputs are difficult to estimate and may be based on unrealistic assumptions.

20 - 26

22.	CFA Examination II (1998)

Based on the information in Exhibit 3, SmileWhite apparently has the higher quality of earnings-for the following reasons:

- SmileWhite amortizes its *goodwill* over a shorter period than does QuickBrush. SmileWhite, therefore, presents more conservative earnings by including larger amounts of goodwill expense than would be recognized if a longer amortization period were used. Thus, SmileWhite's quality of earnings is higher.

- SmileWhite depreciates its *property, plant, and equipment* using an accelerated method, whereas QuickBrush uses a straight-line method. SmileWhite is thus recognizing a larger amount of depreciation expense sooner. Again, the company's income is thus more conservatively stated than QuickBrush's, and SmileWhite, therefore, has the higher quality of earnings.

- SmileWhite's *bad debt allowance* is higher as a percentage of receivables than is QuickBrush's. SmileWhite is recognizing higher bad-debt expenses than QuickBrush. Assuming that there is no substantial difference between the two firms in actual experience for collections, SmileWhite has the higher quality of earnings.

Each of SmileWhite's conservative accounting policies may lead to underreporting of current income because of accelerated recognition of expenses and losses.

23.	CFA Examination II (1998)

23(a).	Security Market Line

i.	*Fair-value plot.* The following template shows, using the CAPM, the expected return, ER, of Stock A and Stock B on the SML. The points are consistent with the following equations:

ER on stock = Risk-free rate + Beta x (Market return – Risk-free rate)

ER for A  = 4.5% + 1.2(14.5% - 4.5%)

= 16.5%

ER for B  = 4.5% + 0.8(14.5% - 4.5%)

= 12.5%

ii.	*Analyst estimate plot.* Using the analyst's estimates, Stock A plots below the SML and Stock B, above the SML.

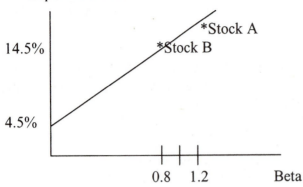

Expected Return

14.5%

4.5%

*Stock A

*Stock B

0.8   1.2         Beta

23(b).  Over vs. Undervalue

**Stock A is overvalued** because it should provide a 16.5% return according to the CAPM whereas the analyst has estimated only a 16.5% return.

**Stock B is undervalued** because it should provide a 12.5% return according to the CAPM whereas the analyst has estimated a 14% return.

24.   CFA Examination II (1999)

24(a)(i) Return on Equity (ROE) = Profit Margin X Asset Turnover X Financial Leverage
*OR*
ROE = (Net Income/Revenue) X (Revenue/Assets) X (Assets/Equity)

(ii) ROE= 510/5140      X 5140/3100 X 3100/2200
          9.9%   X   1.66 X   1.41     = 23.16%

Balance sheet averages may be used for assets and equity.  The calculations become
ROE= 510/5140 X   5140/3025  X   3025/2150
        9.9%       X    1.70 X    1.41   = 23.73%

Beginning of period equity may also be used in calculating leverage as shown below:
ROE= 510/5140 X   5140/3100  X   3100/2100
        9.9%       X    1.66 X    1.48   = 24.32%

(iii) Sustainable Growth = ROE  X  Retention Ratio (RT)
      where RT= 1 - Div. P/O Ratio   or P/O = .60/1.96 = .306; RT= I- .306 = .694

          23.16% X .694 =16.07%   (using end of period balances)
      or 23.73% X .694 =16.47%   (using average assets and equity)
      or 24.32% X .694 =16.88%   (using beginning equity)

24(b).  If the problem were temporary, management could simply accumulate resources in anticipation of future growth.  However, assuming this trend continues longer-term as the

20 - 28

question stated, there are four alternative courses of action that management can take when actual growth falls below sustainable growth:

1. Acquire, merge with, or invest in another company (buy growth). Investing internally is acceptable if the core concepts of increasing earnings growth and using excess cash flow are discussed.
2. Return cash to shareholders by increasing the dividend or the dividend payout ratio
3. Return cash to shareholders by buying back stock
4. Reduce liabilities (decrease leverage or pay off debt)

# CHAPTER 21

## TECHNICAL ANALYSIS

### Answers to Questions

1.  The principle contention of technicians is that stock prices move in trends that persist for long periods of time. Because these trends persist they can be detected by analyzing past prices.

2.  Technicians expect trends in stock price behavior because they believe that new information that causes a change in the relationship between supply and demand does not come to the market at one point in time--i.e., they contend that some investors get the information before others. Also, they believe that investors react gradually over time to new information. The result is a gradual adjustment of stock prices.

3.  The problems encountered when doing a fundamental analysis of financial statements are: (1) much of the information in financial statements is not useful; (2) there are comparability problems for firms using alternative accounting practices; and (3) there are important psychological factors not included in financial statements. Also, with technical analysis it is not necessary to invest until the move to a new equilibrium begins.

4.  The disadvantages of technical analysis are: (1) past price patterns may not be repeated in the future; (2) the intense competition of those using the trading rules will render the technique useless; (3) the trading rules require a great deal of subjective judgment; and (4) the values that signal action are constantly changing.

5.  The mutual fund cash position of 12 percent is relatively high. This would indicate a bullish market because: (1) the theory of contrary-opinion states that mutual funds are the odd-lot trader of the institutional market and typically make the wrong decision by holding excess cash near a trough when they should be fully invested; and (2) the large cash positions of mutual funds represent potential buying power.

6.  Credit balances result when investors sell securities and leave the proceeds with their broker with the intent of reinvesting the funds shortly. Therefore, they can be considered a source of potential buying power. Given this line of reasoning, a decline in credit balances would indicate a decline in potential buying power that is bearish. Another line of reasoning is based on contrary opinion. It is assumed that these balances are generally maintained by small investors who draw them down to invest at the peak, so this is bearish for the contrary opinion technician.

7.  This index indicates what proportion of investment advisory services are bearish and 61 percent is a fairly high ratio. To a contrary opinion technician this is bullish because so many of the services are bearish.

21 - 1

8.    When the ratio of specialist short sales to total short sales is equal to 70 percent, it is relatively high. The technician would consider this bearish because specialists are aggressively selling short and they make good decisions--i.e., you want to follow the smart money. In contrast, if odd-lot short sales increase, it would be bullish because the odd-lotter is typically wrong so when they become very bearish it is probably near the trough.

9.    Debit balances represent borrowing by sophisticated investors, therefore, higher debit balances indicate optimism on the part of these investors. The problem with the debit balance measure is that it only represents borrowing through brokers and it ignores the amount of borrowing from alternative sources.

10.   The Dow Theory contends that stock prices move in waves. Specifically, these waves may be grouped into three categories based upon the period of the wave: (1) major trends for long periods (tides); (2) intermediate trends (waves); and (3) short-run movements for very short periods (ripples). The major trend (the tide) is most important to investors. An intermediate reversal occurs when some investors decide to take profits.

11.   The direction of a price movement accompanied by high volume is more important than if the same price change is associated with light volume. If prices decline (advance) on heavy volume it is bearish (bullish) since it indicates numerous sellers (buyers).

12.   The breadth of the market index is a time series calculated as the cumulative number of net advances or net declines. It indicates a peak or trough in stock prices prior to the peak (or trough) in the aggregate price series by indicating a broadly based decline in the majority of individual stocks. The technician would expect that at a turning point this decline (advance) in the breadth index would be moving in the opposite direction of a rising (falling) market price index series -i.e., the aggregate price series would still be rising (falling) when most individual stocks are beginning to decline (advance).

13.   Technicians following the breadth of market rules might interpret the event as indicative of a possible market peak. Since the DJIA is a value-weighted series confined to 30 large well-known stocks, the past trading period indicates that while the large stocks are still advancing, the majority of individual issues are declining. Due to the technical analyst's belief that information is disseminated on an unequal basis, the technicians would interpret a net cumulative decline as a sign of a market turn that has not been interpreted yet by small investors who hold funds of the large, well-known stocks.

14.   A support level is a price range where considerable demand is expected, while a resistance level is a price range where a large supply is expected. Support and resistance levels exist due to the behavior of a number of investors who are closely monitoring the market and will trade quickly at attractive price levels. Specifically, a support level occurs after a stock has increased in price followed by a brief period of profit-taking at which time some investors who did not get in on the first round decide to take the opportunity to get in. A resistance level occurs after a stock has declined and when it

21 - 2

experiences a recovery, some investors who missed selling at a price peak take the opportunity to sell.

A price break through a resistance level on strong volume would be considered very bullish. This is because as the price rises to the target price set by investors, the supply increases usually causing the price increase to reverse. Thus, a price breakthrough on strong volume would be bullish because it would mean the excess supply is gone.

15.   A moving average line indicates the major trend of a security's price. When daily prices break through the long-term trend from below on heavy volume it is considered a bullish action. The move above the trend line may indicate a new upward change in the trend.

16.   If current prices break through the 50-day MA line from above on heavy volume, technicians would expect a reversal of a rising trend and become bearish. If the 50-day MA line crosses the 200-day MA line from above on good volume, technicians would again expect a reversal in rising prices and become bearish.

17.   Relative strength is the ratio of a firm's stock price to a market price series. If the relative strength ratio is increasing during a bear market it means that the stock is not declining as much as the aggregate market. Under such favorable conditions, the technician would expect the stock to likewise outperform the market in the ensuing bull market.

18.   Technicians recognize that there is no single technical trading rule that is correct all the time--even the best ones miss certain turns or give false signals. Also, various indicators provide different information for alternative segments of the market. Therefore, you don't want to depend on any one technique, but look at several and derive a consensus.

Harcourt, Inc.

# CHAPTER 21

## Answers to Problems

1.   Student Exercise

2.   Student Exercise

3.   Student Exercise

4.   40
     39
     38 X 0
     37 X 0
     36 X 0
     35 X 0
     34 X 0
     33 X 0
     32 X 0
     31 X 0
     30 X 0 X
     29 X 0 X
     28 X 0 X
     27 X 0 X
     26 X 0 X
     25 X
     24 X
     23 X

The price of the stock went to 38 1/2 before declining.  Therefore, at the current price of around 30, the chart could imply a buying opportunity since the price has risen recently from 26 to 30 without a reversal.

5.   Day 4  =  $(11,010 + 11,100 + 11,165 + 11,080)/4 = 44,355/4 = 11,088.75$

     Day 5  =  $(11,100 + 11,165 + 11,080 + 11,070)/4 = 44,415/4 = 11,103.75$

     Day 6  =  $(11,165 + 11,080 + 11,070 + 11,150)/4 = 44,465/4 = 11,116.25$

     Day 7  =  $(11,080 + 11,070 + 11,150 + 11,220)/4 = 44,520/4 = 11,130.00$

     Day 8  =  $(11,070 + 11,150 + 11,220 + 11,130)/4 = 44,570/4 = 11,142.50$

     Day 9  =  $(11,150 + 11,220 + 11,130 + 11,250)/4 = 44,750/4 = 11,187.50$

Day 10 = $(11,220 + 11,130 + 11,250 + 11,315)/4 = 44,915/4 = 11,228.75$

Day 11 = $(11,130 + 11,250 + 11,315 + 11,240)/4 = 44,935/4 = 11,233.75$

Day 12 = $(11,250 + 11,315 + 11,240 + 11,310)/4 = 45,115/4 = 11,278.75$

6.

| Day | 1 | 2 | 3 | 4 | 5 |
|---|---|---|---|---|---|
| Net advances (advances minus declines) | +448 | +95 | +519 | -499 | -193 |
| Cumulative net advances | +448 | +543 | +1062 | +563 | +370 |

# CHAPTER 22

# EQUITY PORTFOLIO MANAGEMENT STRATEGIES

## Answers to Questions

1.  Passive portfolio management strategies have grown in popularity because investors are recognizing that the stock market is fairly efficient and that the costs of an actively managed portfolio are substantial.

2.  Numerous studies have shown that the majority of portfolio managers have been unable to match the risk-return performance of stock or bond indexes. Following an indexing portfolio strategy, the portfolio manager builds a portfolio that matches the performance of an index, thereby reducing the costs of research and trading.

    In an indexing strategy, the portfolio manager's evaluation is based upon how closely the portfolio tracks the index or "tracking error," rather than a risk-return performance evaluation.

3.  There are a number of active management strategies discussed in the chapter including sector rotation, the use of factor models, quantitative screens, and linear programming methods.

    Following a sector rotation strategy, the manager over-weights certain economic sectors, industries or other stock attributes in anticipation of an upcoming economic period or the recognition that the shares are undervalued.

    Using a factor model, portfolio managers examine the sensitivity of stocks to various economic variables. The managers then "tilt" the portfolios by trading those shares most sensitive to the analyst's economic forecast.

    Through the use of computer databases and quantitative screens, portfolio managers are able to identify groups of stocks based upon a set of characteristics.

    Using linear programming techniques, portfolio managers are able to develop portfolios that maximize objectives while satisfying linear constraints.

4.  Three basic techniques exist for constructing a passive portfolio: (1) full replication of an index is where all securities in the index are purchased proportionally to their weight in the index; (2) in sampling the portfolio managers purchases only a sample of the stocks in the benchmark index; and (3) quadratic optimization or programming techniques utilize computer programs that analyze historical security information in order to develop a portfolio that minimizes tracking error.

5. Managers attempt to add value to their portfolio by: (1) timing their investments in the various markets in light of market forecasts and estimated risk premiums; (2) shifting funds between various equity sectors, industries, or investment styles in order to catch the next "hot" concept; and (3) stockpicking of individual issues (buy low, sell high).

6. The job of an active portfolio manager is not easy. In order to succeed, the manager should maintain his/her investment philosophy, "don't panic." Since the transaction costs of an actively managed portfolio typically account for 1 to 2 percent of the portfolio assets, the portfolio must earn 1-2 percent above the passive benchmark just to keep even. Therefore, it recommended that a portfolio manager attempt to minimize the amount of portfolio trading activity. Numerous portfolio turnovers will result in diminishing portfolio profits due to growing commission costs.

7. The four asset allocation strategies are: (1) integrated asset allocation strategy, which relies on current market expectations; (2) strategic asset allocation strategy, which utilizes long-run projections; (3) tactical asset allocation strategy, which assumes that investor's objectives and constraints remain constant over the planning horizon; and (4) insured asset allocation strategy, which presumes changes in investor's objectives and constraints as market conditions change.

8. CFA Examination III (1994)

   Value-oriented investors (1) focus on the current price per share, specifically, the price of the stock is valued as "inexpensive"; (2) not be concerned about current earnings or the fundamentals that drive earnings growth; and/or (3) implicitly assume that the P/E ratio is below its natural level and that the (an efficient) market will soon recognize the low P/E ratio and therefore drive the stock price upward (with little or no change in earnings).

   Growth-oriented investors (1) focus on earnings per share (EPS) and what drives that value; (2) look for companies that expect to exhibit rapid EPS growth in the future; and/or (3) implicitly assume that the P/E ratio will remain constant over the near term, that is, stock price (in an efficient market) will rise as forecasted earnings growth is realized.

9. Stock-market index portfolios are probably more difficult to construct and maintain because securities must frequently be bought and sold in order to reflect cash inflows and outflows, company mergers and acquisitions, etc.

10. There are tradeoffs between using the full replication and the sampling method. Fully replicating an index is more difficult to manage and has higher trading commission costs, when compared to the sampling method. However, tracking error occurs from sampling, which should not be the case in the full replication of the index.

11. The portfolio manager could emphasize or overweight, relative to the benchmark, investments in natural resource stocks. The portfolio manager could also purchase options on natural resource stocks.

22 - 2

# CHAPTER 22

## Answers to Problems

1. $50 million x 1.2 x 1.10 = 66 million

2.

| Month | Portfolio ($R_i$) | $R_i - E(R_i)$ | S&P 500 ($R_m$) | $R_m - E(R_m)$ | $[R_i - E(R_i)]$ x $[R_m - E(R_m)]$ |
|-------|-------|-------|-------|-------|-------|
| Jan | 5.0% | 4.7583 | 5.2% | 5.0333 | 23.9500 |
| Feb | -2.3 | -2.5417 | -3.0 | -3.1667 | 8.0488 |
| Mar | -1.8 | -2.0417 | -1.6 | -1.7667 | 3.6071 |
| Apr | 2.2 | 1.9583 | 1.9 | 1.7333 | 3.3943 |
| May | 0.4 | 0.1583 | 0.1 | -0.0667 | -0.0106 |
| Jun | -0.8 | -1.0417 | -0.5 | -0.6667 | 0.6945 |
| Jul | 0.0 | -0.2417 | 0.2 | 0.0333 | -0.0080 |
| Aug | 1.5 | 1.2583 | 1.6 | 1.4333 | 1.8035 |
| Sep | -0.3 | -0.5417 | -0.1 | -0.2667 | 0.1445 |
| Oct | -3.7 | -3.9417 | -4.0 | -4.1667 | 16.4239 |
| Nov | 2.4 | 2.1583 | 2.0 | 1.8333 | 3.9568 |
| Dec | 0.3 | 0.0583 | 0.2 | 0.0333 | 0.0019 |
| Sum | 2.9 | | 2.0 | | 62.0067 |

$E(R_i) = 2.9/12 = .2417$ 　　　　　 $E(R_m) = 2.0/12 = .1667$

$Var_i = 60.3490/12 = 5.0291$ 　　　 $Var_m = 64.7865/12 = 5.3989$

$\sigma_i = \sqrt{5.0291} = 2.246$ 　　　　 $\sigma_m = \sqrt{5.39889} = 2.3236$

$COV_{i,m} = 62.0067/12 = 5.1672$

$R_{i,m} = \dfrac{5.1672}{(2.24260)(2.3236)} = .9916$ 　　　 $R^2 = (.9916)^2 = .9833$

$\beta_i = \dfrac{5.1672}{5.3989} = .9571$

$\alpha = E(R_i) - (B_i \times E(R_m)) = .2417 - (.9571)(.1667) = .0822$

With a $R^2$ value of .9833, one can conclude that the passive portfolio did closely track the S&P 500 benchmark. The tracking errors were +0.9% (with sign) and 3.3% (without).

3. The annual geometric mean for the equity risk premium is 6.9 percent. Trading costs of 1.5 percent is equal to 21.74% of the equity risk premium.

4. CFA Examination III (1992)

4(a). The following arguments could be made in favor of <u>active management</u>.

Economic diversity – the diversity of the Otunian economy across various sectors may offer the opportunity for the active investor to employ 'top down', sector rotation strategies.

High transaction costs – very high transaction costs may discourage trading activity by international investors and lead to inefficiencies that may be exploited successfully by active investors.

Good financial disclosure and detailed accounting standards – good financial disclosure and detailed accounting standards may provide the well-trained analyst an opportunity to perform fundamental research analysis to identify inefficiently priced securities.

Capital restrictions – restrictions on capital flows may discourage foreign investor participation and serve to segment the Otunian market, thus creating exploitable market inefficiencies for the active investor.

Developing economy and securities market – developing economies and markets are often characterized by inefficiently priced securities and by rapid economic change and growth; these characteristics may be exploited by the active investor, especially one using a 'top down', longer-term approach.

Settlement problems – long delays in settling trades by non-residents may serve to discourage international investors, leading to inefficiently priced securities that may be exploited by active management.

Potential deregulation of capital restrictions – potential deregulation of key industries in Otunia (media and transportation, for example) may be anticipated by active management.

Poorly constructed index – a common characteristic of emerging country indices is domination by very large capitalization stocks which may not capture the diversity of the markets or economy; to the extent that the Otunian index exhibits this poor construction, active management would be favored.

Marketing appeal – it would be consistent for GAC, and appealing to GAC's clients, if GAC were to develop local Otunian expertise in a regional office (similar to GAC's other regional offices) to conduct active management of Otunian stocks.

The following arguments could be made in favor of <u>indexation</u>.

22 - 4

Economic diversity – economic diversity across a broad sector of industries implies that indexing may provide a diverse representative portfolio that is not subject to the risks associated with concentrated sectors.

High transaction costs – indexation would be favored by the implied lower levels of trading activity and thus costs.

Settlement problems – indexation would be favored by the implied lower levels of trading activity and thus settlement activity.

Financial disclosure and accounting standards – wide public availability of reliable financial information presumably leads to greater market efficiency, reducing the value of both fundamental analysis and active management and favoring indexation.

Restrictions of capital flows – indexation would be favored by the implied lower levels of trading activity and thus smaller opportunity for regulatory interference.

Lower management fees – clients would receive the benefit of GAC's cost savings by paying lower management fees for indexation than for regulatory interference.

4(b). A recommendation for active management would focus on short-term inefficiencies in and long term prospects for the developing Otunian markets and economy, inefficiencies and prospects which would not be easily found in more developed markets.

A recommendation for indexation would focus on the factors of economic diversity, high transaction costs, settlement delays, capital flow restrictions, and lower management fees.

5.   CFA Examination III (1995)

Reasons NewSoft shares may not be overvalued compared with shares of Capital Corporation, despite NewSoft's higher ratios of price to earnings (P/E) and ratios of price to book (P/B) include:

**Higher P/E**

1 . **Prices reflect expected future earnings.** If NewSoft's earnings are growing faster than Capital Corp.'s, a higher P/E would be justified.

2.  **Different accounting practices.** Accounting practices affect P/Es based on accounting profits because companies often have different accounting practices (e.g., LIFO/FIFO, depreciation policy, and expense recognition). Historical accounting decisions (e.g., writeoffs) may also affect P/Es. Adjustments for such differences may be required before relative valuations can be properly assessed.

3.  **Cyclical behavior.** Given the cyclical nature of the capital goods sector, the P/E ratio for Capital Corp. may have declined below its five-year average only because recent earnings have risen to a level that analysis indicates is unsustainable.

4. **Difference between accounting and economic profits.** Accounting profits used to calculate P/Es can differ from economic profits and may or may not be sustainable. NewSoft's earnings performance may be understated (e.g., by expensing noncash items such as goodwill). Capital Corp.'s earnings performance may be overstated (e.g., by using low-cost tiers of LIFO inventory).

5. **Differences in industries.** Different industries have different valuation levels given by the market. NewSoft is a technology company, but Capital Corp. is a capital goods company.

6. **Young versus mature industries.** Industries at different points in their life cycles will have different valuations. Young industries often have higher valuations.

**Higher P/B**

1. **Off-balance-sheet assets.** NewSoft may have significant off-balance-sheet assets that are reflected in its stock price but not in its book value. P/Bs have little interpretive value in situations in which intellectual property and human capital are key aspects to company success (e.g., the software industry). Physical plant and equipment are typically small, resulting in high P/Bs.

2. **Nature of assets.** Although physical plant and equipment presumably are a larger portion of Capital Corp.'s total value, the nature of its assets will also affect the validity of using book value as a measure of economic value. Assets such as goodwill and plant and equipment may vary greatly in their balance sheet cost versus economic value. For example, Capital Corp.'s balance sheet might include significant goodwill, raising the company's book value but not its stock price.

3. **Efficient use of assets.** The P/B does not show how efficiently either company is using its assets. To the extent that NewSoft is generating a higher margin of profit with its assets, a higher P/B may be justified.

4. **Obsolete assets.** Some of Capital Corp.'s assets may be functional but obsolete. The company's lower P/B may merely reflect the limited market value of its plant and equipment and the prospective costs of replacement.

6(a). $EU_{pk} = ER_p - (\sigma_p^2/RT_k)$

| Portfolios | Ms. A | Mr. B |
|---|---|---|
| 1 | 8 - (5/8) = 7.38 | 8 - (5/27) = 7.81 |
| 2 | 9 - (10/8) = 7.75 | 9 - (10/27) = 8.63 |
| 3 | 10 - (16/8) = 8.00 | 10 - (16/27) = 9.41 |
| 4 | 11 - (25/8) = 7.88 | 11 - (25/27) = 10.07 |

6(b). Portfolio 3 represents the optimal strategic allocation for Ms. A, while Portfolio 4 is the optimal allocation for Mr. B. Since Mr. B has a higher risk tolerance, he is able to pursue more volatile portfolios with higher expected returns.

22 - 6

6(c).    For Ms. A:    Portfolio 1 = Portfolio 2

$$8 - (5/RT) = 9 - (10/RT)$$
$$RT = 2$$

In other words, a risk tolerance factor of 2 would leave Ms. A in different between having Portfolio 1 or Portfolio 2 as her strategic allocation.

7.    CFA Examination II (1995)

Whether active asset allocation among countries could consistently outperform a world market index depends on the degree of international market efficiency and the skill of the portfolio manager. Investment professionals often view the basic issue of international market efficiency in terms of cross-border financial market *integration or segmentation*. An integrated world financial market would achieve international efficiency in the sense that arbitrage across markets would take advantage of any new information throughout the world. In an efficient integrated international market, prices of all assets would be in line with their relative investment values.

Some claim that international markets are not integrated, but segmented. Each national market might be efficient, but factors might prevent international capital flows from taking advantage of relative mispricing among countries. These factors include psychological barriers, legal restrictions, transaction costs, discriminatory taxation, political risks, and exchange risks.

Markets *do not* appear fully integrated or fully segmented. Markets may or may not become more correlated as they become more integrated since other factors help to determine correlation. Therefore, the degree of international market efficiency is an empirical question that has not yet been answered.

8.    CFA Examination III (1995)

8(a).    The primary characteristics of Constant Mix, Constant Proportion, and Buy and Hold strategies that are related to changes in market values follow.

    1. **Constant mix.** The Constant Mix Strategy maintains a constant percentage exposure to all asset classes at all levels of wealth. The portfolio must be rebalanced to return to its target mix whenever asset values change significantly. Therefore, assets of one class are purchased when their value falls, while assets of another class are sold when their value rises. This strategy is typical of contrarian investors: More funds are put at risk in the asset class whose values have declined, which implies that the investors' risk tolerance is constant. This "buy low, sell high" strategy supplies liquidity to the markets.

    **Market environment for best relative performance.** The Constant Mix Strategy will provide the best relative performance when the capital markets are volatile and trendless (alternatively, choppy and featuring mean reversion).

2. **Constant proportion.** The Constant Proportion Strategy uses "portfolio insurance." Fewer funds are left in the high-risk asset as wealth falls. A floor amount is established, which is invested entirely in low-risk (or risk-free) assets when the market value of the portfolio is equal to the amount of the floor. The remainder of the portfolio is invested in high-risk assets in some multiple of the difference between the floor amount and the market value of the total portfolio. Buying additional high-risk assets is required when their value increases (because portfolio value minus floor amount rises), whereas the sale of high-risk assets is required as their value falls. This liquidity-demanding, trend-following strategy buys the risky asset on strength and sells it on weakness.

   **Market environment for best relative performance.** The Constant Proportion Strategy makes sense for investors whose risk tolerance is highly sensitive to changes in wealth. It provides the best relative performance when the markets are in a steady upward or downward trend.

3. **Buy and hold.** A Buy and Hold Strategy requires neither purchases nor sales once the original portfolio mix has been implemented. Such a strategy, given the absence of turnover, enjoys the advantage of avoiding postformation transaction costs, requires no "asset allocation management" (thereby avoiding management fees), and is blind to changes in market levels. Passive investors holding the market mix of assets often use this strategy. The strategy implies that investors' risk tolerance increases as wealth increases.

   **Market environment for best relative performance.** The relative performance of the Buy and Hold Strategy will typically lie between that of the other two alternatives. The Buy and Hold Strategy produces "market average" performance. It enjoys no "best" relative performance environment but is a good strategy to follow over long periods in the United States, where the primary long-term market trend has been upward.

8(b). **Recommendation:** Given the board's concern about downside risk, the recommended policy would be the Constant Proportion Strategy, with the Buy and Hold Strategy as a second choice. The Constant Mix Strategy provides the best performance only if the capital markets are volatile and trendless. It provides less of what the board considers important, namely, downside protection, than either of the other two strategies.

**Justification:** If opportunity exists to rebalance on a timely basis, the Constant Proportion (portfolio insurance) Strategy provides the best downside protection. If that assumption is not made, the Buy and Hold Strategy can be recommended. The Buy and Hold Strategy typically performs between the other two (which make opposite bets on the volatility and trend of the market) and will do well when markets follow a long-term, generally upward trend. Because the Buy and Hold Strategy is a relatively costless strategy to operate, the absence of turnover will positively affect the results over time.

A secondary reason for considering the Constant Proportion Strategy is that its popularity has waned since the 1987 stock market crash, when the required transactions could not be affected in a timely manner. It may offer a mispricing benefit because of the supply/demand imbalance relative to the Constant Mix Strategy (a portfolio insurance seller).

9. CFA Examination III (1986)

9(a). A futures contract is an agreement to buy or sell an asset at a certain time in the futures for a stated price. Option on futures gives the buyer the right (but not the obligation) to buy or sell a futures contract at a later date at a price agreed upon today. The writer of the call option on futures, upon exercise, establishes a short position in the futures contract at the exercise price. The holder of a put option on futures, upon exercise, establishes a short position in the futures contract at the exercise price. The writer of the put option on futures establishes a long futures position at the exercise price.

Futures and options can affect the risk and return distribution for a portfolio. In effect, being long (short) in futures is identical to subtracting (adding) cash from (to) the portfolio. Long futures positions have the effect of increasing the exposure of the portfolio to the asset; shorting futures decreases the portfolio's probability distribution of returns. Long positions in futures on the portfolio's underlying asset increase the portfolio's exposure (or sensitivity) to price changes of the asset. Shorting futures has the effect of decreasing the portfolio's sensitivity to the underlying asset. Since options provide the choice of whether or not to exercise the option, it means that options do not have a symmetrical impact on returns.

9(b) Buying a put when the investor owns the underlying security has the effect of controlling down side risk. Writing a covered call, on the other hand, limits upside returns while not appreciably affecting loss potential.

# CHAPTER 23

# FORWARD AND FUTURES CONTRACTS

## Answers to Questions

1.  There are many different reasons some futures contracts succeed and some fail, but the most important is demand. If people need a particular contract to expose themselves to or hedge a price risk, then the contract will succeed. Most people use treasury bond futures to gain exposure to or hedge general long-term interest rate risk. The only additional advantage of futures on corporate bonds would be that the investors could gain exposure to changes in the credit spread. Apparently there is little demand for this, either because investors do not want to hedge or gain exposure to this risk or because the underlying market is not liquid enough to support futures. Either way, the lack of futures is motivated by a lack of demand in the asset or futures contract. The lack of chicken contracts most likely derives from a similar lack of demand. It could be that chicken prices are highly correlated with other existing contract prices, so investors do not need the additional chicken contract. Perhaps there are too many different types of chickens to have a single contract that would attract enough trading volume.

2.  Before entering into a futures or forward contract, hedgers have exposure to price changes in the underlying asset. To hedge this risk, hedgers enter into contracts that most closely offset this price risk. The problem is that for most hedgers there is not a contract that exactly matches their exposure. Perhaps, the commodity they use is a different grade or needed in a different location than specified in the contract, so differences in prices between the actual asset the company is exposed to and the asset in the contract may exist and change over time. Likewise, a portfolio manager hedging a stock portfolio may hold a portfolio that is not perfectly correlated with the index future he/she is using to hedge with. To minimize basis risk it is necessary to find the contract that's price is most highly correlated with the price of the asset to be hedged.

3(a).  To hedge price risk, you could enter into a long position in 100,000 gallons worth of gasoline futures.

3(b).  Since you will have to post margin on the futures contract, the price swings in the futures contract will effect how much you earn on the capital posted as margin. If gas prices go up, your margin account will be credited and you will earn more interest. If gas prices go down, your account will be debited and you will earn less interest. If prices go down substantially, you will be required to post additional margin, and therefore tie up additional capital. How this effects your pricing of the forward contract you have sold depends on your opportunity cost of capital.

3(c).  In this case, by using futures you will not be able to match the quantity or time of delivery in the forward contract you sold. This gives rise to two types of risk. Since you will be forced to over or under hedge, you will be exposed to the general price movements in gas one way or the other. Next, if you synthetically create a three month expiration using half two-month and half four-month contracts, then you will be exposed to relative price changes in the two futures contracts in the near term. Later, after the two-month contract expires, you will be forced to hedge a shorter term position with a longer term contract, so again relative near-term and longer-term price differentials will lead to basis risk.

4.   There are two types of basis risk that this hedge is exposed to. The first is from changes in the shape of the yield curve. Since the company wishes to hedge a seven year issue's cost with a ten year contract, the hedge is exposed to changes in the relative level of interest rates between the seven and ten year maturities. Specifically, if the seven-year treasury rate rises more relative to the ten-year rate then the hedge will not completely neutralize the position and lose money for the firm. The second source of basis risk is from the quality spread over treasuries in the Eurobond market. Since the company will have to sell its bonds with a spread over the treasury rate, changes in this spread will also effect the quality of the hedge. Specifically, increases in the spread will lead to losses for the firm.

5.   CFA Examination II (1997)

5(a).   **What Lane Should Do**
To protect his investment from declining interest rates, Mike Lane should purchase, or "go long," $5 million worth of U.S. Treasury five-year-note futures contracts. Lane can actually purchase any of the traded five-year-note futures contracts, depending on what date he actually plans to invest his $5 million.

5(b).   **Effect of Higher Interest Rates on Lane's Position**
If rates increase by 100 basis points in three months, the price of these futures contracts will decline and Lane will have a loss in his long futures position. The loss will show up in his mark-to-market position over time and will require him to post additional margin money.

5(c).   **Return from Lane's Hedged Position vs. Unhedged Return**
Two methods can be used to answer Part C.

One answer is that the return from Lane's hedged position will be lower than the return if he had not hedged. Because of the futures contract's loss in Part B, the higher yield Lane can earn when he purchases a now lower priced (higher yield) U.S. Treasury five-year note in the cash market is "offset" by the loss from the futures contract. The loss is actually added to the now lower price of the U.S. Treasury five-year notes, thus decreasing Lane's realized yield.

A second answer draws from the Clarke reading. The reading expresses the combined futures contract's price and cash market price in terms of "net price." Net price equals the new cash market price plus the original futures price minus the new futures price.

Subtracting net price from 100 gives the investor the realized yield and thus the investor's return from the combined futures and cash markets. Because rates have increased, the new lower cash market price (higher yield) is increased by the loss from the futures contract's position, which reduces realized yield. The reading expresses this net price in several forms, but all are the same formula with rearranged terms.

6. Both Eurodollar and Treasury Bill futures are designed so that the long position benefits from a decline in the respective reference dates (relative to the contract yield) while the short position benefits from a rate increase. In both cases, the purpose of the hypothetical price index is to translate rate declines into price increases—and vice versa—which is a more natural way to think of the contract holder's position. Despite the fact that the underlying rate for these contracts are quoted on different conventions, they can both use the same price index calculation because all that really matters at maturity (or contract unwind) is the number of basis points the settlement price differs from the original contract price, with each basis point being worth $25 (= $1,000,000) x .0001 x 90/360).

7. It is most likely that a single position in an index futures market would be the best hedge. There are several reasons for this. The most important is cost. Since there are no exchange traded futures for individual stocks, entering 50 different positions would have to be done through an over-the-counter derivative dealer. This typically would mean higher transaction costs to cover the fees from setting up the one-off deal, the lower liquidity of individual stocks, and the increased commissions for the dealer. Another disadvantage is the liquidity of the position. Index options are very liquid and can be closed out quickly with little trading cost. Closing the 50 different positions would entail paying many of the start-up costs twice. Finally, it is easy to short an index future but rather hard and more expensive to short the underlying stocks which the OTC dealer would have to do to hedge the position in the 50 different stocks. The only advantage to the 50 different positions is that they would provide a nearly perfect hedge, whereas there would be some basis risk in the index futures position. Since the portfolio is well diversified, this should not be a major problem.

8. CFA Examination II (June 1991)

The fourth factor affecting the price of a stock index futures contract is the risk-free interest rate, usually measured by the Treasury bill rate. Futures prices increase with increases in the risk-free interest rate. Investors can create portfolios having identical levels of risk by either investing directly in a diversified equity portfolio or purchasing an equivalent position in stock index futures and placing the remainder in risk-free assets. The stock portfolio earns the price appreciation of the stocks plus their dividend yield; the futures portfolio earns the price appreciation of the futures plus the risk-free interest rate. Since futures are marked to the market, the futures price will equal the spot price of the stocks at the futures contract's expiration date. Market forces (arbitrage activity) results in stock index futures being priced such that their price is equal to the future value of the current spot price, using the "cost of carry" as the discount rate. The cost of carry is the risk-free interest rate minus the dividend yield on the stock portfolio.

If the risk-free interest rate subsequently increases, it becomes more profitable to purchase the futures/Treasury bill combination than to invest directly in the stocks themselves, because of the higher return on the Treasury bills now available. As a result, the price of the futures contract will be bid up until it is again equal to the future value of the current spot price of the equivalent stock portfolio. There is, thus, a direct and positive relationship between the risk-free interest rate and futures prices.

9. When the index futures price is below its theoretical level, the arbitrage involves buying the futures contract and selling the underlying index of stocks short. When the index futures price is above its theoretical level, the arbitrage involves selling the futures contract and buying the underlying index of stocks. The practicalities of selling the index short make the first type of arbitrage more difficult. First, there is an up-tick rule for short sales that prevents short sales from being possible for all of the index's stocks at the current market price. This is because, on average, about half of the market prices will have just moved down a tick and the up-tick rule prevents short sales until they trade up a tick. Second, margin requirements and limitations on the use of proceeds from short sales demand the use of more capital than long positions in the underlying stocks. Finally, for some stocks there may not be shares available to borrow and then short, or shares borrowed may be recalled by the original owner prior to the arbitrageur's preferred time to close the position.

10. CFA Examination III (June 1989)

If WEC invests in Bunds, they can use the current spot rate to calculate how many bonds they will receive today for $30 million. We can assume WEC is satisfied with the Bund interest rate and motivated primarily by a desire to diversify and reduce interest rate risk. Even if they could guarantee the Deutschemark value of the bonds they will hold, however, they would still face exchange rate risk. A currency futures contract sets the rate for future exchange of marks for dollars. With a prior agreement, like a futures contract, WEC can guarantee their exchange rate six months hence.

Short futures positions will incur losses as the exchange rate rises and gains as the exchange rate falls. The dollar value of the Bunds will change in the opposite direction. A perfect hedge would have WEC buy just enough futures (face value in marks) to cover the marks they will repatriate.

Undesirable Characteristics:
Even a perfect fixed futures hedge does not preserve the entire $30 million. The futures settlement rate for six months hence is almost surely less favorable than the exchange rate today. WEC can hedge but probably will lock in a loss, even without transaction costs. This loss is part of the opportunity cost of hedging - forgoing the chance of exchange rate gains in return for preventing exchange rate losses.

Fixed currency hedges are rarely perfect because German mark futures contracts are for a fixed amount (currently 125,000 DM) and may not be an integer multiple of the number of marks purchased today. A typical fixed futures hedge is either slightly over or under hedged.

Currency futures positions require margin. Losses must be paid daily. If WEC does not liquidate gains on the Bunds to fund losses on the futures, they may need extra cash some time during the six months.

Fixed currency hedging also presents problems when the Bunds mature beyond the six month holding period. WEC will not know exactly how many marks it will need to repatriate six months hence. Hedging by shorting a fixed number of contracts is rarely done unless the foreign investment is a pure discount security.

11. First, enter into a forward position agreeing to exchange pesos for dollars in two months. Then, enter into another forward contract agreeing to exchange those dollars for Swiss francs, also in two months.

12. Because the funds from one country could be converted to another currency and then through the use of forward contracts converted back to the original currency at the same rate, an arbitrage opportunity is available. Investors from the Country B could borrow at the lower rate, convert into the currency of Country A, earn a higher rate of return on the money, and then pay back their loan pocketing the difference in interest payments. The market forces from these transactions would tend to either equalize interest rates or change the forward exchange rates so that the currency of Country A trades at a forward discount.

# CHAPTER 23

## Answers to Problems

1(a).

|  | Price | Adjustment | Margin | Maintenance |
|---|---|---|---|---|
| March 9 | $173.00 | 0 | 3000 | 0 |
| April 9 | $179.75 | -675 | 2325 | 0 |
| May 9 | $189.00 | -925 | 3000 | 1600 |
| June 9 | $182.50 | 650 | 3650 | 0 |
| July 9 | $174.25 | 825 | 4475 | 0 |

Net loss of $4475 - ($3000 + $1600) = -$125
(including maintenance)

Total Return = -125/3000 = 4.17%

1(b).  Cost of Carry = 1.5%+8%=9.5%
Theoretical spot price on March 9
$S = PV(F)$
$S = 173*exp(1.095*.3333)$
$S = $167.61$

Implied May 9 price
$S = $189*exp(-.095*.16667)$
$S = $186.03$

1(c).  Futures (Forwards) unwind without (with) discounting net differential, so

|  | Short Futures | Long Forward | Net |
|---|---|---|---|
| May 9 | -(189 - 173) x100= ($1,600) | (189-173) x 100 x exp(-0.8x .1667) = $1,578.81 | -21.19 |
| June 9 | -(182.5 -173)x100=($950.00) | (182.5 - 173) x 100 x exp(-0.8 x 0.0833)=$943.69 | -6.31 |

This implies that the forwards underhedge with equal notional amounts of forwards and futures.

2(a).  Client A would need to go short 10,000 units of the June 1 contract at $24.95 and long 15,000 units of the September 1 contract at $25.85 The change in value of the two contracts to Client A is
= (24.95-25.85) x 10,000 + (25.85-25.65) x 15,000 = ($2,500.00)

So, you would receive this amount since this is the amount of their losses.

2(b).  You would need to add in the interest received on the margin balance.

Harcourt, Inc.

2(c). If Client B called to default, it would not be to your advantage since they had a long position at $26.40 and the price has declined to $25.85. So you would lose 25,000 x ($26.40-$25.65) = $18,750.00 at expiration, which in present value terms is $18,610.42.

2(d). Yes, you were short the equivalent of 25,000-15,000=10,000 contracts so you would be harmed by a price increase.

3(a). You buy the coffee at 58.56 cents per pound. This will cost 75,000 x ($.5856) = $43,920. Your futures profit will be 75,000 x ($ .592 - $ .5595) = $2,437.50. This reduces the effective price at which you buy the coffee to $43,920-$2,437.50 = $41,482.50. This is an effective price per pound of $41,482.50/75,000 = $ .5531. So you paid 55.31 cents per pound.

Buying two contracts for 75,000 pounds at 55.95 cents/pound leaves 7,000 pounds unhedged and therefore purchased in the spot market for 58.56 cent/lb. The effective price per pound is therefore = (75,000 x 55.95 + 7,000 x 58.56)/82,000 = 56.17 cents/pound.

The difference in price between spot and future is probably due to delivery costs.

3(b). There are a couple of types of basis risk. First the anticipated amount is not exactly hedgable because of the contract size. This means you will either have to over-hedge or under-hedge. Also you may not know the exact amount that you will really need at the future date. If you are really going to purchase the coffee somewhere else and were only using the futures to hedge (i.e. close your position before delivery) then you will be exposed to changes in the relative prices between the market you purchase in and the futures market.

4. CFA Examination III (1983)

In setting up the hedge, the crucial assumption is the hedge ratio as follows:

$ position in Treasury bond futures / $ size of bond issue

Obviously, the easiest assumption is a "naive" hedge where it is 1 to 1 with the bond issue, and in this situation, the 1 to 1 hedge ratio provides a satisfactory offset.

|  | Case 1<br>Interest rates **rise**<br>50 basis points | Case 2<br>Interest rates **fall**<br>50 basis points |
|---|---|---|
| Sell 1000 contracts | | |
| June 'S3 futures at 78.875 | $78,875,000 | $78,875,000 |
| Close-out 1000 contracts | | |
| May '83 | 75,930,000 | 81,840,000 |
| Gain/loss | 2,945,000 | (2,965,000) |
| Present value of | | |
| Increase/decrease Interest ($500,000) for 10 years at 10.5 (6.021) | (3,010,500) | 3,010,500 |
| Net gain/loss | (65,500) | 45,500 |

23 - 7

By hedging, United American Co. can offset some of the loss (or gain) due to the increased or decreased cost of financing due to changing interest rates. Comparison of the gain or loss on the futures contract to the present value of the increased or decreased interest payments must be made as a result of the change in the interest rate level. If United American Co. did not hedge and Case 1 occurred, then the loss would have been $3,010,500 instead of $65,500.

5(a). The price of the bond as of August 1993 will be 97.39193% of par for a total portfolio value of $97,391,930:

$$D = \frac{1.03435}{.039435} - \frac{1.03943 + [40(0.04 - .039435)]}{0.04 \times [(1.039435^{40}) - 1] + .039435}$$

$$P_{Aug93} = \sum_{t=1}^{52} \frac{(.03625 \times 100)}{(1 + 0.37395)^t} + \frac{100}{(1 + 0.37395)^{52}}$$

5(b). The duration portfolio bond:

$$D = \frac{1.037395}{.037395} - \frac{1.037395 + [52(0.03625 - .037395)]}{0.03625 \times [(1.03735^{52}) - 1] + .037395}$$

= 27.741543 - 3.9796244
= 23.761919 six month periods
= 11.88096 years

modified duration = (11.88096/1.037395) = 11.4537

The duration futures bond:

$$D = \frac{1.039435}{.039435} - \frac{1.039435 + [40(0.04 - .039435)]}{0.04 \times [(1.038435^{40}) - 1] + .039435}$$

= 26.358184 − 5.6688275
= 20.689356 six month periods
= 10.3447 years

modified duration = (10.3447/1.039435) = 9.9522

5(c). The calculation of the hedge ratio:

= (11.4527/9.9522) x 1 x (97,391,930/101,125)
= 1.15077 x 963.0846
= 1108.29 contracts
= 1108 contracts

6(a).   Both bonds in portfolio 1 are zero coupon bonds so,

$D_1 = (4/10) \times 14 + (6/10) \times 3 = 7.4$

$ModD_1 = 7.4/1.0731 = 6.896$ years

$$D = \frac{1.0731}{.0731} - \frac{1.0731 + 9 \times (.046 - .0731)}{.046[(1.0731)^9 - 1] + .0731} = 7.4$$

$ModD_2 = 7.4/1.0731 = 6.896$ years

For both portfolios:

$\Delta P/P \cong -6.896 \times .006 = -4.137\%$

6(b).   Though the two portfolios have identical durations, the actual price changes will be different because the portfolios have different convexities. In general, a "barbell" portfolio (i.e. portfolio 1) will have greater convexity, meaning that its value will fall less relative to portfolio 2.

6(c).   To hedge this position
$HR_1 = (6.896/10.355) \times [0.6 \times 1.13 + 0.4 \times 1.03] \times (-10,000,000/109,750) = -66.14$
$HR_2 = (6.896/10.355) \times [1.01] \times (-11,500,000/109,750) = 70.48$

Combining these two gives a net hedge ratio of 4.339. Consequently, the hedge would be to enter into a long position in 4 futures contracts.

7.   CFA Examination II (May 1998)

**Arbitrage transactions.** In a cash-and-carry strategy, which is what this transaction is, the arbitrageur borrows funds at a short-term rate, buys the asset, and sells the futures contract. On the expiration date, the arbitrageur delivers the asset against the futures, repays the loan with interest, and earns a low-risk profit.

- List of transactions
- Borrow funds
- Buy the asset
- Sell futures
- Deliver the asset against the futures
- Repay the loan with interest

**Calculation of arbitrage profits.** The cash-and-carry model, so called because the trader buys the cash good and carries it to the expiration of the futures contract, may be used to explain the pricing relationship between the futures market and the cash (or spot) market. Simplistically, the expected price (or "fair value") of a futures contract is given by the formula:

Futures price = Cash price + Finance charges - Income.

First, determine whether the futures is overpriced or underpriced relative to cash. Calculate the fair value of the futures contract and compare this value to the contract's actual value. If the actual value is greater than the fair value, the futures contract is overvalued, and a cash-and-carry strategy will result in profits; if the actual value is less than the fair value, the futures contract is undervalued and a reverse cash-and-carry strategy will yield profits.

The theoretical futures price is $101 + $2.50 - $4.50 = $99. Because the actual futures (invoice) price is $ 100, a profit of $1 can be obtained by employing a cash-and-carry strategy.

8.

$$\text{IFDY}_{90,180} = \left[ \frac{(180 \times .0750) - (90 \times .0750)}{180 - 90} \right] \times \frac{1}{1 - [(90 \times .0750)/360]}$$

$$= .076433$$

Since the implied forward rate, 7.6433%, is not equal to the explicit futures rate, an arbitrage opportunity is possible, depending on the size of the profit compared to the transaction costs.

- Go long (or lend) at 7.6433% between days 90 and 180 by buying the 180-day paper and selling the 90-day paper in the current spot market.
- Go short (or borrow) at 7.50% between days 90 and 180 in the futures market.

(all transactions are in British pounds)

| Date 0 | 90 | 180 |
|---|---|---|

Buy 180-day paper in spot market
    Pay 96,250                                         Get 100,000

Sell 90-day paper in spot market
    Get 98, 125       Pay 100,000

Sell 90-day paper forward
                    Get   98,125                  Pay 100,000

$96{,}250 = 100{,}000 \times [1 - (180 \times .0750)/360]$

$98{,}125 = 100{,}000 \times [1 - (90 \times .0750)/360]$

23 - 10

On a net basis, for each set of transactions having a face value of £100,000, the arbitrageur receives £1,875 on date 0 and pays £1,875 on date 90. The profit, therefore, is the interest that can be earned on £1,875 for 90 days. For example, 90-day paper having a face value of £1,910.83 perhaps can be purchased for £1,875 (a discount yield of 7.50). The net profit of £35.83 would have to be sufficient to cover transaction costs.

9(a). Recalling the convention that the interest expense on floating-rate debt is determined in advance and paid in arrears, the relevant quarterly LIBOR expenses (rounded to the basis point) are:

*1st Quarter Expense Rate:*

4.60% (i.e., current 90-day LIBOR)

*2nd Quarter Expertise Rate:*

$$IFR_{90,180} = \left[ \frac{(180 \times .0475) - (90 \times .0460)}{180 - 90} \right] \times \frac{1}{1 - [(90 \times .0460)/360]} = 4.84\%$$

*3rd Quarter Expertise Rate:*

$$IFR_{180,270} = \left[ \frac{(270 \times .0500) - (180 \times .0475)}{270 - 180} \right] \times \frac{1}{1 - [(180 \times .0460)/360]} = 5.37\%$$

*4th Quarter Expertise Rate:*

$$IFR_{270,360} = \left[ \frac{(360 \times .0530) - (270 \times .0500)}{360 - 270} \right] \times \frac{1}{1 - [(270 \times .0500)/360]} = 5.98\%$$

Based on a non-amortizing loan balance of $1,000,000 and 90-day quarters, these percentages imply the following sequence of quarterly cash payments:
$11,500 = $1,000,000 x (.046) x (90/360); $ 12,100; $ 13,425; and $ 14,950.

9(b). Although there are four interest payments due, the convention of setting LIBOR at the front-end of a borrowing period means that there are only three uncertain cash flows at the time the funding is originated. This means that the customer will have to "lock in" a 90-day LIBOR on settlement dates 90, 180, and 270 days from now.

This can be done by shorting the following strip of Eurodollar futures contracts: short one 90-day contract, short one 180-day contract, and short one 270-day contract. Notice that this problem would require a short hedge because the floating-rate borrower would need a hedge to compensate him/her when LIBOR rose (i.e., Eurodollar futures prices fall), thereby raising their underlying funding cost.

23 - 11

9(c). If Eurodollar prices are consistent with the series of implied forward rates, we would observe the following prices: 90-day contract: 95.16 =100 - 4.84; 180-day contract: 94.63; and 270-day contract: 94.02.

The annuity that would be equivalent to locking in the preceding series of quarterly cash expenses with the futures strip is calculated as the solution to:

$$\frac{\$11,500}{1+[(.046)(90)/360]} + \frac{\$12,100}{1+[(.0475)(180)/360]} + \frac{\$13,425}{1+[(.050)(270)/360]} + \frac{\$14,950}{1+[(.053)(270)/360]}$$

$$= \frac{\text{Annuity}}{1+[(.046)(90)/360]} + \frac{\text{Annuity}}{1+[(.0475)(180)/360]} + \frac{\text{Annuity}}{1+[(.050)(270)/360]} + \frac{\text{Annuity}}{1+[(.053)(270)/360]}$$

or:
Annuity = (50,325.8353/3.87895) = $12,974.07

Expressing this dollar amount on a percentage basis on terms comparable to LIBOR leaves:

($12,974.07/$1,000,000)(360/90) = 5.19%

10. Since you think that interest rates are going to rise, you would not want to have a net long position in T-bill or Eurobond futures. But, since you also believe that the credit spread between treasuries and LIBOR will narrow, you would want to be short this spread. Let LIBOR be expressed as the T-bill rate (R) plus a spread (S). Then creating a portfolio

1. Shorting the T-bill future (payoff $= N*\Delta R*\Delta T$)
2. Offsetting long position in the Eurodollar future (payoff $= N*\Delta(R+S)*\Delta T$).
Combining these two payoffs gives
Net payoff $= N*\Delta R*\Delta T -N*\Delta(R+S)* \Delta T = -N*\Delta S*\Delta T$. So the portfolio value is not related to R. Hence, if R increases and S decreases ($\Delta S<0$) then the payoff on the portfolio will be positive. If you strongly believed that interest rates were going to increase you could also profit from an additional short position in T-bill futures.

11. We can calculate the theoretical spot price for the index as S $= F*\exp[-(r-d)t] = 614.75*\exp[-(.08-.03)*.25] = 607.11$. Since this is larger than the actual spot price, there is a theoretical arbitrage opportunity, so program trading might take place. This would involve borrowing the money to buy 1 "index share," taking a short position in the futures, and "delivering" the share at the future date. The cash flows would be as follows:

Harcourt, Inc.

|                                      | T = now  | T=9Q days |
|--------------------------------------|----------|-----------|
| 1. borrow 602.25                     | +602.25  | -614.42   |
| 2. buy 1 index                       | -602.25  | S         |
| 3. short future (K=614.75)           | 0        | 614.75 - S |
| 4. receive dividends on index        | 0        | 4.53      |
| Total                                | 0        | $4.86     |

So the arbitrage nets $4.86 in 90 days. This may or may not cover transaction costs or overcome the fact that most investors cannot borrow at the risk-free rate.

12(a). To get a return of 4.25% by converting to CHF it must be the case that a dollar converted today, invested at rate R, and converted back at the end of a year is then worth $1.0425. So,

$$(\$1/.6651) \times (1 + R) \times .6586 = 1.0425$$
$$.990 + .990R = 1.0425$$
$$R = 5.28\%$$

12(b). If the actual rate is 5.5% for a one-year Swiss government bond then the return on investing in CHF would be greater. This can be seen by plugging in R= .055 into the above left-hand side to get

$$(\$1/.6651) \times (1+.055) \times .6586 = 1.0447$$

12(c). An arbitrageur could borrow $250,000 domestically at 4.25%, convert it into 375,883.33 CHF, buy Swiss government bonds, and enter into a forward contract to reconvert the proceeds after a year. After a year invested at 5.5% the arbitrageur would have $396,556.91 which could be converted back into dollars at the forward rate of 0.6586 $/CHF. This would result in $261,172.38 of which $260,625 would be needed to repay the loan plus interest. So the arbitrageur would be left with a $547.38 profit, before commissions.

# CHAPTER 24

# OPTION CONTRACTS

## Answers to Questions

1.  A long straddle consists of a long call and a long put on the same stock and profits from dramatic price movement by the stock. A short straddle involves the sale of a call and a put on the same stock and profits from little or no stock price change. Investors going long would anticipate volatility in excess of that discounted by the options' prices while investors going short would expect volatility below that already discounted. Since volatility enhances option prices, long straddles would tend to pay higher premiums for more volatile options, whereas short straddles must accept lower premiums for less volatile options.

2.  A range forward is actually an option strategy that combines a long call and a short put (or vice versa) through a costless transaction. Because the options will not have the same striking price, the combination is classified as a **range** forward as opposed to an **actual** forward, created by combining long and short options with the same striking price. It is fair to view actual forwards as a special case (or zero-cost version) of range forwards.

3.  CFA Examination II (1993)

    Call options give the owner the right, but not the obligation, to purchase SFr's for a pre-specified amount of domestic currency. Purchasing an at-the-money call option would guarantee the current exchange rate over the life of the option. If the SFr declines in value, the call will not be exercised since francs can be purchased more cheaply in the open market and redeeming the bond issue will be less costly.

    Contrasting characteristics: (1) Currency options are traded worldwide and enjoy a liquid market. (2) Exchange-traded currency option contracts have standard amounts, maturities, etc. (3) Over-the-counter options could be tailored to meet Michelle's needs. (4) The initial cash outflow would be the premium. (5) The use of options preserves the ability to profit. (6) No counterparty credit risk. (7) Must roll to match year obligation.

    Currency forward contracts commit the seller to deliver the specified amount of currency to the buyer on a specified future date at a fixed price. A short position in a forward contract requires delivery.

    Contrasting characteristics: (1) The market for forward contracts is over-the-counter and sometimes may not be as liquid as option or futures market. (2) Forward contracts may be custom-designed for specific applications. (3) Cash does not change hands until a forward contract is settled. (4) Counterparty credit risk. (5) Can best match 5-year obligation.

24 - 1

Currency futures are like forward contracts except the gain or loss on the contract is settled daily under the supervision of an organized exchange. A short position in the futures requires either offset or delivery at expiration.

Contrasting characteristics: (1) Futures are traded in standardized contracts and are highly liquid. (2) Cash is required for daily settlement. (3) A margin account is required. (4) Management and administration costs are higher than with a forward or option contract. (5) No counterparty credit risk. (6) Must roll to match year obligation.

4.   CFA Examination III (1991)

The other three factors affecting the value of call options and the ways that changes in them affect value are:

(1).   Increases in underlying stock volatility. A call cannot be worth less than zero no matter how far the stock price falls, but rising stock prices can increase the call's value without limit. Therefore, the wider the range within which a stock's price can fluctuate (i.e. the greater its volatility), the greater the chance that the option will expire in-the-money, the higher the expected payoff from owning it, and the higher its value. A wider range of probable future prices on the underlying stock increases the probability of higher payoffs in general but because the call's value cannot decline below zero does not symmetrically increase the probability of lower payoffs.

(2).   The risk-free interest rate. Call value increase with increases in interest rates (given constant stock prices) because higher interest rates make the ownership of call options more attractive. The call owner does not pay for the stock until the option is exercised; its owner can, therefore, take advantage of the time value of money by investing free interest rate increases the time value benefit to the call owner, increasing the value of the call option.

(3).   The exercise price of the option. Call values decrease with increases in the exercise price. When a call option is exercised, the payoff is the difference between the stock price at the time of exercise and the exercise (or strike) price. A higher exercise price decreases the expected payoff from the call, thus reducing the option's value.

5.   Put-call parity indicates that a long position in a stock combined with being short a call and long a put (with the same strike price) is a risk-free investment. In other words, no matter what the stock price at expiration, the payoff will be the same. Consequently, any investment in this portfolio should earn the risk-free return. The three-step process for valuing options is to

(1).   Determine a distribution of future stock prices,

(2).   Calculate the cash flows from the option at the future prices, and

(3).   Discount these expected cash flows to the present at the risk-free rate.

It is this final step that is relevant. Cash flows can be discounted at the risk-free rate because of the riskless replicating portfolio strategy.

6. The Black-Scholes model is derived by showing how a portfolio of the underlying asset and risk-free bonds can be created that exactly mimics the price of an option. This involves taking a long position in the underlying asset to replicate a call option. For currency options, the underlying asset can be thought of as risk-free deposits (bonds) in the foreign currency. So, just as stocks pay dividends, foreign deposits pay interest. Therefore, we can just substitute the foreign risk-free rate for the dividend yield when pricing options on currency.

7. If there are no transaction costs, it is only rational to exercise a call option early, immediately before a dividend payment. This is because it will always be more profitable to sell the option and buy the stock in the open market rather than exercise the option, unless there is a dividend. When a firm pays a dividend, the price of the stock usually declines by approximately the amount of the dividend. This has two impacts on the option holder. First, the decrease in the stock price decreases the value of his option. Second, the investor does not get the dividend payment unless he actually has exercised the option and owns the stock. Consequently, if the value of the dividend is greater than C+K-S, it will be beneficial to exercise early. Note, this is most likely to happen for every in-the-money options.

For put options, it may be the case that the interest that could be earned on the proceeds from early exercise are greater than the intrinsic option value (P+S-K), so early proceeds from early exercise is optimal. Using similar logic as above, puts should always be exercised immediately after a dividend (on a dividend paying stock) because the stock's price declines after a dividend, thus making the put more valuable.

8. In the Black-Scholes model, the expected future value of a stock is a function of the risk-free interest rate and the dividend yield. As long as the risk-free rate is greater than the dividend yield, the future expected value will be greater than today's price. The longer the time period, the higher the expected price. So, as time to expiration increases, there are two opposing forces on the value of a European put. First, the increased time to expiration increases the chances of the option being more in-the-money. This increases put value. Second, the higher expected price at expiration decreases the expected value of the put's payoff at expiration and, therefore, decreases the put value. Depending on which of these two effects is larger, the put may increase or decrease in price with an increase in time to expiration.

For a European call option, these two effects work in the same direction, since an increase in expected future price increases the value of a call. Hence, an increase in the time to expiration always increases the value of a European call.

9.   Since the price of an option is positively related to volatility, "buying low vol and selling high vol" is the same as the idea of "buy low, sell high" for any risky asset if the other parameters that affect option prices are fixed. The other factors that affect option prices can be effectively neutralized by holding the appropriate portfolio of options and the underlying asset (beyond the scope of this question). If this is the case, then the risky asset is volatile itself, not the underlying foreign currency.

10.  A decrease in security volatility will cause an increase in both the call and put option values. For example, when the volatility of the underlying asset's price decreases, the call option becomes less valuable since this decreases the probability that the option will be deeper in the money at expiration (a similar scenario is also true for the put option).

11.  On October 19, 1987, implied volatilities sky-rocketed. The jump in implied volatility increased the value of call options more than enough to offset the negative impact of the in the index level.

# CHAPTER 24

## Answers to Problems

1. CFA Examination III (1987)

1(a).
$$\text{Hedge ratio} = \frac{C_u - C_d}{uS - dS} = \frac{20 - 0}{120 - 80} = 0.5$$

$$\text{Implied probability (p)} = \frac{(1 + r) - d}{u - d} = \frac{(1 + 0.1) - 0.0}{1.2 - 0.8} = 0.75$$

$$\text{Call value} = \frac{pC_u + (1 - p)C_d}{1 + r} = \frac{.75(20) + .25(0)}{1 + .01} = 13.6$$

*OR*

### Step 1

Set up binomial tree and calculate the option values at expiration for each ending stock price.

### Step 2

Solve for the amount to invest in the stock and the amount to borrow in order to replicate the option given its value in the up state and its value in the down state. Solve these equations simultaneously.

### Step 3

Use the values derived in Step 2 to solve for the value of the option at the beginning of the period.

*OR*

### Step 1

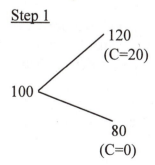

100

120
(C=20)

80
(C=0)

Harcourt, Inc.

<u>Step 2</u>

$$20 = 120 \times D - 1.1 \times B$$
$$0 = 80 \times D - 1.1 \times B$$

$$D = \frac{-1.1(20) - (-1.1)(0)}{120(-1.1) - 80(-1.1)} = \frac{-22}{-44} = 0.5$$

$$C = 80(.5) - 1.1 \times B$$

$$0 = 80(.5) - 1.1 \times B$$

$$B = 40/1.1 - 36.4$$

<u>Step 3</u>

$$C = 50 - 36.4 = 13.6$$

1(b).  The binomial option pricing model is a discrete version of the continuous time Black-Scholes option pricing model. As the number of intervals in the binomial model approaches infinity, the option value derived from this model approaches the option value derived from the Black-Scholes model.

The binomial model is more flexible than the Black-Scholes model because it does not require one to assume constant interest rates and constant variance throughout the horizon. These values can be changed at any of the nodes in the binomial tree. However, the binomial model is more cumbersome to use since accuracy requires that the tree include many nodes.

2.  CFA Examination III (1992)

2(a).  An individual put will hedge an amount of the underlying stock index equal to the underlying value of the put, which in each case here is the respective stock index times $100.

Also, due to the differing betas, the portfolio and the stock indexes are expected to produce gains or losses in proportion to their respective betas. Thus the number of puts required to hedge the portfolio must be adjusted for the betas of the respective stock indexes relative to the beta of the portfolio.

The number and cost of protective puts could be calculated indirectly or directly.

Indirect method:

$$(\beta_{port})(V_{port}) = (\beta_{GAC})(V_{GAC}) = (\beta_{opt})(V_{opt})$$

The indirect method is based on the fact that an overall portfolio's beta is equal to the weighted average of its component betas. Since we are seeking a zero beta portfolio, the left-hand side of the equation can be set to zero.

For the S&P 100:

$$0 = -(1.05)(7,761,700) = (0.95)(V_{opt})$$

$V_{opt} = -(1.05/0.95)(7,761,700)$

$V_{opt} = -8,578,721$

Number of puts = 8,578,721/(365 x 100) = 235

Cost of puts = 235 x \$10.25 x 100 = \$240,875

For the S&P 500:

$$0 = -(1.05)(7,761,700) = (1.00)(V_{opt})$$

$V_{opt} = -(1.05/1.00)(7,761,700)$

$V_{opt} = -8,149,785$

Number of puts = 8,149,785/(390 x 100) = 209

Cost of puts = 209 x \$11.00 x 100 = \$229,900

For the NYSE:

$$0 = (1.05)(7,761,700) = (1.03)(V_{opt})$$

$V_{opt} = -(1.05/1.03)(7,761,700)$

$V_{opt} = -7,912,413$

Number of puts = 7,912,413/(215 x 100) = 368

Cost of puts = 368 x \$6.25 x 100 = \$230,000

Direct method:

The direct method calculates the number of puts by utilizing the hedge ratio (HR).

HR = volatility of hedged security / volatility of hedging instrument

Beta, which measures the movement in a security relative to the S&P 500, serves as a measure of volatility.

For the S&P 100:

Number of puts = (1.05/0.95)(7,761,700)/(365 x 100) = 235

Cost of puts = 235 x $10.25 x 100 = $240,875

For the S&P 500:

Number of puts = (1.05/1.00)(7,761,700)/(390 x 100) = 209

Cost of puts = 209 x $11.00 x 100 = $229,900

For the NYSE:

Number of puts = (1.05/1.03)(7,761,700)/(215 x 100) = 368

Cost of puts = 368 x $6.25 x 100 = $230,000

2(b).   The cost of the S&P 500 and NYSE puts are essentially the same and less than the cost of the S&P 100 puts; other relevant factors in the decision are correlation and liquidity.

While the hedge calculated in Part A is intended to protect GAC's portfolio from a decline, the portfolio does not replicate any of the indices. The hedge could be less than perfect if the price movement of GAC's portfolio does not track the index movement. In this context, the index which has the highest correlation with GAC's portfolio (the S&P 500, 0.95) would be most preferred, while the index exhibiting the lowest correlation with GAC (the S&P 100, 0.86) would be least preferred.

The hedge should be implemented with a minimum of market impact thus another consideration is liquidity. If the hedge transaction represents a disproportionate share of average daily trading volume, the market could move adversely, increasing the cost of the hedge. The required put position represent 2.4% (235/10,000) of average daily trading volume for the S&P 100, 5.2% (209/4,000) for the S&P 500, and 36.8% (368/1,000) for the NYSE. Thus based on trading volume and likely market impact, the S&P 100 would be most preferred, with the S&P 500 also acceptable; the NYSE transaction would clearly be least desirable.

The S&P 500 options would appear to be the preferred protective position, offering the best combination of cost, hedging ability (correlation), and liquidity; the S&P 100 is a relatively costly position and the NYS position is relatively illiquid.

2(c).   The scenario in Part A used options with strike prices equal to the current index value (i.e. "at the money"). Such options have no intrinsic value (the difference between the index value and the strike price) and contain only a time premium. Buying the put at-the-money will enable a hedge of the portfolio with no loss from current levels assuming that the betas used in the GAC hedge are stationary; then decreases in the portfolio value will be offset exactly by increases in the put option value.

24 - 8

As the relationship between the strike price and the index value changes, however, a trade-off enters into the investment decision. If the strike price is below the current index value, then the puts are "out of the money." These options will be less expensive than "at the money" or "in the money" puts; however they expose the portfolio to potential loss, with the difference between the index value and strike price being analogous to the deductible on an insurance policy. For example, if the S&P 500 index is at 400 and the strike price at 390, then GAC's portfolio would be unprotected for the 10 point difference. The portfolio value will decline by 2.5 (10/400) if the index drops to 390 or lower. However, an index value between 390 and 400 at option expiration will not provide any offset to a portfolio decline. The portfolio would have incurred the cost of the option, only to have it expire worthless at expiration.

If the strike price is above the current index value, then the puts are "in the money. These puts will be most expensive, since they include both intrinsic value and a time premium. Buying "in the money" puts is analogous to selling the portfolio at the strike price and owning a call option. If the S&P 500 index is 390 and the strike price is 400, then the portfolio is assured of a 2.6% (10/390) gain (ignoring the cost of the option).

In summary, the protective put strategy will prove a floor value for the portfolio. However, the various index options will each have strike prices different from their respective current index values. Thus the portfolio manager must weigh the trade-off between the cost of the put option (the higher the strike price, the higher the put premium) and the degree of protection sought Revel of assured portfolio value).

2(d). An option pricing model, such as the Black-Scholes or binomial approaches, can be used to establish the fair value of an option and to facilitate value comparisons across different strike prices, different tines to expiration, and different stock index options. To the extent that mispricings can be identified, arbitrage opportunities may be exploited.

The Black-Scholes formula utilizes the current index price and strike price, in conjunction with the risk-free interest rate, the time to expiration, and return volatility, to establish a fair option price. Alternatively, prevailing option prices may used in the model to calculate implied volatility and to facilitate volatility comparisons across strike prices and times to expiration; this also enables assessment of option premiums against implied risk levels. The model can also be used to calculate hedge ratios, the change in portfolio value for a $1 change in index price.

In summary, option pricing models allow the portfolio manager to quantify the relative pricing of options to determine which option gives the most efficient portfolio protection per dollar of cost.

3.     CFA Examination II (1998)

3(a).  **Critique of Belief**
Joel Franklin's belief is incorrect. There are two fundamental kinds of options: American style and European style. An American option permits the owner to exercise the option at

any time before or at expiration. The owner of a European option may exercise it only at expiration. If an option is at expiration, it will have the same value whether it is American or European.

The owner of an American option can treat the option as a European option simply by postponing the decision to exercise until expiration. Therefore, the American option cannot be worth less than the European option. However, the American option can be worth more. The American option will be worth more if circumstances make exercise of the option before its expiration desirable. So, it may have a higher premium.

### 3(b). European-Style Option's Value

The formula to calculate a call option using put-call parity is $c = S + p - Xe^{-rt}$

where
$c =$ the price of a European call option at time t
$S =$ the price of the underlying stock at time t
$p =$ the price of a European put at time t
$X =$ the exercise price for the option
$t =$ time to expiration = one year

Therefore, from the information given,

Call option = $4.408 = \$43 + 4.00 - 45.00e^{-.055}$

### 3(c). Effect of Variables

| | *Effect on Call Option's Value* |
|---|---|
| i. An increase in short-term interest rate | Positive |
| ii. An increase in stock price volatility | Positive |
| iii. A decrease in time to option expiration | Negative |

4(a). Calculate the following parameters, option values, and hedge ratios at each node:

$U = 42/40 = 1.05$
$D = 38.4/40 = .96$
$R = (1.06)^{1/3} = 1.01961$
$r_f = 1.961\%$ per period
$P_u = (R-D)/(U-D) = (1.01961-.96)/(1.05-.96) = .05961/.09 = .662$

4(a)(i). S = 40.32

If the stock moves up the option will be worth \$4.34 ($C_{udu}$); if the stock moves down the option will be worth \$.71 ($C_{udd}$). The value of the option and hedge ratio at this node is

$$C_{ud} = \frac{.662(4.34) + (1 - .662)(.71)}{1.01961} = 2.501/1.01961 = 2.45$$

$$HR_{ud} = \frac{4.34 - .72}{(1.05 - .96) \times 40.32} = 1.00$$

24 - 10

4(a)(ii). S = 42

If the stock moves up the option will be worth \$6.62 ($C_{uu}$); if the stock moves down the option will be worth \$2.86 ($C_{ud}$). The value of the option and hedge ratio at this node is

$$C_u = \frac{.662(6.62) + (1- .662)(2.86)}{1.01961} = 5.34912/1.01961 = 5.246$$

$$HR_u = \frac{6.62 - 2.86}{(1.05 - .96) \times 42.00} = 1.00$$

Note:

$$C_{uu} = \frac{.662(8.31) + (1- .662)(4.34)}{1.01961} = 6.96814/1.01961 = 6.834$$

4(a)(iii). S = 40

If the stock moves up the option will be worth \$5.05 ($C_{uu}$); if the stock moves down the option will be worth \$1.87. The value of the option and hedge ratio at this node is

$$C = \frac{.662(5.05) + (1- .662)(1.87)}{1.01961} = 3.97516/1.01961 = 3.8987$$

$$HR_u = \frac{5.05 - 1.87}{(1.05 - .96) \times 40.00} = 0.8833$$

Note:

$$C_d = \frac{(.662)^2(4.34) + (2)(1- .662)(0.71)}{(1.01961)^2} = 2.38194/1.0396 = 2.29$$

So the riskless portfolio will initially contain 1 call option and be short 0.8833 shares of stock. Since after an initial up move to 42.00 the option can only finish in-the-money, the hedge ratio is 1.00.

4(b).

| Ending Price | Number of Paths | Path Probability | Total Probability |
|---|---|---|---|
| \$46.31 | 1 | $.6075^3 = .2242$ | .2242 |
| \$42.34 | 3 | $.6075^2 \times .3925^1 = .1449$ | .4346 |
| \$38.71 | 3 | $.6075^1 \times .3925^2 = .1449$ | .2808 |
| \$35.39 | 1 | $.3925^3 = .0604$ | .0604 |

4(c).

$$C = \frac{.662^3 (8.31) + (3)(.662^2)(1-.662)(4.34) + (3)(.662)(1-.662)^2 (.71)}{1.06} = 4.50/1.06 = 4.24$$

4(d).

$$P = \frac{(1- .662)^3 (2.61)}{1.06} = 0.1008/1.06 = .095$$

Harcourt, Inc.

Check with put call parity. Does the following hold true:

$$C - P = S - PV(K)$$
$$4.24 - .095 = 40 - 38/1.06$$
$$4.15 = 4.15$$

Put-call parity **does** hold exactly.

5(a).   $u = 33.00/30.00 = 36.00/33.00 = 1.10$      $d = 27.00/30.00 = 24.30/27.00 = 0.90$

$r = (1 + .05)^{1/2} = 1.0247$

$$p = \frac{r - d}{u - d} = \frac{1.0247 - 0.90}{1.10 - 0.90} = .1247/.20 = .6235$$

$C_{uu} = Max [0, 36.30 - 28] = 8.30$
$C_{ud} = Max [0, 29.70 - 28] = 1.70$
$C_{dd} = Max [0, 24.30 - 28] = 0$

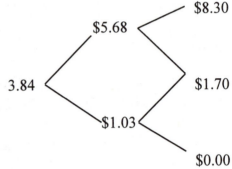

$$C_U = \frac{(.6235)(8.30) + (.3765)(1.70)}{1.024695} = \frac{5.17 + 0.64}{1.024695} = 5.815/1.025 = \$5.68$$

$$C_d = \frac{(.6235)(1.70) + (.3765)(0.00)}{1.024695} = \frac{1.05995}{1.024695} = \$1.03$$

$$C_o = \frac{(.6235)(5.675) + (.3765)(1.0344)}{1.024695} = \frac{3.538 + .3895}{1.024695} = \$3.84$$

$h = (5.675 - 1.0344)/(36.30 - 24.30) = 4.64/12.00 = 0.3867$

5(b)(i). Asian-style      ($33.00 + $36.30)/2  - $28.00 = $6.65

$5.28

($33.00 + $29.70)/2  - $28.00 = $3.35
($27.00 + $29.70)/2  - $28.00 = $0.35

$3.29

$0.21

($27.00 + $24.30)/2 - $28.00 = 0

$$C_U = \frac{(.6235)(6.65) + (.3765)(3.35)}{1.024695} = \frac{4.146 + 1.261}{1.024695} = \$5.28$$

$$C_d = \frac{(.6235)(0.35) + (.3765)(0.00)}{1.024695} = \$0.21$$

$$C_o = \frac{(.6235)(5.28) + (.3765)(0.21)}{1.024695} = \$3.29$$

5(b)(ii). Lookback

max ($33.00, $36.30)- $28.00 = $8.30

$6.89

max ($33.00, $29.70) - $28.00 = $5.00

max ($27.00, $29.70) - $28.00 = $1.70

$4.57

$1.03

max ($27.00, $24.30) - $28.00 = 0

$$C_U = \frac{(.6235)(8.30) + (.3765)(5.00)}{1.024695} = \frac{5.175 + 1.8825}{1.024695} = \$6.89$$

$$C_d = \frac{(.6235)(1.70) + (.3765)(0.00)}{1.024695} = \$1.03$$

$$C_o = \frac{(.6235)(6.89) + (.3765)(1.03)}{1.024695} = \$4.57$$

5(b)(iii). Digital

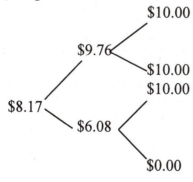

$10.00

$9.76

$10.00

$10.00

$8.17

$6.08

$10.00

$0.00

24 - 13

$$C_U = \frac{(.6235)(10.00) + (.3765)(10.00)}{1.024695} = \frac{6.235 + 3.765}{1.024695} = \$9.76$$

$$C_d = \frac{(.6235)(10.00) + (.3765)(0.00)}{1.024695} = \$6.08$$

$$C_o = \frac{(.6235)(9.76) + (.3765)(6.08)}{1.024695} = \$8.17$$

6(a).   One way is to calculate approximate dividend yield: approximate annual dividend yield = 8/75 = .1067

| Asset Price | Strike | Volatility | T | R(f) | Div. Yield | Put/Call |
|---|---|---|---|---|---|---|
| 75.00 | 70.00 | 0.2000 | 0.25 | 0.0900 | 0.1067 | 1 |
| B-S Value | | | Delta | Gamma | $\phi$~X(1) | $\phi$~X(2) |
| 5.68424 | | | 0.6798 | 0.0406 | 0.6982 | 0.5982 |

Or we could calculate the value ex-dividend: 75 - 2 = 73

| Asset Price | Strike | Volatility | T | R(f) | Div. Yield | Put/Call |
|---|---|---|---|---|---|---|
| 73.00 | 70.00 | 0.2000 | 0.25 | 0.0900 | 0.000 | 1 |
| B-S Value | | | Delta | Gamma | $\phi$X(1) | $\phi$X(2) |
| 5.66469 | | | 0.6946 | 0.0429 | 0.6946 | 0.5946 |

The difference in price is less than 2 cents, much less than the bid-ask spread.

6(b). Using put call parity

P = C - S + PV(D) + PV(K)
P = 5.68 - 75 + (70+2)*exp(-.09*.25)
P= 1.08

6(c).

| Asset Price | Strike | Volatility | T | R(f) | Div. Yield | Put/Call |
|---|---|---|---|---|---|---|
| 75.00 | 70.00 | 0.2000 | 0.25 | 0.0900 | 0.1067 | 1 |
| B-S Value | | | Delta | Gamma | $\phi$X(1) | $\phi$X(2) |
| 7.25695 | | | 0.9649 | 0.0334 | 0.9649 | 0.8649 |

So the price would increase: $1.57

24 - 14

6(d). An increase in the volatility to 30% would increase the call's value. A decrease in the risk-free rate to 8% would decrease the call's value.

7(a).

| Stock Price | Call Value | Hedge Ratio |
|---|---|---|
| $25 | $0.02 | 0.0104 |
| $30 | 0.26 | 0.1003 |
| $35 | 1.32 | 0.3409 |
| $40 | 3.62 | 0.6331 |
| $45 | 7.51 | 0.8438 |
| $50 | 12.00 | 0.9463 |
| $55 | 16.80 | 0.9838 |

$X = \$40; r = .09; T = 6$ months $(0.5); \sigma = 0.25$

$$d_1 = \frac{\ln(S/X) + [r + (\sigma^2/2)]T}{\sigma(T)^{1/2}} \qquad\qquad d_2 = d_1 - \sigma(T)^{1/2}$$

For example, if $S = 25$

$$d_1 = \frac{\ln(25/40) + [.09 + (.25^2/2)](0.5)}{(.25)(0.5)^{1/2}}$$

$$= \frac{-.47 + [.09 + .03125](0.5)}{(.25)(.7071)} = \frac{-.47 + .060625}{.17678} = -.409375/.17678 = -2.31$$

$d_2 = -2.31 - (.25)(0.5)^{1/2} = -2.31 - .17678 = -2.49$

$N(d_1) = 1 - .9896 = 0.0104$ $\qquad\qquad N(d_2) = 1 - .9936 = 0.0064$

$C = S(N(d_1)) - Xe^{-rT}(N(d_2)) = 25(0.0104) - 40e^{-(.09)(.5)}(.0064) = 0.26 - 0.24 = \$0.02$

7(b). The call value for each level of stock price is lower than those shown in Table 24.1 because:
   (1) A decrease in time to expiration (one year to six months) causes a decrease in the call value.
   (2) A decrease in security volatility $(\sigma)$ causes a decrease in the call value.

7(c). For $S = 40$

$P = Xe^{-rT}(N(-d_2)) - S(N(-d_1)) = 40e^{-(.09)(.5)}(.4325) - 40(.3669) = 16.539 - 14.676 = \$1.86$

where $N(-d_1) = 1 - .6331 = .3669$ and $N(-d_2) = 1 - .5675 = .4325$

8(a).   Call:

| Future Price | Strike | Volatility | T | R(f) | Div. Yield | Put/Call |
|---|---|---|---|---|---|---|
| 46.50 | 46.50 | 0.2300 | 0.50 | 0.0545 | 0.000 | 1 |
| Future Option | | | Delta | Gamma | d(1) | d(2) |
| 4.14286 | | | 0.1150 | 0.0524 | 0.1150 | -0.1150 |

Put:

| Future Price | Strike | Volatility | T | R(f) | Div. Yield | Put/Call |
|---|---|---|---|---|---|---|
| 46.50 | 46.50 | 0.2300 | 0.50 | 0.0545 | 0.000 | -1 |
| Future Option | | | Delta | Gamma | d(1) | d(2) |
| 4.14286 | | | -0.1150 | 0.0524 | 0.1150 | -0.1150 |

8(b).   You have created a long forward on a future. An investor that is bullish on the futures price would take a long position in this synthetic forward.

| 9(a). | Asset Price | Strike | Volatility | T | R(f) | Div. Yield | Put/Call |
|---|---|---|---|---|---|---|---|
| | 653.50 | 670.00 | 0.1600 | 0.25 | 0.0650 | 0.0280 | 1 |
| | B-S Value | | | Delta | Gamma | $\phi$X(1) | $\phi$X(2) |
| | 15.48 | | | -0.1860 | 0.0074 | -0.1873 | -0.2673 |

9(b).

| Asset Price | Strike | Volatility | T | R(f) | Div. Yield | Put/Call |
|---|---|---|---|---|---|---|
| 653.50 | 670.00 | 0.1751 | 0.25 | 0.0650 | 0.0280 | 1 |
| B-S Value | Market Price | Difference | Delta | Gamma | $\phi$X(1) | $\phi$X(2) |
| 17.40 | 17.40 | 0.00 | -0.1628 | 0.0068 | -0.1640 | -0.2515 |

So, the option has an implied volatility of 17.51%.

9(c).   The market price may differ from the estimated price for the following reasons:

1. The quote may be stale. That is the market maker may not have adjusted the price to reflect new market conditions.
2. Is this a bid or ask price? The ask price win have a higher implied volatility than the bid price or the midpoint.
3. We are making the assumption that dividends are paid continuously, when in fact they are clumped together. So our estimate of the effective dividend yield may be incorrect.
4. Black-Scholes model may not be the correct pricing model.

10(a). The volatility estimates are calculated as:

|  |  |
|---|---|
| Period A | 0.2708 |
| Period B | 0.2570 |

10(b).

| Asset Price | Strike | Volatility | T | R(f) | Div. Yield | Put/Call |
|---|---|---|---|---|---|---|
| 120.63 | 115.00 | 0.2570 | 0.17 | 0.0742 | 0.0365 | 1 |
| B-S Value | Market Price | Difference | Delta | Gamma | $\phi X(1)$ | $\phi X(2)$ |
| 8.72 | 12.25 | 3.53 | 0.5608 | 0.0265 | 0.5643 | 0.4583 |

The market price is much higher than the calculated BS price. This implies that if all of the other parameters of the model are correct, the implied BS volatility is much higher than the historical volatility. This could be because of recent developments in the stock. Another more controversial explanation is that implied volatilities have a risk-premium built into them such that implied volatilities are on average higher than realized historical volatilities.

11(a).

| | Cost/Contract | x 31,250 |
|---|---|---|
| long 1.44 Call | 0.0422 | $1,318.75 |
| short 1.48 Call | 0.0255 | $ 796.88 |
| long 1.40 Put | 0.0260 | $ 812.50 |
| short 1.44 Put | 0.0422 | $1,318.75 |

| June USD/GBP | Net Initial 1.44 Profit | Long Call 1.48 Profit | Short Call 1.40 Profit | Long Put 1.40 Profit | Short Put 1.44 Profit | Total Net Profit |
|---|---|---|---|---|---|---|
| 1.36 | $15.63 | 0 | 0 | 1250 | -2500 | ($1,234.38) |
| 1.40 | $15.63 | 0 | 0 | 0 | -1250 | ($1,234.38) |
| 1.44 | $15.63 | 0 | 0 | 0 | 0 | $15.63 |
| 1.48 | $15.63 | 1250 | 0 | 0 | 0 | $1,265.63 |
| 1.52 | $15.63 | 2500 | -1250 | 0 | 0 | $ 1,265.63 |

11(b).

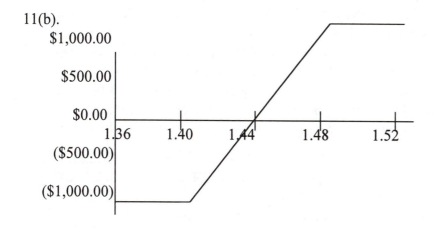

This position resembles a bull vertical spread. The purchaser of this portfolio is probably moderately bullish on the exchange rate. We see this from the willingness to give up the extreme upside in exchange for limiting the downside.

11(c). This is a simple application of put-call parity

C - P = FX * exp(-rf * dt) - K *exp(-rd *dt)

where FX is the exchange rate,

rd (rf) is the domestic (foreign) risk-free rate,

dt is the time to expiration.

C - P = 1.385*exp(-.07*.1667) - 1.44*exp(-.05*.1667) = ($0.0591)

12.     CFA Examination III (1986)

12(a).  A straddle-type option strategy called a conversion would involve writing (selling) 40 calls and buying 40 puts on the underlying Government bond portfolio. The investor receives the option premium less commissions for the calls and pays the option premium plus commissions for the puts.

12(b).  The breakeven market prices for the underlying Government bonds are calculated as follows:

| | |
|---|---|
| Portfolio Manager Sells Dec 112 Calls | @ 1.65 |
| Buys Dec 109 1/2 Puts | @ 2.25 |
| Portfolio Manager Receives: | (.60) / $ 100 par value |
| Less Commission of: | (.10) / $ 100 par value |
| Resulting in Total Net Option Receipts of: | (.70) / $100 par value |

Currently, the market price of the bond is $111.00. The breakeven market price on the upside is equal to the call exercise price plus (less) the total net option premiums received (paid). The breakeven price on the downside is equal to the put exercise price less (plus) the total net option premiums received (paid).

Upside: 112.00 - .70 = 111.30
Downside: 109.50 + .70 = 110.20

12(c).  Presently the market price of the bond at $111.00 is about in the middle of breakeven range. If the bond price increases 0.27% [(111.30 - 111)/111] or decreases 0.72% [(111 - 110.20)/111], then the strategy would breakeven. These percentage price changes are much less than one standard deviation of past price changes on the underlying bonds (10% standard deviation). Thus, based on past evidence, it is unlikely that this strategy would add to return. But this is all right because this strategy is essentially a risk minimization, return protection strategy designed to lock in already achieved returns.

13(a)

| Price of ARB Stock at Expiration | Initial Cost | Profit on Call #1 Position | Profit on Call #2 Position | Net Profit on Total Position |
|---|---|---|---|---|
| 40 | ($1.72) | $0.00 | $0.00 | ($1.72) |
| 45 | ($1.72) | $0.00 | $0.00 | ($1.72) |
| 50 | ($1.72) | $0.00 | $0.00 | ($1.72) |
| 55 | ($1.72) | $5.00 | $0.00 | $3.28 |
| 60 | ($1.72) | $10.00 | $0.00 | $8.28 |
| 65 | ($1.72) | $15.00 | ($10.00) | $3.28 |
| 70 | ($1.72) | $20.00 | ($20.00) | ($1.72) |

Harcourt, Inc.

13(b).

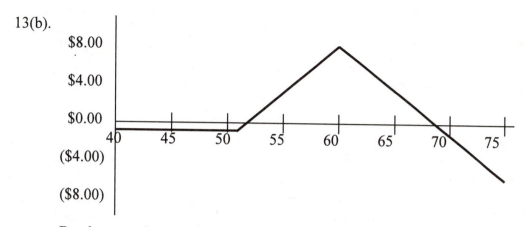

Breakeven points are $51.72 and $68.28. Maximum profit occurs at $60.

13(c). The user of this position is betting on low volatility (that prices will stay between breakeven points). The holder has limited liability for substantial price declines and unlimited liability for substantial price increases.

14. Consider the following put option transactions: (i) long one put #1; (ii) short two puts #2, and (iii) long one put #3. The net initial cost of this set of transactions is $0.83 (= 1.70 + 6.47 - 3.67 - 3.67) and its terminal payoffs for a variety of potential expiration date SAS stock prices are:

| SAS Price (Expiration) | Value of Put #1 | Value of Put #2 | Value of Put #3 | Cost of Options | Net Profit |
|---|---|---|---|---|---|
| 20 | 15.00 | -40.00 | 25.00 | 0.83 | -0.83 |
| 25 | 10.00 | -30.00 | 20.00 | 0.83 | -0.83 |
| 30 | 5.00 | -20.00 | 15.00 | 0.83 | -0.83 |
| 36 | 0.00 | -10.00 | 10.00 | 0.83 | -0.83 |
| 40 | 0.00 | 0.00 | 5.00 | 0.83 | 4.17 |
| 45 | 0.00 | 0.00 | 0.00 | 0.83 | -0.83 |
| 50 | 0.00 | 0.00 | 0.00 | 0.83 | -0.83 |
| 55 | 0.00 | 0.00 | 0.00 | 0.83 | -0.83 |
| 60 | 0.00 | 0.00 | 0.00 | 0.83 | -0.83 |

Graphing these payoffs would lead to the same illustration as shown in Figure 24.22.

15. CFA Examination III (May 1997)

The suggested strategy is essentially a zero-premium collar, which is constructed by selling a call option with enough premium to fund the purchase of the put option. In this case, at-the-money protection (provided by the put) is more expensive than the out-of-money call. Therefore, the strategy requires the sale of two calls to finance one put. The call is not struck (sold) at the money because the fund manager, Ken Webster, does not want to incur the opportunity cost for a 1.05 percent rise above the S&P 500 Index's

24 - 19

current 668 level. By selling two 675 calls, the manager would expose the portfolio to incurring losses (from the calls) at twice the rate of the underlying portfolio's appreciation. The portfolio would experience full market participation within the 665-675 range (plus the premium received from selling the collar). The strategy will underperform if the index has appreciated beyond 675 at expiration date and outperform if the index has declined below 665 at expiration.

15(a). **Potential Returns**

    i.    **Index rises to 701.** This rise would cause a substantial loss to the combined portfolio. An increase above the 675 call's strike price would require an increase above 1.05 percent (668 to 675) in the S&P 500, at which time the call would be in the money. Because two calls were sold for every put bought in the collar, the collar would lose at twice the rate of the underlying portion of the portfolio against which it was written for any appreciation of the S&P 500 above 675. (The portfolio would realize a slight increment in return because of the premium [per collar traded] generated by the collar [2 x 4.30 - 8.05 = 0.55 per collar].)

    ii.    **No change.** The combined portfolio would experience only a slight gain as a result of the premium (per collar traded) generated by the collar (2 x 4.30 - 8.05 =0.55 per contract). Both the put and the call would expire worthless. Therefore, the change in the portfolio would mirror the S&P 500 at 668.

    iii.    **Index declines to 635.** This decline would cause a slight loss to the combined portfolio because of the unhedged portion (668 to 675); then, the put hedge would take effect. Below 675.55, the put option guards against losses on a one-for-one basis. (The portfolio would realize a slight increment in return because of the premium [per collar traded] generated by the collar [2 x 4.30 - 8.05 = 0.55 per collar].)

15(b). **Effect of Scenarios on Delta**

    i.    **Index rises to 701**. The initial delta of the out-of-the-money calls was 0.36. As the call option got into the money and time expired, the delta of each call would approach 1.0. As the put option went out of the money and time expired, the delta of each put would approach zero.

    ii.    **No change.** The delta of both the put and call would approach zero as they both went out of the money and time was expiring.

    iii.    **Index declines to 635.** The initial delta of the out-of-the-money put was -0.44. As the put option got into the money and time expired, the delta of each put would approach 1.0. As the call option went out of the money and time expired, the delta of each call would approach zero.

### 15(c). Pricing

Compared with the historical volatility of the market (12 percent), the calls (Part *ii*) are priced relatively cheaper (11 percent) and the puts (Part *i*) are priced relatively more expensive (14 percent). The suggestion is that the collar (Part *iii)* is relatively expensive.

### 15(d). Wasting Asset

The options used to replicate the collar are "wasting assets" because they are worthless after the expiration date. Therefore, after 30 days, the strategy would have to be assessed and reestablished if desired. The profit or loss on the trade would depend on the market price as outlined in Part A and would be equal to the option's intrinsic value. Collars do not hedge away risk; they change the risk profile of the portfolio.

# CHAPTER 25

## SWAP CONTRACTS, CONVERTIBLE SECURITIES, AND OTHER EMBEDDED DERIVATIVES

### Answers to Questions

1.      CFA Examination III (1994)

1(a).   An interest rate swap is a customized risk-management vehicle. In a pension portfolio (i.e., investment) context, an interest rate swap would be represented by an agreement between two parties to exchange a series of interest money cash flows for a certain period of time (term) based on a stated (notional) amount of principal. For example, one party will agree to make a series of floating-rate coupon payments to another party in exchange for receipt of a series of fixed-rate coupon payments (or vice versa, in which case the swap would work in reverse). No exchange of principal payments is made.

1(b).   Strategies using interest rate swaps to affect duration or improve return in a domestic fixed-income portfolio can be divided into two categories:

*Duration modification.* Swapping floating- for fixed-rate interest payments increases portfolio duration (and vice versa, decreases duration when the portfolio is the floating-rate recipient). This method of modifying duration can be used either to control risk (e.g., keep it within policy guidelines/ranges) or to enhance return (e.g., to profit from a rate anticipation bet while remaining within an allowed range).

*Seeking profit opportunities in the swap market.* Opportunities occur in the swap market, as in the cash markets, to profit from temporary disequilibrium between demand and supply. If, in the process of exploiting such opportunities, portfolio duration would be moved beyond a policy guideline/range, it can be controlled by using bond futures contracts or by making appropriate cash-market transactions.

If a strategy calls for a large-scale reorientation of the portfolio's characteristics in a manner that swaps could achieve, their use for implementation of the strategy would act to reduce transaction costs (thus improving portfolio return) and might also permit transactions to be effected more quickly or completely than through conventional trading mechanisms.

2.      An interest rate swap is an agreement to exchange a series of cash flows based on the difference between a fixed interest rate and a floating interest rate on some notional amount. A fixed rate receiver would get the difference between a fixed rate and a floating rate if the fixed rate was above the floating rate, and pay the difference if floating was above fixed. The fixed rate is set so that no cash changes hands upon initiation of the deal. This can be thought of as:

i. A series of forward contracts on the floating rate because forward contracts also have no initial cash flow and will net the `1ifFerence between the floating rate and the forward rate (which acts like a fixed rate). To make the analogy precise, only one forward rate is chosen but it is chosen such that the sum of the values of all the contracts are zero. The fixed rate receiver is like the short position in the interest rate forwards, because if interest rates go up, she loses.

ii. A pair of bonds, one with a floating-rate coupon the other with a fixed-rate coupon (both selling at par with the same face value and maturity). Being the fixed-rate receiver in the swap is the same as being long the fixed-rate bond and short the floating-rate bond. As long as the floating rate is less than the fixed rate, the coupon payment from the fixed-rate bond will cover the interest due on the floating rate bond and the difference is profit. If the floating rate is above the fixed rate then the fixed-rate receiver must make up the difference. Since the bonds are of the same face amount, there is no net cash flow at the beginning or end of the agreement.

3. To have zero value at origination, the present vale of the expected cash flows from the swap must be zero. This implies that if there is an upward sloping yield curve, the expected cash flows to the floating payer will come at the beginning of the swap and be offset by expected payments by the floating payer at the end of the swap. The only way this is possible is if the fixed rate is somewhere between the current floating rate cow) and the implied floating rate later in the contract (high).

4. You are essentially holding a two-year swap agreement that requires you to pay 7% in exchange for floating. Since the market rate for the same swap is 6.5%, if your counterparty defaulted you would be able to replace the swap at a lower rate. Thus, it would be to your benefit for your counterparty to default, and you would realize an economic gain.

5. You have created an off-market swap where you are paying a fixed rate of 7%. This is seen by analyzing the portfolio of long a 7% cap and short a 7% floor. If interest rates are above 7%, then the cap pays the difference between 7% and the floating rate, and the floor is out-of-the money. If interest rates are below 7%, then you must pay the difference between floating and 7%, and the cap is out-of-the-money. Since the market rate is a fixed rate of 8% for the same maturity and you only have to pay 7%, you will have to pay money up-front to get the cap and floor. In other words, the cap costs more than you will get from selling the floor.

6. CFA Examination III (1995)

6(a). The purchase of an interest rate receiver's swaption would modify O the risk characteristics of a fixed-income portfolio and (2) the return characteristics of a fixed-income portfolio, in the following manner:

(1). The interest rate receiver's side of the swaption provides the right to receive a fixed interest rate and pay a variable rate. The swaption behaves as a call option on a bond with leverage arising from paying the variable rate. The transaction increases the duration of the portfolio, but because of the option aspect, convexity would be greater for an interest rate decrease than for an interest rate increase. Risk increases but not symmetrically.

(2). If interest rates rise, the option will not be exercised and the loss will be limited to the premium paid to enter the swaption. That is, the effect of a rate rise is the loss of the premium. Downside risk is limited. If interest rates decline, the option will be exercised and the portfolio's return enhanced. The return is enhanced because it receives the higher interest rates (strike rates) instead of the lower prevailing market rates, which offsets reinvestment rate risk in a declining interest rate environment. Overall, the larger the decline in rates, the larger the return enhancement effect.

6(b). The following are major disadvantages of using swaptions to help manage risk in a fixed-income portfolio:

(1). Swaptions are illiquid instruments whose use incurs transaction costs. Because transaction costs are measured by the bid-ask spread employed by the counterparty, the more custom-made the swaption the larger the spread and the larger the transaction cost if the instrument is not held to term.

(2). Swaptions have a credit risk that can be much higher than that of exchange-traded securities such as futures contracts or standard options. Because owning the instruments can be highly profitable to buyers if interest rates decline, swaptions can also be very costly to sellers. Hence, the importance of controlling credit risk is increased.

(3). A swaption purchase imposes a return-reducing cost on the portfolio (the premium).

The following are minor disadvantages:

(1). As with most derivative instruments, using swaptions complicates performance measurement. This disadvantage is not directly related to risk control or portfolio management.

(2). Because no standard contracts exist for swaptions, they are subject to legal risks (e.g., a party may be able to nullify a contract or be forced into litigation before honoring a contract).

(3). Swaptions potentially introduce accounting risk. Financial Accounting Standards Board standards continue to evolve. Issues such as the validity of treating swaptions as a form of off-balance sheet financing must also be considered.

(4). Using a derivative based on a yield set in the swap market to hedge against a yield set in the capital market exposes the portfolio to the potential for basis risk.

25 - 3

7.   CFA Examination III (1995)

7(a).   The problem here is to sell equities and reinvest the proceeds with the skilled fixed-income manager, without changing the split between the existing allocations to the two asset classes. The solution is to turn to derivative financial instruments as the means to the end: selling enough of the existing fixed-income exposure and bringing in enough of the equity exposure to get the desired mix result.

The following are distinct derivatives strategies that the board could use to increase the Fund's allocation to the fixed-income manager without changing the present fixed-income/equity proportions:

**Strategy 1 - Use futures:**  One strategy would be to sell futures on a fixed-income index and buy futures on an equity index.

Selling the futures eliminates the fixed-income index return and risk, while keeping the skilled fixed-income manager's extra return. By being long the equity index, the portfolio obtains the index return and risk, keeping its exposure to the equity market.

**Strategy 2 - Use swaps:** A second strategy would be to use over-the-counter (OTC) swaps.

BI would swap a fixed-income index return for an equity index return in a notional amount large enough to keep the skilled manager's extra return while eliminating the fixed-income market return and replacing it with the equity market return.

**Strategy 3 - Use option combinations:** A third strategy would use put and call options to create futures-like securities.

Buying put options and selling call options on a fixed-income index, while selling put options and buying call options on a stock index, would achieve the same result as the appropriate futures position.

7(b).   The following are advantages and disadvantages of each strategy identified and explained in Part A:
**Strategy 1 - Use futures**

*Advantages:*
1.   Futures contracts are liquid instruments.
2.   Transaction costs are low.
3.   Credit risk is negligible because the securities are marked to market daily.

*Disadvantages:*
1. If the holding period is long, rollover (transaction) costs are incurred.
2. Standard contract forms are limited, so contracts may not exist on the index or instrument needed. Tracking errors may create basis risk between the index and the performance benchmark.

25 - 4

## Strategic 2 - Use swaps

*Advantages:*

1.  Swaps can be tailored to fit the desired investment horizon, eliminating (or reducing) rollover costs.
2.  Swaps can be contracted for a specific index dike the performance benchmark) even if there is no futures contract on it.
3.  The desired adjustment goal can be accomplished through a single transaction.

*Disadvantages:*

1.  A counterparty credit risk is created that can be much larger than with other types of instruments.
2.  Swap agreements are illiquid instruments, and disposals can be both difficult and expensive.
3.  Transaction costs are large because of typical "tailoring" of a given swap.

## Strategy 3 - Use option combinations

Buying put and call options on fixed income index (synthetic short position) and buying call and selling puts on stock index (synthetic long position)

*Advantages:*

1. Transaction costs are low.
2. Credit risks are small.

*Disadvantages:*

1. Rollover(s) may be necessary.
2. The "right" option may not be available when needed or at all.
3. Holders may exercise the put option and end the hedge.

A generic disadvantage of any strategy is that returns are automatically eroded by the costs of establishing and maintaining the strategies, of meeting margin requirements, if any, and of unwinding them, if necessary.

8.      CFA Examination III (1995)

8(i).   From BI's perspective, the major risk it would eliminate under this transaction is represented by participation in the EAFE Index (to the extent that this participation has been reduced), the return on which is now being paid to the counterparty bank.

BI has reduced its international equity exposure. The market risk, formerly present in that part of the total participation that has now been swapped out in exchange for S&P Index exposure, has been eliminated.

8(ii).  From BI's perspective, the major risk that is retained after this transaction (i.e., not eliminated) is the risk of tracking error between BI's international equity portfolio and the EAFE Index. This potential tracking error arises from differences between the portfolio and the index in terms of country weights and security selection. Thus, as the correlation coefficient between BI's portfolio and the index is probably less than 1.0, a basis risk is retained.

To the extent that significant differences in composition now exist (either in terms of country weights or security selection), BI's return experience could be quite different from that expected when the decision to change the exposure was made. In effect, the transaction is a bet that U.S. stocks will outperform EAFE stocks in U.S. return terms. The market risks inherent in all such exposures still apply, including exposure to global equity markets. Because the EAFE return is dollar denominated, the BI international equity portfolio is still exposed to currency risk either hedged or unhedged.

8(iii). From BI's perspective, risks created under this transaction include:

**1. Counterparty credit risks.** BI now has contractual relationships with two banks that it did not have before, creating a new risk dimension that will require monitoring and ongoing evaluation. This credit risk is, in effect, an added element of cost and uncertainty that must be considered in assessing the cost/benefit outcomes expected to result from the transaction.

2. **Return risks arising from spread changes between LIBOR and T-bill rates.** If the initial or expected spread between these two markets moves against BI, it will find its realized return to be different from its expected return. This will, in effect, increase the cost of the move and reduce its efficacy.

3. **Return risks arising from differential S&P 500 Index and EAFE Index performance.** Future relative performance levels are uncertain. Thus, BI's new risks include not only a spread risk in terms of the S&P Index (added) versus the EAFE Index (reduced) but also spread risk between the actual portfolio and the index portfolios.

4. **Risk related to the one-year term of the transaction.** If BI wants to reverse or modify the original move away from international to U.S. equity exposure or to change the LIBOR/T-bill markers, new complications arise. Liquidity risk is now present. Changing or undoing the contracts with the counterparty banks may be impossible or unduly costly. A risk of being "frozen-in-place" and being unable to take advantage of new circumstances or avoid new dangers has been introduced. A corollary risk is that the one-year term does not equate with the "temporary" reduction intent of the bond's proviso. A risk of overstaying a temporary reduction has been introduced and may manifest itself in liquidity or additional expense terms.

5. **Rollover risk.** BI may be unable to renew the contracts on satisfactory terms if the board wants to do so at the expiration of the original one-year term.

6. **Lower diversification.** BI has temporarily reduced its diversification because it has decreased its international equity exposure and increased its domestic equity exposure.

7. **Risk of mismatched notional amounts.** If the swaps have variable notional amounts, there is risk that the notional amounts upon which the swap payments are based may become mismatched as the return experience of the EAFE and S&P 500 indexes diverge.

25 - 6

8. **Regulatory, legal, or accounting risk.** BI has added the risk that the regulatory, legal, or accounting treatment of these swaps may be changed unfavorably during the term of the contracts.

9. **Benchmark measurement.** The benchmark should measure the portfolio manager's execution of the strategies for which he or she is responsible. If the board changes the strategy, it may need to change the benchmark.

9. CFA Examination III (1997)

9(a). **Transactions Needed to Restore Balance**

   i. **Futures.** The most straightforward way to restore the portfolio's 50 percent bonds/50 percent equity allocation *and* restore (lengthen) the duration is for the plan to purchase a $200 million equity index (i.e., S&P 500 Index) futures position and a $200 million *fixed* (i.e., long-duration Treasury) bond futures position.

   ii. **Swaps.** Entering into two swaps will restore the 50 percent bond/50 percent equity allocation. On the fixed-income side, the floater's impact on portfolio duration (shortening) will be offset if the plan enters into a $200 million receiver interest rate swap in which it pays T-bill (plus 50 basis points [bps]) and receives fixed (long-bond) exposure. On the equity side, rebalancing also requires a $200 million swap in which the plan pays T-bill (plus 50 bps) returns and receives equity index return. This transaction could be accomplished with one swap--that is, swapping $400 million of floating-rate returns for a 50/50 blend of fixed-income and equity returns.

9(b). **Advantages and Disadvantages of Using Futures**

**Advantages:**
- Futures contracts do not expose the plan to credit (counterparty) risk, as swaps do.
- Although volume and liquidity in futures contract trading vary among markets and indexes, futures pricing for many major market indexes is generally tight enough that exchange-traded futures offer flexibility, observable prices, and ease of entry and exit. Buying or selling the contract is simpler and more certain in the open market than is identifying a willing counterparty to negotiate a reverse swap.
- Implementing a futures position is easier than implementing a swap because of the smaller denominations possible for futures.
- Because of regulations, swaps cannot be used for certain cases for which futures may be used.
- Futures may be mispriced (below fair value).

**Disadvantages:**
- A futures contract involves the buyer in rollover risk during the two-year period. The swap approach transfers the rolling risk to the counterparty.

- Futures must be marked to market and involve maintenance margins.
- The buyer incurs the risk of tracking error--related to the futures contract vs. the underlying security (basis risk) or the futures contract vs. the hedged asset. Standard futures contracts do not lend themselves to customization in terms of underlying assets or maturities.
- Futures may be mispriced (above fair value).
- Futures require two transactions to achieve the same result as one swap.

10.    The difference between warrants and regular options comes from the difference in issuer. Unlike a regular call option, when a warrant is exercised the shares purchased are new shares created by the company. Since the shares have identical rights as existing shares and have been purchased at a discount to existing shares (otherwise the warrants wouldn't be exercised) the value of existing shares is watered down. This depresses the value of the stock. Consequently warrants are less valuable than regular options since regular options have no affect on the capital structure of the firm.

Firm's may wish to issue warrants if the floatation costs are lower or if they are worried about not being able to sell enough new stock. Warrants can be used to "force" the issuance of new shares.

11.    Convertible bonds and preferred stock are both very similar to an ordinary bond (or perpetuity) and a call option on the firm's common stock. This is because these instruments give the holder the option but not the obligation to trade in the existing asset for common stock, much the way a call option gives its holder the right but not the obligation to purchase shares at a prospected price. Since call options have upside potential and a limited downside, these traits are passed on to the convertible bonds and preferred stock. The pricing of these securities must take into account the optionality embedded in the issue.

12.    Structured notes must satisfy several criteria to be successfully issued. Most important is that the payoff structure be one that appeals to investors. Perhaps it helps get around some legal restrictions or provides a payoff that is not available in other traded securities. Investors will not take on the additional hassle of owning structured notes unless there is some benefit to them. It must also be the case that the payoff of the note is well defined. It must be based on an easily measured index or price that is not subject to interpretation or manipulation. You will never see a structured note whose payoff depends on the number of "nice days" in New York or the price of an illiquid stock or commodity.

Issuers usually rely on investment banks to know what the needs or preferences of prospective investors are. Frequently, investment banks will know that a client wants a certain type of structured note and will approach prospective issuers to put the deal together.

# CHAPTER 25

## Answers to Problems

1.  The fixed-rate receiver will receive 5.48%.

| Date | Fixed-Rate | LIBOR | Converted FR-LIBOR (-1) | Net Cash Flows |
|---|---|---|---|---|
| 2/10/99 | 5.48% | 5.00% | | |
| 8/10/99 | 5.48% | 5.30% | 0.11% | $11,968.75 |
| 2/10/00 | 5.48% | 5.85% | -0.20% | ($22,250,000) |
| 8/10/00 | 5.48% | 6.00% | -0.76% | ($84,984.37) |
| 2/10/01 | 5.48% | 5.60% | -0.91% | ($102,093.75) |

2(a).  Company W will want to enter into a receive-fixed pay floating swap with semiannual payments for 5 years with a notional principal of USD 35M. The current quote on this swap is 5.47%. Company X will want to enter into a pay-fixed receive floating swap with semi-annual payments for 4 years with a notional principal of USD 50M. The current quote on this swap is 5.45%.

2(b).  The two swaps are not matched perfectly. The first mismatch is the size of the notional principal. Since Company W's swap is for USD 15M less than Company X's the dealer is exposed to a USD 15M receive-fixed swap for the first four years. The second mismatch is maturity. Company W's swap is one year longer, so after four years, the dealer will be exposed to a USD 35M pay-fixed swap.

3.  The key is to recognize that the combination of buying the cap and writing a floor at the same strike rate generates the same settlement cash flows as a pay-fixed swap. The fixed rate on the swap would equal the strike rate on the cap and floor.

Consider first the 8 percent cap-floor combination. The treasurer could buy the cap for 413 basis points (the market maker's offer) and sell the floor for 401 basis points (the market maker's bid). The net is an up-front outflow of 12 basis points (times the notional principal). Because the 8 percent pay-fixed swap would not entail an initial payment, the 8 percent cap-floor combination can be rejected.

Consider next the 7 percent cap-floor combination. The treasurer could buy the cap for 597 basis points and sell the floor for 320 basis points, resulting in a net up-front outflow of 277 basis points. The fixed rate on the synthetic swap would be 7 percent however, not 8 percent. The attraction of the cap-floor alternative turns on the trade-off of a present value of 277 basis points versus a three-year annuity of 100 basis points (actually a 12-period annuity of 25 basis points per quarterly period). Using the three-year fixed rate of .20 percent, the present value of the savings is 263.57 basis points; that is,

25 - 9

$$\sum_{t=1}^{12} \frac{25}{(1+ .00820/4)^t} = 263.57$$

Because the 263.57 basis points are less than the up-front cost of 277 basis points, the 7 percent cap-floor combination can be rejected as well.

Consider finally the 9 percent cap-floor combination. The treasurer could buy the cap for 220 basis points and sell the floor for 502 basis points, resulting in a net up-front inflow of 282 basis points. The fixed rate on the synthetic swap would be 9 percent. Because the initial receipt exceeds the present value of the higher swap coupon (i.e. 282 > 263.57), this combination should be considered. Is it definitely better? Perhaps so in terms of cash flow and the time value of money, but the treasurer would also have to consider the tax and accounting treatment of the difference in the options premiums to confirm the benefit.

4(a).  Issue the Traditional FRN and enter <u>one pay-fixed</u> swap:

[(LIBOR + 0.25%) x (365/360)] + [9.20% - LIBOR x 365/360)]
= 9.20% + (0.25% x 365/360) = 9.4535%

Issue the Bull Floater and enter <u>one receive-fixed</u> swap:

[(18.40% - LIBOR) x (365/360)] + [(LIBOR x 365/360) - 9.10%)]
= (18.40% x 365/360) - 9.10% = 9.5556%

Issue the Bear Floater and enter <u>two pay-fixed</u> swaps (or one with twice the notional principal):

[(2 x LIBOR - 9.10%) x (365/360)] + [2 x {9.20% - (LIBOR x 365/360)}]
= (2 x 9.20%) - (9.10% x 365/360) = 9.1736%

Note that the Bull/swap combination is fixed only for LIBOR < 18.40%, since the coupon on the Bull Floater would be zero if LIBOR > 18.40% while the net settlement payout on the swap increases. The Bear/swap combination is fixed only for LIBOR @ 4.55%. If LIBOR < 4.55%, the coupon of the Bear Floater remains zero while the net settlement payout on the swap increases.

4(b).  Issue one $25 million tranche as a Traditional FRN and a second $25 million tranche as a Bull Floater:

(1/2) [(LIBOR + 0.25%) x 365/360] + (1/2) [(18.40% - LIBOR) x (365/360)]
= (1/2) (0.25% x 365/360) + (1/2) (18.40% x 365/360) = 9.4545%

25 - 10

4(c).   Student exercise

4(d).   As suggested by its name, investors in a Bull Floater are "bullish" on bonds, expecting bond prices to rise. Since the coupon rate on the Bull Floater is inversely related to LIBOR, these investors must expect the future path for LIBOR to be steady or falling.

4(e).   Investors in a Bear Floater are "bearish" on bonds, expecting bond prices to be falling. So, as market rates (and LIBOR) rise, the coupon rate on the Bear Floater rises even faster, in fact, at twice the rate. An investor who buys the Bear Floater as a hedge must be exposed to higher levels for LIBOR.

| Event | Exposure | Hedge (Buy Bear floater) |
|---|---|---|
| LIBOR rises | Lose | Gain |
| LIBOR falls | Gain | Lose |

This could occur, for instance, if the investor had long-term, fixed-rate assets funded by short-term or variable-rate liabilities. The duration gap would be positive.

5(a).   Eurobond: 5 years (n)
                    11.5% annual interest ($115 annual payment)
                    Current price = 99.625 (percent of par)
        i = 13.12%

        AUD bond: 5 years-semiannual (10 = n)
                    10.25% + 1% = 11.25% annual rate ($56.25 semi-annual interest)
                    Current price = 100 (par)
        i = 5.92% x 2 = 11.92%

        Based upon the above calculations, the AUD bond provides a higher return.

5(b).   3 years remaining (6 semi-annual periods)
        i = 10.75% (annually) or 5.375% (semiannually)

$$PV = \sum_{t=1}^{6} (\$56.25/(1 + .05375)^6 + 1000/(1 + .05375)^6$$

        = AUD 1027.70  or AUD 102,770,000 (in total)

6.      First of all, recognize that at the current exchange rates, USD 25 million translates in JPY 3,186,750,000 (the product of USD 25,000,000 and JPY 127.47/USD) and GBP 12,736,264 (USD 25,000 divided by USD 1.82/GBP). These become the principal amounts governing the transaction. Then:

6(a). The desired swap could be accomplished by combining the following transactions:
- "pay 4.92% Japanese yen, receive US dollar LIBOR" currency swap
- "receive 9.83% British sterling, pay US dollar LIBOR" currency swap, resulting in a "pay 4.92% yen, receive 9.83% sterling," which represents your offer swap rate in yen and your bid rate in sterling.

6(b). After swapping principal amounts at the origination date, the cash flow exchanges on first settlement date from the counterparty's standpoint are calculated as follows:

Yen payment = $(0.0492) \times (183/365) \times (JPY\ 3,186,750,000) = JPY\ 78,608,828$

and

Pound receipt = $(0.0983) \times (183/365) \times (GBP\ 13,736,264) = GBP\ 686,390$

The full set of cash exchanges, which will be known at the inception of the deal, is:

| Settlement Date | Days in Settlement | Payments (Millions) | Receipts Millions) |
|---|---|---|---|
| Initial | -- | GBP 13.736 | JPY 3,186.75 |
| 1 | 183 | JPY 78.61 | GBP 0.69 |
| 2 | 182 | JPY 78.18 | GBP 0.68 |
| 3 | 183 | JPY 78.61 | GBP 0.69 |
| 4 | 182 | JPY 78.18 | GBP 0.68 |
| 5 | 183 | JPY 78.61 | GBP 0.69 |
| Final | 182 | JPY 3,186.75 and JPY 78.18 | GBP 13.736 and GBP 0.68 |

7(a). The MTM value of the swap was the present value of the dollar inflows converted to francs at the spot rate, less the present value of the franc outflows. The reduction in the dollar interest rate from 12.72 percent to 10.20 percent raised the value of the swap (and the default loss), and the reduction in the franc rate from 14.88 percent to 12.78 percent lowered the value. Adding the appreciation in the dollar relative to the franc from FRF 8.4435/USD to FRF 9.4829/USD suggests that the net effect should have been a positive MTM value. This result is confirmed by the following calculations:

$$PV_{USD} = \frac{USD12,720,000}{1.1020} + \frac{USD112,720,00}{(1.1020)^2} = USD10,361,84$$

$$PV_{FRF} = \frac{FRF125,639,280}{1.1278} + \frac{FRF969,989,280}{(1.1278)^2} = FRF874,012,546$$

25 - 12

$$\text{Value} = \frac{\text{USD}104{,}361{,}843}{\text{USD}0.105453/\text{FRF}} - \text{FRF}874{,}012{,}546 = \text{FRF}115{,}640{,}124$$

The default by the counterparty caused the French corporation to lose FRF 115,640,124, the market value of the swap that had become an asset.

7(b).  The at-market, plain vanilla currency swaps that were available in the market on April 15, 1988, were priced such that the French corporation could receive a fixed rate of 10.20 percent in dollars and pay a fixed rate of 12.78 percent in francs. If the corporation wanted an off-market swap to receive 12.72 percent (an additional 252 basis points in dollars), it would need to pay a higher rate in francs. First calculate the value in francs of 252 basis points in dollars:

$$\frac{252\text{ bps}}{1.1020} + \frac{252\text{ bps}}{(1.1020)^2} = \frac{x}{1.1278} + \frac{x}{(1.1278)^2}$$

or, $x = 260.7375$ bps

The off-market swap fixed rates would be 12.72 percent in dollars versus 15.387375 percent in francs (15.387375 percent = 12.78 percent + 2.607375 percent). The principal on the swap would be USD 100 million = FRF 948,290,000.

The scheduled cash flows on the two-year swap from the perspective of the French corporation would be:

| Date | Receive | Pay |
|---|---|---|
| April 15, 1989 | USD 12,720,000 | FRF 145,916,938 |
| April 15, 1990 | 112,720,000 | 1,094.206.938 |

The MTM value of the currency swap can also be measured as the present value of the lost (or gained) cash flows from entering into a replacement swap at current rates. Because the remaining scheduled and replacement cash receipts are the same, the value of the swap is the difference between the payments. Those differences are FRF 20,277,658 on April 15,1989, and FRF 124,217,658 on April 15, 1990. Discounting those amounts by 12.78 percent provides the value of the swap.

$$\text{MTM Value} = \frac{\text{FRF}20{,}277{,}658}{1.1278} + \frac{\text{FRF }124{,}217{,}658}{(1.1278)^2} = \text{FRF }115{,}640{,}383$$

Note that the value of the swap obtained by the replacement swap method is virtually identical to the more direct mark-to-market method (differing only because of rounding).

8(a).  With these estimates, the settlement payments can be calculated as follows:

*March 2:*

Floating-rate payment = (0.0350 - 0.0010) x ($50,000,000) x (90/360) = $425.000

Equity-index receipt =[(477.51 - 463.11)/463.111 x ($50,000,000) = $1,554,706
So the *net receipt;* the fund expects would be ($1,554,706 - $425,000) = $1,129,706

*June 2:*
Floating-rate payment = (0.0325 - 0.0010) x ($50,000,000) x (92/360) = $402,500

Equity-index receipt = [(464.74 - 477.51)/477.51] x ($50,000,000) = -$1,337,145
So the n*et payment* the fund owes would be ($1,337,145 + $402,500) = $1,739,645

*September 2:*
Floating-rate payment = (0.0375 - 0.0010) x ($50,000,000) x (92/360) = $466.389

Equity-index receipt =[(480.86 - 464.74)/464.74] x ($50,000,000) = $1,734,303
So the *net receipt* the fund expects would be ($1,734,303 - $466,389) = $1,267,914

*December 2:*
Floating-rate payment = (0.0400 - 0.0010) x ($50,000,000) x (91/360) = $492,917

Equity-index receipt = [(482.59 - 480.86)/480.86] x ($50,000,000) = $179,886
So the *net payment* the fund owes would be ($492,917 - $179,886) = $313,031

8(b).   It is also quite common for equity swaps to be based on a notional principal amount that varies directly with the level of the underlying index. If, for instance, the swap participants had agreed to let the initial notional principal of $50 million vary over time, it would have been adjusted up on March 2 to $51.555 million. This adjustment is calculated as [$50 million (1 + [(477.51 - 463.11)/463.11]). That is, each settlement date, the notional principal is adjusted up (down) by the percentage of capital appreciation (depreciation) in the starting level of the index. This adjustment process, which is equivalent to adding the gross equity settlement payment to the initial notional principal, simulates the return that investors with direct stock positions would obtain inasmuch as their actual equity exposure would rise or fall with market conditions. In contrast, a fixed notional principal in an equity swap is equivalent to an asset allocation strategy by which the equity exposure is kept constant.

9.      CFA Examination III (1996)

9(a).   To achieve Ames' goal, HSF would enter into a two-year swap agreement as the fixed rate payer. In return for agreeing to make quarterly cash flow payments based on the two-year swap fixed rate of 5.5%, HSF would receive a cash flow based on the three-month LIBOR that prevailed at the beginning of the settlement period. Each quarterly swap settlement payment would be made on a ret basis, the direction of which would depend on the difference between that period's LIBOR and 5.5%. There would be no exchange of (notional) principal.

9(b).   If the candidate uses the interest rate information provided in the question, the amount of the cash flow would be the difference in the fixed rate and the Eurodollar rate multiplied times the notional amount times the fraction of annual time period. The calculation would be (.055 - .051) x $ 10,000,000 x 1/4 = $10,000. The direction: the endowment pays this cash flow at the end of the first period.

25 - 14

[NOTE: Candidates may use different practices in calculating the holding period of the swap (e.g., 92 days/360 or 365 days) which may produce slightly different solutions.

[IMPORTANT NOTE: Technically, insufficient information was provided in market convention of determining LIBOR at the *start* of the settlement period but paying the cash flow at the end. Thus, the September 30, 1996 settlement payment will be based on the three-month spot LIBOR that prevailed on June 30, 1996. The September 1996 Eurodollar futures rate of 5.1% (as established on June 30, 1996) will be floating rate for the second swap settlement payment, which will be made on December 30, 1996. Since the problem does not provide the current (i.e., June 30, 1996) three-month LIBOR, there is no way to answer the question correctly as it is written.]

9(c).    A pay-fixed swap can be viewed as either: (1) lengthening the duration of a floating rate liability, or (2) shortening the duration of a fixed-rate asset. In HFS's case, the second interpretation is appropriate. By reducing asset duration, HFS has moved to a more defensive posture against the anticipated increase in short-term rates. Said differently, by converting its fixed-rate asset into a synthetic floating-rate note, HFS is now in a position to receive larger coupon cash flows if Ames' interest rate forecast is correct.

9(d).    A plain vanilla interest rate swap is an agreement that requires two counterparties to exchange cash flows on a periodic basis, with one of these cash flows based on a fixed interest rate and the other tied to a variable (i.e., floating) reference rate index. In general, the cash flow for either side of the swap on a given settlement date is calculated as [(Rate) x (Notional Principal) x (% of Year covered by Settlement Period)]. For two risk-neutral counterparties to agree to such an exchange without requiring (or being willing to make) a front-end premium payment, the sum of the discounted expected values of these cash flow streams must be equal.

Although all but the first floating-rate cash flow settlement payment on the swap will not be known at the time the agreement is originated, they can be locked in using a strip of Eurodollar futures contracts. For a two-year, quarterly settlement swap negotiated in June 1996, which has a total of eight settlement dates, the following sequence of LIBOR can be established: Payment #1: three-month spot LBOR in June 1996; Payment #2: September 1996 Eurodollar futures rate, as established in June 1996; Payment #3: December 1996 Eurodollar futures rate, as established in June 1996; etc. Thus, the floating rate side of the swap contract can be fully hedged in June 1996 with Eurodollar futures positions extending out to the March 1998 contract.

With these future LIBOR levels established, the swap fixed rate can then be calculated as the time-weighted average of this sequence. That is, the fixed rate can be thought of as the yield that generates an annuity equal (in present value terms) to the variable cash flows associated with the future LIBOR payments tied to the strip of Eurodollar futures contracts. (By way of an analogy, the swap fixed rate is to the strip of forward LIBOR what a bond's yield-to-maturity is to the underlying term structure of zero-coupon discount rates.)

Harcourt, Inc.

9(e). HFS's pay-fixed swap position (with a fixed rate of 5.5%) could be replicated with an interest rate collar by: (1) purchasing an interest rate cap, which can be viewed as a portfolio of European-style call options on LIBOR, at a strike rate of 5.5 %; and (2) selling an interest rate floor, which is a portfolio of European-style put options on LIBOR, at the same strike rate. If, on a given settlement date, LIBOR is above 5.5 %, HFS will receive a settlement check from the cap seller. Conversely, if LIBOR is less than 5 %, HFS will have to make a settlement payment to the floor buyer. If the cap sell/floor buyer is the same company, these arc the identical settlement exchanges that would occur on a swap with a fixed rate of 5.5%.

In general any 'long cap, short floor" combination (i.e., collar) done with the same strike rate, maturity date, and settlement terms will recreate a pay-fixed swap under those same conditions. However, only when that common strike rate is equal to the prevailing swap fixed rate will the collar have no net front-end cost to either counterparty. This result is the swap equivalent of the put-call parity condition.

10.   The Spanish pension fund would buy El Oso Grande, enter three swaps (each for a notional principal equal to the par value of the FRN or, equivalently, one swap with three times the notional value) to receive the fixed rate of 13.35 percent and write three floors at a strike rate of 8 percent (or, again, one with three times the notional amount).

The role of the floors is to create a fixed-rate asset even when LIBOR is less than 8 percent. Neglecting the floors, if LIBOR 2 8 percent, the return will be (3 x LIBOR - 24 percent) + (3 x 13.35 percent - 3 x LIBOR). The LIBOR flows, net out by design, and the return is 16.05 percent. If LIBOR < 8 percent, the return will be (3 x 13.35 percent - 3 x LIBOR) > 16.05 percent. Writing the floors in effect sells off the potential for a higher return if LIBOR is low. The receipt of 420 basis points (3 x 140 basis points for each floor) raises the fixed rate of return above 16.05 percent.

The net cost of the position is only 95.8 percent of par, the cost of the FRN less the premium received on writing the floors. So the all-in, semiannual fixed rate of return is 17.34 percent, calculated as

$$95.80 = \sum_{t=1}^{10} \frac{8.025}{(1 + y/2)^t} + \frac{100}{(1 + y/2)^{10}}$$

Payoff to EOG is,
Coupon = max(0, 3*LIBOR - 24%)

So the bondholder's exposure is the equivalent of long 3 floaters and long a floor. We can rewrite the payoff as
Coupon = max[0, 3*(LIBOR - 8%)]
Coupon = 3*max[0, LIBOR - 8%]

25 - 16

So to convert this to straight fixed, the fund would need to undertake 3 receive fixed swaps and sell 3 floors at 8%.

This gives a new coupon of (where AFP = amortized floor premium)
New Coupon= $3*\max[0, \text{LIBOR-8\%}] + 3*13.35 - 3*\text{LIBOR} + 3* \min[0,\text{LIBOR-8\%}]+\text{AFP}$
New Coupon= $3*[\text{LIBOR} - 8\%] + 3*13.35 - 3*\text{LIBOR} + \text{AFP}$
New Coupon= $3*\text{LIBOR} - 24\% + 3*13.35 - 3*\text{LIBOR} + \text{AFP}$
New Coupon= $16.05\% + \text{AFP}$

PVIFA(AFP,13.5%) = 140
AFP = 40bp
New Coupon = 16.05% + .40% = 16.45%

11(a). Conversion value = 48.852 shares x 12.125 = $592.33
The conversion option embedded is this bond is currently out of the money since the conversion value is below the current market price of the bond.

11(b). Conversion parity price = Bond price/conversion ratio = 965/48.852 = $19.75

11(c). Payback = $\dfrac{\text{Bond Price} - \text{Conversion Value}}{\text{Bond Income} - \text{Income from equal investment in common stock}}$

$= (965 - 592.33)/(76.25 - 0) = 372.67/76.25 = 4.88$ years

Sold the bond for $965.00 and used the proceeds to purchase 79.588 shares (=$ 965.00/$12.125) of Bildon Enterprise stocks, the payback period would be 4.88 years.

11(d). $\$965.00 = \sum\limits_{t=1}^{14} \dfrac{38.125}{(1 + y/2)^t} + \dfrac{1000}{(1 + y/2)^{14}}$

Solving for y = 4.147% (semiannual) or 8.29% (annual)

$\$917.61 = \sum\limits_{t=1}^{14} \dfrac{38.125}{(1 + .04625)^t} + \dfrac{1000}{(1 + .04625)^{14}}$

This means that the net value of the combined option is $47.39, $965.00 minus $917.61.

12(a). SEK issued a two-year silver-linked note. The bull tranche has its principal redemption amount increase directly with silver price movement. The investor is able to purchase a fixed-income security that also allows for participation in silver price movements. In exchange for accepting a lower-than-market coupon, buyers of the bull tranche will receive a redemption value that exceeds their purchase price if the gold index increases.

25 - 17

12(b). Bull Redemption:

USD 1,000 + [(spot silver price per ounce – USD 4.46) x USD 224.21525)]

12(b)(i). If spot silver = USD 4.96 per ounce

$= 1000 + (4.96 – 4.56)(224.21525) = 1000 + 89.69 = \$1,089.69$

12(b)(ii). If spot silver = USD 3.96 per ounce

$= 1000 + (3.96 – 4.56)(224.21525) = 1000 + (-134.53) = \$865.47$

12(c). Since SEK is effectively short gold across the bull segment, to hedge the position SEK would long gold in the futures market.

SEK If silver = USD 4.35 per ounce

$= 1000 + (4.35 – 4.56)(224.21525) = 1000 + (-47.09) = \$953.91$

$$1001.25 = \sum_{t=1}^{2} 65/(1 + y)^t + 952.91/(1 + y)^2$$

$y = 4.42\%$

13(a). The bond's cash flows can be broken down depending on two mutually exclusive possibilities; either the NYSE index exceeds 166 after three years or it does not:

| NYSE Index | $CF_1$ | $CF_2$ | $CF_3$ |
|---|---|---|---|
| < or = 166 | 3 | 3 | 103+0 |
| > 166 | 3 | 3 | $103 + [100 \times (NY_3 - 166)/166]$ |

Thus, you receive the same cash flows as a straight bond which pays a 3% coupon and is redeemable at par plus the additional cash flows associated with 0.60241 (=100/166) units of a call option on the NYSE index which pays a dollar for each point the index exceeds 166 at maturity.

13(b). A regular bond without the embedded index option would have to sell for 71.65%, or:

$$P = [3/(1.0765)] + [3/(1.0765)^2] + [103/(1.0765)^3] = \$87.94$$

Guinness was able to sell the SPEL for 100.625, meaning that the value of the option feature must satisfy:

$100.625 = 87.94 + (Bond's Option Value)$

so that the bond's option feature is worth \$12.685. (Recall that this represents only about 60% of a regular NYSE index call option struck at 166.) The bond's option value is

25 - 18

purely a time premium since the option is currently out of the money (i.e., the index value of 134 is less than the exercise price of 166).

14(a).

$$d_1 = \frac{\ln(35/50) + [.052 + (.34^2/2)](5)}{.34(5)^{.5}} = \frac{-0.3567 + [.052 + .0578](5)}{.7603} = 0.1923/.7603$$

$$= .25$$

$d_2 = .25 - .34(5)^{.5} = -.51$

$N(.25) = .5987$

$N(-.51) = .3050$

$c(t) = 35(.5987) - 50[e^{-.052(5)}(.3050)] = 20.9545 - 50[.7711)(.3050)]$
$$= 20.9545 - 11.7593 = 9.195$$

$q = 10,000/100,000 = 0.1$

$w(t) = 9195/1.1 = 8.36$

14(b). Since the stock price before exercise must be $5,200,000/100,000 = $52, then all warrants will be exercised. Then the warrant holder will purchase 10,000 shares at $50 per share, thus injecting $500,000 of new capital into the firm. Then the firm will be worth $5,700,000/10,000 = $51.82.

14(c). The warrant was originally worth $8.36. At expiration, the warrant was only 2 points in-the-money and with the dilution effect, it was worth only 2/1.1 = 1.82. This is a percentage decrease in value of (1.82/8.36) - 1 = -0.7823. Meanwhile the stock price increased from $35 to $52, an increase of $8.57. Obviously, the warrant lost considerable value even though the stock price gained significantly in value. The reason is that when the warrant was purchased all of its price was its time value (it was not in-the-money). During the life of any warrant or option, it will lose all of its time value. The large time value reflects the volatility and long time to expiration. Ultimately at expiration, the warrant finished barely in-the-money. The warrant holder gained a little in intrinsic value but lost so much time value because the stock price, in spite of its large percentage move, still did not change by enough over the warrant's life.

# CHAPTER 26

# PROFESSIONAL ASSET MANAGEMENT

## Answers to Questions

1.  Private management and advisory firms typically develop a personal relationship with their clients, getting to know the specific investment objectives and constraints of each. The collection of assets held can then be tailored to the special needs of the client. Conversely, a mutual fund offers a general solution to an investment problem and then markets that portfolio to investors who might fit that profile.

    Special attention comes at a cost and for that reason private management firms are used mainly by investors with substantial levels of capital, such as pension funds and high net worth individuals. Conversely, individual investors with relatively small pools of capital are the primary clients of investment companies.

    The majority of private management and advisory firms are still much smaller and more narrowly focused on a particular niche in the market. A wide variety of funds are available, so an investor can match almost any investment objective or combination of investment objectives.

    Management and advisory firms hold the assets of both individual and institutional investors in separate accounts, which allows for the possibility of managing each client's portfolio in a unique manner. Conversely, investment companies are pools of assets that are managed collectively. Investors in these funds receive shares representing their proportional ownership in the underlying portfolio of stocks, bonds, or other securities.

2.  Based upon Table 26.1 there has been a rapid increase in the number of large asset management firms. Much of this asset growth can be explained by the strong performance of the U.S. equity markets during this period, but there has been a trend toward consolidating assets under management in large, multiproduct firms.

3.  After the initial public sale of the investment company the open-end fund will continue to sell new shares to the public at the NAV with or without a sales charge and will redeem (buy back) shares of the fund at the NAV. In contrast, the closed-end fund does not buy or sell shares once the original issue is sold. Therefore, the purchase price or sales price for a closed-end fund is determined in the secondary market.

4.  Two prices are provided for closed-end investment companies: (1) the NAV which is computed the same as any open-end fund, and (2) the current market price of the shares as determined in the secondary market (e.g., the NYSE). In the majority of cases the shares are selling at a discount to NAV of about 5-20 percent--i.e., the current market price is 5-20 percent below the NAV.

Harcourt, Inc.

5.	The load fund charges a sales commission of about 7.5 –8 percent when you buy the fund shares. Therefore, when you buy the shares you only get securities worth about 92- 92.5 percent of what you invest. In contrast, with a no-load fund you pay only the NAV (i.e., there is no sales commission). Notably, in order to purchase a no-load fund it is necessary to directly contact the fund to buy or sell shares.

6.	A common stock fund only invests in common stock and typically will not acquire any bonds with the possible exception of convertible bonds. A balanced fund will invest in stocks and in bonds in various proportions depending upon their outlook for the market. Because of the combination of stocks and bonds you would expect the balanced fund to have lower risk and return than a pure common stock fund.

7.	You definitely should care about how well a mutual fund is diversified. One of the major advantages of a mutual fund is instant diversification, so it truly is important. Given the CAPM, it is known that the market only pays for systematic risk so it is important to eliminate unsystematic risk, which is the purpose of diversification. A portfolio that is completely diversified will be perfectly correlated with the market portfolio ($R^2 = + 1.00$).

8.	The net return for a fund is the return after all research and management costs. The gross return is before these expenses. The net return is the return reported to the stockholder since all expenses have been allowed for in the NAV. To compute the gross return it is necessary to compute the expenses of the fund and add these back to the ending NAV and compute the returns with these expenses added back. Typically, the average difference in return is about one percent a year, but this varies by fund. As an investor, it is the net return that is important because these are the returns that you derive.

9.	Just because only half do better than buy-and-hold on the basis of risk-adjusted return does not mean you ignore them because there are other functions that investment companies perform that are important. These other functions include diversification, flexibility, and record keeping. To derive these other advantages it may be necessary to give up some of the return.

10.	It is questionable whether good performance will continue during two successive short-term periods because in many cases it could be a random event of a couple of winners that are not repeated. Empirically, such superior performance has not been consistent beyond what you would expect by chance.

11.	Managers are often compensated with a base salary and a bonus that depends on the performance of their portfolios relative to those of their peers. Therefore, a manager with a relative poor performance midway through a compensation period could be more likely to increase the risk of the portfolio in an effort to increase his/her final standing. Of course, altering fund risk to enhance his/her own compensation suggests that some managers may not always act in their client's best interest.

12. Soft dollars are generated when a manager commits the investor to paying a brokerage commission that is higher than the simple cost of executing a stock trade in exchange for the manager receiving additional bundled services from the broker. One example would be for a manager to route her trades through a non-discount broker in order to receive security reports that the brokerage firm produces.

13(a). To derive a quick view of recent performance you can look at a recent quarterly review in *Barron's*; the Mutual Fund Scoreboard in *Business Week*, the annual Forbes review.

13(b). The long-run analysis and address for the funds are best derived from the Weisenberger *Investment Companies* book.

# CHAPTER 26

## Answers to Problems

1.  Initial number of shares $= \dfrac{\$50,000}{\$8.00} = 6,250$

    Current NAV = $75,800/6,250 shares = $12.13

2.  Load fund = ($1,000 - $80) x 1.15 = $1,058.00
    Represents a 5.80 percent growth

    No-load fund = ($1,000 x 1.12) - 11.20 = $1,108.80
    Represents a 10.88 percent growth

    The no-load fund offers an extra $50.80 over the load fund for a $1,000 investment held over a one-year time period. The difference in percent growth is 5.08 percent.

3.

| Period | NAV | Premium/Discount | Market Price |
|--------|--------|------------------|--------------|
| 0 | $10.00 | 0.0 | $10.00 |
| 1 | 11.25 | -5.0 | 6.25 |
| 2 | 9.85 | +2.3 | 12.15 |
| 3 | 10.50 | -3.2 | 7.30 |
| 4 | 12.30 | -7.0 | 5.30 |

3(a).   $10.00 = 5.30(PV\ 4\ years)$    Average return per year = -14.68%
        $1.8868 = 1/(1+x)^4$            (using calculator)
        $(1+x)^4 = .5300$
        $1+x = (.5300)^{.25}$
        $1+x = .8532$
        $x = -.1468$

3(b).   $10.00 = 12.30(PV\ 4\ years)$    Average return per year = 5.31%
        $0.8130 = 1/(1+x)^4$             (using calculator)
        $(1+x)^4 = 1.230$
        $1+x = (1.230)^{.25}$
        $1+x = 1.0531$
        $x = 0.0531$

3(c).   $6.25 = 12.15(PV\ 1\ year)$    Average return per year = 94.40%
        $0.5144 = 1/(1+x)$             (using calculator)
        $(1+x) = 1.9440$
        $x = 0.9440$

3(c).   $11.25 = 9.85(PV\ 1\ year)$    Average return per year = -12.44%
        $1.142 = 1/(1+x)$             (using calculator)
        $(1+x) = .8755$
        $x = -.1244$

4(a).    <u>Client 1</u>

| | | | | | | | |
|---|---|---|---|---|---|---|---|
| .0100 | x | 5,000,000 = | 50,000 | .0100 | x | 5,000,000 = | 50,000 |
| .0075 | x | 5,000,000 = | 37,500 | .0075 | x | 5,000,000 = | 37,500 |
| .0060 | x | 10,000,000 = | 60,000 | .0060 | x | 10,000,000 = | 60,000 |
| .0040 | x | <u>7,000,000</u> = | <u>28,000</u> | .0040 | x | <u>77,000,000</u> = | <u>308,000</u> |
| | | 27,000,000 | 175,500 | | | 97,000,000 | 455,500 |

4(b).    175,500/27,000,000 = .0065          455,000/97,000,000 = .004696
                        = 0.65%                                 = 0.47%

4(c).    Costs of management do not increase at the same rate as the managed assets because substantial economies of scale exist in managing assets.

5.       CFA Examination II (May 1997)

      Potential conflicts of interest in each situation are as follows:

I.      **Serving on a board:** A conflict may exist between the fiduciary duties owed to clients and the duties owed to shareholders of the company.
OR
Investment personnel who serve as directors may receive compensation, such as securities or options to purchase securities, for serving on the board, which could raise questions about trading decisions they make for clients that might affect the value of those securities.
OR
There could be a perception that information not available to the public is used by the portfolio manager in the investment management business.

II.     **Purchasing IPOs for self: Because opportunities to participate in IPOs are limited,** participation in an initial public offering may have the appearance of appropriating an attractive investment opportunity away from clients.
OR
An investment professional who owns IPO stock may have an incentive to recommend that clients purchase those issues on the secondary market to increase .the likelihood that the investment professional will personally gain through the stock ownership.
OR
Because opportunities to participate in IPOs are limited, the receipt of the IPO may be perceived as an incentive to make future investment decisions for the benefit of the party making the IPO available rather than for clients.
OR
Participation in an IPO may be viewed as an award for past or future services.

III.    **Investment recommendations involving a firm client:** A research analyst who provides recommendations to clients on a company for which the analyst's employer is the primary underwriter may be influenced by the employer to provide favorable research on the company. This relationship thus calls into question the analyst's independence and objectivity.

OR

There could be a perception that information obtained through the investment management business and not available to the public is used by the research analyst in making the recommendations.

    **IV.**    **Performance-based fee:** Although performance-based investment management fees are permissible in many cases, such fees may place the portfolio manager's interests in conflict with a client's interests. The fee structure may give the portfolio manager an incentive, in order to achieve better performance, to take greater risks in managing a portfolio than would be consistent with a client's investment objectives.

OR

A portfolio manager may take investment action or make a recommendation that discriminates in favor of the performance-based fee accounts.

OR

A portfolio manager may spend additional time and effort on performance-based fee account to the detriment of non-performance-based fee accounts.

6(a).   Beginning value =      $27.15 x 257.876 = $7,001.33
Capital gain/dividends =  $1.12 x 257.876 =   288.82
Ending value =           $30.34 x 257.876 =  7,823.96

$$\text{Return} = \frac{(\$7,823.96 - \$7,001.33) + 288.82}{\$7,001.33} = 15.87\%$$

6(b).   Assuming that the tax rate of 30% is applied to all cash flows:
($7,823.96 - $7,001.33) + 288.82 = $1,111.45
$1,111,45(1 - .30) = $778.02
Return = $778.02/$7,001.33 = 11.11%

6(c).   Alternatively, the $1,111.45 could be reinvest at the year-end NAV of $30.34. The investor could purchase $1,111.45/$30.34 = 36.63 shares

7.

| Stock | Year 1 | Year 2 | Proportion | Dollar Liquidated | No. of shares |
|-------|--------|--------|------------|-------------------|---------------|
| A | $4,525,000 | $4,875,000 | 5.63% | $297,594 | 6,104 |
| B | 5,710,500 | 5,568,750 | 6.44% | 339,943 | 13,735 |
| C | 5,437,500 | 4,642,500 | 5.37% | 283,401 | 22,892 |
| D | 10,019,950 | 11,327,500 | 13.09% | 691,485 | 7,020 |
| E | 8,701,000 | 9,625,000 | 11.12% | 587,557 | 9,401 |
| F | 11,025,000 | 13,475,000 | 15.57% | 822,579 | 10,683 |
| G | 6,784,000 | 8,189,560 | 9.46% | 499,930 | 12,942 |
| H | 4,193,750 | 2,406,250 | 2.78% | 156,889 | 16,787 |
| I | 4,333,500 | 12,352,500 | 14.28% | 754,056 | 27,470 |
| J | 6,412,500 | 6,784,200 | 7.84% | 414,140 | 5,494 |
| K | 3,665,310 | 4,317,810 | 4.99% | 263,580 | 5,311 |
| L | 2,723,560 | 0 | 0.00% | 0 | 0 |
| M | 0 | 2,962,500 | 3.42% | 180,845 | 9,157 |
| | $73,531,570 | $86,526,570 | 100.00% | $5,282,000 | |

7(a).  Portfolio value of   $73,531,570
Cash   3,542,000
Expenses   (730,000)
Net Asset Value   $76,343,570/5,430,000 = $14.06

7(b).  Portfolio value of   $86,526,570
Cash   2,873,000
Expenses   (830,000)
Net Asset Value   $88,569,570/5,430,000 = $16.31

Growth = ($16.31 - $14.06)/$14.06 = 16.0%

7(c).  $2,873,000/$16.31 = 176,149.61 shares

7(d).  500,000 - 176,149.61 = 323,850.39 shares or $5,282,000 (based on NAV of $16.31)

Each stock's percentage of portfolio was calculated arriving at the percentages presented in the table. Each percentage was applied to the $5,282,000 to arrive at the $ amount for each stock that must be liquidated. Finally, each stock price (Year 2) was divided into the liquidation amount per stock to determine the number of shares of each stock that would have to be sold.

8(a).  (1)  3 percent front-end load = $100,000 (1 - .03) = $97,000
$97,000 (1 + .12)^3 = $97,000(1.4049) = $136,278

(2)  0.50 percent annual deduction
Year 1: $100,000(1 + .12) = $112,000 (1 - .005) = $111,440
Year 2: $111,440(1 + .12) = $124,812.80(1 - .005) = $124,188.74
Year 3: $124,188.74(1 + .12) = $139,091.38(1 - .005) = $138,395.93

(3) 2 percent back-end load
$$\$100,000(1 + .12)^3 = \$100,000(1.4049) = \$140,492.80$$
$$\$140,492.80(1 - .02) = \underline{\$137,682.94}$$

Choice (2) with ending wealth of $138,395.93

8(b).  (1) 3 percent front-end load = $100,000 (1 - .03) = $97,000
$$\$97,000 (1 + .12)^{10} = \$97,000(3.10585) = \underline{\$301,267.28}$$

(2) 0.50 percent annual deduction
$$\$100,000(1 + .12)^{10} (1 - .005)^{10} = \$100,000(3.10585)(.9511)$$
$$= \underline{\$295,400.54}$$

(3) 2 percent back-end load
$$\$100,000(1 + .12)^{10} = \$100,000(3.10585) = \$310,584.82$$
$$\$310,584.82(1 - .02) = \underline{\$304,373.12}$$

Answer would change, now choice (3) with ending wealth of $304,373.12

8(c).  Front-end load takes the money out right away, thus reducing your initial deposit.

The annual fee is usually less than one percent, which is a small amount and based on the example the preferred choice for a holding period of three years.

Back-end loads, although usually a smaller percentage than a front-end load, the dollar amount has grown during the holding period. However, back-end loads are not due until the fund is liquidated, in this case, a long period of time.

9.  CFA Examination II (1995)

9(a).  The following AIMR Standards of Professional Conduct apply to Clark if C&K provides all three functions on a combined basis.

1.  According to AIMR Standard V, Disclosure of Conflicts, C&K must disclose to its clients any material conflict of interest relating to the firm that might be perceived by clients to influence C&K's objectivity. If the Europension Group is hired as a pension consultant and it recommends to the client that C&K International be hired to manage the pension portfolio, C&K needs to disclose to the client C&K's interest in the affiliate. If C&K International executes pension portfolio securities transactions through Alps Securities, C&K needs to disclose to clients C&K's interest in the affiliate so that they can decide whether C&K's self interests are compromising its interests.

2.  According to AIMR Standard VI.A, Disclosure of Additional Compensation Arrangements Compensation, C&K must inform its customers and clients of compensation or other benefit arrangements concerning its services to them that are in addition to compensation from them for such services. Therefore, C&K needs to disclose to clients that C&K earns through its affiliates additional compensation in the management of portfolios and in brokerage transactions.

3.  According to AIMR Standard VI. B, Disclosure of Referral Fees, C&K must inform prospective customers or clients of any considerations paid or other benefits delivered to any of its affiliates for recommending to them (the clients or customers) services of a sister organization. Such disclosure should help the customer or client evaluate any possible partiality shown in any recommendation of services or evaluate the full cost of such services.

4.  According to AIMR Standard III. G, Fair Dealing with Customers and Clients, C&K must deal fairly with all customers and clients when taking investment actions. Alps Securities needs to deal fairly with all customers when executing security orders and not favor the pension clients of C&K International over the other customers of Alps Securities.

9(b).  The following AIMR Standards of Professional Conduct apply to this situation:

1.  According to AIMR Standard III. C1, Portfolio Investment Recommendations and Actions, C&K must, when taking an investment action for a specific portfolio or client, consider its appropriateness and suitability for such a portfolio or client. In considering such matters, C&K must consider the needs and circumstances of the client. C&K must also use reasonable judgment to determine the applicable relevant factors. According to these requirements, C&K should consider differences in relevant factors in various countries. If the duties, practices, and customs in that country stipulate a particular pension fund asset allocation, then C&K may reasonably be expected to respect this practice. Because his clients and pension beneficiaries specifically want to conform to conservative asset allocation practices in their country, C&K may reasonably be expected to respect its clients' investments policies.

2.  According to AIMR Standard VII. C, Fiduciary Duties, Clark should determine applicable fiduciary duties in that country and comply with them. Clark must also determine to whom the duties are owed and what asset allocation is best suited to the investment objectives of the respective clients together with the investment conditions and circumstances in the host country. If the prevailing fiduciary practice stipulates a particular asset allocation, C&K may have to respect that practice. Therefore, the practice of allocating at least 80 percent of pension fund assets to fixed-income securities may be appropriate within the context of this European country's practices, as opposed to a North American context.

9(c).  The following AIMR Standards of Professional Conduct apply in this situation.

1.  According to AIMR Standard II. A, Required Knowledge and Compliance, Clark must comply with the AIMR Standards of Professional Conduct and the accompanying Code of Ethics. Although local laws, rules, and regulations may not relate specifically to the use of material nonpublic information, any violation of another standard would be considered a violation of Standard II. A. Therefore, the latter standard applies.

26 - 9

2.   According to AIMR Standard II. B, Prohibition Against Assisting Legal and Ethical Violations, Clark must not knowingly participate in any act that would violate the AIMR Standards of Professional Conduct. Lacking specific local or other regulatory requirement in a country, or when the AIMR Standards impose a higher degree of responsibility or higher duty than that required by local or other law or custom, Clark is held to the AIMR Standards.

3.   According to AIMR Standard II. C, Prohibition Against Use of Material Nonpublic Information, Clark cannot use insider information in his investment actions. Specifically, Clark must not take investment actions based on material nonpublic information if (1) such actions violate a special or confidential relationship with an issuer or with others, or (2) such information was disclosed to him in a breach of a duty or was misappropriated. If a breach of duty exists, Clark should try to achieve public distribution of the information.

10(a). Based upon a market return (S&P) of 13.3%, Portfolio A had an average annual return of only 10.2% (underperformed), while Portfolio B with an average annual return of 15.4% outperformed the market.

10(b). Additional risk measures such as standard deviation and risk/return measures should be calculated. Portfolio style (value, growth, market-oriented or small-capitalization) should be identified. What fees are involved (front-load, back-load, management, etc.). What is the expense ratio? What is the portfolio turnover rate? What are the funds' objectives and constraints? Consistency of results - the reported results are for the last five years, what about the previous 5 or 10 years? Same portfolio manager, or has there been a change?

10(c). Since Portfolio C has an average return of 13.2% which is close to the index return of 13.3%, with a beta of .99, I would assume that the portfolio manager was had designed the portfolio to replicate the index. Portfolio A has a lower than market beta which would explain the lower than market return, following a very conservative investment approach.

10(d). Portfolio B has a much higher beta value than either of the two other portfolios and the market, thus one would expect a higher return for the portfolio – more risk, more return. Probably this portfolio has been investing in high return stocks such as technology companies, thus explaining the lower diversification level.

# CHAPTER 27

# EVALUATION OF PORTFOLIO PERFORMANCE

## Answers to Questions

1. The two major factors would be: (1) attempt to derive risk-adjusted returns that exceed a naive buy-and-hold policy and (2) completely diversity - i.e., eliminated all unsystematic risk from the portfolio. A portfolio manager can do one or both of two things to derive superior risk-adjusted returns. The first is to have **superior timing** regarding market cycles and adjust your portfolio accordingly. Alternatively, one can consistently **select undervalued stocks.** As long as you do not make major mistakes with the rest of the portfolio, these actions should result in superior risk-adjusted returns.

2. Treynor (1965) divided a fund's excess return (return 'less' risk-free rate) by its beta. For a fund not completely diversified, Treynor's "T" value will understate risk and overstate performance. Sharpe (1966) divided a fund's excess return by its standard deviation. Sharpe's "S" Value will produce evaluations very similar to Treynor's for funds that are well diversified. Jensen (1968) measures performance as the difference between a fund's actual and required returns. Since the latter return is based on the CAPM and a fund's beta, Jensen makes the same implicit assumptions as Treynor - namely, that funds are completely diversified. The information ratio (IR) measures a portfolio's average return in excess of that of a benchmark, divided by the standard deviation of this excess return.

3. For portfolios with $R^2$ values noticeably less than 1.0, it would make sense to compute both measures. Differences in the rankings generated by the two measures would suggest less-than-complete diversification by some funds - specifically, those that were ranked higher by Treynor than by Sharpe.

4. As suggested above, Jensen defines superior (inferior) performance as a positive (negative) difference between a manager's actual return and his CAPM-based required return. For poorly-diversified funds, Jensen's rankings would more closely resemble Treynor's. For well-diversified funds, Jensen's rankings would follow those of both Treynor and Sharpe. By replacing the CAPM with the APT, differences between funds' actual and required returns (or "alphas") could provide fresh evaluations of funds.

5. The IR can be viewed as a benefit-cost ratio that assesses the quality of the investor's information deflated by unsystematic risk generated by the investment process.

6. Since the return for selectivity is the difference between overall performance and the required return for risk, if the overall performance exceeds the required return for risk, the portfolio experiences a positive return for selectivity. In the example, the required return would have to be less than -0.50 in order to experience a positive selectivity value. Common sense tells us that a negative required return for assuming risk is not realistic.

7.   A high $R^2$ value of .95 implies that the portfolio is highly diversified and, thus, the diversification term will be minimal. By definition, if we have a selectivity value of a positive 2.5 percent and a minimal diversification term, net selectivity will be a positive value.

8(a).   CFA Examination I (June 1991)

The returns of a well-diversified portfolio (within an asset class) are highly correlated with the returns of the asset class itself. Over time, diversified portfolios of securities within an asset class tend to produce similar returns. In contrast, returns between different asset classes are often much less correlated, and over time, different asset classes are very likely to produce quite different returns. This expected difference in returns arising from differences in asset class exposures (i.e., from differences in asset allocation) is, thus, the key performance variable.

8(b).   Three reasons why successful implementation of asset allocation decisions is more difficult in practice than in theory are:

A.   Transaction Costs - investing or rebalancing a portfolio to reflect a chosen asset allocation is not cost-free; expected benefits are reduced by the costs of implementation.

B.   Changes in Economic and Market Factors - changing economic backgrounds, changing market price levels and changing relationships within and across asset classes all act to reduce the optimality of a given allocation decision and to create requirements for eventual rebalancing. Changes in economic and market factors change the expected risk/reward relationships of the allocation on a continuing basis.

C.   Changes in Investor Factors - the passage of time often gives rise to changes in investor needs, circumstances or preferences which, in turn, give rise to the need to reallocate, with the attendant costs of doing so.

In summary, even the "perfect" asset allocation is altered by the very act of implementation, due to transaction costs and/or changes in the original economic/market conditions and, as time passes, changes in the investor's situation. These impediments to successful implementation are inherent in the process, mandating ongoing monitoring of the relevant input factors. In practice, the fact of change in one or more of these factors is a "given;" constant attention of the degree and the importance of the effects required.

9.   The difference by which a manager's overall actual return beats his/her overall benchmark return is termed the total value-added return and decomposes into an allocation effect and a selection effect. The former effect measures differences in weights assigned by the actual and benchmark portfolios to stocks, bonds and cash "times" the respective differences between market-specific benchmark returns and the overall benchmark return. The latter effect focuses on the market-specific actual returns 'less" the corresponding market-specific benchmark returns "times" the weights assigned to each market by the actual portfolio. Of course, the foregoing analysis implicitly assumes that the actual and benchmark market-specific portfolios (e.g., stocks) are risk-equivalent. To be otherwise would invalidate this analysis.

10. CFA Examination III (1991)

Use of a "benchmark portfolio" has been proposed as a potential solution to the difficulty of distinguishing real active management skill from mere random results. By identifying the investment style, an appropriate benchmark can be developed which provides a reference point by which to judge the active management results. An appropriate benchmark would represent the characteristics that the manager's portfolio would exhibit in the absence of active investment management; i.e., a passive representation of a money manager's investment process.

A benchmark which serves as an effective tool for investment performance evaluation possesses the following characteristics:

Unambiguous - the names and weights of securities comprising the benchmark are clearly delineated.

Investable - the option is available to forgo active management and simply hold the benchmark as a representation of the style.

Measurable - it is possible to readily calculate the benchmark's return on a reasonably frequent basis.

Appropriate - the benchmark is consistent with the manager's investment style or biases.

Reflective of current investment opinions - the manager has current knowledge of the securities which make up the benchmark.

Specified in advance - the benchmark is constructed prior to the start of an evaluation period.

The "median manager" approach is an example of a commonly used benchmark whose value is seriously compromised as a measurement tool due to its lack of the above-listed characteristics. While the median-manager result is capable of being measured, most critically the median manager benchmark is not specified in advance. The median manager is identified only ex post.

Because the median manager is not known in advance, neither the manager being evaluated nor the client has the option to invest in the median manager's portfolio. Further, the median manager is ambiguous in that the portfolio composition is unavailable for inspection before or after the evaluation period.

In addition, the median manager's portfolio most likely contains securities of which the manager being evaluated has no current investment knowledge. Finally, the median manager benchmark is unlikely to be appropriate because of the high probability that the median manager's investment style will not be identical to that of the manager being evaluated.

27 - 3

Other factors favoring benchmark portfolios over the median manager approach are their ability to be used as the basis of performance fees and calculation of various risk-adjusted performance measures (Sharpe ratio, Treynor value, Jensen ratio, etc.). Moreover, benchmark portfolios do not suffer the "survivorship bias" of the median manager approach.

11. CFA Examination III (1991)

11(a). The basic procedure in portfolio evaluation is to compare the return on a managed portfolio to the return expected on an unmanaged portfolio having the same risk, via use of the CAPM. That is, expected return ($E_p$) is calculated from:

$$E_p = E_f + (E_m - \beta_p)$$

Where $E_r$ is the risk-free rate, $E_m$ is the unmanaged portfolio or the market return and $\beta_p$ is the beta coefficient or systematic risk of the managed portfolio. The benchmark of performance then is the unmanaged portfolio. The typical proxy for this unmanaged portfolio is some aggregate stock market index such as the S&P 500.

11(b). The benchmark error often occurs because the unmanaged portfolio used in the evaluation process is not "optimized." That is, market indices, such as the S&P 500, chosen as benchmarks are not on the evaluator's **ex ante** mean/variance efficient frontier. Benchmark error may also occur because of an error in the estimation of the risk free return. Together, these two sources of error will cause the implied Security Market Line (SML) to be mispositioned.

11(c). The main ingredients are that the true risk-free rate is lower than the measured risk-free rate and the true market is above the measured market. The result is under-performance relative to the true SML rather than superior performance relative to the measured SML.

11(d). The fact that the portfolio manager has been judged superior based on several different benchmarks should not make me feel any more comfortable because all the benchmarks could have errors, which means that you are simply computing different errors. It is shown by Roll that if the various indexes are perfectly correlated, a proportionate difference will exist in the error. Notably, all of these indexes are very highly correlated.

11(e). All of the discussion by Roll is not directed against the CAPM theory, but is concerned with a **measurement problem** involved in finding a valid benchmark, i.e., an unmanaged portfolio that is mean/variance efficient. The theory is correct and valid. The problem is implementing the theory in the real world where it is difficult to construct a true "market portfolio."

12. When measuring the performance of an equity portfolio manager, overall returns can be related to a common total risk or systematic risk. Factors influencing the returns achieved by the bond portfolio manager are more complex. In order to evaluate performance based on a common risk measure (i.e., market index), four components must be considered that differentiate the individual portfolio from the market index. These components include:

27 - 4

(1) a **policy effect, (2) a rate anticipation effect,** (3) an **analysis effect,** and (4) a trading effect. Decision variables involved include the impact of duration decisions, anticipation of sector/quality factors, and the impact of individual bond selection.

13.    CFA Examination III (June 1982)

13(a). **Yield-to-maturity.** This is the expected return on the bond based upon the beginning price. Assuming no changes in the market, it is made up of the accrued coupon payments; an expected price change to amortize the differ e between par and the beginning market price' and the "roll effect," which is due to changes in yield-to-maturity due to the slope of the yield curve and the fact that the bond's maturity declined during the holding period.

13(b). The **interest rate effect** is an analysis of what happened to the bond's price due to a change in market interest rates during the period. Specifically, the analysis involves relating what should have happened to the price of the portfolio bond taking into account the change in yields for treasury securities of a comparable maturity and assuming the same spread as at the beginning of the period.

13(c). The **sector/quality effect** examines what should have happened to returns based upon changes in sector/quality differentials during the period. You begin with a matrix of differential returns for the bonds in different sectors (corporates, utilities, financial, telephone) and quality (Aaa, Aa, Baa) relative to the returns for Treasury bonds of the same maturity. As an example, the matrix will indicate that the return difference for an Aa corporate bond during the period was one percent more or less than a similar maturity Treasury bond. Put another way, it indicates what happened to bonds of this quality and sector during this period relative to Treasury bonds.

13(d). The **residual return** is what is left of total return after taking account of yield to maturity, the interest rate effect, and the sector/quality effect. It is as follows:

**Total Return = Yield to Maturity+Interest Rate Effect+Sector / Quality Effect + Residual Return**

# CHAPTER 27

## Answers to Problems

1.   CFA Examination III (June 1985)

1(a).   The risk adjusted returns of the two equity portfolios are computed as follows:

$$\text{Risk Adj Returns} = \frac{(\text{Realized returns - risk free rate})}{\text{beta}} + \text{risk free rate}$$

Good Samaritan Equity Portfolio:

(11.8% - 7.8%)/1.20 + 7.8 % = 3.3 % + 7.8 % = 11.1 %

Mrs. Atkins' Equity Portfolio:

(10.7% - 7.8%)/1.05 + 7.8 % = 2.8 % + 7.8 % = 10.6 %

Both portfolios outperformed the S&P 500 both on an absolute basis and on a risk adjusted basis. The Good Samaritan portfolio outperformed Mrs. Atkins' portfolio by more than a full percentage point before risk adjustment, but by only one-half percentage point after risk adjustment. These differences are small enough to be within the range of normal statistical variation and are therefore not meaningful in judging performance.

1(b).   Factors which could account for the differences in *total account performance* would include the following:

*Different asset mixes between stocks, bonds, arid short term reserves.* Clearly, a higher proportion of equity investments would have improved the total portfolio return for Mrs. Atkins.

*The use of taxable bonds versus tax exempt bonds.* Since Mrs. Atkins' bonds were tax exempt whereas the Good Samaritan bonds were undoubtedly taxable, Mrs. Atkins' portfolio return would be adversely affected unless an adjustment were made for *after-tax* returns.

Mrs. Atkins' portfolio is *riot* since it contains only eight equity issues (other than Merit Enterprises). This creates a higher potential for specific risk to affect the portfolio return in any given year.

The *objectives and constraints* under which the two portfolios are operating are probably *quite different.* The higher beta of the Good Samaritan portfolio suggests that it may have been managed with less restrictive constraints than Mrs. Atkins' portfolio.

The relatively short *time period* (i.e., twelve months) is *too short* to make a truly meaningful evaluation of relative performance of the two portfolios. A complete market cycle would be more appropriate.

Harcourt, Inc.

2(a).

$$S_P = \frac{.15 - .07}{0.50} = \frac{.08}{.05} = 1.60$$

$$S_Q = \frac{.20 - .07}{.10} = \frac{.13}{.10} = 1.30$$

$$S_R = \frac{.10 - .07}{.03} = \frac{.03}{.03} = 1.00$$

$$S_S = \frac{.17 - .07}{.06} = \frac{.10}{.06} = 1.67$$

$$\text{Market} = \frac{.13 - .07}{.04} = \frac{.06}{.04} = 1.50$$

2(b).

$$T_P = \frac{.15 - .07}{1.00} = \frac{.08}{1.00} = .0800$$

$$T_Q = \frac{.20 - .07}{1.50} = \frac{.13}{1.50} = .0867$$

$$T_R = \frac{.10 - .07}{.60} = \frac{.03}{.60} = .0500$$

$$T_S = \frac{.17 - .07}{1.10} = \frac{.10}{1.10} = .0909$$

$$\text{Market} = \frac{.13 - .07}{1.00} = \frac{.06}{1.00} = .0600$$

|        | Sharpe | Treynor |
|--------|--------|---------|
| P      | 2      | 3       |
| Q      | 4      | 2       |
| R      | 5      | 5       |
| S      | 1      | 1       |
| Market | 3      | 4       |

2(c).  It is apparent from the rankings above that Portfolio Q was poorly diversified since Treynor ranked it #2 and Sharpe ranked it #4. Otherwise, the rankings are similar.

3.  CFA Examination I (1994)

3(a).  The Treynor measure (I) relates the rate of return earned above the risk-free rate to the portfolio beta during the period under consideration. Therefore, the Treynor measure shows the risk premium (excess return) earned per unit of systematic risk:

$$T_i = \frac{R_i - R_f}{\beta_i}$$

Harcourt, Inc.

where: $R_i$, = average rate of return for portfolio i during the specified period,
$R_f$ = average rate of return- on a risk-free investment during the specified period
$\beta_i$ = beta of portfolio i during the specified period.

| Treynor Measure | Performance Relative to the Market (S&P 500) |

$$T = \frac{10\% - 6\%}{0.60} = 6.7\%$$    *Outperformed*

Market (S&P 500)

$$T_M = \frac{12\% - 6\%}{1.00} = 6.0\%$$

The Treynor measure examines portfolio performance in relation to the security market line (SML). Because the portfolio would plot above the SML, it outperformed the S&P 500 Index. Because T was greater than $T_M$, 6.7 percent versus 6.0 percent, respectively, the portfolio clearly outperformed the market index.

The Sharpe measure (S) relates the rate of return earned above the risk free rate to the total risk of a portfolio by including the standard deviation of returns. Therefore, the Sharpe measure indicates the risk premium (excess return) per unit of total risk:

$$S = \frac{R_i - R_f}{\sigma_i}$$

where: $R_i$ = average rate of return for portfolio i during the specified period,
$R_f$ = average rate of return on a risk-free investment during the specified period,
$\sigma_i$ = standard deviation of the rate of return for portfolio i during the specified period.

| Sharpe Measure | Performance Relative to the Market (S&P 500) |

$$S = \frac{10\% - 6\%}{18\%} = 0.222\%$$    *Underperformed*

Market (S&P 500)

$$S_M = \frac{12\% - 6\%}{13\%} = 0.462\%$$

The Sharpe measure uses total risk to compare portfolios with the capital market line (CML). The portfolio would plot below the CML, indicating that it underperformed the market. Because S was less than *SM,* 0.222 versus 0.462, respectively, the portfolio underperformed the market.

3(b). The Treynor measure assumes that the appropriate risk measure for a portfolio is its systematic risk, or beta. Hence, the Treynor measure implicitly assumes that the portfolio being measured is fully diversified. The Sharpe measure is similar to the Treynor measure except that the excess return on a portfolio is divided by the standard deviation of the portfolio.

For perfectly diversified portfolios (that is, those without any unsystematic or specific risk), the Treynor and Sharpe measures would give consistent results relative to the market index because the total variance of the portfolio would be the same as its systematic variance (beta). A poorly diversified portfolio could show better performance relative to the market if the Treynor measure is used but lower performance relative to the market if the Sharpe measure is used. Any difference between the two measures relative to the markets would come directly from a difference in diversification.

In particular, Portfolio X outperformed the market if measured by the Treynor measure but did not perform as well as the market using the Sharpe measure. The reason is that Portfolio X has a large amount of unsystematic risk. Such risk is not a factor in determining the value of the Treynor measure for the portfolio, because the Treynor measure considers only systematic risk. The Sharpe measure, however, considers total risk (that is, both systematic and unsystematic risk). Portfolio X, which has a low amount of systematic risk, could have a high amount of total risk, because of its lack of diversification. Hence, Portfolio X would have a high Treynor measure (because of low systematic risk) and a low Sharpe measure (because of high total risk).

4(a). Portfolio MNO enjoyed the highest degree of diversification since it had the highest $R^2$ (94.8%). The statistical logic behind this conclusion comes from the CAPM which says that all fully diversified portfolios should be priced along the security market line. $R^2$ is a measure of how well assets conform to the security market line, so $R^2$ is also a measure of diversification.

4(b).

| Fund | Treynor | Sharpe | Jensen |
|---|---|---|---|
| ABC | 0.975(4) | 0.857(4) | 0.192(4) |
| DEF | 0.715(5) | 0.619(5) | -0.053(5) |
| GHI | 1.574(1) | 1.179(1) | 0.463(1) |
| JKL | 1.262(2) | 0.915(3) | 0.355(2) |
| MNO | 1.134(3) | 1.000(2) | 0.296(3) |

4(c).

| Fund | t(alpha) |
|---|---|
| ABC | 1.7455(3) |
| DEF | -0.2789(5) |
| GHI | 2.4368(1) |
| JKL | 1.6136(4) |
| MNO | 2.1143(2) |

Only GHI and MNO have significantly positive alphas.

5(a). (Information ratio) $IR_j = \alpha_j/\sigma_u$ where $\sigma_u$ = standard error of the regression

$IR_A = .058/.533 = 0.1088$

$IR_B = .115/5.884 = 0.0195$

$IR_C = .250/2.165 = 0.1155$

5(b). Annualized $IR = (T)^{1/2}(IR)$

Annualized $IR_A = (52)^{1/2}(0.1088) = 0.7846$

Annualized $IR_B = (26)^{1/2}(0.0195) = 0.0994$

Annualized $IR_C = (12)^{1/2}(0.1155) = 0.4001$

5(c). The higher the ratio, the better. Based upon the answers to part a, Manager C would be rated the highest followed by Managers A and B, respectively. However, once the values are annualized, the ranking change. Specifically, based upon the annualized IR, Manger A is rated the highest, followed by C and B. (In both cases, Manager C is rated last). Based upon the Grinold-Kahn standard for "good" performance (0.500 or greater), only Manager A meets that test.

6(a).

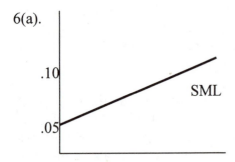

6(b). Overall Performance $= R_a - R_f = .15 - .05 = .10$

6(c). Selectivity $= R_a - R_x(\beta_a) = .15 - .11 = .04$

6(d). Risk $= [R_x(\beta_a) - R_f] = .11 - .05 = .06$
where $R_x(\beta_a) = .05 + 1.2(.10 - .05) = .11$

7(a). Overall performance (Fund 1) $= 26.40\% - 6.20\% = 20.20\%$
Overall performance (Fund 2) $= 13.22\% - 6.20\% = 7.02\%$

7(b). $E(R_i) = 6.20 + \beta(15.71 - 6.20)$
$= 6.20 + \beta(9.51)$
Total return (Fund 1) $= 6.20 + (1.351)(9.51) = 6.20 + 12.85 = 19.05\%$
where 12.85% is the required return for risk
Total return (Fund 2) $= 6.20 + (0.905)(9.51) = 6.20 + 8.61 = 14.81\%$
where 8.61% is the required return for risk

7(c)(i). Selectivity$_1$ = 20.2% - 12.85% = 7.35%

Selectivity$_2$ = 7.02% - 8.61% = -1.59%

7(c)(ii).Ratio of total risk$_1$ = $\sigma_1/\sigma_m$ = 20.67/13.25 = 1.56

Ratio of total risk$_2$ = $\sigma_2/\sigma_m$ = 14.20/13.25 = 1.07

$R_1$ = 6.20 + 1.56 (9.51) = 6.20 + 14.8356 = 21.04%

$R_2$ = 6.20 + 1.07 (9.51) = 6.20 + 10.1757 = 16.38%

Diversification$_1$ = 21.04% – 19.05% = 1.99%

Diversification$_2$ = 16.38% – 14.81% = 1.57%

7(c)(iii). Net Selectivity = Selectivity – Diversification

Net Selectivity$_1$ = 7.35% - 1.99% = 5.36%

Net Selectivity$_2$ = -1.59% - 1.57% = -3.16%

7(d). Even accounting for the added cost of incomplete diversification, Fund 1's performance was above the market line (best performance), while Fund 2 fall below the line.

8. CFA Examination III (June 1995)

8(a). The following briefly describes one strength and one weakness of each manager.

### 1. Manager A

**Strength.** Although Manager A's one-year total return was slightly below the EAFE Index return (.0 percent versus -5.0 percent, respectively), this manager apparently has some country/security return expertise. This large local market return advantage of 2.0 percent exceeds the 0.2 percent return for the EAFE Index.

**Weakness.** Manager A has an obvious weakness in the currency management area. This manager experienced a marked currency return shortfall compared with the EAFE Index of 8.0 percent versus -5.2 percent, respectively.

### 2. Manager B

**Strength.** Manager B's total return slightly exceeded that of the index, with a marked positive increment apparent in the currency return. Manager B had a -1.0 percent currency return versus a -5.2 percent currency return on the EAFE index. Based on this outcome, Manager B's strength appears to be some expertise in the currency selection area.

**Weakness.** Manager B had a marked shortfall in local market return. Manager B's country/security return was -1.0 percent versus 0.2 percent on the EAFE Index. Therefore, Manager B appears to be weak in security/market selection ability.

Harcourt, Inc.

8(b). The following strategies would enable the Fund to take advantage of the strengths of the two managers and simultaneously minimize their weaknesses.

1. **Recommendation:** One strategy would be to direct Manager A to make no currency bets relative to the EAFE Index and to direct Manager B to make only currency decisions, and no active country or security selection bets.

   **Justification:** This strategy would mitigate Manager A's weakness by hedging all currency exposures into index-like weights. This would allow capture of Manager A's country and stock selection skills while avoiding losses from poor currency management. This strategy would also mitigate Manager B's weakness, leaving an index-like portfolio construct and capitalizing on the apparent skill in currency management.

2. **Recommendation:** Another strategy would be to combine the portfolios of Manager A and Manager B. with Manager A making country exposure and security selection decisions and Manager B managing the currency exposures created by Manager A's decisions (providing a "currency overlay").

   **Justification:** This recommendation would capture the strengths of both Manager A and Manager B and would minimize their collective weaknesses.

9(a)(i). $.6(-5) + .3(-3.5) + .1(0.3) = -4.02\%$

9(a)(ii). $.5(-4) + .2(-2.5) + .3(0.3) = -2.41\%$

9(a)(iii). $.3(-5) + .4(-3.5) + .3(0.3) = -2.81\%$

Manager A outperformed the benchmark fund by 161 basis points while Manager B beat the benchmark fund by 121 basis points.

9(b)(i). $[.5(-4 + 5) + .2(-2.5 + 3.5) + .3(.3 -.3)] = 0.70\%$

9(b)(ii). $[(.3 - .6)(-5 + 4.02) + (.4 - .3)(-3.5 + 4.02) + (.3 -.1)(.3 + 4.02)] = 1.21\%$

Manager A added value through her selection skins (70 of 161 basis points) and her allocation skills (71 of 161 basis points). Manager B added value totally through his allocation skills (121 of 121 basis points).

10. CFA Examination III (June 1985)

10(a). Overall, both managers added value by mitigating the currency effects present in the Index. Both exhibited an ability to "pick stocks" in the markets they chose to be in (Manager B in particular). Manager B used his opportunities not to be in stocks quite effectively (via the cash/bond contribution to return), but neither of them matched the passive index in picking the country markets in which to be invested (Manager B in particular).

|  | Manager A | Manager B |
|---|---|---|
| Strengths | Currency Management | Currency Management |
| | Stock Selection | Stock Selection |
| | | Use of Cash/Bond Flexibility |
| | | |
| Weaknesses | Country Selection | Country Selection |
| | (to a limited degree) | |

10(b). The column reveals the effect on performance in local currency terms after adjustment for movements in the U.S. dollar and, therefore, the effect on the portfolio. Currency gains/losses arise from translating changes in currency exchange rates versus the U.S. dollar over the measuring period (3 years in this case) into U.S. dollars for the U.S. pension plan. The Index mix lost 12.9% to the dollar reducing what would otherwise have been a very favorable return from the various country markets of 19.9% to a net return of only 7.0%.

11.      $I = E + U$
    $11\% = 10 + U$
     $1\% = U$

| | 10-Year AA Bonds | 5-Year A Bonds | 25-Year B Bonds |
|---|---|---|---|
| M | 1.50 | 1.00 | 3.00 |
| S | -0.40 | -0.60 | -1.20 |
| B | .25 | .50 | .75 |
| C | 1.35 | .90 | 2.55 |
| I | 11.00 | 11.00 | 11.00 |
| R | 12.35 | 11.90 | 13.65 |

where

| | S |
|---|---|
| AAA | -.2 |
| AA | -.4 |
| A | -.6 |
| BBB | -.8 |
| BB | -1.0 |
| B | -1.2 |

and

$M = .2 \times 5 + .1 \times \phantom{0}5 = 1.50 \ (10 \ Yr.)$
$M = .2 \times 5 + .1 \times \phantom{0}0 = 1.00 \ (\phantom{0}5 \ Yr.)$
$M = .2 \times 5 + .1 \times 20 = 3.00 \ (25 \ Yr.)$

27 - 13

12.     CFA Examination III (June 1994)

12(a).  Evaluation begins with selection of the appropriate benchmark against which to measure the firms' results:

*Firm A.* The Aggregate Index and "Managers using the Aggregate Index" benchmark are appropriate here, because Firm A maintains marketlike sector exposures. Performance has been strong; Firm A outperformed the Aggregate Index by 50 basis points and placed in the first quartile of managers' results.

*Firm B.* Firm B does not use mortgages; therefore, the Government/Corporate for both index and universe comparisons would be the appropriate benchmark. Although Firm B produced the highest absolute performance (9.3 percent), it did not perform up to either the Index (9.5 percent) or other managers investing only in the Government/Corporate sectors (third quartile).

*Firm C.* Like Firm A, this firm maintains broad market exposures and should be compared with the Aggregate Index for both index and universe comparisons. Performance has been good (30 basis points ahead of the index and in the second quartile of manager results) but not as good as Firm A's showing during this relatively short measurement period.

12(b).  Firm A does not show an observable degree of security selection skill (-10 basis points); nor does it appear to be managing in line with its stated marketlike approach. Some large nonmarketlike bets are driving return production (e.g., duration bets, +100 basis points; yield curve bets, +30 basis points; and sector-weighting bets, -70 basis points) and account for its +50 basis-point better-than-benchmark total return.

Firm C's ability to anticipate shifts in the yield curve correctly is confirmed by the analysis (its +30 basis points accounts for all of its observed better than-benchmark outcome). In addition, its claim n to maintain marketlike exposures is also confirmed (e.g., the nominal differences from benchmark in the other three attribution areas).

12(c).  Firm C produced the best results because its style and its expertise were confirmed by the analysis; Firm A's were not.

13(i).  Dollar-Weighted Return

Manager L:
$$500,000 = -12,000/(1+r) - 7,500/(1+r)^2 - 13,500/(1+r)^3 - 6,500/(1+r)^4 - 10,000/(1+r)^5 + 625,000/(1+r)^5$$
Solving for r, the internal rate of return or DWRR is 2.74%

Manager M:
$$700,000 = 35,000/(1+r) + 35,000/(1+r)^2 + 35,000/(1+r)^3 + 35,000/(1+r)^4 + 35,000/(1+r)^5 + 625,000/(1+r)^5$$
Solving for r, the internal rate of return or DWRR is 2.98%

27 - 14

13(ii). Time-weighted return

Manager L:

| Periods | HPR |
|---------|-----|
| 1 | $[(527,000 - 500,000) - 12,000]/500,000 = .03$ |
| 2 | $[(530,000 - 527,000) - 7,500]/527,000 = -.0085$ |
| 3 | $[(555,000 - 530,000) - 13,500]/530,000 = .0217$ |
| 4 | $[(580,000 - 555,000) - 6,500]/555,000 = .0333$ |
| 5 | $[(625,000 - 580,000) - 10,000]/580,000 = .0603$ |

$$\text{TWRR} = [(1 + .03)(1 - .0085)(1 + .0217)(1 + .0333)(1 + .0603)]^{1/5} - 1$$
$$= (1.143)^{1/5} - 1 = 1.02712 - 1 = .02712 = 2.71\%$$

Manager M:

| Periods | HPR |
|---------|-----|
| 1 | $[(692,000 - 700,000) + 35,000]/700,000 = .03857$ |
| 2 | $[(663,000 - 692,000) + 35,000]/692,000 = .00867$ |
| 3 | $[(621,000 - 663,000) + 35,000]/663,000 = -.01056$ |
| 4 | $[(612,000 - 621,000) + 35,000]/621,000 = .04187$ |
| 5 | $[(625,000 - 612,000) + 35,000]/612,000 = .0784$ |

$$\text{TWRR} = [(1 + .03857)(1 + .00867)(1 - .01056)(1 + .04187)(1 + .0784)]^{1/5} - 1$$
$$= (1.1658)^{1/5} - 1 = 1.03094 - 1 = .03094 = 3.094\%$$

13(iii). Dietz approximation method $= \dfrac{EV - (1 - DW)(\text{Contribution})}{BV + (DW)(\text{Contribution})} - 1$

In this case, $DW = (91 - 45.5)/91 = 0.50$

Manager L:

| Periods | HPY |
|---------|-----|
| 1 | $[(527,000 - (1 - .50)(12,000)]/[500,000 + (.50)(12,000)] - 1$ |
| | $= (527,000 - 6,000/(500,000 + 6,000) - 1 = 521,000/506,000 - 1 = .0296$ |
| 2 | $(530,000 - (1 - .50)(7,500)]/[527,000 + (.50)(7,500)] - 1$ |
| | $= 526,250/530,750 - 1 = -.0085$ |
| 3 | $(555,000 - (1 - .50)(13,500)]/[530,000 + (.50)(13,500)] - 1$ |
| | $= 548,250/536,750 - 1 = .0214$ |
| 4 | $(580,000 - (1 - .50)(6,500)]/[555,000 + (.50)(6,500)] - 1$ |
| | $= 576,750/558,250 - 1 = .0331$ |
| 5 | $(625,000 - (1 - .50)(10,000)]/[580,000 + (.50)(10,000)] - 1$ |
| | $= 620,000/585,00 - 1 = .0598$ |

Manager M:

| Periods | HPY |
|---|---|
| 1 | $[(692,000 - (1 - .50)(-35,000)]/[700,000 + (.50)(-35,000)] - 1$ |
| | $= (692,000 + 17,500/(700,000 - 17,500) - 1 = 709,500/682,500 - 1 = .0396$ |
| 2 | $(663,000 - (1 - .50)(-35,000)]/[692,000 + (.50)(-35,000)] - 1$ |
| | $= 680,500/674,500 - 1 = .0089$ |
| 3 | $(621,000 - (1 - .50)(-35,000)]/[663,000 + (.50)(-35,000)] - 1$ |
| | $= 638,500/645,500 - 1 = -.0108$ |
| 4 | $(612,000 - (1 - .50)(-35,000)]/[621,000 + (.50)(-35,000)] - 1$ |
| | $= 629,500/603,500 - 1 = .0431$ |
| 5 | $(625,000 - (1 - .50)(-35,000)]/[612,000 + (.50)(-35,000)] - 1$ |
| | $= 642,500/594,500 - 1 = .0807$ |